COVID-19 and Risk Society across the MENA Region

COVID-19 and Risk Society
across the MENA Region

Assessing Governance, Democracy, and Inequality

Edited by
Larbi Sadiki and Layla Saleh

I.B. TAURIS

LONDON • NEW YORK • OXFORD • NEW DELHI • SYDNEY

I.B. TAURIS

Bloomsbury Publishing Plc

50 Bedford Square, London, WC1B 3DP, UK

1385 Broadway, New York, NY 10018, USA

29 Earlsfort Terrace, Dublin 2, Ireland

BLOOMSBURY, I.B. TAURIS and the I.B. Tauris logo are trademarks of Bloomsbury Publishing Plc

First published in Great Britain 2023

Cover design by www.paulsmithdesign.com
Cover image © Giulia Fiori Photography/Getty Images

A catalogue record for this book is available from the British Library.

A catalog record for this book is available from the Library of Congress.

ISBN: HB: 978-0-7556-4388-2
PB: 978-0-7556-4389-9
ePDF: 978-0-7556-4390-5
eBook: 978-0-7556-4391-2

Typeset by Deanta Global Publishing Services, Chennai, India

To find out more about our authors and books visit www.bloomsbury.com and sign up for our newsletters.

For Zidane and Tayeb

Contents

MENA Risk Society and the "Pandemic Condition"

Larbi Sadiki and Layla Saleh

Introduction

At the interlocking levels of polity, economy, and society, global changes wrought by the COVID-19 pandemic prompt investigation, reflection, and deliberation by academics, civic activists, and political practitioners. In the middle (and aftermath) of widespread uncertainty and the "collapse" of taken-for-granted functions of states, economies, and international institutions, it is apropos to reconsider some widely held conceptions. How do crises bring to the fore the contradictions in the discourses and practices seeking to ensure democracy, freedoms, and socioeconomic rights through the national, regional, and global actors and institutions? This compelling question is far from abstract. Lives and livelihoods, many already precarious, have been bulldozed off-track in the wake of the pandemic and policy responses aiming (or claiming) to contain it. Hence, it is fitting to reflect on how social scientists can engage in research aimed at problem-solving to confront enormous challenges heightened by COVID-19. These range from inequality and human indignity to contracting opportunities compounded by resurgent authoritarianism in many Arab settings. Prior to March 2020, the Middle East and North Africa (MENA) was already in the throes of intense tumult and trenchant violent conflict, particularly since the onset of the 2011 Arab Spring uprisings and counterrevolutions. These have played out not only in the Arab states but have also ricocheted to other states in the region, such as Iran (Holliday 2015). The pandemic has piled on difficulties of health, sustenance, and aspirations to security and emancipation. COVID's woes in this region may be understood through a sort of duality. Its blows have, on the one hand, followed the trajectory of some global patterns. At the same time, the pandemic's impact has played out in regionally specific ways. The collection of chapters in this edited volume collectively seek to untangle how COVID-19 unfolds in the MENA region. That is, the book attempts to probe the contours and configurations of its "pandemic condition," with special reference to issues of socioeconomic (in)equalities, (self) governance, civic engagement, and democracy. An eye to problem-solving research, the "reflexivity" dimension, further enhances the empirical, country-level analyses attuned to major trends exacerbated or initiated by the virus. This introductory chapter lays out the book's twin theoretical framework of "regional risk society" and reflexivity; explains the quasi-ethnographic approach adopted in its various chapters; and lays out the structure of the ensuing volume.

The COVID-19 pandemic is at the time of writing too new for any deep or systematic analysis to have emerged in any number of research genres, including traditional academic scholarship or more policy-oriented work. The state-of-the-art on the pandemic, that is, remains in its rudimentary in 2020. Philosophical-cultural readings (Lal 2020) include warning of a "new barbarism" in the pandemic age (Zizek 2020), and personalized musings on ideological divergences (e.g., libertarian, authoritarian) shaping incommensurate responses to the pandemic in a world already beset by food crises and global warming (Zizek 2021). Such accounts are more impressionistic than empirical-conceptual. Others have sought to trace the rapid spread of the disease and initial responses by international organizations in wide-ranging narratives (Koley and Dhole 2021). Some have reflected on early harbingers of the coronavirus that should have warned policymakers of its imminent eruption (MacKenzie 2020), as well as on the failures of policymaker responses to the pandemic across the world (Horton 2020).

Beyond damage assessments, few studies engaged in more focused analysis of what we term "pandemic risk" in areas such as knowledge (education, teaching-learning) (Likzuli 2020) or civic capacities within MENA. Research from 2020 that did directly venture into the region seemed to capture only "snapshots" that public opinion polls can offer. Arab Barometer surveys in Algeria, Jordan, Lebanon, Morocco, and Tunisia, for instance, suggest that Arab populations' assessments of government responses to COVID vary, with 58 percent of Tunisians versus 75 percent of Jordanians rating their government positively as of December 2020 (Abufalgha 2020). People appear to apportion blame between citizen behavior (a quarter to a third in the countries surveyed) and insufficient responses by governments (between 1 and 7 percent), and inadequacy of healthcare system (8–17 percent) (Abufalgha 2020). These surveys, however, cannot account for dynamism and change inherent to government-citizen or state-society interactions in confronting risk. Such an enterprise requires more in-depth, qualitative research that is interpretive, with a touch of ethnography—as our book tries to do. Thus, this volume addresses and seeks to fill this important gap of deep, situated case studies (Lowi 1964) within the MENA region that are not confined to single moments in time catalogued in public opinion work. This we do through our exploration of knowledge capacity-development within and between a sampling of MENA cases. To offset some of the "uncertainty" even within social science predictions (Varnum, Huthcerson and Grossman 2021), contextualized analysis can go a long way. Stepping into the social science void, this book seeks to offer quasi-ethnographic accounts from across the region to examine pandemic impacts and response in the MENA region rigorously, systematically, through the prism of risk society.

This introductory chapter conceptualizes the universality *and* specificities of lived COVID experiences first, through Arendt's "human condition." Additionally, it offers Beck and Gidden's notion of "risk society" as a window to parsing both the (lack of) preparedness and (in)effectiveness of responses in MENA, as a region and within the countries that comprise it. This, we argue, calls for a COVID-era reflexivity. Next, we present a regional overview of COVID-risk society through basic statistics and snippets of what have largely been shortcomings and failures in political-economic grappling with the pandemic across the region. Finally, we call for an adoption of an "ethnographic sensibility" which, coupled with reflexivity, can provoke deeper engagement in research and thought-practice in the direction of easing sociopolitical inequalities and stimulating civic engagement. Thus do we situate the country case studies presented in the book's chapters. These are mini and tentative "quasi-ethnographies of the pandemic" through which we collectively seek to understand the commons alongside the local specificities of the most glaring iteration of MENA "risk society," its COVID condition.

The "Pandemic Condition"

Our overarching objective is to begin to parse what we call here the "pandemic condition" as lived experience in the MENA region. To this end, Arendt's *The Human Condition* helps us begin to consider this pandemic with its universal reach, precipitated by some of modern life's most acute ailments: unfettered capitalist drive for accumulation, disregard for the environment, the development of biological weapons, and escalating contests for power between rival states and their respective economies. (Here the United States and China spring to mind.) States, societies, and individuals muster differentially distributed toolkits (material, scientific, civic, ideational) to confront disease and economic disaster. Local, national, regional, and international actors are *not* equally prepared to fight the pandemic. In both theory and practice, such a recognition poses the question of how to approach the universal plague in ways amenable to identifying widespread patterns while simultaneously disentangling the specificities of local experiences (Arendt's "plurality"). Our analytical imperative here is to look for both the commonalities and the contextualized realities of this twenty-first-century iteration of the "human condition." A return to Arendt enables us to grasp the shared experiences and intersecting layers of modern life, *vita activa*. In so doing, her work, like Beck's, helps us zoom in on consequential pitfalls and discrepancies of "modernity." For Arendt, the natural, the human-made ("artifice"), and the social-political worlds intersect in the respective concepts of labor, work, and action. Human being, nature, and object come together perpetually in myriad "condition"-ing. No part of lived human reality is not touched by other human beings and their activities: "human existence is conditioned existence, it would be impossible without things . . . [which are its] conditioners" (Arendt 1998, 9). These things have in turn been constructed and "fabricated" through human encounters with nature and biology, the living and non-living. There is no blank page on which to script human life, no escape from human interdependence—whether for good or ill. COVID-19 has brought such interpenetration of humans, their physical and mental efforts, the things they build, and their encounters with their environments into sharp relief.

And yet, for Arendt, "the conditions of human existence . . . never condition us absolutely" (1998, 11). Agency is always a potentiality for which to carve out analytical (and practical) space. Even, we suggest, in the face of devastating structural catastrophes. Extending Arendt's concept, then, we approach the (foreseeable) future as an extended instance of the twenty-first-century "human condition." It follows that we should seek to understand the scope and limits of its "conditioning" in various locales. Attempting to resist pandemic inertia (of polities, economies, societies, activisms, value systems, etc.) in theory and practice, we proceed with this type of analytical curiosity. Grappling with COVID-19 should engender problem-solving thinking. It is not enough to get bogged down in simple critique, that is—a point to which we will return in the discussion of reflexivity.

MENA "Regional" Risk Society

Investigating the logics and instances of the "pandemic condition," we invoke Ulrich Beck and Anthony Giddens's (1992) concept of "risk society." This notion helps to underscore the severity of the pandemic for human development and (in)humane sharing of the burdens afflicting the region's states and societies as a result of COVID-19. It strikes a chord as we seek to both make meaning out of the pandemic *and* to chart pathways for ways to understand and even mitigate COVID destruction. Risk society is characterized by "distributional conflicts over 'bads'" (and not "goods"), in contests over "how the risks accompanying goods production . . . can be distributed, prevented, controlled and legitimized" (Beck, Giddens, and Lash 1992, 6). Further, Beck has offered the notion of risk as "manufactured uncertainty" that results from human-made (not natural) problems spilling out of modernization (1998, 12–13). Risks, he says, include environmental disasters and new illnesses, for example, that arise from technological, scientific, and industrial development.

Beck conceives of this "second modernity" as one of reflexive (rather than linear) modernization that can bring about "its own change through unwanted side effects" (Wimmer and Quandt 2007, 338). Reflexive modernization can thus, in a new "Enlightenment" ideal, induce "criticism" and "self-criticism" (Beck 1998, 20). He pays special attention to the role of industry and science. Rather than merely bringing about improvements in people's lives according to the liberal rubric of progress, they themselves contribute to or even create risks (Beck 1998, 14–16). *Social* science has a role to play, argues Beck: by being more "reflective" than "professional," it can move away from excessive positivism to deeply and critically consider how to address the contemporary challenges of risk society (Wimmer and Quandt 2007, 345). We thus approach COVID-19 as a clear and dire manifestation of Beck's "risk society." This global pandemic, unpredictable in its outbreak and its rapid-fire spread, has crippled polities, economies, and societies. It has arguably resulted from the toxic combination of capitalist structures and practices on the one hand, and scientific-technological developments on the other. Advancement-turned-vulnerability is the name of the game.

Risk society and its dangers are not neatly boxed within single countries. Instead, they permeate the territorial demarcations of modern states. The COVID-19 pandemic, the focus of our study, clearly illustrates this. Thus, we also further draw on Beck's concept of "world risk society." Here, there is a threefold "de-bounding of uncontrollable risks" (Beck 2002, 41). It is *spatial* (problems pushing through nation-state boundaries), *temporal* (unforeseeably longer time frame), and *social* (accountability and culpability are indeterminate) (2002, 41). Ecological, global financial, and global terrorist risks are all examples (Beck 2002, 41–2). We can add the pandemic to the roster. Since risk can resonate internationally and transnationally, Beck urges "cooperation" and multilateralism for problem-solving in such cases, ideally within "cosmopolitan states" whose rights- and justice-based values make them more inclined to exactly such synergism (2002, 47–9, 50). The globalization of risk has implications not only for problem-solving in the policy realm but also in social science. Hence, Beck shuns what he calls "methodological nationalism" that deals with nation-states as the cornerstone of social science analysis, as a "socio-ontological given" (Beck 2002, 51). Instead, he argues that social science must be made more "transnational" (elsewhere, "cosmopolitan") from concept-building to theorizing to methodological implementation, in addition to its structural features (2002, 53). Following Beck, then, we take the pandemic to be a manifestation of "world risk society." In this volume, we go beyond the "methodological nationalism" he decries in social science, toward a "transnationalism" that remains focused on the MENA region. Going too global may come at the price of losing the specificity of local/regional context in the conceptualization and measurement of concepts and the tracing of patterns.

Hence, our take on Beck's global risk society zeroes in on the MENA region. Shared cultural, economic, political characteristics emanating from geographic proximity and overlapping histories necessitate region-wide examinations of politics (Korany 2020). MENA countries also experience common patterns of risk society. These include relatively "dependent" status in world affairs, from Palestine and Kuwait to Morocco and Syria. We contend that such recipient positionality extends to the problems arising from risk society. As Beck notes, "in the so-called periphery," policies and decisions in confronting world risk society are made elsewhere in the "center," involving an "exogenous process" outside the former's control (2002, 42). In fact, he adds, risk is unequally distributed across a world riven with inequality, its dangers sometimes "exported" across time and space by the powerful in the direction of the less powerful (2008, 7). Investigating the pandemic's pathways, as expression and exacerbation of risk in MENA's numerous countries, impels us to adopt a regional focus: what we call "regional risk society." At the same time, our analytic strategy further aids us as we seek to avoid abstracting Arab states and societies of their agency. Thus, we stress the comparative uniqueness of states and regions dealing with risks not of their own making. That is, the risk inducers of modernity (capitalism, industrialization, technological progress, etc.) that Beck has suggested are not of local (Arab) origin—a logic that extends to the coronavirus. Yet, the Arab states and their societies, like other developing countries, must suffer the consequences of such risk as the architects of Western modernization do, albeit through distinct experiences.

We are aware of criticisms leveled at Beck's risk society. For example, some theorists take Beck to task for presenting as novel risks that are not really new (or modern) in the history of human existence (Rasborg 2012, 5–6). Beck's conceptualization of risk is "too simple," leaving undifferentiated disparate phenomena of risk development and the "rationalities" through which to observe and assess it (Rasborg 2012, 10–14).

Importantly, speaking of a single "world risk society" is too reductive to account for the variegated and staggered processes of modernization and "counter-modernization" (Rasborg 2012, 16–19). What justifies its use here in this volume is not subscription of a view of "total risk" as perhaps contended by Beck. It is not how class *per se* relates to risk. Rather, it is how risk engulfs the world's peripheries relative to the industrialized states that form the center of global economic, scientific, technological and even military prowess. These peripheries in MENA, almost invariably ex-colonized states and societies, display insecurities and vulnerabilities exacted on them by adoption of development models (modernization-cum-liberalization, dependence, etc.) and implements of power (Western tutelage and authoritarian rule tolerated by the West). So risk may not be "total," as conceived by Beck within new modernity. It is, however, "situated" risk with own specificities. In particular, how risk is not in any small measure, as regards political, socioeconomic, or social vulnerabilities and woes, created by ex-colonized but a variant of that experienced by the ex-colonizers. Indebtedness to the ex-colonizers debilitates the economies of the ex-colonized. The techne of oppression, militarization, and securitization that prop up delegitimized regimes and elites are made available to the ex-colonized by the ex-colonizers. Failed development models following different economic itineraries, socialist or liberal, account for a big share of the brands of risk found in MENA. Examples include wars and their aftermath in the region. And so on, such that MENA risk society becomes a fitting frame through which to examine, critique, and reimagine its "pandemic condition."

Global COVID Risks

In tracing COVID-19's repercussions on economies, polities, and societies, some global trends have taken shape since early 2020. The pandemic's breathtakingly rapid spread revealed drawbacks of the much-vaunted "flows" of globalization. The movement of people, it turns out, carries with it potential dangers to human health and livelihoods. Early into the pandemic, debates raged about coronavirus' damage to capitalism, and which markets, businesses, and economic practices, were more amenable to recovery. Comparisons abounded with the 2008–9 recession, or even the Great Depression of the 1920s. Some argue that COVID-19 has shown the unreliability of employment, irresponsible lending practices given climbing household debt, and the dangers of weakened public sectors (Mazzucato 2020). Crumbling healthcare infrastructure not just in MENA countries like Tunisia but also in established OECD democracies (e.g., the United Kingdom and even the United States) are telling. In 2020, the World Bank predicted a 5.2 percent contraction in economic growth across the world. Nosediving per capita income would be followed by dramatically declining investment, an "erosion of human capital" because of time missed at work and in school, and major disruptions in international trade and supply chains (World Bank 2020). Already under strain, developing countries would suffer more than the rest, predicted the World Bank early on. Rising joblessness and poverty heighten inequality.

Political freedoms, too, have been another casualty, rendering full and equal citizenship more insecure. International groups have been monitoring rollbacks in human rights and democracy set in motion as governments responded to COVID-19 by policing movement and expression (International IDEA 2020). Democratic advocates have stressed that authoritarian states and even some governments who came to power in democratic elections have instituted policies going against the grain of democracy. Abuse of emergency powers, the curbing of free speech, and circumventing the rule of law are some indicators. Governance of the pandemic is further complicated by the absence of globally (or even regionally) systematic approaches. From mask refusers and "anti-vaxers" to intra-GCC travel bans, pandemic policy itself has become a space for political contention within and between states. According to early assessments, the pandemic seemed to be feeding into nationalism and even "reinforc[ing] the nation-state" from scientific expertise to interstate relations (e.g., United States versus China) (Woods et al. 2020). Scrutinizing state-society and state-transnationalism dynamics, we can tentatively point to shifts, in power and prominence, in favor of the state. This is a worrying trend in the MENA region where authoritarianism is the prevalent form of rule shaping relations between those who govern and those being governed. Taken together, these global pandemic tendencies are cause for vigilance in research and civic-political practice springing from values of human dignity, freedom, and equality.

Regional Overview: MENA's COVID-Risk Society

The Limits of Risk-as-Security

COVID-19 prompts us to ask deeper questions about the nature and causes of vulnerability and risk, as well as attendant responses by policymakers, civil society, scholars, and activists. For the last two decades at least, MENA crises and "risks" as such have been dealt with through the lens of security. The US playbook, particularly its War on Terror policies of invasion, occupation, incarceration, torture, and extensive surveillance has been especially instructive for Arab autocrats. A view of "risk" as pertaining to potential for terrorism or extremism has been echoed in the work of scholars and analysts. Pinar Bilgin asserts that the very notion of the "Middle East" as a region is couched in Western security concerns related to the price of oil, the Arab-Israeli conflict, restraining Islamism, blocking ascendance of a "hegemon," and cultivating regimes amicable to the United States and its allies (2004, 28). This is a "top-down" understanding of security, she continues, one that places primacy on "externally" directed threats (to the United States, or NATO, or their friends in the region). On the one hand, then, what we consider here risk-as-security seems to dovetail with external interests and the perpetually problematic knowledge-power dyad explored by Said and others with respect to the "Orient" or the "Middle East." On the other hand, a focus on risk as "security" has long been readily adopted by autocratic regimes who, under the guise of participation and cooperation in the US War on Terror, have gleefully moved to quell hints of opposition and dissent. Counterrevolutionary policies and power takeovers reacting to the popular Arab

Spring uprisings and revolutions (Sadiki 2015) have comfortably reverted back to similar confrontation of "risks" in the form of "terrorism" and "extremism." Egypt's Sisi, for whom "risk" of terrorism/extremism/state security inheres in the Muslim Brotherhood (Moussa 2015) is one example. Syria's Assad, where revolutionaries, opposition activists (Saleh 2017, 140–78) and militants all constitute "terrorist" infiltrators seeking to sow seeds of discord according to the script of an international conspiracy, is another.

Reliance on a security frame to deal with risk through emergency laws, illegal arrests, lack of due process, and deeply entrenched *mukhabarat* (security and intelligence apparatus) practices in the name of snuffing out the faintest threat to autocratic stability, has coincided with another feature of the region's politics. Deep fragmentation, particularly since the US invasion of Iraq, has worked against regional cooperation on any number of issues, including risks not framed by a strict security mindset. Sectarianized and tribalized politics, violence, shifting alliances, and regional (re)alignments spilled into conflictual stances and interventions propelled by the 2011 "Arab Spring." Some initially promising uprisings spiraled into internationalized war (Libya, Syria, Yemen), while other already war-torn contexts sank into further violence (Iraq).

Enter the pandemic. In the COVID-19 era, a securitized notion of risk by the region's policymakers has proven ineffective, paradoxically itself compounding risk. COVID-19 thus prompts us to rethink what risk *is* in the MENA region. For both policy and analysis, developments over the past two years seem to suggest that a move away from risk-as-security/instability is in order. It is worth remembering that inattention to or neglect of inequalities, citizens' distributional needs, and the state's fractious relationship with society are some identical factors to those that caught Arab autocrats off guard in 2011. These same "risks" have again come to the fore in the pandemic, and in attempts to repel it, throughout the region. Insufficient concern for the roots and symptoms of risks beyond security arguably complicates state and regional-level responses to the pandemic. COVID-19, then, at once reveals and augments MENA's "regional risk society." Thus, this volume's investigation of the region's manifold risk, as unearthed by the pandemic.

Trends and Patterns

We tentatively identify several interrelated trends that we conceptualize as MENA-level "risks" that have come into sharp relief in the COVID era. First, the risk-as-security preoccupation, whether against internal rebellion or external infiltration and intervention, has worked against cooperation among MENA states. Even before 2011, the region was already notorious for weakly institutionalized regionalism incapable of addressing the most intractable conflict of all, the Israeli occupation of Palestine. Internal and externally waged conflicts have precluded predispositions, let alone institutions, that facilitate joint or coordinated crisis management of problems such the socioeconomic and health challenges brought on by COVID. Regional frictions even became the backdrop to policies of aid (GCC assistance to Tunisia) or travel restrictions vis-à-vis "sister" states in the region (Saudi-Emirati travel ban). Thus, risk-as-security in MENA has hindered pandemic preparedness in two ways. First, by diverting attention from (non-security) sources of "risk," such as unequal distribution, weak or absent individual freedoms, constrained civic space, and securitized politics. Additionally, by fortifying fragmentation and *weak* regional cooperation (Legrenzi and Calculli 2013) where rivalry supersedes cooperation by a wide margin. This has been the case even for a subregion like the GCC, as the 2017–21 blockade/crisis demonstrated.

Second, economic underdevelopment has stood out as both cause and consequence of profound vulnerability to the pandemic. The world's premier International Financial Institutions have focused on the economic consequences of COVID-19, also tentatively forecasting the speed and scope of economic and financial recovery. In this regard, some trends are discernible across the region. First, MENA has been no exception to the global contraction of economies. Lockdown measures in particular set Arab economies back considerably. Remittances were expected to fall by 12 percent and foreign direct investment by 82 percent, and low oil prices (atop travel restrictions) stalled the vital tourism sector, even as the government delayed taxes and offered loans to small businesses in 2020 assessments of Tunisia, for instance (OECD 2020). Poor healthcare infrastructure in the North African country, particularly in underserved marginalized regions, set in motion expansive healthcare procurement (funded by a Central Bank loan) by the health ministry to reach 2,000 ICU beds (OECD 2020). Unsurprisingly, the UN concluded in 2020 that COVID-19 will serve as a setback to the UN Sustainable Development Goals (2020). Countries and regions better situated to cope with the pandemic are the ones who have progressed further in the SDGs: namely, South Asia (UN 2020, vi). Arab states, on the other hand, exhibit wide variance in their performance pre-COVID. One serious gap in assessing preparedness has been the lack of reliable data on indicators such as poverty, income inequality, and the conditions of workers, particularly in the Gulf region (UN 2020, 38). The World Bank (2021c) has reported on skyrocketing public debt across MENA countries. Borrowing, according to the agency, has pushed up projected rates by about 8 percent, to an average of 54 percent, as high as 93 percent in oil-importing countries (e.g., Egypt, Jordan, Lebanon, and Tunisia). There is irony in the World Bank's recommendations that countries exercise greater "transparency" and better "fiscal prioriti[zation]." The greater the indebtedness and accumulation of international loans, of course, the smaller the space for governments to set budgets or allocate stipends and other public spending for the most vulnerable. Domestic priorities and prerogatives fall to the wayside in economic-political dependencies induced by watchful guards of global capitalism, such as the IMF and the World Bank.

Third and relatedly is the problem of inequality and skewed distribution. Within the MENA region, not all risks are borne equally. This inequality is superimposed on MENA's positionality within the global hierarchy, recounted previously. One IMF "Regional Economic Outlook" stressed the unevenness of impact and potential bounce-back in the MENA region. Severity of the pandemic infection and contagion patterns, socioeconomic structural difficulties including indebtedness and unemployment rates, access and distribution of the vaccine, and the centrality of tourism to the region's economies (e.g., Morocco and Tunisia) will all be factors that determine how fast or slow recovery can be (IMF 2021a, 1–7). The GCC states, for instance, were ahead of other Arab states in rolling out the vaccine by early 2021. These "early inoculators," also countries with extensive "fiscal space" (e.g., Qatar-GCC), where oil prices have begun to bounce back, are in a relatively favorable position. They are better positioned to administer economic and fiscal convalescence than deeply indebted countries with high youth unemployment and late/slow vaccination (e.g., Tunis), conflict-afflicted states (e.g., Syria), or politically unstable countries (e.g., Sudan) (IMF 2021a, 2–8). Emphasizing what we consider here risk, the IMF highlights the extreme "uncertainty" surrounding economic prospects in what is largely an unpredictable path of the virus and government policy measures (e.g., lockdowns) that can hamper recovery (IMF 2021a, 9). The IMF notes that COVID-19 brought to the fore deep inequalities in the region, and the extreme vulnerabilities of particular groups such as youth, women, and small companies. The danger is that inadequate state responses in the economic and "social protection" realms may deepen poverty and perhaps even threaten social cohesion in the direction of "unrest" by discontented publics (IMF 2021a, 10).

To flesh out these second and third trends, Table 1.1 offers a comparative snapshot of COVID-19 socioeconomic risk within a sample of MENA countries. The numbers may not be fully accurate or reliable, since access to information can be limited under authoritarianism and in states/territories beleaguered by war or occupation. Nevertheless, data for each of the five indicators exhibits variation within the region. Preparedness or vulnerability to the pandemic is measured here through the Human Development Index (HDI) and the number of hospital beds (per 10,000 people). At the highest end of HDI are the Gulf states, with the UAE coming in first at .866), and war-torn Yemen coming in last at .463. Hospital beds range from 32 per 10,000 in Libya to 7.1 per 10,000 in Yemen. Youth unemployment, a persistently high problem for years in a trend not unrelated to the Arab Spring uprisings (Palencia 2015), later exacerbated by COVID-19, also differs across MENA. Gas-rich Qatar has the lowest youth unemployment rate registered at 0.5 percent, while Tunisia (35.8 percent), Jordan (37.3 percent), Palestine (40 percent), and violence-stricken Libya (49.5 percent) show markedly higher rates in 2019. In terms of the actual pandemic, the number of cases per million according to official statistics begin at 1,465 in Syria (where government numbers are likely underestimates) to 153,282 in Bahrain. Fatality rates were highest in Tunisia (1,825 per million) and lowest in Algeria (107), based on officially reported numbers. Finally, the table displays vaccination rates—the real test for dealing with the extended "pandemic condition" particularly in terms of mobility (travel) and even the ability to work or study face-to-face. Here, the Gulf small states have the consistently highest rates: 72.9 percent in the UAE, 65.17 percent in Qatar, and 62.96 percent in Bahrain. On the other hand, vaccination in Yemen (0.4 percent) and Syria (0.5 percent) as of August 2021 was almost nonexistent. Financial largesse and relative stability (no war, no sanctions) seem to correspond with country-level access to the vaccine. The worldwide trend of poorer countries in the developing world being the last to vaccinate was in 2020 acutely experienced in MENA. An exception to this tendency was Tunisia. Under Kais Saied's "vaccine diplomacy" shortly before his July 25 power grab, the country which managed to secure 6 million doses from Arab and other international donors in June/July 2021 as its pandemic reached an apex (Reuters 2021).

Table 1.1 Indicators of COVID-19 "Risk" in MENA

Country	Youth Unemployment Rate (2019)[a]	Human Development Index (HDI)[b]	Hospital Beds (Per 10,000)	COVID-19 Cases/ 1 M[c]	COVID-19 Deaths/1M	COVID-19 Vaccination Rate (% Population Vaccinated)
Algeria	29.7	.759	19	4,186	107	1.65
Bahrain	7.3	.838	17.4	153,282	783	62.96
Egypt	26.5	.700	14.3	2,731	159	1.82
Iran	25.5			51,949	1,148	3.75
Iraq	25.2	.689	13.2	43,069	477	1.23
Jordan	37.3	.723	14.7	75,941	990	24.89
Kuwait	15.7	.808	20.4	93,646	550	21.62
Lebanon	17.1	.730	27.3	85,849	1,174	14.33
Libya	49.5	.708	32	40,415	560	5.4
Morocco	22.3	.676	10	20,306	295	30.89
Palestine	40	.690		61,219	692	8.37
Qatar	0.5	.848	12.5	81,618	214	65.17
Saudi Arabia	29.6	.857	22.4	15,204	237	32.05
Syrian Arab Republic	20.8	.549	14	1,465	108	.05
Tunisia	35.8	.739	21.8	52,182	1,825	12.6
United Arab Emirates	7.2	.866	13.8	70,008	200	72.9
Yemen	24.2	.463	7.1	239	46	.04

[a] *Source*: World Bank (2021a). from the ILO.
[b] Source for HDI and Hospital Bed numbers: UNDP (2021), p. 20.
[c] Data as of August 16, 2021. Source for COVID cases, fatalities, and vaccination: World Bank (2021b) MENA Crisis Tracker.

A fourth trend taking shape as an aspect of pandemic-induced regional risk is the shaky status of democracy and human rights in the MENA region. Alex De Waal (2021) cautions that the "Euro-American 'war on disease' narrative" can work against democracy, and counter to the efforts of activists working against injustice and inequality. War-like language-turned-policy runs parallel to states of emergency, which feeds into autocratic tendencies and encourages problematic policing even within democracies (De Waal 2021, 9–12). Western states and policymakers are not alone in employing this martial language. Its parallel exists among Arab leaders, too, whose promises and justifications in the first two years of the pandemic were often prefaced by *al-harb 'ala corona* (war on corona, alternatively COVID). Throughout the MENA region, from the Arab Gulf to Turkey to the Arab Maghreb and Jordan, Iraq, and Syria, human rights and public freedoms have taken a toll. It is as though Arab autocrats, and even new democrats (Tunisia), have sought to reconquer public space claimed by mobilized publics in the early days of the Arab Spring. This COVID-era "return of the state" has taken several forms. The most dramatic setback for democracy in the region was Tunisian president Kais Saied's sudden consolidation of power, including the freezing of Parliament, on July 25, 2021. He declared his "exceptional measures" the new law in town on a day when public protests had decried government incapacity to stave off the pandemic's impact, the deadliest in the region. More broadly, International IDEA has found that all countries in the Middle East have put in place at least one measure that is "concerning" or potentially concerning with respect to democracy and human rights. These include postponing elections that are already far from "clean" (Oman). More common casualties are freedoms of expression, association, assembly, movement (lockdowns), and even religion (closing mosques) coupled with "us[ing] excessive force" in implementing measures like lockdowns and curfews (23–7). Media freedoms in particular are under threat, as in government fines for supposed "fake news" from Saudi Arabia and the UAE (IDEA 2021, 30) to Algeria and Morocco (Kacha 2020). Moreover, electronic surveillance by the state is a twenty-first-century form of Foucault's (1978) biopower that "disciplines" and regulates to makes people "docile." Qatar's EHTERAZ app (Aljazeera 2020), and other versions in Bahrain and Kuwait (Statt 2020) have raised questions about digital privacy (Amnesty 2020), possibly used as entry points for "mass surveillance." Strict state policies of monitoring and control, on and off-line, have not always had the (presumably intended) effect of quieting dissent, however. Repressive lockdowns and restrictions on the use of public space in the Arab world beleaguered by inequalities from Algeria to Lebanon have spurred alternative activisms, from food drives to online campaigns (Fahmi 2021). When six people died in an Amman hospital due to insufficient oxygen, protests by Jordanians already suffocating under pandemic restrictions popped up across the country from Irbid to Karak to Aqaba, and the health minister was sacked (AlKhalidi 2021). Algeria's *Hirak* movement is one example where protests moved online (Mestek 2020, 26–9). In Tunisia, dissent and protest, particularly expressing socioeconomic and social justice demands, picked up despite restrictions on public space and mobility, especially in late 2020 to early 2021 (Ghannouchi 2021, 26–9). This paradox, previously at work in some Arab Spring protests in 2011–2 whereby government crackdowns helped instigate further mobilization in Syria (Saleh 2018) or Yemen (Manea 2015), calls for further investigation, taken up by some of this book's chapters.

A fifth important trend across the region relates to conflict. Policy studies have speculated in a general sense on how COVID-19 is set to impact existing violence and war. The pandemic's toll on international politics, conflict, and diplomacy has been projected as dire (International Crisis Group 2020). With their compromised health systems, conflict-ridden locales (e.g., Libya, Gaza, Syria, Yemen) are more vulnerable to infection and contagion. Access by international organizations and aid groups is more difficult in places such as Idlib (Syria) and Yemen (ICG 2020, 3–4). Internally displaced persons and refugees (more than 70 million in a 2019 estimate) likely suffer more in their substandard and crowded living conditions, such as the Al-Hol Syrian refugee camp where 70,000 people reside (ICG 2020, 4). Densely populated northern Syria, home to four million people (many displaced by the war), witnessed high levels of COVID-19 contagion in October 2021. Already weak healthcare infrastructure was further battered by successive and "severe" pandemic waves. Oxygen deficiencies, low screening and vaccination levels (3%), and inadequate numbers of healthcare workers afflicted the region from Idlib to Afrin, Al-Bab, and Raqqa. Violent attacks against doctors in Iraq have spiked (Latfa et al. 2021) during the pandemic. Reported levels of gender-based violence have also surged, with domestic violence comprising three quarters (UNFPA 2020). Moreover, international mediation and diplomacy efforts are made more difficult by the pandemic, especially given travel restrictions (ICG 2020, 6–7). State-society tensions will likely simmer (e.g., through protest) as governments impose lockdowns, struggle to keep up healthcare provision, provide economic relief, and intervene in basic freedom of movement (ICG 2020, 6–9). These countervailing tendencies are evident in Libya. Renewed (internationalized) civil war violence wreaked further havoc on the country's healthcare infrastructure. Yet popular protests against both the GNA and General Haftar's LAAF's tepid pandemic response in late 2020 may have served as an impetus to relaunch internationally mediated negotiations (El Gomati 2020). Still, the accord promised by the ceasefire agreement of 2020 did not prevent the cancellation of the scheduled December 2021 elections. Hence, social, economic, and public health measures against COVID-19 are inextricable from conflict patterns in the MENA region, necessitating "multidimensional" approaches to dealing with these challenges (Kenney and Harrison 2020). Such preliminary conclusions point to the utility of a holistic, region-wide examination of pandemic risks and responses in addition to national-level analyses. The mounting evidence thus far does not always bear out international prescriptions for cooperation. Exploring such a paradox calls for sustained and systematic inquiry, especially in the Arab world, where COVID-19 arguably magnifies the scope and spillovers of rampant conflict (Mulroy 2021). A year into the pandemic, the International Crisis Group noted that "COVID-19 hasn't re-invigorated peacemaking" around the globe, failing to dull long-standing tensions and conflicts including in the MENA region (e.g., US-Iran) (Atwood 2021).

The indicators and trends discussed above present an ominous and regionally skewed picture, hinting at extensive pandemic impact which countries in MENA are differentially equipped to handle. Conflict, underdevelopment, and inequality are entangled in risks that make for desperately limited pandemic preparedness. Thus, some global institutions have suggested at least general policy responses to what we term here the panoply of COVID-19 risk. Important to "sustainable, inclusive, job-rich, and greener economies" are cooperation at the regional and international levels. Digitization in particular can amplify state responses to changing socioeconomic environments, as can improved "governance, transparency, and accountability" (IMF 2021, 11–12). Similarly, the UN advises "solidarity and partnerships" in confronting ongoing crises, including between "policymakers, business, civil society, and the scientific community" (UN 2020, vii). Considering the outlook for a "new development paradigm" in the wake of the pandemic, the UNDP stresses the low "institutional capacity" (medical, equipment, communication) rendering Arab states ill-equipped to confront crises (2020, 158). These compound existing "structural challenges" and less than stellar achievements regarding the Sustainable Development Goals (UNDP 2020, 158). Needed are "integrated solutions" to deal with a number of risks from inequality, unemployment, "political suppression," and polarization through balancing health and economic responses (UNDP 2020, 162). The UNDP advises bolstering state capacity through greater regional integration, improved public services, and honing "more appropriate skills" among the people allowing their entry into changing (e.g., digital) economies (2020, 163). In a conflict-ridden and explosive environment such as the Middle East, the International Crisis Group advises cooperation between governments and UN bodies. They can establish synergies in offering humanitarian aid, financial support, and even debt relief after "needs assessments" about specific areas of vulnerability. In addition to maintaining the pace of regional and international mediation efforts in conflict situations, support for civil society (including NGOs and independent media) can counteract rumor-mongering and political exploitation related to the pandemic (ICG 2020, 14). However, such policy recommendations remain somewhat vague. More substantive and actionable explorations of the manifold problems instigated or exacerbated by COVID-19 in the region are necessary. This is where scholars can step in, carrying out more in-depth, fine-grained, and contextualized analyses of both risk and possible solutions to mitigate it. Enter the "reflexivity" that can be the positive upshot of "risk society."

Action Research and Reflexivity

Reflexivity is a valuable research practice needed more than ever in unscrambling pandemic-era risk across the MENA region. Like all intellectual pursuits, it involves meaning-making, but goes a step further in its orientation toward problem-solving. Moreover, reflexivity seeks to insert research and researchers *inside* COVID-19, toward greater ownership of the pandemic that has been dominated by technocratic recommendations and governance from without, for example, the WHO or the IMF. The underlying question propelling such reflexivity is the drive to identify COVID-19-related problems—often new iterations of long-standing risks. In this chapter, we have pointed out possible directions for further investigation: underdevelopment, inequality, dependencies, freedoms and democracy, conflict. Thus, we seek to begin activating basic tenets of action research, which angles to re-merge theory and praxis via social science (Coghlan and Brydon-Miller 2014). This type of research is one that builds on actual experiences of researchers as well as participants, understood as more than simply "respondents" (Coghlan and Brydon-Miller 2014, 20–1). The aim is for the knowledge produced to be more reflective of realities of the people it studies, and useful in "transforming th[e] world" (Coghlan and Brydon-Miller 2014, 21). Research that takes up such issues, as the ensuing chapters seek to do, becomes a space that exudes an ethos of reflexivity, in its examination of political, socioeconomic, demographic, and even military issues. This stance can elevate scholars from mere analysts to critical problem-solvers, producing research that *matters* to the quality of human life. Becoming quasi-ethnographers of the pandemic is one-way researchers can take up this challenge.

The complexities of our normatively laden topic, COVID-19's socioeconomic and political impact on MENA, call for multi-disciplinarity to explore new types of power at work in governing and administering the pandemic and the populations, institutions, processes, and social relations it (potentially) infects. As the "return of the state" becomes more and more prominent, much can be gleaned from investigating how states exercise their power and control. Tracking applications, testing procedures and results, vaccination accolades that have become travel and even dining requirements, all interact with more traditional forms of policing, evident in lockdowns. Thus, the state is powerful vis-à-vis the populations it governs, even when that state lacks the capacity (in knowledge and resources) to ward off the pandemic, as in the case of most MENA countries. State power penetrates and controls the (sometimes digitized) bureaucracy, the school and university, the media, technology itself, and even tribes (Sadiki 2020, 10–12). Foucault's well-known insight that power is the control over *life* as well as death, the "right of death and power over life" (1978, 133), resonates loudly in the age of the pandemic.

Not unlike Foucault, Arendt also delves into some (knowledge) practices that exert control over individuals and societies. Unthinking same-ness emerges as the norms of society interweave with the toolkits of social science (statistics, experiments, "laws"), she cautions. Merged thus, they extinguish the "paradoxical plurality of unique beings" that is the "basic condition of thought and speech," the realm of politics and by extension true freedom (Arendt 1958, 175–6). We interpret here a reflexivity in Arendt's work. This is a drive to fashion the world into "what the world is always meant to be, a home for men [*and women*, we would add] during their life on earth" (Arendt 1958, 173). It involves aspiring to and realizing the "freedom" of the political in "action" underpinned by morality, away from the disastrous "belie[f] that we deal with ends and means in the political realm" (Arendt 1958, 220, author addition). Arendt seems open to optimism so long as the possibility of "thought" exists, that is, "wherever men live under the conditions of political freedom" (Arendt 1958, 324). This begs the question: freedom from what? We venture to reinterpret what Arendt valorizes as freedom from "necessity" as instead being freedom as freedom from want. That is, deprivation (*hirman*), marginalization, lives bereft of dignity—all too common throughout the MENA region. Working toward this freedom is the purview of "action research," decidedly non-positivist in ontology and epistemology. Embracing pluralism (from ontology to epistemology to methodology) and multi-disciplinarity is one-way researchers can delve into life under COVID-19, the "pandemic condition," in problem-solving mode.

In addition to Arendt, Beck's, and Habermas's more explicit reflexivity can guide us in conceptualizing the leap from theory to practice as problem-solving, with respect to COVID's destructive path. Critically approaching the pandemic should prompt Beck's "reflexive modernization" recounted earlier. That is, "possibility of a creative (self-)destruction" (Beck, Giddens and Lash 1992, 2). Tailored to the context at hand, such reflexivity necessitates rethinking enduring problems prevalent in (mostly) postcolonial MENA polities and economies. Theory can couple with practice, we suggest, what Beck refers to as "public, political and scientific reflection" (Beck, Giddens and Lash 1992, 6). The aim is to untangle sociopolitical dynamics and begin to reverse inequality in the direction of greater civic engagement, inclusion, full citizenship, access to social welfare, raised environmental awareness, etc. COVID-19 (and other potential pandemics) is a novel form of human-made risk concocted by modernity's hazards, from science to technology to environmental degradation. In practicing reflexivity, practitioners (in politics, civil society, business) and scholars can adopt a Habermasian dialogic stance. Here, Habermas's (1984) communicative action is a useful concept. It is by nature pluralist, participatory, intersubjective, agential, dispersed, and inclusive. Communicative action thus lends itself to including diverse inputs and widening participation in debates relevant to public life. Contributions can be formal (legislation and policymaking), or they can stem from informal advocacy and communal action (by civil society groups). Such communicative rationality can jump-start multidirectional dialogue in the MENA region. Animated by an ethos of mutuality and collaboration, local (national), regional (intra-MENA), and international exchanges can counteract some of the zero-sum, nationalist policies in health, science, and anti-COVID measures that have run rampant over the past two years. Moreover, this dialogic, reflexive sensibility of a MENA risk society (Sadiki and Saleh 2020) can enhance (critical and action) research in similar fashion.

Quasi-Ethnography of the Pandemic?

There is much to critique in the seemingly ubiquitous adoption of the "war on COVID" discourse that, as feminists point out, may prop up patriarchy, racism, and even authoritarianism (Enloe 2020). Subsequent "securitization" of the spaces and people that may (potentially) spread it is already cause for alarm. However, social science examinations of wartime may lend some analytical insights to our present investigation. The COVID-19 pandemic seems to have become a common scheme through which to probe political, socioeconomic, and cultural life. We may take notes from those who research "war as experience" (Sylvester 2013). Sylvester's approach, for instance, interrogates how war shapes and is shaped by lives and structures at various levels and interactions of society, polity, and economy. In line with an "action research" orientation, understanding the "pandemic condition" similarly lends itself to ethnography (see also Sadiki and Saleh 2021). This includes "engaged ethnography," replete with practices of "solidarity and *praxis*" through involvement with resistance against hegemonic forces such as neoliberalism (Mathers and Novelli 2007). Ethnography as critical and interpretive (rather than positivist) research practice is imbued with constant ethical engagements (dilemmas, decisions), as research(er) meets world and vice versa, making it a necessarily "improvisational" enterprise (Cerwonka and Malkki 2007). In approaching the pandemic, reflexive researchers can learn from ethnographic studies of war. Stephen Lubkemann's research on war and displacement in Mozambique skirts the temptation to approach "war as an 'event' that suspends social processes" (2008, 1). Instead, he posits that war is a "transformative social condition" inclusive of, but not fixed solely on, violence (Lubkemann 2008, 1). In a similar vein, Elisabeth Wood (2008) suggests placing "social networks" at the center of war analysis. She argues that doing so allows for exploring a range of experiences from mobilization to socialization to shifts in identities, economies, and gender relations.

In parallel fashion to war, perhaps, the pandemic may have altered sometimes seemingly "frozen" individual and collective lives. Yet the subsequent sociopolitical dynamics stemming from these changes—which is after all the stuff of social science research—warrant serious investigation. Such explorations are the required precursor for any solution-oriented reflexivity. Even in pandemic times, people of all stripes—from political elites to activist and ordinary citizens to the downtrodden and marginalized—maneuver within tightening spaces. They have not been shorn of agency. The "action and speech" that for Arendt comprises politics has not receded by the wayside. It follows that *changes* in the ways people perform or pursue the civic and the political, whether from the center or the margins, cry out for full-bodied scholarly attention. The lines of inquiry are many. How has public space "liberated" by Arab Spring protestors shrunk, reconquered by the military and security forces imposing lockdown curfews, as the state makes a comeback? In what ways has civic space contracted as public health is securitized through the "governmentality" rules of Foucault's biopolitics: tracking devices, age categorizations of "vulnerable" populations, security checkpoints, temperature readings as entry cards to public and private buildings? How has the "sociality" of pandemic socioeconomic and political life been transformed, from earning livelihoods (virtually or under lockdown) to political participation, civic mobilization, constraints on political freedoms, and "emergency law" operation? What are the stocks of values utilized, nurtured, and learned, or disregarded in such relations and interactions?

Ethnographic approaches can probe these patterns more convincingly and holistically than country or region-level indicators generated by the World Bank, the UN, or the WHO. To this end, tapping into various social science and humanities disciplines and their "texts," from political science to economics to sociology and even literature (cooke 2020), enriches research. Spiking unemployment numbers do not do full justice to the everyday struggles of job searches when social distancing, mask-wearing, restaurant and store closures, and unavailability of public transportation become the new (gatekeeping) rules in town. Rates charting voter turnout may not explain the rage expressed at the political class as elites vacation in lavish resorts (e.g., Tunisia's Mechichi government Sousse excursion) while much of the population wades through socioeconomic uncertainty and insecurity. The contextualized and granular data (co) generation that is the strength of ethnography can fill in these blanks to illuminate political orientations, attitudes, values, and attendant behavior, ruly (voting) or unruly (protests, sit-ins). Official data (even if reliable) on cash transfers to needy populations from Tunisia to Jordan cannot convey how *hirman* has redoubled in COVID times. Budget cuts announced by governments in the Gulf, and chronicles of thousands of workers sent home to Egypt (or Jordan, Tunisia, Nepal, and more) are just the beginning. On their own, these kinds of indicators cannot adequately explain the motivations, mindsets, and backgrounds of the more and more Tunisians choosing the treacherous *harqah* journey on death-boats to escape life without work, without futures, languishing in café after café. Nor can they represent the frustrations and deprivations of life in Idlib's refugee camps and cities without running water, or under occupation in Palestine as rapid vaccination campaigns in Israel garner international acclaim. For more regional perspectives, ethnographies of the pandemic can facilitate examinations of the interconnections emanating from what we have termed "MENA risk society." Researcher, citizen/resident, and political elite can pool their repertoires of experiences, observations, analyses, and suggestions that become kernels for more effective policies and even bottom-up initiatives to constrain creeping inequalities. Some areas of such synergy can be upgrading health services, more even-handed negotiations of international loans, braving travel restrictions, improving health infrastructure, prioritizing aid distribution, amplifying civil society recommendations, inclusive legislating, and more. The list is long.

Reflexivity in Pandemic "Quasi-Ethnography"

One challenge facing a quasi-ethnographic approach is striking a balance between the global, regional, and local. The goal is to unearth localized (national or subnational level) specificities which are further contextualized within the region as well as globally. Such nuance has ontological and epistemological implications relating to the blinkered experiences of COVID in differently situated states and societies. It may not be sufficient to speak of "two pandemics" manifesting differently, sometimes counterintuitively in infection and death rates (Schellekens and Diego Sourrouille 2020). We can begin to surmise instead "many pandemics" across and within countries, within MENA and outside it. Acknowledging the "multiple dimensions of inequality" in the Global South (GRIP Secretariat 2020) is one promising starting point. Appeals to more international "openness" and "collaboration" in scientific knowledge and data (Kityui 2020) additionally point to globally *un*equal access not just of material but also ideational resources and infrastructures. Such imbalanced distribution of knowledge practices, with their pivotal role in *governing* the pandemic's impact and consequences, makes for another stratum of variation in pandemic experiences across and within regions. Thus, we suggest that an ethnographic research trajectory can begin to unpack a fuller gamut of pandemic problems, including breakdowns in knowledge economies (Mckee and Stuckler 2020). Investigations must be grounded in empirical data, coupled with an understanding of the multiple realities, or the different ontologies, of local-national-regional-global life in the shadow of the pandemic. In turn, this may require multiple epistemologies, as researchers reflexively pursue a kind of "control" over researching the pandemic outside the policy-cum-knowledge agendas of global power-holders (UN, IMF, WHO, etc.). This is especially pressing for developing countries (most of MENA). Scholars residing in or studying much of the "Global South" may be well-situated to interrogate both the practices and the edicts, informed by if not embodying neoliberalism, of economic-scientific management of COVID-19.

A quasi-ethnographic sensibility lends itself to the reflexivity of knowledge practice, to account for both the "positive" and the "normative" dimensions of investigating the "pandemic condition" in MENA risk society. Ethnographies of the pandemic, in this volume, involve explorations of both top-down (elite-level) and bottom-up (citizen, civil society) discourses and behaviors to examine local knowledge (e.g., Swidler 1986). Hence, compassionately, ethically informed ethnographic research practices may facilitate creative, collaborative thinking, spilling from academia to policy circles and back. This is aimed at not just at understanding but also problem-solving in the spirit of Giddens's and Beck's "reflexive modernization." Researchers in this book, therefore, draw on a number of approaches/methods, blended in complementary fashion for the benefit of "triangulating" both methods *and* data sources (Carter et al. 2014). The intent is to enhance data validity and reliability through variously combining interviews, analysis of social media, participant observation/field accounts, content analysis, and even policy analysis.

Important to bear in mind is the element of life-research "risk" interface in the eclectic methodologies with an ethnographic thrust. Travel limitations and social distancing measures rendered, at least for some time during the height of the pandemic, in-person fieldwork difficult if not impossible. Social scientists have begun to reflect on new pandemic-induced challenges of access to the field site and the increasing prevalence of "digital ethnography" (e.g., Ghosh 2020). Because of the pandemic, virtual or digital ethnography was popularized as a "fully legitimate method of inquiry" (Krause et al. 2021, 267). It can involve increased reliance on digital forms of data (online news sources, social media posts, videos) in addition to the "multisited" research gone digital through online forms of communication with interviewees (Zoom interviews, chat via various social media platforms) (DeHart 2020). Researchers visit the research sites in "disembodied" form (Hine 2008, 262–4). Online interviews with diplomats and activists, "virtual" attendance of online civil society or academic events, and/or immersion in social media platforms and exchanges, form the crux of data collection in this investigation. The chapters in this book collectively attempt to broach a form of cutting-edge research in online ethnography and qualitative research. The volume's contribution is at once conceptual (MENA risk society), empirical (situated case studies), and *methodological* as the authors delve into the shifting contours of pandemic research. "Risk" flows into research practice, then, here as limited face-to-face interactions and access to research sites. At the same time, our reflexive orientation allows for developing researcher capacity building through new modes of data collection and distanced immersion in the field.

Across cases, participant observation in its various forms enriches the book's chapters. These span conducting interviews and focus groups, curating media (print newspapers), scrutinizing online sources and perhaps partaking in online exchanges, scouring online, off-line, and in-person instructions for the latest public health measures, and immersion in the plethora of state interventions and COVID-countering policies imposed on residents, citizens, and visitors (now all too familiar delineations). Particularly in the as-yet under-researched MENA COVID context, a quasi-ethnographic perspective adds plenty to research. The texture of affect (anxiety, anger at the state); the vacillation of state policies (closures, lockdowns, curfews, and their implementation or lack thereof by police); and social patterns of behavior (mask-wearing, congregating in crowds, lining up in front of pharmacies) come alive. For instance, we (this chapter's authors) were in Tunis as the pandemic was just starting in February–March 2020. It had not yet reached alarming global proportions. That spatio-temporal moment serves as a rough ethnographic "baseline" to which we might compare the unfolding and then climaxing of the COVID-19 roller-coaster. Our experiences and observations upon returning to Tunis for fieldwork over a year later in June–July 2021, at the juncture when the COVID crisis seemed to peak, were palpably distinct. The country's healthcare system struggled to new degrees in confronting the mounting infection rate and death toll recounted above. This time, life in Tunis had a markedly different "feel": (temporarily) abandoned restaurants and shops, early café closures, 8 p.m. curfews, limited mobility between cities and governorates. Above all, shared anxiety, unsettled-ness, a sense of impending doom, and intense dissatisfaction with the state's responses were unmistakably detectable among workers, business owners, and professionals we spoke to. Pandemic risk had almost a material quality in the demeanors, conversations, newly acquired habits (e.g., purchasing and spending, going out or staying indoors), dispositions and emotions (grief, loss, bewilderment, resignation) and concerns of seemingly all and sundry. This was a tense build-up to the events of July 25: President Kais Saied's power grab, freezing of parliament, and single-handed concentration of powers that has been since a huge setback for the country's democratization. Witnessing firsthand what has arguably been the pandemic's most dramatic consequentiality for politics, from the street protests to screaming newspaper headlines to café chatter, has given us a sharper appreciation—in addition to more fine-grained data—of the very high stakes of "MENA risk society" as it played out in Tunisia. Similarly, our participant observer contributors to this volume witnessed various iterations of COVID's progression in a number of countries (Italy on EU-MENA; Palestine; Morocco; Turkey, etc.). When documented and "written" into scholarly accounts of the pandemic by researcher as interlocutor and reader as interpreter, awareness borne of an ethnographic sensibility adds a bit of "situated knowledge" that self-consciously keeps the eye and the pen on the locale. This enhances, we argue, the resulting text—never a "stable" authorial account but one that is read, and reread, by various audiences. Writing the pandemic, so detrimental and debilitating to lives and livelihoods, is replete with conceptual, practical, and normative urgency. The task carries implications of which the reflexively oriented researcher must be cognizant.

Overview of the Book

This introductory chapter has laid out the theoretical and methodological framework for our collective exploration of MENA risk society. The book next turns to MENA's Gulf

Cooperation Council subregion (Bahrain, Kuwait, Oman, Qatar, Saudi Arabia, and the UAE). In Chapter 2, Beverley Milton-Edwards examines Gulf "risk society" inherent in the failings of international and regional institutions to foment cooperation and stabilization in the pandemic era. Disadvantaged because of their "small" capacities and cadres, the Gulf states Kuwait, Qatar, and the UAE thus improvised devices to ensure their own survival and resilience. Caught like other states unprepared for COVID-19, their "pandemic diplomacy," particularly the international dispensation of aid, has made them more relevant within the unstable international system. Taking on the "risk society" dimensions of labor and migration, in Chapter 3 Abdul Ghaffar Mughal and Ali Alshawi illustrate economic disparities between oil-wealthy GCC countries and the labor-exporting economies in the "Gulf migration corridor," exemplified in the case of Pakistan. Diversification and nationalization of the Gulf economies have been two almost contradictory goals. The irony is that COVID-19 offered the GCC just the opportunity to expand economic nationalization. The chapter further offers policy prescriptions that could detract from the "risk society" of entangled and codependent economies. Rounding off the investigation of the Gulf, Hela Miniaoui and Anis Khayati take a broader look at the economic "risk society" engendered by the COVID-19 in Chapter 4. They discover, however, that Gulf associational life was somewhat energized by the very pandemic. With an eye to diversification, Miniaoui and Khiyati suggest some policies that could minimize "risk society" and further shock-proof the Gulf economies in the ongoing pandemic.

Traveling West to the Maghreb, the book then approaches some of MENA's North African countries. The next two chapters linger on questions of governance, democracy, and rights. In Chapter 5, Mohammed Elhachimi compares Algeria, Moroccan, and Tunisian pandemic policies. Structurally, the countries suffer from a common "three-dimensional trap" of social inequality, the absence of regional integration, and weak economic self-reliance. This rendered them woefully unprepared for the pandemic onslaught. To perversely compensate, perhaps, states have retracted some of the rights and stepped back from democratic advances of the last decade. Aisha Kedaoui closely examines Morocco's authoritarian "risk society" in Chapter 6, arguing that the state took advantage of COVID-19 to enact violence and crack down on citizens. Political liberalization, and with it democratization and the protection of human rights, have become increasingly uncertain in the monarchy as pandemic policymaking precludes participation and transparency. The Moroccan Ministry of Health's junior status to the Ministry of the Interior is indicative of the police and securitization approach of COVID-19 management.

MENA risk society moves eastward. Mohammed Moussa and Takayuki Mokota take up the uncertainty of Egypt's risk society in Chapter 7. They draw on Timothy Mitchell's notion of the state, in addition to Beck, illustrating the Egyptian body-politic's growing precarity in the realm of health. Science and politics grow ever cozier, even as Egypt's dependencies on international organizations and corporations call into question the state's capacity to provide the very "good" needed most in COVID: public health itself. Shifting to a context of multidimensional violence, in Chapter 8 Basem Ezbidi investigates pandemic "risk society" in Israeli-occupied Palestine. Enormous discrepancies emerge between Israel's outsize capacities and those of the

Palestinian territories to confront the virus. The Gaza blockade, a "captured economy," and incessant Israeli transgressions against Palestinian rights confound the latter's efforts to manage COVID-19. The burdens of risk society are not equally encountered by occupier and occupied. At the same time, Palestinians have been subject to increasingly authoritarian measures by the Palestinian Authority itself, leaving them doubly vulnerable.

Assem Dandashly focuses on Lebanon's risk society in his Chapter 9 case study, suggesting that the country to an extent was able to manage the pandemic. He critically interrogates four indicators of COVID-19 crisis management: decision-making, communication especially social media, collaboration and coordination, and trust and public acceptance of government and its policies. Inequality, corruption, and financial crisis have complicated Lebanon's efforts to cope with COVID-19.

Utilizing a gender security studies lens, Ravza Altuntaş-Çakır, Ayşegül Gökalp Kutlu, and Fatmanur Delioğlu examine what could be termed a "refugee risk society" in Chapter 10. They ask how Syrian women have weathered the pandemic in neighboring Turkey. These women's insecurities span domestic violence, forced marriages, departures from formal education, obstacles to online learning, unemployment, and difficulty accessing healthcare services. This version of security as risk, therefore, necessitates widening its purview to encompass gendered human security. Moving to Iran, in Chapter 11, Maziyar Ghiyabi puts forth a bottom-up, localized perspective of dealing with pandemic "risk society." He points to "technologies of trust," solidarity, and mutual help networks that have helped blunt the damage of lived pandemic experience in Iran. Ghiyabi calls this the "pedagogy of the virus" as people discover avenues and forge relations helping them survive COVID-19.

Next, Pietro Marzo and Renata Pepicelli shed light on the risk society of foreign policy with respect to EU-MENA relations. In Chapter 12, they demonstrate that the pandemic's impact on MENA countries could have in theory reenergized long-controversial interactions between the two. However, the EU has chosen to turn inward, focusing on domestic and European-level policy priorities. Migration, economic ties, and (resurgent) authoritarianism remain fraught issues across these sets of Mediterranean actors. In Chapter 13, Mudar Kassis delves into the counterrevolution dynamic of the post-Arab Spring political scene. He presents some reflections on how the popular uprisings ("dignity revolutions") of 2011 were forestalled by new and old elites who thwarted mobilization against neoliberal authoritarianism. His risk society is one of counterrevolution, energized and intensified by the pandemic. The aspirations expressed by dignity revolutions may have become an ever more distant possibility. Concluding the volume, Larbi Sadiki and Layla Saleh comment on the significance and analytical utility of the risk society frame to understand its unfolding in MENA. They recap the main findings of the book, suggesting comparative linkages to other regions' pandemic experience. Finally, the brief chapter reflects on avenues for future research on COVID in this region and elsewhere.

Investigating pandemic risk for the understanding of the "pandemic condition" defies ready-made social science indicators and recommendations. It is an undertaking that adheres neither to delineations between national-regional sociopolitical inquiry nor to demarcations between "empirical" and "normative" analyses and interpretations. It is with these caveats in mind that we embark on a tentative exploration of COVID-19's socioeconomic and political repercussions in MENA, through the lens of "regional risk society" undergirded by a posture of reflexivity. The assortment of chapters contained in this volume seek together to kick off a social science discussion of the many faces and facets of vulnerability and responsiveness to the pandemic throughout the region. Our contention is that (quasi)ethnographic accounts of the pandemic, further boosted by the ethos and praxis of "action research" can begin to unearth the transformations wrought across the region, as well as the magnification of status quo problems and challenges. In a world of advancing technology and globalization's many gains, the pandemic brings to light the risk-response dynamic. Pressing questions emerge, with bearing on life and sustenance, freedom and dignity, dreams and prospects, for hundreds of millions of MENA resident-citizens. Uncertainty, unpredictability, and instability loom large. They unsettle taken-for-granted assumptions about the role of the state, the acquiescence of citizens, the sustainability of (under)development, the legitimacy of long-standing regimes, the outlook for democratic freedoms, and the resolvability of sharp or violent conflicts. In research, advocacy, and policy, we ignore the quandaries of risk society at our peril. Neglecting the localized-regionalized vagaries of MENA risk society may prove to be the biggest risk of all.

References

Abufalgha, Mohamed. (2020). "Arabs' Evaluations of their Governments' Responses to COVID-19," *Arab Barometer*, https://www.arabbarometer.org/2020/12/arabs-evaluations-of-their-governments-response-to-covid-19/ (accessed August 26, 2021).

Al-Khalidi, Suleiman. (2021). "Protests Erupt in Jordan after COVID-19 Hospital Deaths Scandal," *Reuters*, March 15, https://www.reuters.com/article/us-health-coronavirus-jordan-protests-idUSKBN2B60QY (accessed July 20, 2021).

Aljazeera. (2020). "Qatar Makes COVID-19 app Mandatory, Experts Question Efficiency," *Aljazeera*, May 26, https://www.aljazeera.com/news/2020/05/qatar-covid-19-app-mandatory-experts-question-efficiency-200524201502130.html (accessed May 20, 2021).

Amnesty International. (2020). "Qatar: Contact Tracing app Security Flaw Exposed Sensitive Personal Details of More than One Million," *Amnesty International*, May 26, https://www.amnesty.org/en/latest/news/2020/05/qatar-covid19-contact-tracing-app-security-flaw/. (accessed March 10, 2022).

Arendt, Hannah. (1998 [1958]). *The Human Condition*, 2nd ed. Chicago: The University of Chicago Press.

Atwood, Richard. (2021). "A Year of COVID and Conflict: What the Pandemic Did and Didnt' Do," *International Crisis Group*, April 2, https://www.crisisgroup.org/content/year-covid-and-conflict-what-pandemic-did-and-didnt-do (accessed April 27, 2021).

Beck, Ulrich. (1998). " Politics of Risk Society," in Jane Franklin (ed.), *Politics of Risk Society*, 9–22. Cambridge: Polity Press.

Beck, Ulrich. (2002). "The Terrorist Threat: World Risk Society Revisited," *Theory, Culture and Society*, 19 (4): 39–55.

Beck, Ulrich. (2008). "World at Risk: The New Task of Critical Theory," *Development and Society*, 37 (1): 1–21.

Beck, Ulrich, Anthony Giddens and Scott Lash. (1992). *Reflexive Modernization: Politics, Tradition and Aesthetics in the Modern Social Order*. Stanford: Stanford University Press.

Bilgin, Pinar. (2004). "Whose 'Middle East'? Geopolitical Inventions and Practices of Security," *International Relations*, 18 (1): 25–41.

Carter, Nancy, Denise Bryant-Lukosius, Alba DiCenso, Jennifer Blythe and Alan J. Neville. (2014). "The Use of Triangulation in Qualitative Research," *Oncology Nursing Forum*, 41 (5): 545–7.

Cerwonka, Allaine and Liisa H. Malkki. (2007). *Improvising Theory: Process and Temporality in Ethnographic Fieldwork*, 3–10. Chicago: The University of Chicago Press.

Coghlan, David and Mary Brydon-Miller. (2014). "The Action Turn," in *The SAGE Encyclopedia of Action Research*, 18–21. London: SAGE.

Cooke, Miriam. (2020). "Literature in the Arab Postcolony," in Larbi Sadiki (ed.), *Routledge Handbook of Middle East Politics: Interdisciplinary Inscriptions*, 88–101. London: Routledge.

DeHart, Monica. (2020). "Thinking Ethnographically in Pandemic Times," *Social Science Research Council*, https://items.ssrc.org/covid-19-and-the-social-sciences/social-research -and-insecurity/thinking-ethnographically-in-pandemic-times/ (accessed April 22, 2021).

De Waal, Alex. (2021). *New Pandemics, Old Politics: Two Hundred Years of War on Disease and its Alternatives*. Cambridge: Polity.

El Gomati, Anas. (2020). "Libya and the COVID-19 Lifecycle: From Distraction to Dissidence," *Istituto Affari Internazionali*, November 6, https://www.iai.it/en/pubblicazioni /libya-and-covid-19-lifecycle-distraction-dissidence. (accessed March 11, 2022).

Enloe, Cynthia. (2020). "COVID-19: 'Waging War' Against a Virus is NOT What We Need to Be Doing," *Women's International League for Peace and Freedom*, https://www .wilpf.org/covid-19-waging-war-against-a-virus-is-not-what-we-need-to-be-doing/ (accessed June 15, 2021).

Fahmi, Georges. (2021). "Can Protest Movements in the MENA Region Turn COVID-19 Into an Opportunity for Change?" *Chatham House*, April 29, https://www .chathamhouse.org/2020/04/can-protest-movements-mena-region-turn-covid-19 -opportunity-change (accessed July 15, 2021)

Foucault, Michel. (1978). *The History of Sexuality, Volume 1: An Introduction*, trans. Robert Hurley. New York: Pantheon Books.

Ghannouchi, Cyrine. (2021). "The COVID-19 Outbreak in Tunisia: Politics, Policies, and Public Dissent," Arab Hub for Social Protection from COVID and Tunisian Forum for Economic and Social Rights (FTDES), Working Paper 1.

Ghosh, Banhishikha. (2020). "Digital Ethnography During the COVID-19 Pandemic," https://www.zora.uzh.ch/id/eprint/199780/1/DIGITALETHNOGRAPHYDURIN GTHECOVID-19PANDEMIC.pdf (accessed April 22, 2021).

GRIP Secretariat. (2020). "#1 Miniseries: COVID-19 and Global Dimensions of Inequality," https://gripinequality.org/2020/03/miniseries-covid-19-and-global -dimensions-of-inequality/ (accessed July 28, 2020).

Habermas, JÜRgen. (1984). *The Theory of Communicative Action, Vol. I, Reason and the Rationalization of Society*. Boston: Beacon Press.

Hine, Christine. (2008). "Virtual Ethnography: Modes, Varieties, Affordances," In Nigel Fielding, Raymond M. Lee and Grant Black (eds.), *SAGE Handbook of Online Research Methods*, 257–270. London: SAGE.

Holliday, Shabnam J. (2015). "Iran's Own Popular Uprising and the Arab Spring," in Larbi Sadiki (ed.), *Routledge Handbook of the Arab Spring*, 527–37. London: Routledge.

Horton, Richard. (2020). *The COVID-19 Catastrophe: What's Gone Wrong and How to Stop It*. Cambridge: Polity.

International Crisis Group. (2020). "COVID-19 and Conflict: Seven Trends to Watch," https://www.crisisgroup.org/global/sb4-covid-19-and-conflict-seven-trends-watch (accessed April 26, 2021).

International IDEA. (2020). "The Global Monitor of COVID-19's Impact on Democracy and Human Rights-A One-Stop Tool to Hold Governments to Account," July 7, https://www.idea.int/news-media/events/global-monitor-covid-19%C2%B4s-impact -democracy-and-human-rights-one-stop-tool-hold (accessed May 20, 2021).

International IDEA. (2021). "Taking Stock of Regional Democratic Trends in Africa and the Middle East Before and During the COVID-19 Pandemic," https://www.idea.int/ sites/default/files/publications/regional-democratic-trends-Africa-Middle-East-before -and-during-COVID-19.pdf (accessed May 20, 2021).

International Monetary Fund. (2021). *Regional Economic Outlook, Middle East and Central Asia: Arising from the Pandemic: Building Forward Better*, https://www.imf.org /en/Publications/REO/MECA/Issues/2021/04/11/regional-economic-outlook-middle -east-central-asia (accessed May 20, 2021).

Kacha, Yasmine. (2020). "In a Post-COVID-19 World, 'Fake News' Laws, a New Blow to Freedom of Expression in Algeria and Morocco/Western Sahara?" *Amnesty International*, https://www.amnesty.org/en/latest/news/2020/05/in-a-post-covid19 -world-fake-news-laws-a-new-blow-to-freedom-of-expression-in-algeria-and -morocco-western-sahara/ (accessed March 10, 2022).

Kenney, Steven and Ross Harrison. (2020). "Middle East Conflcit and COVID-19--A View from 2025," *Middle East Institute, Strategic Foresight Initiative*, https://www.mei .edu/publications/middle-east-conflict-and-covid-19-view-2025 (accessed May 1, 2021).

Kityui, Mukhisa. (2020). "Why the Global Science Community Must Come and Stay Together Beyond the Coronavirus Pandemic," *UNCTAD*, https://unctad.org/en/pages/ newsdetails.aspx?OriginalVersionID=2357 (accessed July 28, 2020).

Koley, Tapas Kumar and Monika Dhole. (2021). *The COVID-19 Pandemic: The Deadly Coronavirus Outbreak*. London: Routledge.

Korany, Bahgat. (2020). "Travelling the Middle East Without a Map: Three Main Debates," in Larbi Sadiki (ed.), *Routledge Handbook of Middle East Politics: Interdisciplinary Inscriptions*, 70–87. London: Routledge.

Krause, Peter et al. (2021). "COVID-19 and Fieldwork: Challenges and Solutions," *PS: Political Science and Politics*, 54 (2): 264–9.

Lafta, Riryadh, Noor Qusay, Meighan Mary, and Gilbert Burnham. (2021). "Violence against Doctors in Iraq during the Time of COVID-19," *PLoS ONE*, 16 (8): e0254401, https://doi.org/10.1371/journal.pone.0254401.

Lal, Vinay. (2020). *The Fury of COVID-19: The Politics, Histories and Unrequited Love of the Coronavirus*. New Delhi: MacMillan India.

Legrenzi, Matteo and Marina Calculli. (2013). "Regionalism and Regionalization in the Middle East: Options and Challenges," *International Peace Institute*, https://www.ipinst

.org/wp-content/uploads/publications/ipi_e_pub_regionalism_me.pdf (accessed August 27, 2021).

Likzuli, Fadilah. (2020). *Al-Tadris 'an Bu'd wa Rihanat al-Islah fi Dhil Ja'ihat COVID-19*. Majallat al-Bahith li al-Dirasat al-Qanuniyyah wa al-Qadhai'yyah, Vol. 17.

Lowi, Theodore J. (1964). "American Business, Public Policy, Case Studies, and Political Theory," *World Politics*, 16: 677–693.

Lubkemann, Stephen C. (2008). *Culture in Chaos: An Anthropology of the Social Condition in War*. Chicago: University of Chicago Press.

Mackenzie, Deborah. (2020). *Covid-19: The Pandemic that Should Never Have Happened and How to Stop the Next One*. New York: Hachette Books.

Manea, Elham. (2015). "Yemen's Arab Spring: Outsmarting the Cunning State?" in Larbi Sadiki (ed.), *Routledge Handbook of the Arab Spring*, 160–72. London: Routledge.

Mathers, Andrew and Mario Novelli. (2007). "Researching Resistance to Neoliberal Globalization: Engaged Ethnography as Solidarity and Praxis," *Globalizations*, 4 (2): 229–49.

Mazzucato, Mariana. (2020). "Coronavirus and Capitalism: How will the Virus Change the Way the World Works?" *World Economic Forum*, April 2, https://www.weforum.org/agenda/2020/04/coronavirus-covid19-business-economics-society-economics-change (accessed March 11, 2022).

McKee, Martin and David Stuckler. (2020). "If the World Fails to Protect the Economy, COVID-19 will Damage Health Not Just Now but also in the Future," *Nature Medicine*, 26: 640–2, https://doi.org/10.1038/s41591-020-0863-y.

Médecins Sans Frontiers. (2021). "Press Release: Worst Wave yet of COVID-19 in Northern Syria Overwhelms Health System," October 13, https://www.msf.org/health-system-overwhelmed-northern-syria-most-severe-covid-19-outbreak-yet (accessed March 10, 2022).

Mestek, Yahia M. L. (2020). "Algeria: Politics and Protests in Coronavirus Times," in *The Politics of Pandemics: Evolving Regime-Opposition Dynamics in the MENA Region*. ISPI and Atlantic Council, 26–37, https://www.ispionline.it/it/pubblicazione/politics-pandemics-evolving-regime-opposition-dynamics-mena-region-28410 (accessed March 11, 2022).

Moussa, Mohammed. (2015). "Contemporary Islamist Discourses on the State in Egypt: Before and After the Arab Spring," in Larbi Sadiki (ed.), *Routledge Handbook of the Arab Spring*, 240–52. London: Routledge.

Mulroy, Mich, Eric Oehlerich and Amanda Blair. (2021). "COVID-19 and Conflict in the Middle East," *Middle East Institute*, January 21, https://www.mei.edu/publications/covid-19-conflict-middle-east (accessed May 2, 2021).

National Endowment for Democracy. (2020). "A Call to Defend Democracy," June 25, https://www.ned.org/call-to-defend-democracy/ (accessed March 15, 2022).

OECD. (2020). *COVID-19 Crisis Response in MENA Countries*, https://www.oecd.org/coronavirus/policy-responses/covid-19-crisis-response-in-mena-countries-4b366396/ (accessed July 27 2020).

Palencia, Maria Blanco. (2015). "Youth and Technology in a Bottom-Up Struggle for Empowerment," in Larbi Sadiki (ed.), *Routledge Handbook of the Arab Spring*, 420–31. London: Routledge.

Rasborg, Klaus. (2012). "'(World) Risk Society' or 'New Rationalities of Risk'? A Critical Discussion of Ulrich Beck's Theory of Reflexive Modernity," *Thesis Eleven*, 108 (1): 3–25.

Reuters. (2021). "Tunisia Vaccinates More than Half a Million People in a Day," August 9, https://www.reuters.com/world/africa/tunisia-vaccinates-more-than-half-million-people-day-2021-08-08/ (accessed August 26, 2021).

Sadiki, Larbi. (2015). "The Arab Spring: The People in IR," Chapter 15 in Louise Fawcett (ed.), *International Relations of the Middle East*, edition 4, 325–55. Oxford: Oxford University Press, 2016.

Sadiki, Larbi. (2020). "Writing Middle East Politics: A Field in Transit," in Larbi Sadiki (ed.), *Routledge Handbook of Middle East Politics: Interdisciplinary Inscriptions*, 1–18. London: Routledge.

Sadiki, Larbi and Layla Saleh. (2020a). "Reflexive Politics and Arab 'Risk Society'? COVID-19 and Issues of Public Health," *Orient: German Journal for Politics, Economics and Culture of the Middle East*, 61 (3): 6–20.

Sadiki, Larbi and Layla Saleh. (2020b). "The Arab World Between a Formidable Virus and a Repressive State," *OpenDemocracy*, April 6, https://www.opendemocracy.net/en/north-africa-west-asia/arab-world-between-formidable-virus-and-repressive-state/ (accessed March 15, 2022).

Sadiki, Larbi and Layla Saleh. (2021). "Mulahathat min Tunis wa al-Khalij al-Arabi: Nahwa Inthnoghraphia li Ja'ihat Corona?" in Rima Majed (ed.), *Rethinking Social Transformations: Inequalities in the Arab World In Light of COVID-19*, 145–59. Arab Forum for Alternatives, https://bit.ly/3wgh8se (accessed April 7, 2020).

Saleh, Layla. (2017). *US Hard Power in the Arab World: Resistance, the Syrian Uprising, and the War on Terror*. London: Routledge.

Saleh, Layla. (2018). "Civic Resilience During Conflict: Syria's Local Councils," *Journal of Arab and Muslim Media Research*, 11 (2): 135–55.

Schellekens, Philip and Diego Sourrouille. (2020). "COVID-19 Mortality in Rich and Poor Countries: A Tale of Two Pandemics?" World Bank, Policy Research Working Paper 9260, https://openknowledge.worldbank.org/handle/10986/33844 (accessed July 28, 2020).

Statt, Nick. (2020). "Gulf States Using COVID-19 Contact Tracing apps as Mass Surveillance Tools, Report Says," *The Verge*, June 16, https://www.theverge.com/2020/6/16/21293363/covid-19-contact-tracing-bahrain-kuwait-mass-surveillance-tools-privacy-invasion (accessed May 20, 2021).

Swidler, Ann. (1986). "Culture in Action: Symbols and Strategies," *American Sociological Review*, 51 (April): 273–286.

Sylvester, Christine C. (2013). *War as Experience: Contributions from International Relations and Feminist Analysis*. London: Routledge.

United Nations. (2020). *Sustainable Development Report 2020: The Sustainable Development Goals and COVID-19*. Cambridge: Cambridge University Press, https://sdgindex.org/reports/sustainable-development-report-2020/ (accessed May 1, 2021).

United Nations Development Programme (UNDP). (2020). *Compounding Crises: Will COVID-19 and Lower Oil Prices Lead to a New Development Paradigm in the Arab Region?* https://www.arabstates.undp.org/content/rbas/en/home/library/crisis-response0/undp-regional-report--compounding-crises--will-covid-19-and-lowe.html (accessed April 27, 2021).

United Nations Development Programme (UNDP). (2021). *Compounding Crises: Will COVID-19 and Lower Oil Prices Lead to a New Development Paradigm in the Arab Region?* https://www.arabstates.undp.org/content/rbas/en/home/library/crisis-response0/undp-regional-report--compounding-crises--will-covid-19-and-lowe.html (accessed March 15, 2022).

United Nations Population Fund Iraq. (2020). "COVID-19 Exacerbating Gender-Based Violence in Iraq," November 25, https://iraq.unfpa.org/en/news/covid-19-exacerbating-gender-based-violence-iraq (accessed March 13, 2022).

Varnum, Michael, Cendri Huthcerson and Igor Grossman. (2021). "Everyone was Wrong on the Pandemic's Societal Impact," *Foreign Policy*, March 18, https://foreignpolicy.com/2021/03/18/pandemic-social-science-predictions-wrong/ (accessed May 2, 2021).

Wimmer, Jeffrey and Thorsten Quandt. (2007). "Living in the Risk Society: An Interview with Ulrich Beck," *Journalism Studies*, 7 (2): 336–47.

Wood, Elisabeth Jean. (2008). "The Social Processes of Civil War: The Wartime Transformation of Social Networks," *Annual Review of Political Science*, 11: 539–61.

Woods, Eric Taylor, Robert Schertzer, Liah Greenfeld, Chris Hughes and Cynthia Miller- Idriss. (2020). "COVID-19, Nationalism, and the Politics of Crisis: A Scholarly Exchange," *Nations and Nationalism*, 26 (4): 807–25.

World Bank. (2020). "The Global Economic Outlook During the COVID-19 Pandemic: A Changed World," June 8, https://www.worldbank.org/en/news/feature/2020/06/08/the-global-economic-outlook-during-the-covid-19-pandemic-a-changed-world (accessed July 20, 2021).

World Bank. (2021a). "Unemployment, Youth Total (% of Total Labor Forces Ages 15–24) (Modeled ILO Estimate)," https://data.worldbank.org/indicator/SL.UEM.1524.ZS (accessed August 26, 2021).

World Bank. (2021b). *MENA Crisis Tracker-8/16/2021*, https://documents1.worldbank.org/curated/en/280131589922657376/pdf/MENA-Crisis-Tracker-August-16-2021.pdf (accessed March 15, 2022).

World Bank. (2021c). "MENA Economies Face Rapid Accumulation of Public Debt: Strong Institutions Will Be Key to Recovery," https://www.worldbank.org/en/news/press-release/2021/04/02/strong-institutions-will-be-key-to-mena-recovery-amid-rapid-accumulation-of-public-debt (accessed August 27, 2021).

Zizek, Slavo. (2020). *Pandemic! Covid-19 Shakes the World*. Cambridge: Polity.

Zizek, Slavo. (2021). *Pandemic! 2: Chronicles of a Time Lost*. Cambridge: Polity.

Part I

The Gulf

2

Small States of the Arab Gulf

Diplomatic Dimensions of a Pandemic

Beverley Milton-Edwards

Introduction

The outbreak of the COVID-19 pandemic in early 2020 came at a time of unprecedented instability and diplomatic fissure in the relations among Arab Gulf countries and the Gulf region more generally. These fissures, in the realm of foreign policy, were evident in a number of spheres, including Gulf Cooperation Council (GCC) relations, wider Gulf and regional strategic power balances, as well as elements of bitter and rivalrous engagement at a bilateral level with the Trump administration.

Developments across the globe appeared at once to both shake old certainties about the international system, including foreign relations and diplomacy, while at the same time reinforcing state-centric nationalist positioning and sharpening superpower rivalry. This shone a light on concerns about the increasing fragility of international consensus building, associated institutions, norms and values. In essence, the leaders of individual countries were alone while at the same time had to continue to be seen to adhere to norms that urged diplomatic cooperation and international unity.

As the world moves from the mitigation of the pandemic to forms of reemergence based on developments in vaccine provision, it is important to interrogate how diplomacy has fared, especially for small states. For the purposes of this chapter, we will look at three small states in the Arab Gulf region: Kuwait, Qatar, and the United Arab Emirates (UAE). By working with discourse on small states at a conceptual nexus with niche diplomacy, the possibilities and limits for policy are explored.

Diplomacy for resilience, especially by small states such as those discussed in this chapter, is often overlooked. The complex connections and interfaces, perceived threats, narrative-making, and action are ignored in favor of basic dynamics of power and the modern international system. Yet, just as the end of the Cold War created cognizance about the possibility of a changing balance of power and changed international system, the COVID-19 pandemic is doing the same.[1] The notion of risk society and its relation to forms of modernity highlight how the international system and diplomatic relations matter. We argue that the pandemic has been consciously utilized as a tool of more significant diplomatic assertion and resilience by small states such as Kuwait, Qatar, and the UAE. This is part of wider conceptions of responsiveness to threat perceptions and power projection in a regional and global context. Uncertain that the international system and state hegemons therein can be relied upon and in a context where regional cooperation is still disappointingly weakened, these forms of assertion may prove to be a natural response. Existing structures for diplomatic action, alliance-building, and cooperation, established in the wake of the Iraqi invasion of Kuwait in 1991 have perpetuated rather than weakened the concerns of these small states. Hence, COVID-19 has exacerbated these institutional failings and writ large their consequences in terms of a fragile security order in the region. It has also brought to the fore the ways in which these states, though small, have resources which allow them to shape politics in their own image.

In this chapter, the first section offers a conceptual structure for discussion through the prism of small state and niche diplomacy. The following section then specifically addresses the issue of resilience of the thee small Arab Gulf states under examination. The third section "Pandemic Politcs" section addresses the COVID-19 pandemic and its strategic impacts on foreign policy before "Pandemic Diplomacy as Niche Policy" situates these responses as pandemic diplomacy. By situating the pandemic and diplomacy in this way, the conclusion of this chapter considers the policy implications in terms of soft power and niche-diplomacy, cognition of threat, cooperation, and future security dilemmas, as such small states seek to not only survive but thrive on the global stage.

Small States Big World

International relations literature provides a rich conceptual seam and varied discourses on statehood and sovereignty. Academic debate has been normatively centered on the nation-state and ensuing discourse is engaged with realist ideas of power within the international system. One prevailing assumption within much of the discourse had focussed on state power in relation to the size of a country.

Throughout the Cold War, when the international system was subject to organizing frames of a world order dominated by big (and even superpower) states, it was "naturally" assumed that medium and small states would organize to shelter in the polar realms of one power or the other. As such small- and medium-sized states were assumed to recognize and "enact" their subordinate status in a variety of diplomatic realms as well. This has implications in terms of the "focus from the power the state possesses to the power that they exercise," delimiting the possible and the impossible in the conduct of diplomatic relations.[2] Given the assumed relationship between state-power and size differentials at work, the notion that small states somehow constituted forms of diminished resilience entered normative discourse. Within such international orders, small states were perceived as being unable to wield power in the ways that larger states can.[3] This perspective points to diplomacy and power in an international system moulded by dominant-subordinate state-to-state relationships privileging big or strong states over small or weak states.

In such conceptualizations, disparities of power matter for small states because they are normatively assumed to be in an almost unceasing for battle for status analogous to big or strong states.[4] Though as an aside, Hey also argues that this can be somewhat ameliorated if the small state is also wealthy.[5] In general though, for small states, these disparities have implications for the connected jurisdictions of national interest, security, and foreign policy. Some academic discourse then dwells on the particular set of vulnerabilities that small states exhibit in building or being forced into external relations essentially characterized as security shelter.[6] Here shelter is defined as the "diplomatic, economic, societal and political alignment response of structurally weak states."[7]

The post–Cold War literature's fixation with small states is mostly contextualized in relation to structure-agency opposition, which we contend privileges Eurocentric biases and the assumed authority of related governance norms. Furthermore, this had the effect of emphasizing the orthodox perspective that small states were unwanted stresses on the international system. It revealed a tension between an emerging post–Cold War order that was increasingly typified by the phenomenon of small states and the inherent challenges of a power differential of cooperative or alliance behaviors.

With respect to foreign policy, small states were perceived as exhibiting a range of behaviors labelled as neutrality, balancing, and bandwagoning.[8] Such roles are not intrinsically powerful but are considered second or third order in relation to large states characterized as predominantly hard power actors.[9] These realist perspectives absent small states in terms of having sufficient power to effect change or impact on international norms and system behaviors. Moreover, in such contexts, the geostrategic context in which small states exist are assumed to place additional foreign policy considerations particularly with respect to alliance-building or cooperative behaviors to deter larger dominance-seeking neighbors. As Jesse and Dreyer assert, "inherent in this line of thought is the logic that 'smallness' is built as a weaker set of capabilities . . . small states must therefore have a more limited range of policy options."[10] Limited or not, small states must remain resilient and enact agency through the means available to them.

Riyal Politik: Resilience and Agency

Discourse on small states and foreign policy is evolving and dynamic. Some contributions have begun to argue that some, if not many, small states have proved to be resilient and enduring. This, in turn, means that there is something to be said about particular forms of power or agency of such small states in the international system. This form of agency is framed as forms of so-called niche diplomacy or norm entrepreneurship.[11] We are arguing here that forms of resiliency may indeed accrue to small states, especially those that are resource rich, through niche diplomacy such as those found in foreign policy approaches to pandemic response. The necessary caveat here is that while such approaches can create a measure of agency, it is limited by contingencies of power within the international system. Nevertheless, this bears attention in the pandemic context where international leadership and norm determination enter a form of flux or uncertainty.

Countries like the UAE, Kuwait, and Qatar are characterized as small or even micro sovereign entities. Because these entities exist in the geostrategic context of the Gulf, their status as small is also determined in relation to their larger neighbors including Saudi Arabia, Iraq, and Iran. Historically, these larger neighbors have indeed acted as an existential threat against these small states.[12] Academic writing has tended to emphasize the fact that the strategic ambitions and related foreign policies of Kuwait, Qatar, and the UAE, can be more effectively leveraged because they are wealthy states.[13] Ulrichsen, for example, argues that this permits such countries to punch above their weight, "Qatar, and to a lesser extent the United Arab Emirates were able to demonstrate how small states could play a role in international affairs out of all proportion to their size."[14]

Here the emphasis for small states is on particular forms of power and more specifically soft power.[15] In the context of a global pandemic like COVID-19, these small Arab Gulf states already possess a diplomatic track record in fields directly related to public health emergency responses including medical aid, health support, and humanitarianism. The mechanisms of soft power, while raising issues of transparency and accountability, are nevertheless viewed internally and externally as durable and resilient mechanisms. This has been a means by which such states can not only raise their profiles but sustain them and thus create forms of resilience and protection.[16]

The UAE, for example, has "consciously developed" an array of soft-power credentials nested within its strategic approach to national interest and the foreign policy nexus.[17] Under the soft-power umbrella lay the policy of humanitarian and development assistance. Indeed, according to the OECD, by 2018, the UAE was the world's largest donor of development assistance in proportion to its gross national income.[18] Gökalp addresses the strategic objectives harnessed to foreign policy,

> Humanitarian aid has been an integral and strategically formulated component of the country's foreign aid to serve the business and long-term economic interests of the Emirates in the Middle East, Africa and the rest of the world as well. The humanitarian aid sector has been embraced, especially by Dubai, as an innovative 21st century enterprise to practice, given the global potential to capitalize on the recent trend of privatization and commercialization of humanitarianism.[19]

For sure, aspects of this manifestation of soft-power projection accounts for the recognition of the UAE in the international system. The drawback is that with increased recognition comes visibility and a concurrent expectation that such states act within a set of norms and values especially where ally relationships are concerned.

These expressions of sovereignty evidenced in the soft-power attributes of countries like the UAE, Kuwait, and Qatar are further reflected in the decision to carve out particular diplomatic niches for themselves. Increasingly though, these niches have led to forms of competition and even hostile rivalry between such states. In Qatar, for example, Khatib contends that niche diplomacy has been the outcome of a foreign policy disposition reflecting political pragmatism, adaptation, and the establishment of linkages that often transcend normative organizing categories of diplomatic relations.[20] Fromm develops this argument further by claiming that states like Qatar and the UAE serve as indispensable "bridging" representatives between their region and the rest of the world.[21] Evidence of such an assertion is not difficult to discover and, in the case of Qatar, was powerfully demonstrated in August–September 2021 by the crucial bridging role it played between the United States and authorities in Afghanistan. Designing and implementing foreign policy that validates this conception of power has created a strongly held ideational perception of small states "punching above their weight." Narrative-perpetuation and branding around these perceptions allows dimensions of "small-statedness" to diminish especially when arraigned against increasingly disinterested larger and regionally external states. As such, discourse on small states needs to be reappraised.

Niche diplomacy offers the potential for small states, therefore, to enhance their position in the international system. The literature focuses on impact within foreign policy and highlights the "creative use of diplomatic talents or entrepreneurship" for more effective diplomacy.[22] By examining the amplification of power by small states like the UAE, Kuwait, and Qatar on the global stage, it is easy to understand how niche diplomacy nests with the construction of narratives of power and agency around them. Cooper further argues that as such these small countries "identify and fill niche space on a selective basis through policy ingenuity and execution."[23] The drawback of such an approach, exemplified by Cooper and Nye, is that much of the emphasis on power is through agency as a bridging actor to a powerful large country. Moreover, this agency, specifically as it applies to the states discussed in this chapter, is so very reliant on assumptions about state resources derived from hydrocarbon wealth in non-democratic settings. Here the ethnography reflects differently in terms of norms of an international system traditionally set by larger countries. The point here is that niche diplomacy theory is still being explored from a neorealist tradition and its attendant assumptions about the international order.[24]

Crucially, small state power as niche diplomacy also directs us to attenuated meanings offered by Kamrava as "subtle power."[25] This discourse is helpful in shining a light on forms of governance and decision-making that are often hidden. This also places forms of meaning that might otherwise be withheld for small states operationalizing policy in niche realms.[26] Indications of the efficacy and meaning of such discourse is, we argue, discernible when examining the foreign policies of these small states in relation to the outbreak of the COVID-19 global pandemic.

Pandemic Politics

The one globally defining event of 2020 was the COVID-19 virus and its spread as a pandemic. Aside from the public health implications and effects on the global economy, one important dimension of the pandemic was that it appeared to require different approaches to international relations and diplomatic policy. As such the politics of the pandemic had implications for small, medium, and large states alike.

While for small Arab Gulf states like Kuwait, Qatar, and the UAE, the domestic impacts of the unfolding pandemic were of importance, it was simultaneously clear that how foreign policy and diplomacy was created and enacted would have significant implications as well. In fact, the pandemic highlighted a number of exogenous factors where reliance on the diplomatic capacity of the state would be key to secure national interest through pandemic responses.

In theory the pandemic presented a new form of security dilemma for such small states. It left them disadvantaged against medium and larger states that had the capacity to rapidly deploy state and citizen assets to mitigate, combat, and find a sustainable route from the pandemic. Such capacities revolved around public health treatments and responses, vaccine development and/or procurement, research and development, and alliance-building and cooperation.

The distinctive character of these states and sources of revenue combined with geostrategic susceptibility at a time when the politics of the Gulf were considered highly unstable, manifested in specific vulnerabilities that the pandemic exposed. The economies of the countries under examination in this chapter are, with some variation, dependent on hydrocarbon earnings. The UAE, compared to Kuwait, is the least dependent as it pursues policies of economic diversification.[27] This reliance meant that during the initial phase of the pandemic, as the global economy ground to a halt, demand for energy resources to primary export bases in Asian countries shrank and state earnings were hit hard. The resources at the disposal of the state were constrained yet pandemic politics for these small states demanded that resources be diverted to protection of status and power in the international system.

In the initial phases of the pandemic, there was also a growing sense of alarm within the international system that the world order and the role of global power competition would be exacerbated rather than relieved by the common concern to combat COVID. Indeed, and as national security discourse expanded to include public health threats through the prism of existential crisis, international cooperation appeared to decrease. The opportunities for small states to up the ante and power-up on a global stage also went into rapid decline. As Walt has argued, "COVID-19 has accelerated the shift in power from West to East and put further limits on globalization, leading to a world less open and prosperous . . . nor did it usher in a new era of global cooperation . . . Globalization is in reverse, and international cooperation to defeat the pandemic has been half-hearted at best."[28]

This emerging discourse is, furthermore, dominated by scrutinizing big powers and global organizations, rarely turning the spotlight on small states and their future in this international system of change and uncertainty. Yet, the COVID-19 pandemic and related impacts on economies, social order, and diplomatic relations have already impacted the way small states work, exposed their vulnerability and seen them emerge as the victims of "weaponized interdependence" and rivalries.[29] Some refer to this as deplorable, unprecedented, and a sign that globalization is in almost fatal decline.[30] These issues affect the ways in which countries like Kuwait and Qatar address their foreign policy agenda and crisis management approach.

There is already evidence that the impacts of the pandemic on countries like the UAE, Kuwait, and Qatar demanded that they alter foreign policy and their narrative supports to project resilience, and maintain soft-power credentials. This can be framed as pandemic politics with diplomacy operationalized in an international system that has become increasingly typified by nation-states that are inward-looking, protectionist, nationalistic, and economically cautious. It also reflects the weakening of the multilateral system with its attendant norms and values.[31] This did not augur well for small states like Kuwait, Qatar, and the UAE.

Pandemic Diplomacy as Niche Policy

The responses of all the states studied in this chapter reflect a strategic approach to enhance existing narratives throughout the pandemic. The added dimension here is that, on occasion, such narratives have been competitive and clearly an attempt to demonstrate diplomatic weight and indispensability of one over the other. This is clearly demonstrated in the adaptation of aspects of preexisting humanitarian diplomacy policies and gestures into what I call pandemic diplomacy. Pandemic diplomacy is defined by COVID-19-specific foreign policy initiatives to augment existing niches and supplement where national interest determines strategic protectionism.

It creates new meanings and extends resilience within foreign policy realms to consolidate meanings attached to these states playing an outsized role in a global context. It is evidenced both in the realm of diplomatic initiatives to provide aid to combat the pandemic and project meanings about what these states represent in an evolving international order. It is also part of consciously constructed narratives designed to compete against each other to prove their "indispensability" as part of the ways in which large state actors order their strategic interest in the Gulf region. When other countries have floundered in both their national and international responses to the pandemic or appeared to prioritize other issues, these countries were able to appear to head the humanitarian wave signified through narratives of global cooperation. This view is evident in the speech of the UAE's minister of state for international cooperation in May 2021, "International cooperation is a really important mechanism that we as government officials have been speaking about for decades. The pandemic has shown us what can happen when we truly do cooperate with one another, but also what doesn't happen when we don't."[32] This may well be very different from the way in which such countries treat the ideation of global cooperation in a domestic context, where, in fact, COVID-19 has led to state policies of securitization, and insecurity for the extremely large populations of migrant workers resident there.

Returning to the global level, however, the very presence of these state actors early in the pandemic, where others were absent or played a minor role, is epitomized by generous-gesture responses. Kuwait, for example, made a major donation in early April 2020 of $60 million to the World Health Organization (WHO) COVID-19 Strategic Preparedness and Response plan. This singled it out as one of the largest donors at that point in the pandemic (WHO, 2020). The initial epicenter of the pandemic was China—a country recognized as extremely important to the economic resilience of small Arab Gulf states. All three countries moved with some degree of diplomatic nimbleness to publicize donations of much-needed health and medical supplies to the Chinese authorities. Kuwait's leaders, for example, announced a decision to give $3 million worth of medical supplies to be sent to Wuhan. Doha announced the donation of supplies as well as free air freight of aid to China on the national carrier Qatar Airways. The UAE also made early donations of medical supplies to China and were "rewarded" when Chinese authorities marked the country out for especial thanks during the initial phase of the pandemic. Focusing in on the more immediate needs within the Gulf region, there then followed shared step provision of humanitarian assistance by all three countries to neighboring Iran where the pandemic was in danger of overwhelming the population and its rulers.[33]

Interestingly, despite differences in national crisis management in the domestic context, all three countries have shown similar patterns of policy practice, messaging, and anticipation of consolidated niche status in their foreign policy approaches to the pandemic. These approaches center on preexisting brand narratives as humanitarian actors promoting international solidarity and unity. Note, for example, the ways in which this was signified in the decision in early February 2020 by Emirati leaders to have iconic buildings, including the Burj al Khalifa, lit up with the colors of the Chinese flag and slogans of solidarity.[34] As the pandemic prolonged and endured throughout 2020 and into 2021, these showcase gestures formed an important dimension of the utilization of soft power and broader diplomatic objectives. Qatar, for example, assiduously utilized dimensions of its preexisting brand power, specifically Qatar Airways, to boost its humanitarian credentials during the pandemic.[35] Qatar Airways claims that as part of the COVID-19 humanitarian response effort, it has facilitated flights for over one million people to travel across the world back to their home countries and played its part in transporting over 100,000 tonnes of medical equipment and aid relief during the pandemic. Both the UAE's Etihad Airways and Emirates airline were cited by the government as having bolstered "their fleets of freighters to keep critical commercial goods like pharmaceuticals and medical devices moving and to assist in the delivery of international humanitarian relief assistance overseas" and were frequently featured in government messaging allied to diplomatic response efforts during the pandemic.[36]

Competition between UAE and Qatar aviation is legendary and cut-throat so it should have been no surprise that foreign policy narratives of the pandemic frequently referred to the role that national carriers such as Emirates or Qatar Airways played during the pandemic. Such rivalry, it has also been argued, led to Doha being targeted by anti-Qatar elements disinformation campaigns waged throughout the blockade against the country by UAE, Bahrain, Egypt, and Saudi Arabia from June 2017 to January 2021.[37]

Narrative frame of niche diplomacy as it relates to humanitarian emergencies has been a key feature of all three countries under discussion in this chapter. These narratives have also been allied to resource deployment in relation to medium-term to long-term development issues as a strategic arm of foreign policy, particularly in other Arab or Muslim-majority countries.[38] Humanitarianism and developmental aid resources and how they are deployed, however, has been critiqued. Much of that critique has centered on opaque donor and beneficiary relationships and the fungibility of aid at a nexus with security agendas and terrorism.[39] Furthermore, the assiduousness with which certain foreign policy agendas were maximized through trend-lines of aid and assistance practice has been framed in part of a wider discourse about "dinar diplomacy" and influence.[40] These critiques, notwithstanding, there is now increasing evidence of all three countries enhancing their humanitarian aid budgets to cooperative agreements for distribution with major UN and other mechanisms. Indeed, Gulf countries like Kuwait have been regarded as playing a leading role in creating governmental frameworks allied to foreign policy objectives.[41]

During the COVID-19 pandemic this form of leverage, along with direct aid disbursements, has been palpable. Kuwait, for example, led with response initiatives focussing on the least developed countries tied to the coordinating platform led by the OPEC International Fund for Development (OFID) of the Arab Coordination Group (ACG). In late May 2020 a pledge of $10 billion was jointly made by the member groups, including the Kuwait Fund and Qatar's Fund for Development (QFFD) and OFID to allocate to COVID-19 responses.[42] QFFD—nested directly within the Ministry of Foreign Affairs—also contributed COVID-19 aid into regions where it traditionally operated. Hence, early programmatic responses from QFFD saw donations of funding for health centers, mobile clinics, and into national health funds, such as in Jordan, for refugees and internally displaced peoples.[43] The UAE's own claims around COVID-19 assistance situate itself as accounting for "80% of international aid and assistance during the pandemic."[44] This assistance, like Kuwait and Qatar, has included medical and food aid, field clinics and hospitals, as well as "in-kind" aid to WHO worth some $10 million. Similarly, the UAE directed aid to China, as well as European countries. To this end Galeeva has gone as far to assert that such assistance allowed the UAE to achieve a form of global status similar to large/strong states such as China or the United States, supporting "the generally recognised value of foreign aid as a mechanism for winning international influence and status, while underlining the emergence of the UAE as a potentially 'strong' state on the global stage."[45]

We contend, however, that such responses do not take account of the limited evidence of the necessary strategic adjustments to leverage these aid initiatives even in the short-to-medium term. Yes, it could be argued that the UAE, for example, has benefited from a new channel of relations with China wrought by its pandemic response but there is so much more to account for China's strategic balancing during the pandemic. UAE has served as part of the Phase III trials for Chinese Sinopharm being the first country to register it in December 2020. UAE's vaccine-making (Abu Dhabi-based tech company, G42, teamed up with China's Sinopharm) to start producing the Hayat injection has tied it to China, while at the same time leaving it somewhat as an outlier due to skepticism about the efficacy of Sinopharm among Western countries.

More important here, for all three countries, has been the diplomatic value of gestures and statements that have envisioned themselves as part of a bigger and more global response. Yet all too often these gestures were singularly nationalistic in objective and have been characterized by forms of short-termism that make it difficult to convert into diplomatic leverage. So while it has been asserted that humanitarian aid and assistance can be perceived as a "quiet tool" and diplomatic resource for the many smaller states to power-up and gain visibility in a variety of arenas, it has also been weaponized.[46] Moreover, dimensions of such aid have, according to some arguments, been used as part of a securitizing narrative against Qatar by the UAE. Barakat, for example, argues that the blockade "further politicised Gulf humanitarian action. The blockading states labelled Qatar a 'terror financier', singling out its humanitarian aid as one arm of a controversial foreign policy that supports Islamist movements across the Arab world."[47] The riposte to such assertions is evident in the ties forged by Qatar with international institutions—such as the UN—and their gold standard mechanisms of aid transparency and accountability—as an essential component of their COVID-19 agenda. The COVID-19 crisis and the attendant strategic decision-making in aid and assistance from such countries, it is argued, amounts to nothing more than a new facet of politicized aid.[48] While some have been optimistic that the pandemic and diplomatically informed aid and assistance creates new opportunities for international cooperation, most have tended to see it as lacking this kind of impact.

Conclusion: Ethnographies of a Pandemic and Niche Diplomacy

As discussed through this chapter, small Arab Gulf countries have always attempted to project power and consolidate their sovereignty through embedding foreign policy approaches in niche realms that permitted them to punch above their weight. This has added an important dimension to the resilience and endurance of such states, especially when they have faced or endured forms of existential threat from large states.

Moreover, in terms of "risk society" and an opportunity for "reflexive modernization" there are noticeable absences with respect to diplomacy as a form of governance in responses to the pandemic.[49] While it is true that dimensions of a particular global moral and norm agenda are evident or addressed in some of the emergent diplomatic responses to the pandemic, it must reside within a wider realm where other factors determine the maintenance of the existing order and ultimately the preservation of the political and allied governing status quo. Indeed, the countries under examination in this chapter demonstrated significant resilience. While it is true that some internal vulnerabilities were exposed, the notion that the pandemic might draw such countries to some form of revolutionary dynamic proves ill-founded.

In terms of capacities for governance, as expressed through the national interest and a foreign policy agenda, these countries' experiences of the pandemic hint at forms of structural strength—especially around well-resourced public health and economic responses domestically as well as foreign aid and assistance budgets. This, in comparison to the structural inequalities prevalent among poorer and more vulnerable states in the Arab region, points to the enduring vulnerabilities of the region more generally to crisis and the attendant limits of help that even resource-rich states in the region can offer.

The overpowering effect of the global pandemic required states within the international system to endure what has become an unprecedented cycle of infection, lockdown, ease, infection, and lockdown. Additionally, foreign policy not only moved into a realm of emergency management and reaction but policymakers were required to come up with responses to an unprecedented global event. In the Gulf, Kuwait, Qatar, and the UAE were already located in a strategic environment where interstate cooperation and the institutions that were supposed to embody those norms were almost fatally weakened.

While in the past such states have relied on forms of sheltering with larger states, the pandemic has coincided with other security developments within the Gulf to create moments of circumspection. In seeking to alter approaches, foreign policy elites in these countries initially looked to multilateral forums as the most important entry points and found them reduced in terms of capacity to meet the demands of cooperation during a global pandemic. Hence, the strategic value of such small states attempting to conduct diplomatic business as usual faltered and had to be modified. This has important consequences in terms of diplomacy. Some have gone as far as to argue that the longer the pandemic endures the higher the risk of an "evisceration" of international cooperation.[50]

Moreover, for countries like the three under discussion in this chapter, the pandemic has demonstrated that soft-power credentials now need to expand and evolve to incorporate global public health policy and diplomacy, digital diplomacy, nations, and economies. With healthcare and digital working featuring much more prominently in international system policy planning, it can also be contended that R&D is key. Thus, despite mixed responses, the decision by the UAE to partner with China in vaccine production is evidence of a strategic foreign policy goal forming distinct features of "health diplomacy."[51]

The efforts and resources pledged and distributed by Kuwait and Qatar during the initial phase of the pandemic breaking out, first in China, then the Middle East and beyond can, in part, be considered constitutive of pandemic diplomacy. This is because it signifies the ways in which these countries have used resources to power-up through the pandemic, especially in relation to showcase contributions to WHO, GAVI, and other global initiatives such as vaccine production to tackle the public health crisis. This permits these countries to make claims around the ethical and moral good. The limits of pandemic diplomacy, however, are also exposed. While the pandemic may have invited reflexivity by government and then incorporated into their foreign policy stances, it is also limited by the nature of the collective bargain between state and citizen in such countries. This is particularly pertinent to the realm of foreign policy where power has remained decidedly vertical and the so-called collective voice is in fact determined by narrow political and ruling elite interests. Agency has been superimposed in the name of the diverse (and often contentious and conflicting) constituencies of citizens and residents that reside in these three countries affecting their future place in the world.

In terms of policy critique, the diplomatic responses from the three countries demonstrated that even with available capacities, and in the case of some such as Qatar the political motivation, their efforts were simply not up to meeting the larger and more endemic pandemic fragility in areas of conflict such as Israeli-occupied Palestine and in particular Gaza. In just such a context, it was not just the ways in which COVID-19 affected a population, placed under an unjust siege by Israel for more than a decade, but the weaponization of aid and vaccines that engendered further vulnerability and additional burdens.[52] Indeed, it could be argued that the Palestinian refugee population of the Gaza Strip, West Bank, and occupied East Jerusalem have become pawns in a diplomatic humanitarian response part of Gulf dispute and tension over wider political issues such as normalization policies with Israel. The reach of the state and preexisting political fissures and foreign policy battles often prevailed in a regional setting though at a level of global responsiveness the policy practices enacted by all three countries went some way in demonstrating moral values and norms associated with humanitarian practice and thus the associated normative diplomatic kudos and recognition from other state actors in the international system was accrued. In particular, Kuwait and Qatar appeared through their diplomatic approach to COVID assistance programs to enact burden-sharing as a global good. The UAE emerges as more strategic in its approach, securing its own national interest through its relationship with China— particularly in the field of vaccine procurement and production.

Nevertheless, pandemic diplomacy has created resilience for the small states under scrutiny in this chapter. There were important instances of burden-sharing from these resource-rich countries in fighting the pandemic which, at the time, mitigated some but by no means all risks within the region. It has revealed itself to have many of the same features of niche diplomacy efforts in the past—including a strong humanitarian dimension, and real strategic leverage achieving best benefit when serving the purpose of bolstering preexisting bilateral relations and security-sheltering practices.

Notes

1 Rasmussen (2001).
2 Steinmetz and Wivel (2016, 7).
3 Fox (1959).
4 Hey (2003, 75).
5 Hey (2003, 76).
6 Antola (2002).
7 Bailes, Thayer, and Thorhallsson (2006, 9).
8 Walt (1987, 17).
9 Handel (1981).
10 Jesse and Dreyer (2016, 32).
11 Henrikson (2005).
12 Milton-Edwards (2018).
13 Wohlforth et al. (2018).
14 Ulrichsen (2013).
15 Nye (2004).
16 Khatib (2013, 418).
17 Antwi-Boateng and Alhashmi (2021, 1).
18 Emirates (2018).
19 Gökalp (2020, 3).
20 Khatib (2013).
21 Fromm (2017).
22 Cooper (1997, 9).
23 Cooper (1997, 3).

24 Fromm (2017, 24).
25 Kamrava (2017).
26 Henrikson (2005, 71).
27 Malik and Nagesh (2021, 215).
28 Walt (2021).
29 Drezner, Farrell and Newman (2021).
30 Wright (2020).
31 Tooze(2019).
32 Al Hashimy2021.
33 Rosen (2020).
34 See: https://www.thenationalnews.com/uae/burj-khalifa-lights-up-red-in-solidarity
   -with-china-over-coronavirus-1.973205
35 Brannagan and Giulianotti (2018).
36 See: https://www.arabianbusiness.com/transport/444745-covid-19-etihad-reveals
   -5-new-cargo-destinations-on-passenger-aircraft and https://www.skycargo.com/
   media-centre/emirates-skycargo-scales-up-network-and-operations-for-transport-of
   -essential-commodities/
37 Jones (2020).
38 Sezgin and Dijkzeul (2015).
39 Warde (2007).
40 Assiri (1991).
41 ElKahlout (2020).
42 OFID (2020).
43 MENAFN (2020).
44 https://u.ae/en/information-and-services/justice-safety-and-the-law/handling-the-
   covid-19-outbreak/humanitarian-efforts
45 Galeeva (2021).
46 Young (2015).
47 Barakat (2019, 67).
48 Soubrier (2020).
49 Beck, Giddens, and Lash (1992). See also Sadiki and Saleh (2020).
50 Wright (2020).
51 Alexander and Mazzucco (2021).
52 Abu Amer (2020).

References

Abu Amer, Ahmad (2020). "UAE Steps up Medical Aid to Gaza," *Al Monitor*, December
   22, https://www.al-monitor.com/originals/2020/12/uae-qatar-aid-gaza-compete-health
   -coronavirus.html (accessed October 5, 2021).
Al Hashimy, Reem. *UAE Minister of State for International Cooperation*, https://www
   .gavi.org/news/media-room/corporations-charities-and-governments-step-support
   -equitable-covid-19-vaccine (accessed May 23, 2022).
Alexander, Kristian and Leonardo Jacopo Maria Mazzucco. "Insight 261: Vaccine
   Diplomacy–The UAE Tries to Balance Hard Times with Soft Power," *MEI-NUS*, https://
   mei.nus.edu.sg/publication/insight-261-vaccine-diplomacy-the-uae-tries-to-balance
   -hard-times-with-soft-power/ (accessed September 7, 2021).

Antola, Esko (2002). "The Future of Small States in the EU," in M. Farrell, S. Fella and M. Newman (eds.), *European Integration in the 21st Century*, 69–86. London: Sage.

Antwi-Boateng, Osman and Amira Ali Alhashmi. (2021). "The Emergence of the United Arab Emirates as a Global Soft Power: Current Strategies and Future Challenges," *Economic and Political Studies*, 10 (2): 1–20.

Assiri, Abdul-Reda. (1991). "Kuwait's Dinar Diplomacy: The Role of Donor-Mediator," *Journal of South Asian and Middle Eastern Studies*, 14 (3): 24–32.

Bailes, Alyson J. K., Bradley Thayer and Baldur Thorhallsson. (2006). "Alliance Theory and Alliance 'shelter': The Complexities of Small State Alliance Behaviour," *Third World Thematics: TWQ J*, 1 (1): 9–26, 14.

Barakat, Sultan (2019). "Priorities and Challenges of Qatar's Humanitarian Diplomacy," *CMI Brief*, 7: 6p.

Beck, Ulrich, Anothny Giddens and Scott Lash. (1992). *Reflexive Modernization: Politics, Tradition and Aesthetics in the Modern Social Order*. Stanford: Stanford University Press.

Brannagan, Paul M. and Richard Giulianotti. (2018). "The Soft Power–Soft Disempowerment Nexus: The Case of Qatar," *International Affairs*, 94 (5): 1139–57.

Cooper, Andrew F. (1997). "Niche Diplomacy: A Conceptual Overview," in A.F. Cooper (eds.), *Niche Diplomacy. Studies in Diplomacy*, 1–24. London: Palgrave Macmillan.

Drezner, Daniel W., Henry Farrell and Abraham L. Newman, eds. (2021). *The Uses and Abuses of Weaponized Interdependence*. Washington, DC: Brookings Institution Press.

Elkahlout, Ghassan (2020). "'Hearts and Minds': Examining the Kuwaiti Humanitarian Model as an Emerging Arab Donor," *Asian Journal of Middle Eastern and Islamic Studies*, 14 (1): 141–57.

Emirates News Agency. (2018). http://wam.ae/en/details/1395302680710 (accessed September 14, 2021).

Fox, Annette Baker (1959). *The Power of Small States*. Chicago: Chicago University Press.

Fromm, Nicholas (2017). *Constructivist Niche Diplomacy: Qatar's Middle East Diplomacy as an Illustration of Small State Norm Crafting*. Hamburg: Springer.

Galeeva, Diana. (2021). "'Weak' and 'Strong' States in Pandemic Times: Power and Influence During a Global Health Crisis," *The RUSI Journal*, 166 (2): 1–9.

Gökalp, Deniz. (2020). "The UAE's Humanitarian Diplomacy: Claiming State Sovereignty, Regional Leverage and International Recognition," CMI Working Paper.

Handel, Michael (1981). *Weak States in the International System*. Totowa, NJ: Frank Cass.

Henrikson, Alan K. (2005). "Niche Diplomacy in the World Public Arena: the Global 'Corners' of Canada and Norway," in J. Melissen (ed.), *The New Public Diplomacy. Studies in Diplomacy and International Relations*, 67–87. London: Palgrave Macmillan.

Hey, Jeanne A. K. (2003). *Small States in World Politics: Explaining Foreign Policy Behavior*. London: Lynne Rienner.

Jesse, Neal G. and John R. Dreyer (2016). *Small States in the International System: At Peace and at War*. Lanham, MD: Lexington Books.

Jones, Marc Owen (2020). "Disinformation Superspreaders: The Weaponisation of COVID-19 Fake News in the Persian Gulf and beyond," *Global Discourse: An Interdisciplinary Journal of Current Affairs*, 10 (4): 431–7.

Kamrava, Mehran (2017). "Qatari Foreign Policy and the Exercise of Subtle Power," *International Studies Journal (ISJ)*, 14 (2): 91–123, http://hdl.handle.net/10822/1048298 (accessed May 23, 2022).

Khatib, Lina. (2013). "Qatar's Foreign Policy: The Limits of Pragmatism," *International Affairs*, 89 (2): 417–31.

Malik, Monica and Thirumalai Nagesh. (2021). "Fiscal Sustainability and Hydrocarbon Endowment per Capita in the GCC," in Giacomo Luciani and Tom Moerenhout (eds.), *When Can Oil Economies Be Deemed Sustainable?*, 215–53. Singapore: Palgrave Macmillan.

MENAFN (2020), "Int'l Donors Contribute 187 m to Support Jordan's COVID-19 Efforts," May 21, https://menafn.com/1100203448/Intl-donors-contribute-187m-to-support -Jordans-COVID-19-efforts (accessed July 19, 2021).

Milton-Edwards, Beverley (2018). *Contemporary Politics in the Middle East*, 4th ed. Cambridge: Polity.

Nye, Joseph S. (2004). *Soft Power: The Means to Success in World Politics*. Cambridge: Public Affairs.

OFID (2020). *Communique*, https://opecfund.org/news-stories/us-10-billion-joint-covid -19-response-for-developing-countries (accessed July 19, 2021).

Rasmussen, Mikkel Vedby (2001). "Reflexive Security: NATO and International Risk Society," *Millennium*, 30 (2): 285–309.

Rosen, Laura (2020). "Coronavirus Spur Humanitarian Outreach to Iran," *Al Monitor*, https://www.al-monitor.com/pulse/originals/2020/03/coronavirus-spur-humanitarian -outreach-iran.html (accessed July 13, 2021).

Sadiki, Larbi and Layla Saleh. (2020). "Reflexive Politics and Arab 'risk Society'? COVID-19 and Issues of Public Health," *Orient*, 60 (3): 12–13.

Sezgin, Zeynep and Dennis Dijkzeul. (2015). *The New Humanitarians in International Practice: Emerging Actors and Contested Principles*. London: Routledge.

Soubrier, Emma (2020). "Gulf Humanitarian Diplomacy in a Time of Coronavirus, AGSIW," https://agsiw.org/gulf-humanitarian-diplomacy-in-the-time-of-coronavirus/ (accessed July 13, 2021).

Steinmetz, Robert and Anders Wivel (2016). *Small States in Europe: Challenges and Opportunities*. New York: Routledge.

Tooze, Adam (2019). "Everything You Know about the Global Order is Wrong," *Foreign Policy*, January 30, https://foreignpolicy.com/2019/01/30/everything-you-know-about -global-order-is-wrong/ (accessed June 5, 2021).

Ulrichsen, Kristian Coates (2013). "From Mediation to Interventionism: Understanding Qatar's Arab Spring Policies, Global Affairs," http://eng.globalaffairs.ru/number/ From-Mediation-to-Interventionism-16170 (accessed September 7, 2021).

Walt, Stephen M. (1987). *The Origins of Alliance*. Ithaka: Cornell University Press.

Walt, Stephen M. (2021). "Authoritarians Look Worse Now; The World After the Coronavirus, American Enterprise Institute," 2 January, https://www.aei.org/op-eds/the -world-after-the-coronavirus/ (accessed September 26, 2021).

Warde, Ibrahim (2007). *The Price of Fear, the Truth Behind the Financial War on Terror*. Berkeley: University of California Press.

Wohlforth, William C., Benjamin De Carvalho, Halvard Leira and Iver B. Neumann (2018). "Moral Authority and Status in International Relations: Good States and the Social Dimension of Status Seeking," *Review of International Studies*, 44 (3): 526–46.

WHO. "The Strategic Partnership with Kuwait 202-21," Kuwait (who.int) (accessed May 23, 2022).

Wright, Thomas (2020). "Stretching the International Order to its Breaking Point, Order from Chaos," *Brookings*, April 6, https://www.brookings.edu/blog/order-from-chaos /2020/04/06/stretching-the-international-order-to-its-breaking-point/ (accessed September 6, 2021).

Young, Karen E. (2015). "The Limits of Gulf Arab Aid: Energy Markets and Foreign Policy," Reflections' Working Paper Series, 1, 43–53.

3

Accelerating AI-led Structural Transformation of the GCC Migration Regimes in the Wake of COVID-19 and the Implications for the Labor-Exporting Countries

Abdul Ghaffar Mughal and Ali A.Hadi Alshawi

Introduction: The Fourth Industrial Revolution and the Future of Work

The contemporary industrial revolution is dramatically transforming life as we know it, contributing to risk society in MENA and across the world.[1] The technologies of what has been called the "Second Machine Age"[2] encompass automation, robotics, additive manufacturing, the Internet of Things (IoT) and, most importantly, artificial intelligence (AI). AI is akin to a general-purpose technology (GPT) that can transform whole societies, like the steam engine and electricity during the first and the second industrial revolution, respectively.[3] Machines that require human-level intelligence can not only collect and process data better and infinitely faster than human beings, but they can also learn and make decisions on their own. AI, driven by increasingly inexpensive computing power, is becoming ubiquitous. What was science fiction is becoming a reality. Termed the "fourth industrial revolution" or "Industry 4.0" or "4IR," the contemporary digital revolution in information and communication technologies (ICT) has been transforming lives in areas as diverse as medicine and entertainment. With the onset of COVID-19, this transformation has received a shot in the arm.

The AI-led digital revolution has profound implications for the future of work. A consensus seems to be emerging among scholars, policymakers, and thought-leaders to the effect that the upcoming AI-driven workforce transitions would be huge but will vary by occupation and sector. In about 60 percent of occupations, at least one-third of the constituent activities could be automated.[4] Activities most susceptible to automation include both low-skill manual and high-skill mental ones.[5] Along with routine low-end jobs, many middle-income occupations, with programmable cognitive skills, such as accounting, mortgage origination, paralegal work, and back-office transaction processing will have the largest employment declines.

While eliminating certain jobs or specific components of certain activities, automation creates new jobs and products. Highly skilled professionals whose work does not follow set rules will have a growing demand for their services. These include professionals such as doctors, engineers, scientists, accountants, analysts, IT professionals, managers, executives, educators, creative artists, performers, entertainers, and builders of infrastructure. Some relatively low-skill non-routine manual and service jobs in unpredictable environments and/or where telecommuting or "telemigration" is non-feasible are also expected to survive the technological onslaught. These include unprogrammable occupations, such as home-health aides, nursing assistants, teaching assistants, domestic servants, and gardening. In other words, the growth of employment across occupations will look like a barbell with a lot of poundage on either end of the bar.[6]

The ongoing digital revolution is increasingly recognized as a "process of creative destruction" (à la Schumpeter). Automation boosts productivity as businesses adopt automation only when it enables them to produce more or higher-quality output with the same or fewer inputs. Rising income from enhanced productivity is expected to create more demand for not only leisure and luxury goods but also for investment in the economy.

Perhaps the clearest expression of the impact of 4IR on employment can be seen in the growth of "platform capitalism" creating new jobs as well as investment opportunities. The ability of machines to collecting, processing, and exchanging large amounts of data quickly and cheaply has laid the foundations of digital network platforms such as UBER, Upwork, Airbnb, Alipay, Baidu, WeChat, Venmo, CashApp, and a host of others. More importantly, by connecting businesses and clients to workers, digital platforms are transforming labor processes with significant implications for the future of work.[7]

COVID-19 has accelerated the adoption of technologies of 4IR by businesses, government, and individuals. In fact, it has accelerated changes that were already underway, both in society and at work. Specifically, it accelerated three broad trends that may reshape the post-pandemic future of work: "remote work, e-commerce (growing three to five times faster than before the pandemic), and automation, with up to 25 percent more workers than previously estimated potentially needing to switch occupations."[8] A significant technological change that attended upon the onset of COVID-19 is telepresence/remote work, particularly the widespread use across the globe of ZOOM, a technology that had existed for years but the simultaneous adoption by all solved the collective action problem establishing a norm.[9] Thanks to the advancements in ICT, educational institutions, healthcare facilities, and workplaces across the globe have been able to maintain continuity through digital innovations.[10]

The new business model associated with digital platforms allows platforms to organize work without investing in capital assets or hiring employees. Instead, they mediate between the workers and clients and manage the entire work process with algorithms. These tasks may include carrying out translation, legal, financial, and patent services, design, and software development on freelance and contest-based platforms; solving complex programming or data analytics problems within a designated time on competitive programming platforms; or completing short-term tasks, such as annotating images, moderating content, or transcribing a video on microtask platforms.[11] Use of digital platforms and related technological innovations like cloud computing and the use of big data and algorithms have been expanding.

Digital labor platforms offer new markets for businesses and more income-generating opportunities for workers, including those who were previously outside the labor market. The new business model associated with digital platforms allows platforms to organize work without investing in capital assets or hiring employees. The low-cost advantage of platform capitalism makes them particularly attractive to low-income countries.

For many in the developing world who lost their jobs in the wake of COVID-19, digital labor platforms have offered opportunities to earn some income. Many businesses have relied on digital labor platforms to keep operating, reach new markets and reduce costs. Digital labor platforms are not only a unique way to address youth unemployment, but it is also particularly conducive to female labor force participation in countries like Pakistan, where sociocultural factors dampen women's participation in the labor market.[12] In short, online work offers an unprecedented opportunity to address some of the chronic structural problems of surplus labor economies. Indeed, digital platforms can shrink the wage gap between the developing and the developed world as businesses typically offer uniform wage rates regardless of the nationality of workers.[13] This is a far cry from the norm in Gulf Cooperation Council (GCC) where discriminatory wage practices are even legally sanctioned. In developing countries, such platforms are regarded as a promising source of work opportunities, leading many governments to invest in digital infrastructure and skills.[14]

The dramatic growth of remote work in the wake of the coronavirus pandemic has accelerated the trend of labor market globalization, with significant ramifications for another global megatrend: the growth of virtual international labor mobility. From the perspective of international labor migration, digital platform capitalism could be a game-changer.

In the era of 4IR, the most in-demand skills are slated to be increasingly technology-related, specifically in the fields of Science, Technology, Engineering, and Math (STEM). Also expected to grow in demand are a set of soft skills that complement automated and technologically driven jobs.[15] Alongside growing demand for specific skills, an essential aspect of 4IR is that general soft skills will grow in demand in formerly mostly technical occupations. Analytical thinking and innovation, active learning, problem-solving, critical thinking, and creativity are listed as the top five skills for 2025 in the Future of Jobs Report 2020[16] (WEF 2020). Not surprisingly, language skills, especially English, are among the most-demanded soft skills.[17] Creative and interpersonal skills will be in greatest demand in sectors such as sales, human resources, healthcare, and education. Healthcare workers, for instance, might see a redefinition of their roles toward the translation and communication of data produced by new technologies that allow for the automation of diagnosis and personalization of treatments.

In the wake of 4IR, what will be the post-pandemic future of work in the Gulf migration corridor?

While economic rents derived mainly from the natural resources but also from the pro-native Kafala (sponsorship) system have delivered dramatic improvements in the living standard of nationals in most GCC countries and have enabled them to build an impressive infrastructure over the last half-century, many labor-exporting countries whose human capital underwrote the phenomenal growth of the oil-rich Gulf states find themselves near the bottom of the pyramid of prosperity. Indeed, many countries of origin in the Gulf migration corridor found themselves ill-prepared to cope with the coronavirus pandemic and its devastating socioeconomic impact, with the education sector taking the biggest hit. The coronavirus pandemic has brought the issue of the digital and income divide between the GCC and the labor-exporting countries into the limelight.[18]

The dominant approach taken by international organizations like the WB, IMF, or ILO tends to focus narrowly on maximizing the net benefits of international migration. Considering the growing divergence between the countries of origin and countries of destination in the Gulf migration corridor, it is time to reframe the issue and ask *how migration fits into the broader development paradigm amid the ongoing structural changes in the global economy.*[19]

Such resistance is expected to grow in the wake of the ongoing digital revolution, and it should be regarded as a critical juncture for restructuring and reconceptualizing of the whole issue of international labor migration as a development strategy.[20]

As a result of automation, a significant number of people may need to shift occupational categories and learn new skills in the years ahead. Indeed, in the wake of 4IR, the world is on the cusp of an educational revolution.[21] In general, the current educational requirements of the occupations that may grow are higher than those for the jobs displaced by automation. Within the context of 4IR, the task for educators needs to be redefined in terms of transmission of needed skills in a fast-changing world to future cohorts, while creating greater incentives for students to enroll in STEM as well as vocational training programs. Education culture must also foster lifelong learning and better educate on, identify, and evaluate impactful soft skills. Lifelong learning of adults is imperative as the pace of technological change has accelerated beyond imagination.

We address this issue with a special focus on a major Gulf labor supplier, that is, Pakistan. A review of academic literature and policy documents on the nexus between migration and development in Pakistan shows little evidence of anchoring strategic thinking on mainstreaming *international labor migration* in the overall development paradigm amid the worldwide digital revolution.

What makes education so unique amid 4IR is that it will be relatively inexpensive, interactive, and virtual.[22] Ceteris paribus, all one needs is access to the Internet and a computer to interact with the instructor and co-learners across the globe. Little investment in physical infrastructure is required for many subjects. Interaction is particularly relevant for educating adults as adults do not do well sitting in classrooms.[23]

Structural Transformation in GCC, the Kafala System, and the Employment Outlook in the Gulf Migration Corridor

The development path chosen by most Gulf states has hinged upon the twin foundations of natural resources and cheap foreign labor. Few countries in recorded economic history have been dependent on temporary foreign workers to the extent that the GCC countries have been. As of 2020, the proportion of foreign population was 87 and 89 percent in Qatar and the UAE, respectively.[24] The kafala system constitutes the defining characteristic of the migration regime prevalent in the Gulf states.[25] While hydrocarbon resources are generally believed to be the source of wealth of the Gulf states, the magnitude of economic rents[26] generated by the kafala system that governs the employment and residency of foreign workers have been enormous. Economic rents over the last half century have taken various forms: wages withheld or unpaid by employers, underpayment of wages, extended hours of work, little or no overtime, and forced labor.[27]

Thus, the nature of the structural transformation in the resource-rich GCC can only be understood in the context of the kafala system in the Arab Gulf states.

Increasingly concerned about legitimizing dynastic rule, Gulf regimes allowed Gulf nationals to extract rents from foreign labor by giving them near total control over expatriates.[28] The system requires all foreign workers to have an in-country sponsor (*kafeel*), usually a national who is also their *de jure* employer[29] and is responsible for their visa and legal status.

Given the high earnings threshold required to bring family members, most migrant workers are forced to live without their loved ones for years, even decades. Those who do bring face economic hardships. Unlike citizenship rights granted to children of migrants in most advanced countries of destination, children born to migrant workers in GCC countries have few rights. As integration and assimilation is actively discouraged, they typically receive their education in private schools where access and efficiency are directly related to the ability to afford tuition.[30] The bulk of students in the United Arab Emirates and Qatar today are children of migrant workers attending private schools.

The labor market in the Gulf can be characterized as a buyers' market. Surrounded by labor-surplus economies of Asia and Africa with an unlimited supply of cheap labor[31] for the foreseeable future, Gulf countries of destination find themselves in the enviable position of discriminating monopsonists.[32] No worker organizations exist to protect workers' rights in the Gulf.

Labor markets are segregated by national status. Nationals who are predominantly employed in the public sector in most GCC receive high salaries with extraordinary perks and job security. Regardless of the sector of work, compensation of foreign workers is almost always significantly lower than those of nationals for comparable work. Even when nationals are employed in the private sector, their status and employment conditions are highly favorable relative to comparable foreign workers. In short, government-sanctioned employer control over the mobility of foreign workers is the hallmark of the kafala system and is a significant source of economic rent.

The kafala system is a double-edged sword. While generating substantial rents for the nationals, the kafala system has been detrimental to productivity in the Gulf countries of destination in three ways: first, it engenders a "rentier mentality" among nationals severing the link between pay and performance, which is the sine qua non of efficiency;[33] second, it discourages automation and encourages labor-intensive technology as cheap foreign labor under the kafala system generates enormous economic rent; third, the transactional approach to expatriates relying exclusively on extrinsic rewards is shown to have a dampening effect on the motivation of workers.[34] According to IMF, *labor productivity*, estimated as non-oil output per worker, has declined in Qatar, the United Arab Emirates, and the kingdom between 2004 and 2014.[35] In contrast with labour productivity, total factor productivity signifies technological innovation.[36] Overall, GCC scores low on innovation.

In addition to labor productivity, total factor productivity (TFP), which measures the degree of efficiency of *both capital and labor* in the production process and is highly correlated with technological innovation, has also declined. The Global Innovation Index (GII) provides a cross-country relative performance assessment of innovation and is compiled annually. Several indicators in GII reports through the years provide indirect confirmation of the stagnant and declining productivity in the Gulf states (with the possible exception of the Emirates).[37]

In addition to the adverse implications for productivity, high proportion of foreign workers has qualitatively different political implications for the sparsely populated GCC than for the countries of destination in the West. The GCC governments are fully aware of the dark side of the kafala system. Faced with the unintended consequences of the kafala system, they have devised specific policies to promote the representation of nationals in the workforce.

In light of the expected surge of alternative energy sources and the shift away from fossil fuels, the critical question facing the Gulf monarchies is whether they will be able to sustain their growth once their oil and gas revenues dry up and provide enough jobs, and/or if a black swan-type event (COVID-19 being one) causes dramatic shifts in supply/demand conditions in the energy and/or regional labor market. Thus, the Gulf states have been making concerted efforts to diversify their economies. Given an extremely low population to natural resources ratio (to varying degrees), "the demographic imbalance now arguably supersedes all other concerns for both governments and citizens alike."[38] Not surprisingly, they aim at not only diversifying away from natural resources and leapfrogging (jumping technological generations) into a high value-added knowledge-based digital economy[39] but also at reducing their heavy dependence on foreign labor through nationalization (Saudization, Qatarization, and Emiratization) of the workforce. In the face of persistent youth unemployment, particularly in Saudi Arabia, which has been suffering from a high youth unemployment, and the perceived political risks involved in continued dependence on foreign labor, they have introduced many workforce nationalization policies, including quotas for nationals, restrictive visa policies, and sanctions for noncompliance (Alsahi 2020).

While the Gulf monarchies have achieved some success in diversifying their economies, given the well-documented reluctance of nationals to work in the private sector, the goal of nationalization of labor has evaded them despite repeated initiatives.[40] Thus, the vision of a high value knowledge-based economy with labor-saving technology appears to be a sound strategic choice. An economy with a high proportion of knowledge-intensive activities is expected to facilitate the participation of nationals in the private sector and help achieve the twin goal of nationalization of the workforce and economic diversification.[41]

This has hitherto been a daunting challenge for the Arab Gulf states. While oil is the primary source of revenue for the GCC governments, the biggest employment sector is the construction industry, followed closely by wholesale and retail trade and public administration. Gulf monarchies have made progress, albeit limited, toward creating a diversified economy, with the UAE being ahead of most Gulf states. Even before the onset of the COVID-19 pandemic, migrant destination countries of the Gulf sought to diversify their economies and promote capital- and technology-intensive industries. National development strategies have propelled this transition and generally aim at leveraging automation and digitalization while diversifying into several high-growth sectors.[42] These moves have accelerated since the beginning of the COVID-19 pandemic. *Indeed, COVID-19 has offered a unique opportunity to GCC countries to square the circle of diversification of the economy and nationalization of the workforce. Data shows that COVID-19 intensified the GCC workforce nationalization policies.*[43] The automation agenda received a shot in the arm and was accelerated in the wake of the pandemic.[44]

Digitalization and automation are transforming the employment landscape of GCC. In addition to the ongoing digital and automated transformation, the growing participation of women, particularly in Saudi Arabia, has been changing the employment landscape against low-skilled workers.

Given the structural dependence of GCC on foreign workers, the role played by their work-visa regimes is likely to be crucial in facilitating or retarding progress toward realizing the national objective of diversification into high-value digital economies along with the nationalization of the workforce. As expected, Gulf states also seek to become more attractive for skilled foreign workers. UAE has been at the forefront of introducing pro-skill reforms in the visa regime. Saudi Arabia has embarked on a pro-skill visa regime with a vengeance. Notwithstanding the absence of an explicit pro-skill immigration policy, rules and unwritten criteria make the recruitment and living arrangements for high-skilled migrants simpler and less costly. Typically, highly skilled foreign workers and professionals are offered tax-free income, employer-provided furnished accommodation, tuition allowance for children, generous excess baggage allowance, permission to sponsor domestic servants, paid vacations, and many other privileges.

The push by GCC toward diversification into a high-value digital economy drawing upon the synergy between highly skilled human capital and advances in ICT had intensified a skill bias in their migration regimes that predates the onset of the COVID-19 pandemic. The COVID-19 pandemic has only put this strategy on steroids, particularly in Saudi Arabia, distinguished by the highest rate of youth unemployment in GCC and growing economic hardships attending upon its foreign policy adventures. In the wake of COVID, an increasing push toward a pro-skill immigration policy is noticeable. It is evident from the recently announced so-called green card schemes in both UAE and Saudi Arabia.[45]

UAE has eclipsed all other GCC in terms of a strategic shift toward the labor demand anticipated in the wake of the fourth industrial revolution.[46] The tilt toward a pro-skill migration regime was evident from the increasing proportion of skilled migrants in UAE and the growing levies on, and exodus/deportation of, low-skilled migrant workers in Saudi Arabia.

While the fundamentals of the kafala system in all Gulf states are similar, the diversity and liberal atmosphere of the Emirates may have made the Emirates (and Qatar to some extent) relatively more attractive to highly skilled professionals and entrepreneurs from certain parts of the world. The Emirates leads the rest of GCC in terms of penetration of 4IR technologies and the relative share of skilled migrant workers. UAE's economy offers a preview of the coming future transformation of the oil-rich Gulf. According to the 2020 Network Readiness Index (NRI), the UAE places in the top quartile, ranking 30th among 134 countries.

Lacking hydrocarbon resources, Dubai has been diversifying its economy for decades and is a growth dynamo among the emirates of the UAE. In large measure, the superior performance of the UAE is explained by the significantly higher proportion of knowledge workers in the Emirates (40 percent[47] as against 35 percent for Saudi Arabia and Qatar's 12.6 percent—as of 2020).[48] thanks to some success in diversifying the economy into a financial, education, and logistics hub requiring highly qualified workers.

GCC have undertaken measures to tailor the education system to the vision of a high-value diversified digital economy. The UAE, for example, actively encourages youth to shift away from studying business and finance, typically seen as preparation for government jobs, and move toward STEM skills, especially engineering.[49] The UAE had spurred this change with various strategic measures to spark reforms in its education system. Spurred by its 2015 National Innovation Strategy, the UAE launched several initiatives to attract students toward STEM education, such as the Mohammed bin Rashid Smart Learning Program, Think Science, and Emirates Skills. The Fourth Industrial Revolution strategy, launched in 2017, focuses on advanced sciences and artificial intelligence research.[50] Significant educational reforms were undertaken in Saudi Arabia under King Abdullah who launched in 2005 the King Abdullah Overseas Scholarship Program, presumably the largest government-sponsored scholarship program in history.[51]

What future changes are expected in the GCC labor market, in general, and demand for foreign workers, in particular? Accelerated adoption of AI and other technologies of 4IR in GCC will directly affect the future demand for skills and the sectoral composition of the foreign workforce in these countries. Skills in demand are slated to be more technologically relevant, built on STEM (Science, Technology, Engineering, and Math) fields, and steeped in a diverse set of soft skills that complement automated and technologically driven jobs, such as computer programming, the ability to handle and manage hardware and network infrastructure, and data management.[52] The employment to population ratio of migrants by gender shows significant differences between Saudi Arabia and the Emirates—the proportion in Saudi Arabian population of female migrants is less than 15 percent; it is about 60 percent for males. The comparable figures for the Emirates are over 55 percent for females and close to 95 percent for males.[53] Potential factors increasing labor demand include mega projects in Gulf countries of destination, such as NEOM, Dubai Expo, and FIFA. Demand for foreign workers is expected to slow down in Qatar following FIFA 2022. Social preferences for public sector jobs by nationals is expected to persist. Potential factors dampening demand for foreign workers include success in nationalization of the workforce and automation. Unpredictable factors include oil prices and lower economic growth.[54] The pandemic has created a massive demand for digital skills, and post-COVID, the demand is likely to persist.

The Perils of Specialization in Low-Skill Migration in the Wake of 4IR[55]

Considering the significant contribution of remittances to the current account and alleviation of poverty among migrant households, the divergence of the countries of origin and countries of destination in the Gulf migration corridor seems puzzling. It would be illogical to hold migration per se responsible for the arrested convergence of the countries of origin and countries of destination as the counterfactual could have been worse.

Specialization in unskilled temporary migration is akin to specialization in low-value export commodities.[56] The opportunity to emigrate impinges on the human capital formation decision of would-be migrants in countries of origin. A positive probability of becoming employed abroad without enhanced skills and high educational attainment alters workers' incentives. The pre-migration per worker investment in human capital is smaller than had the probability of emigration without a high level of human capital had been zero.

There is considerable empirical evidence to the effect that large international earnings differentials for low-skilled workers negatively impact human capital investments in countries of origin. It has been called "the forsaken schooling phenomenon."[57] Most recently, Abdulloev, Epstein, and Gang (2020) have detected the "forsaken schooling phenomenon" in the Central Asian-Russian migration corridor which has numerous similarities with the Gulf migration corridor.[58] They show that having completed their compulsory schooling at ages 16–17, young people in three Central Asian migrant-sending countries—the Kyrgyz Republic, Tajikistan, and Uzbekistan, are forsaking additional schooling because of opportunities to emigrate to high-paying low-skilled jobs in Russia.[59]

The labor markets in GCC are segmented by nationality, with the nationals predominantly employed in the public sector with guaranteed job security while the private sector remains dominated by foreign workers governed by the kafala system.[60] Low-skilled foreign workers are more affected by the automation progress than nationals.[61] The coronavirus pandemic in the backdrop of 4IR has brought the costs into the limelight. The curse has been aggravated with the accelerated adoption of AI and automation in GCC with the onset of COVID-19.

Media reports have been highlighting the plight of migrant workers in the Gulf states for years. The plight of low-skilled workers was brought into the limelight during the pandemic. While GCC has provided access to testing vaccination, asymmetric treatment of nationals and non-nationals in the Gulf is well-documented.[62] Following the onset of COVID, media reports have highlighted the locking up of low-wage workers in overcrowded compounds, with scarce regard to physical distancing, hygiene, and isolation from infected individuals. Unlike the workers' power bubble witnessed in the developed countries in the wake of generous stimulus checks, "[t]he pandemic thus exposed, more aptly than ever, migrants' lack of agency and control of their mobility patterns in the Gulf."[63]

The following section illustrates the perils of specialization in exporting low-skilled labor using Pakistan as a textbook case.

I4.0 and the Future of Work in Pakistan

Of all the countries of origin to GCC, few face the political and economic challenges that Pakistan is confronting at the present juncture. A country of 220 million people, Pakistan is the sixth largest emigration country in the world. Since 1971, more than 11 million Pakistanis have emigrated for employment through official channels.[64] Both push-and-pull factors lie at the root of the emigration pressure. Pakistan's labor force is expected to grow by 138 million people by 2030 or about 30 percent, implying more mouths to feed and a commensurate need for job creation.[65] Between 2008 and 2014, the labor force grew by 3.3 percent a year, while job creation, at around 3 percent, barely matched the rate of new entrants to the labor force.[66]

In the face of the country's mounting economic challenges, the opening of the Gulf labor market following the oil boom starting the oil price spurt in 1973 offered policymakers a much-needed vent for surplus labor. Already, by 1975, Pakistani expatriates constituted 58.1 percent of the total non-Arab expatriates in the Gulf.[67] The number of Pakistani labor migrants seeking opportunities abroad annually increased significantly from some 200,000 departures in 2006 to over 900,000 in 2015.

The bulk of Pakistan migrant workers in the Gulf is low and semi-skilled and is heavily concentrated in a limited set of occupations. About 96 percent of all migration from Pakistan is to the Gulf and is heavily concentrated in two destinations (Saudi Arabia and the United Arab Emirates). At 53.9 percent, it is more than half of their total emigrant population.[68] They are, on average, young, male, educated, and not

Table 3.1 Pattern of Emigration from Pakistan as of 2019

Population of Pakistan	216 million
Stock of migrants abroad	
Total departures in 2019	625,203[a]
Share of women migrant workers (1971–2019)	0.4
GCC countries	96 percent
Remittances: billion during 2019	US$21.84
Remittances from the Arab States (mostly GCC)	60-65 percent
Remittances as a share of GDP in 2019	7.9 percent
Workers migrating through personal contacts 2019	47 percent
Workers emigrating through registered overseas employment promoters (OEPs)	53 percent
Licensed OEPs in 2019	2,062

Sources: United Nations, Department of Economic and Social Affairs, Population Division (2019). World Population Prospects, 2019, Online Edition. Rev. 1.; MOP&HRD, 2015, and the State Bank of Pakistan. (BE&OE, 2019)

from the very poorest households.[69] Those going to Europe are also more likely to be unmarried. A barbell pattern of emigration by skill is evident, with low-skilled migrants concentrated in the Gulf and medium- and high-skilled migrants in the West. At 0.4 percent of all migrant workers, the share of women is significantly lower than in other South Asian countries. Sociocultural factors and a lack of agency in decision-making processes within the family context are the two main reasons for the minuscule share of women among Pakistani migrants.[70]

To our knowledge, no emigration policy has ever been formally adopted in Pakistan. Export of labor to the Gulf following the oil boom was low-hanging fruit, and successive governments have tacitly encouraged emigration for both political and economic reasons as an easy way out of the chronic balance of payments deficit, poverty, youth unemployment, and as a bulwark against potential social unrest. An entrenched bureaucracy with vested interests also militates against any strategic thinking that might challenge the status quo. Domestic labor policies at both the federal and provincial levels in Pakistan aim to lower barriers to emigration.

Remittances and the development of work-related skills and competencies achieved abroad have contributed to economic growth and poverty reduction among migrant households in Pakistan.[71] Migrant remittance inflows from the Gulf constituted 7.9 percent of Pakistan's GDP in 2019.[72] The corresponding figure for Bangladesh and India was 5.5 percent and 2.8 percent, respectively (see Figure 3.1).[73] Despite the significant benefits accruing to the migrant households and to the macroeconomy, Pakistan finds itself at the bottom of the lower-middle-income group, ranking 174/225 on a per capita GDP (PPP) close to Myanmar. Pakistan is a textbook case of the dismal performance of the social sector for a lower-middle-income country. In terms of multidimensional poverty, which is at 38.3 percent, Pakistan presents a bleak picture in comparison with that of India (27.9 percent) and Bangladesh (24.6 percent).[74] The majority of households do not have living wages, particularly given the low rate of women's labor force participation and large household size. Even the lower-middle class is reeling under the unbearable pressure

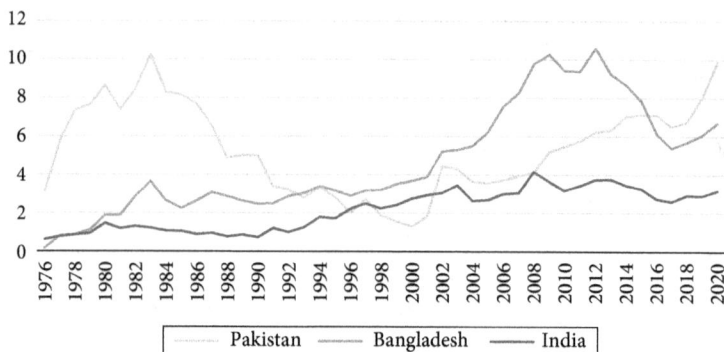

Figure 3.1 Personal remittances, received (% of GDP) 1976–2020. *Source*: World Bank. https://databank.worldbank.org/indicator/NY.GDP.PCAP.CD/1ff4a498/Popular-Indicators#

of the ever-rising inflation tax.[75] A large section of the poor in Pakistan cannot afford a sufficient and nutritious diet despite the overall growth in food production in recent years. According to the UN World Food Program (WFP), more than 20 percent of Pakistan's population is undernourished, and nearly 45 percent of children younger than 5 years of age are stunted. Corruption is institutionalized, and for a large section of the population, it is the only way to survive. However, capital flight has worsened the impact of corruption.

The impacts of the COVID-19 pandemic are further exacerbating Pakistan's macroeconomic and fiscal challenges as thousands of workers either returned or were forcibly deported from the Gulf.[76] In a recent study based on Pakistan Social and Living Standards Measurement (PSLM) survey, Hasan et al. (2021) find that only 10 percent of jobs in Pakistan could be done from home, with rural areas doing worse than urban centers. In addition, many of Pakistan's male workers are in low-skill, low-paying service industries and could not work from home.

Education spending is generally considered a productive expenditure. Disproportionate expenditure on defense has diverted valuable resources away from human capital investment. Education in Pakistan is still marked by a twin deficit (i.e., poor educational attainment of the population, in general, and women's still poorer educational attainment).[77] The average years of schooling in Pakistan at 8.3 lag significantly behind those of India (12.2) and Bangladesh (11.6). As late as 2020, 6 percent of children in Pakistan were still not enrolled in primary schools. The impact of COVID-19 on the education of children in Pakistan has been devastating. With no ready digital infrastructure capable of delivering live remote instruction, countries like Pakistan had to rely on ad hoc methods to deliver instruction, such as television broadcasts of school lessons; "Education: From disruption to recovery," UNESCO, unesco.org.

Hasan et. al highlighted Pakistani students' home-schooling challenges, given the low television and Internet access rates. With schools and training institutions closed and the economy shrinking, many young people have been losing out at a crucial time in their lives.

Discussion

COVID-19 has revealed the inherent risk society of a more connected world, highlighting the unequal prospects for the digitally advanced and resource-rich GCC and the digitally backward and resource-poor labor-surplus economies in the Gulf migration corridor.

Specialization in low-skilled migration is akin to the export of low-value products. *The AI-led transformation of GCC and its ramifications for temporary labor migration of low-skill workers carries significant and qualitatively different risks and opportunities for the labor exporting economies. COVID-19 has offered a unique opportunity to GCC countries to square the circle of nationalizing the workforce while diversifying the economy.*

Notwithstanding the widely reported abuse and exploitation of migrant workers in the Gulf, low- and semi-skilled migrant workers are highly vulnerable to automation in the wake of the ongoing digital transformation in GCC.

The effects of permanent emigration and temporary migration may be very different. Permanent emigration may cause an increase in innovation in the countries of origin by causing low-skilled wages to increase. For instance, rising wages following mass emigration to the United States in the nineteenth century induced technological change in Europe.[78] As for temporary migration, Anderson, Karadja, and Prawitz (2017) find little support for channels connected to return migration, such as human or economic capital accumulation abroad. This argument clearly becomes stronger if return migrants are low-skilled and working in dead-end jobs in countries of destination.

A recent World Bank study on Pakistan has identified many impediments to maximizing the benefits of international labor migration.[79] Lack of diversification in countries of destination and occupational niches makes Pakistan highly vulnerable to the vagaries of the Gulf political economy. In addition to exogenous shocks associated with markets, throughout the migration and work process migrant workers are faced with various market failures, ranging from intermediaries' rent-seeking behaviors to the rent-extraction by employers.[80] While officially all migration to the Gulf is temporary, with initial contracts ranging from one to three years, there is mounting evidence that temporary migration is often permanent, a fortiori within the Gulf migration corridor. Thus, being unable to earn and save enough to return home to upgrade their standard of living, many migrants are stuck beyond their planned separation from their loved ones in the Gulf countries of destination.

Are there are silver linings for countries of origin like Pakistan in the wake of the structural transformation of the GCC and the global economy? In our view, DigiTech offers the prospect of breaking out of the low-skill migration trap. *The real challenge will be to manage the phased transition to the new employment landscape in the Gulf migration corridor.*

Countries of origin need to ensure that emigrants can upgrade their skills on a continual basis to meet the fast-changing requirements of the labor market.

A political economy analysis of the kafala system and historical evidence suggests that the adoption of automation in GCC will be slow. First, a critical mass of knowledge workers and highly skilled professionals is necessary before oil economies can be reincarnated into knowledge-based digital economies.[81] Second, Gulf states' exclusivist and segregationist approach to immigration is likely to deny them the full advantages of the new technologies.[82] Third, dismissal of workers in many countries and industries and the rising global unemployment rate will increase the relative supply of workers willing to accept low salaries and conditions in the short run. Increased supply of cheap labor will dampen the incentives for structural transformation and is likely to slow down the automation process.[83]

The COVID-19 pandemic has created a "critical juncture"—a moment in which fundamental changes are possible.[84] The post-COVID labor markets in the Gulf will be shaped by the rapid societal penetration of DigiTech, reduced international demand for fossil fuel in the context of growing international preference for a greener economy, within GCC competition, particularly between the Emirates and the Kingdom to diversify into tourism and entertainment as major non-oil growth sectors, and the changing geopolitical context.[85]

The AI-led digital revolution is a double-edged sword. It has the potential to widen the gulf between the high and the low-income countries. It can also be enabling if the global digital divide can be bridged. "Over a long period of time, the main force in favor of greater equality has been the diffusion of knowledge and skills." However, education has been incredibly expensive, and at least, in part explains insufficient commitment of resources to education in many developing countries. According to UNICEF, suitable investments in education could lead to a return of 19.3 percent for girls and 12.2 percent for boys. Increasing development expenditure on education by 10 percent per year would add one percentage point to GDP growth.[86] The technologies of 4IR have opened a huge window of opportunity to overcome the challenge of universal access to education at all levels in resource-constrained developing countries. Success will depend upon reaping the digital dividends.

While irregular migration from Pakistan to Europe receives a lot of media attention, the creative solutions that the youth have been devising offers a silver lining. Nature does not like vacuums. The market for "digital entrepreneurship," a multibillion dollar industry, is growing at a rapid rate and is thirsty for young talent. Today, more than 60 percent of the population of Pakistan is under the age of 30. Pakistan has an estimated 3–4 million youth taking advantage of global connectivity and the digital economy to link with job opportunities internationally.[87] According to the Online Labor Index (OLI),[88] online labor supply of Pakistani workers has been increasing. It is remarkable that while India supplies more than one-third of online freelance labor, at about 12 percent, Pakistan supplies more than twice that of India on a per capita basis. It is an endogenous response to economic incentives in the market that can be influenced by the government or the private sector.[89] However, due to limited access and slow speed, only a small proportion of the youth have managed to break into the national or international market. There is a potential for demographic dividend here. The youth of labor-exporting countries like Pakistan are well placed to be in the driver's seat of this vibrant future.[90] With the right investments, this large cohort of young people has the potential to yield an important demographic dividend to contribute to social development and economic growth. "Technology can unleash the career potential of Pakistani youth."[91]

Notwithstanding the global digital divide and the gendered access to it, there are many Pakistani women who are excelling in the digital scene, be it via digital media, digital arts, or digital technology. With the pandemic came a greater reliance on digital media and devices that helped work, communicate, learn, and even play at home.[92] One of the unintended consequences of the COVID pandemic has been the enhanced prominence of English as the global lingua franca. It is among the most-demanded soft skills.[93] Here also Pakistan has a comparative advantage over many developing and emerging economies.

While there is little evidence of strategic thinking on the mass emigration of workers to the Gulf on the part of policymakers in Pakistan, there appears to be recognition of the value of digital platform in solving the problem of youth unemployment. Some small initiatives launched by the current administration in Pakistan appear to be highly promising. The Digital Youth Summit (DYS) established in KPK with assistance from the WB has grown into a premier platform for connecting youth, policymakers, and the private sector around emerging trends in the digital economy. "The Digital Hunar Programme is expected to serve trainees not only in learning new digital skills but will also prepare them for the job market," said Sania Nishtar.[94] Such programs need to be scaled up. A 2016 World Bank report observes that "India and Pakistan have more advanced digital identification systems than high-income North American countries, pointing to the potential for 'leapfrogging' that these technologies offer."[95]

Higher wages for labor make the business case for a shift to automation adoption stronger in rich countries including GCC. However, companies in low-wage countries may also benefit from automation to boost productivity. The need to ride the wave of the fourth industrial revolution beyond consideration of short-term costs is required to enhance quality, achieve tighter production control, and move production closer to end consumers in high-wage countries.[96]

There are some flies in the ointment. Automation, even when slow in adoption, is likely to create downward pressure on wages for the unskilled and semi-skilled workers in occupations with shrinking demand. This will require massive investment in upskilling the affected workers.

Policy Implications

What is the way forward to mitigate Gulf risk society? Our approach is exploratory and aims at generating debate and serious reflections rather than definite policy prescriptions.

As regards GCC, *given the low population base and the strategic goal of reduced dependence on foreign workforce, the accelerated adoption of AI-led automation by resource-rich GCC in the wake of COVID-19 offers the Gulf states a unique opportunity to square the circle of diversifying the economy while nationalizing the workforce that has long evaded them.* With the onset of COVID-19, most countries of destination, including the Gulf states, have embarked on the AI-led structural transformation with a vengeance.

In this unfolding scenario, the de facto policy of *specialization in low-skilled mass emigration* pursued by countries of origin like Pakistan is demonstrably doomed. We reflect on strategies that would mitigate the adverse effects of 4IR on the countries of origin while leveraging the potential gains from technological advances.

COVID-19 pandemic has created a "critical juncture"—a moment in which fundamental changes are possible. There are measures that can be undertaken in the short run, and there are measures that require long-term planning. To begin with, labor export-dependent economies need to leverage the technologies of the fourth industrial revolution and redirect investment toward digital infrastructure to maximize the benefits of digital capitalism.

Conditions for a gradual phasing out of a low-skill emigration are favorable for several reasons. First, the momentous impacts of technological change (e.g., self-driving cars) are unfolding gradually and can take decades from the birth of the invention to its commercialization.[97] Second, for structural reasons discussed earlier, transformation into a high-value knowledge-based economy is likely to be slow in GCC.[98] Third, the demand for certain forms of occupational skills required for infrastructure and building in the Gulf countries of destination is likely to be sustained due to the lack of enthusiasm among GCC nationals for TVET despite GCC governments' investments as part of their economic vision[99] and the preference of nationals for the public sector jobs. These occupations consist of architects, engineers, electricians, carpenters, and other skilled tradespeople, as well as construction workers.

Given the slow pace of nationalization of the workforce in GCC as discussed above, a complete rupture from the past patterns of emigration in the short run will neither be necessary nor advisable. In the short term, most policy recommendations proposed by international organizations like the World Bank and ILO are sound. To summarize, efforts to diversify markets (countries of destination) and upgrade export quality (skills of labor) are required.

It is estimated that investments in technical and vocational education and training (TVET) could lead to a 7 percent gain in worker productivity and better employment prospects. Employment-related training yields a 200 percent overall return on investments and expanding decent work would help Pakistan slash inequality—a major triumph, since reducing inequality by just 1 Gini point would produce an economic growth of 5 percent over the next five years.[100] Thus, the real challenge is to continuously calibrate the link between secondary and post-secondary education and the changing skill requirements in the market. That's where we really need investment.[101]

In the medium term, there is an urgent need to diversify in multiple dimensions. The extent to which the destination markets are concentrated in Gulf countries, occupations, and sectors are limited. Unlike the countries of destination of the West that are facing an ever-aging population, GCC will have a growing population with the share of youth and working-age population (15–64) increasing. Given the high fertility rate of nationals in Saudi Arabia, and a population pyramid comparable to labor-surplus economies like that of Pakistan, young foreign professionals face a higher degree of competition in the labor market, depressing real wages even further.[102]

To maximize the benefits of labor export, countries of destination with the greatest direct and indirect benefits of migration need to be tapped. Would-be migrants are voting by their feet. Irregular migration from Pakistan to Europe via Turkey and other channels is a regular phenomenon.[103] The increased flow of irregular migration to Europe in recent years by would-be migrants is the strategy undertaken by the most enterprising and daring youth. The increased flow may be attributed to the growing exposure of the would-be migrants (thanks largely to the social media) to the vast gulf in living standards between the quality of life between the countries of destination in the West and GCC.[104] Given the risky nature of the adventure, there is a "romantic appeal" to irregular migration for the young.[105]

The exodus of skills to the Gulf and the countries of destination in Europe has different implications at both the micro and the macro levels. First, there is a vast gulf in living standards and access to public goods between the Western countries of destination and GCC.[106] More important, the liberal democracies have an active immigration and integration policy. Most have incorporated international student mobility into their immigration and integration strategy. Second, while economic drivers are predominant for migration from Pakistan, higher education opportunities are the second most prevalent motive for potential migrants toward Europe. Given the pro-skill immigration policy most Western countries pursue, international students pursuing advanced degrees are a prime target for recruitment in most Western countries of destination. The exodus of talent has reached an unprecedented level.[107] Many women have clearly shown their interest in other regions such as Europe, where both the service sector and more professional opportunities are available and where gender and labor rights and protections are more strongly enforced. Highly skilled Pakistani diaspora has thrived under open pluralist and competitive conducive socioeconomic conditions. The swift upward mobility of Pakistani diaspora in the West amply testifies to this effect.

Ceteris paribus, the benefits of migration to Europe and other advanced countries of the West greatly outweigh the benefits of migration from the Gulf. Social remittances from advanced countries in terms of learning and soft skills will be highly important in the post-pandemic globalized labor market. Scholars have highlighted the importance of knowledge networks that international migration can create.[108] It is imperative that countries of origin explore labor emigration channels beyond the Gulf.

Pakistan needs to explore a variety of diversification options. The Ministry of Foreign Affairs must be engaged to identify promising sectors in current countries of destination, and conduct ongoing emerging market analysis regarding trades, skills, and sectors available in countries of destination to help broaden the geographic scope of opportunities. This is highly desirable in countries outside of the GCC region, particularly China, and the emerging markets in Europe and South East Asia.[109]

The Chinese population pyramid is becoming top heavy. Just like Japan with rising income levels and an aging population, China is likely to become an immigrant receiving country for cheap labor if current trends of growing aging population continues and the share of the working-age population continues to decline. China has experienced a labor shortage and rising wages, The dramatic development of its labor market signals that China is entering a new stage of economic development.[110] "As China is increasingly globalized, an immigration boom in China is inevitable."[111] Few countries have the potential to serve as middlemen for China. In light of the ever-growing economic integration with the Chinese economy in the wake of the $62 billion China Pakistan Economic Cooperation (CPEC),[112] the potential demand for Pakistani bilingual workers will come not only from China but also from other countries that wish to do business with China. To maximise the benefits from labour migration, Pakistan can draw upon the experience of projects such as the "Pilot Project Addressing Labor Shortages Through Innovative Labor Migration Models" (PALIM) project, implemented in 2019 by Enabel—Belgium's development agency—in partnership with Flanders and Morocco.[113]

With managed transition out of the low-skill trap and the right policies in place—including targeted investments in tertiary and TVET education and skills training in the digital economy, and the efficient management of labor migration flows—the digital economy in labor-exporting countries like Pakistan can make a significant contribution to advancing decent work and inclusive economic growth at the global, regional, and national levels.[114]

It would be naïve to assume that just because the proposed strategic shift is sound, it would be warmly received by policymakers. A political economy analysis needs to be conducted to identify who is likely to resist change and determine the potential gains to winners and how the losers can be brought on board with shared benefits. We intend to carry out an empirical analysis to address these issues in the sequel to this chapter.

Conclusion

COVID-19 has unearthed the risk society of a more connected world, highlighting the unequal prospects for the digitally advanced and resource-rich GCC and the digitally backward and resource-poor labor-surplus economies in the Gulf migration corridor. *The accelerated adoption of AI-led automation by resource-rich GCC in the wake of COVID-19 has offered the Gulf states a unique opportunity to square the circle of diversifying the economy while nationalizing the workforce that has long evaded them.* The AI-led transformation of GCC and its ramifications for international labor migration carry significant and qualitatively different risks and opportunities for the labor-exporting economies. In this unfolding scenario, labor export-dependent economies can make a virtue of necessity by leveraging the technologies of the fourth industrial revolution and redirecting investment toward digital infrastructure to reduce emigration pressure by enabling the young people to equip themselves to seize the opportunities offered by digital capitalism. Success will depend upon reaping the digital dividends.

Notes

1 Sadiki and Saleh (2020, 6–20).
2 A seminal study on the societal impact of 4IR is Brynjolfsson and McAfee (2014).
3 Trajtenberg (2019), in Agrawal, Gans, and Goldfarb (2019).
4 McKinsey (2021).
5 McKinsey (2021).
6 Autor (2020).
7 Rani et al. (2021).
8 McKinsey (2021).
9 Autor (2020).
10 Nicola (2020).
11 WEF (2016).
12 Pages 241–8.
13 At the present time, labor supply on online web-based platforms exceeds demand, putting downward pressure on earnings (Rani et al. 2021, 21). However, the present imbalance in supply and demand may not last long.
14 Rani et al. (2021, 18).

15 Gagnon and Gagnon (2021).
16 WEF (2020).
17 British Council (2018).
18 Mughal, Abdul Ghaffar, Sadiq M. Sait, Jitendra Roychoudhury, and Rym Ayadi. "Leveraging digital technology to bridge the global knowledge divide: The promise of MOOCs revisited."
19 See Baldwin (2019). Baldwin anticipates a fundamental shift in the global international exchange with the growing trade in services previously thought to be non-tradable.
20 This article is inspired by the seminal work of Ulrich Beck and Tony Giddens on risk society and the pathbreaking study of Thomas Piketty on inequality. See Beck, Giddens, and lash (2018), Piketty (2018).
21 Autor (2020).
22 Autor (2020). Massive online open courses (MOOCs) have been in existence since 2010 but only with the onset of the coronavirus pandemic, they took off.
23 Ibid.
24 https://gulfmigration.grc.net/media/graphs/Figure_1percentageofnationalsnon -nationals%202020.pdf.
25 Months into the pandemic, Qatar technically cancelled this policy. See Qatar (2020).
26 Broadly defined, economic rent refers to any unearned benefit received by a nonproductive factor, such as the one associated with natural resources, possession of unique talents, or monopolistic behavior.
27 The exploitation of low- and semi-skilled workers in GCC is widely documented by scholars, Human Rights Watch, and Amnesty International. Highly cited studies include: Gardner (2011), Sonmez et al. (2011), Auwal (2010), Vora and Koch (2015), Arnold (2019), Jarallah (2009), Afsar (2009), Minaye (2012), Murray, (2013).
28 The seminal work in theorizing the nature of the implicit social contract between the Gulf monarchies and the national population is by Beblawi (1987).
29 Many businesses are substantially owned by foreigners, but the law requires nationals as partners who must also be legally responsible for the foreign workers. GCC nationals receive a fee for this "service," illegal as it may be.
30 Ranju, K.
31 Abella (2017).
32 In economic jargon, a perfectly discriminating monopsonist is one who can "perfectly discriminate" by paying each worker his or her reservation wage (the lowest wage the worker is willing to work for instead of the equilibrium wage in a competitive labor market). See Naidu, Nyarko, and Wang (2016).
33 Soto, Raimundo, and Vásquez (2011). See Beblawi (1987) for the original formulation of the 'rentier mentality' hypothesis.
34 See Pink (2011), Altman (2020).
35 IMF (2014).
36 Fassio, Kalantaryan and Venturini (2015).
37 Dutta, Lanvin, and Wunsch-Vincent (2020). The 2021 GII report shows negative productivity growth in all three major economies of GCC.
38 Ulrichsen (2014). Cited in Forstenlechner & Rutledge (2010).
39 On the concept of leapfrogging, the seminal work is by Gerschenkron (1962). On the overall logic of a knowledge-based economy, see Stiglitz (1999); On the concept of leapfrogging in the context of resource-rich Gulf states, see Ewers and Malecki (2010), Djeflat (2009).

40 See Behar (2013), Behar (2015), Baldwin-Edwards (2011), Table 3. See Peck (2017) for the dismal performance of the *Nitaqat* policy in Saudi Arabia. Peck (2017).
41 Fattouh and Sen (2021).
42 Supply, their impact on labor, and demand in Abu Dhabi Dialogue corridors. "Abu Dhabi dialogue." p. 4.
43 Alsahi (2020).
44 Abu Dhabi Dialogue, p. 13.
45 https://www.uaecabinet.ae/en/details/news/golden-card-permanent-residency -system-for-uaes-expats-launches. For Saudi residency schemes, see https://saprc.gov .sa/#/. Eleonora Ardemagni. October 28, 2021. https://carnegieendowment.org/sada /85676
46 Abu Dhabi Dialogue, p. 12.
47 Share of 'Knowledge Workers' in the Labor Force (2022).
48 World Bank (2020).
49 British Council (2018).
50 Abu Dhabi Dialogue, pp. 6, 12.
51 Mughal (2021).
52 Abu Dhabi Dialogue, p. 11; ILO, 2018.
53 ILO (2021).
54 ILO (2019).
55 The argument in this section is inspired by the groundbreaking study by Reinert (2019). Cimoli, Dosi, and Stiglitz (2009). The argument is analogous to the argument in favor of specializing in high-tech exports, as in Reinert (2019).
56 Korinek and Stiglitz (2021).
57 See also Abdulloev, Epstein, and Gang (2020), Stark, Helmenstein, and Prskawetz (1998).
58 It should be pointed out though that most citizens of ex-Soviet republics can enter Russia without visa; thusthe worst excesses of the kafala system are not witnessed in the Central Asian-Russian migration corridor.
59 Ibid.
60 World Bank Group (2018).
61 Aus dem Moore et al., 2018. Abu Dhabi Dialogue, p. 9.
62 See Sadiki and Saleh (2020). To quote, "Existing structures set in place upon the founding of Arab postcolonial states have perpetuated inequality, within and between them. COVID-19 has not created these problems. Rather coronavirus virus has made these 'pathologies' more pronounced" (pp. 6–7).
63 ICMPD, p. 28.
64 ILO (2020a).
65 McKinsey (2021).
66 WB (2018, 5).
67 Castles and Delgado Wise (2008).
68 ILO (2021). Table 2. p. 10.
69 GCC hosts use the initial costs of migration as a de facto means to restrict and regulate the inflow of Asian contract workers. Ilahi and Jafarey (1999).
70 ILO (2020a); Hahn-Schaur (2021). About half of all 29.7 million migrants from Asia (excluding Iran and Central Asia) in 2019 in Arab states (GCC plus Jordan and Lebanon) were females. Table 6.
71 BE&OE (2019). [general support?] Table 6.
72 ILO (2021, 2020b).

73 Only Sri Lanka and Nepal, with 9.1 and 29.9 percent, exceeded Pakistan.

74 Multidimensional poverty rectifies the shortcomings of the general poverty index in terms of monetary income. Thus, in Pakistan, only 4.4 percent of the population lives in monetary poverty, but 38.3 percent lives in multidimensional poverty. Global Multidimensional Poverty Index 2021. Unmasking disparities by ethnicity, caste, and gender. https://ophi.org.uk/global-mpi-report-2021/.

75 Chronic Inflation has become a structural feature of Pakistan's economy. See Zulfiqar (2019).

76 The rise of remittances . . .

77 Mughal (2021).

78 Andersson, Karadja, and Prawitz (2017).

79 WB (2018, 6).

80 WB (2018, 7).

81 There is a vast literature on increasing social returns to scale in the accumulation of human capital. See the seminal paper by Azariadis and Drazen (1990).

82 Like GCC, Singapore has been heavily dependent upon immigration. The defining difference between them is the integration policy of Singapore with a highly pro-skill bias of the immigration policy. See Perry (2017).

83 Abu Dhabi Dialogue, p. 7.

84 "In the analysis of path-dependent institutions, the concept of critical juncture refers to situations of uncertainty in which decisions of important actors are causally decisive for the selection of one path of institutional development over other possible paths." Capoccia (2015). Institutions are broadly defined as "organizations, formal rules, public policies, political regimes, and political economies." change" (Capoccia, 2015, 2).

85 For conceptual tools to navigate the region's turbulent politics, see Sadiki (2020).

86 For conceptual tools to navigate the region's turbulent politics, see Sadiki (2020).

87 Pakistani Youth See Opportunity in a Globalized Economy February 10, 2016. https://www.un.org/youthenvoy/2016/02/pakistani-youth-see-opportunity-in-digital-economy/.

88 The Online Labor Index (OLI) created by the Oxford Internet Institute is the first economic indicator that provides an online gig economy equivalent of conventional labor market statistics. It measures the supply and demand of online freelance labor across countries and occupations by tracking the number of projects and tasks across platforms in real time.

89 Rani et al. (2021, 44).

90 Ferguson (2017).

91 https://blogs.worldbank.org/endpovertyinsouthasia/supporting-pakistans-digital-transformation.

92 Pakistani Women Paving the Way for A Digital Pakistan October 13, 2021.https://www.fuchsiamagazine.com/2021/10/13/5-pakistani-women-paving-the-way-to-a-digital-pakistan/.

93 British Council (2018).

94 ILO (2020b).

95 World Bank (2016). The report highlights the efficiency of Benazir Income Support Program (BISP) which utilizes blockchain technology, World Bank, 2016, Moreover, the report gives high marks to the Punjab Citizen Feedback Model.

96 Abu Dhabi Dialogue.

97 As noted by Autor, the largest labor market effects that we're seeing right now are from existing information technologies that are two decades old (Autor, 2020).

98 Farzanegan and Thum (2020).

99 Khan et al., 2017. Enrolment in vocational programs at the upper secondary level is less than 2 % in Oman, Saudi Arabia and Qatar, 2.5% in the UAE mostly limited to male students (UNESCO-UNEVOC, 2018).

100 UNICEF, 5.

101 Autor (2020).

102 For instance, the market for drivers has been facing serious competition from nationals. Uber reports more Saudi female drivers. October 4, 2021, https://www.arabnews.com/node/1941251/business-economy. Saudi Arabia's female-only rival to Uber sees growth in first year of operations. June 14, 2021. 23:22. https://www.arabnews.com/node/1876641/business-economy.

103 The number of undocumented Pakistani immigrants arrested by Turkish security forces between 1995-November 2006 was 50000 – second only to Iraq. Castels and Wise, Table 12.

104 The US Consul General in Islamabad, David Donahue, maintains that patterns of migration are changing: "We are seeing a rural population apply, whereas previously it had been an educated class." https://www.thenewhumanitarian.org/report/14891/pakistan-irin-special-report-population-exodus.

105 Hahn-Schaur (2021, 3).

106 The US Consul General in Islamabad, David Donahue, maintains that patterns of migration are changing: "We are seeing a rural population apply, whereas previously it had been an educated class." https://www.thenewhumanitarian.org/report/14891/pakistan-irin-special-report-population-exodus.

107 https://www.thenewhumanitarian.org/report/14891/pakistan-irin-special-report-population-exodus.

108 Referring to the positive externalities of migration, Castles and Wise observe, "Knowledge networks need not of course only be about producing things in order to contribute to development. The knowledge brought home may be about democratic principles, more effective governance, new ways of raising children, new lifestyles, etc." (p. 70).

109 World Bank (2018, Xv).

110 Cui, Meng, and Lu (2018).

111 Donglin (2017), Mathews (2020), Noh (2014).

112 http://cpec.gov.pk/index.

113 Abu Dhabi Dialogue, p. 13.

114 ILO. Skills shortage.

References

Abdulloev, Ilhom, Gil S. Epstein and Ira N. Gang. (2020). "Migration and Forsaken Schooling in Kyrgyzstan, Tajikistan, and Uzbekistan," *IZA Journal of Development and Migration*, 11 (1): 1–27.

Abella, Manolo. (2017). "The High Cost of Migrating for Work to the Gulf," *Migration to the Gulf: Policies in Sending and Receiving Countries*: 221.

Afsar, Rita. (2009). *Unravelling the Vicious Cycle of Recruitment: Labour Migration from Bangladesh to the Gulf States*. Geneva: ILO.

Agrawal, Ajay, Joshua Gans and Avi Goldfarb (2019). *The Economics of Artificial Intelligence: An Agenda*. Chicago: National Bureau of Economic Research and University of Chicago Press.

Alsahi, H. (2020), "COVID-19 and the Intensification of the GCC Workforce Nationalization Policies," *Arab Reform Initiative*, November 10, www.arab-reform.net /publication/covid-19-and-the-intensification-of-the-gcc-workforcenationalization -policies/ (accessed January 21, 2022).

Altman, Morris. (2020). *Worker Satisfaction and Economic Performance*. London: Routledge.

Anderson, David, Mounir Karadja and Erik Prawitz. (2017). "Mass Migration, Cheap Labor, and Innovation," Manuscript, Inst. Internet. Economic Studies, Stockholm University.

Arnold, F. (2019). *Asian Labor Migration: Pipeline to the Middle East*. Routledge.

Autor, David. (2020). "MIT Economist David Autor Speaks at an Enterprise for Society-E4S Event at IMD on the Future of Jobs," filmed January 29, TED video, 10:57, https:// www.youtube.com/watch?v=KHk1RbLHOLc&t=3306s (accessed January 21, 2022).

Auwal, M.A. (2010). "Ending the Exploitation of Migrant Workers in the Gulf," *Fletcher Forum of World Affairs*, 34: 87.

Azariadis, Costas and Allan Drazen. (1990). "Threshold Externalities in Economic Development," *The Quarterly Journal of Economics*, 105 (2): 501–26.

Baldwin, Richard. (2019). *The Globotics Upheaval: Globalization, Robotics, and the Future of Work*. Oxford: Oxford University Press.

Baldwin-Edwards, M. (2011). *Labor Immigration and Labor Markets in the GCC Countries: National Patterns and Trends*, [online]. London: London School of Economics. *Global Governance*.

Beblawi, Hazem. (1987). "The Rentier State in the Arab World," *Arab Studies Quarterly*: 383–98.

Beck, U., A. Giddens, and S. Lash. (1994). *Reflexive Modernization: Politics, Tradition and Aesthetics in the Modern Social Order*. Stanford University Press.

Behar, A. (2013). "Labor Market Reforms to Boost Employment and Productivity in the GCC," In Annual Meeting of Ministers of Finance and Central Bank Governors.

Behar, M.A. (2015). *Comparing the Employment-Output Elasticities of Expatriates and Nationals in the Gulf Cooperation Council*. International Monetary Fund.

British Council. (2018). *Future Skills Supporting the UAE's Future Workforce*. British Council, www.britishcouncil.ae/sites/ default/files/bc_futureskills_english_1mar18_3 .pdf (accessed November 18, 2021)

Brynjolfsson, Erik and Andrew McAfee. (2014). *The Second Machine Age: Work, Progress, and Prosperity in a Time of Brilliant Technologies*. WW Norton & Company.

Capoccia, G. (2015). *Critical Junctures and Institutional Change Advances in Comparative Historical Analysis in the Social Sciences*. 147–80.

Castles, Stephen and Raúl Delgado Wise. (2008). *Migration and Development: Perspectives from the South*. Universidad Autónoma de Zacatecas, 91.

Cimoli, M., G. Dosi, and J.E. Stiglitz (2009). "The Political Economy of Capabilities Accumulation: The Past and Future of Policies for Industrial Development," *Mario Cimoli, Giovanni Dosi and Joseph E. Stiglitz*.

Cui, Yuming, Jingjing Meng and Changrong Lu. (2018). "Recent Developments in China's Labor Market: Labor Shortage, Rising Wages and Their Implications," *Review of Development Economics*, 22 (3): 1217–38.

Curtis, John. (2017). *Singapore: Unlikely Power*. Oxford: Oxford University Press.

Djeflat, A. (2009). *Building Knowledge Economies for Job Creation, Increased Competitiveness, and Balanced Development*. Unpublished paper presented at the World Bank Middle East and North Africa, Tunis.

Donglin, Han. (2017). "Is China Ready for Foreigners? Public Attitudes Towards Immigration in China," *China: An International Journal*, 15 (2): 120–43.

Dutta, S., B. Lanvin, and S. Wunsch-Vincent (eds.). (2020). *Global Innovation Index 2020*. Johnson Cornell University.

Ewers, M.C. and E.J. Malecki. (2010). "Leapfrogging into the Knowledge Economy: Assessing the Economic Development Strategies of the Arab Gulf States," *Tijdschrift Voor Economische en Sociale Geografie*, 101 (5): 494–508.

Farzanegan, M.R. and M. Thum. (2020). "Does oil Rents Dependency Reduce the Quality of Education?" *Empirical Economics*, 58: 1863–911.

Fassio, C., S. Kalantaryan and A. Venturini. (2015). *Human Resources and Innovation: Total Factor Productivity and Foreign Human Capital*. Robert Schuman Centre for Advanced Studies Research Paper No. RSCAS, 43.

Fattouh, Bassam and Anupama Sen. (2021). "Economic Diversification in Arab Oil-Exporting Countries in the Context of Peak Oil and the Energy Transition," in G. Luciani and T. Moerenhout (eds.), *When Can Oil Economies Be Deemed Sustainable?*, 73–97. Singapore: Springer Nature, p. 365.

Ferguson, Alexander. (2017). *Unleashing the Potential of Pakistan's Youth to Contribute to the Global Economy*, May 4, https://www.worldbank.org/en/news/speech/2017/05/03/unleashing-the-potential-of-pakistans-youth-to-contribute-to-the-global-economy (accessed February 9, 2021)

Forstenlechner & Rutledge. (2010). "Unemployment in the Gulf: Time to Update the 'social contract,'" *Middle East Policy*, 17 (2): 38–51.

Gagnon, Catherine and Jason Gagnon. (2021). "Migration in Asia: What Skills for the Future?," 4.

Gardner, A.M. (2011). "Gulf Migration and the Family," *Journal of Arabian Studies*, 1 (1): 3–25.

Gerschenkron, A. (1962). *Economic Backwardness in Historical Perspective: A Book of Essays* (No. HC335 G386). Cambridge, MA: Belknap Press of Harvard University Press.

Hahn-Schaur, Katharina. (2021). "Awareness Raising and Information Campaigns on the Risks of Irregular Migration in Pakistan," 4.

Hasan, Syed M., Attique Rehman, and Wendong Zhang. (2021). "Who Can Work and Study from Home in Pakistan: Evidence from a 2018–2019 Nationwide Household Survey," *World Development*, 138: 105–97.

Ilahi, Nadeem and Saqib Jafarey. (1999). "Guestworker Migration, Remittances and the Extended Family: Evidence from Pakistan," *Journal of Development Economics*, 58 (2): 485–512, p. 509.

ILO. (2019). *Preparing for a Brighter Future of Work*. Report for the 5th Ministerial Consultation of the Abu Dhabi Dialogue, Dubai, October 16–17.

ILO. (2020a). *Female Labor Migration from Pakistan: A Situation Analysis*, https://www.ilo.org/global/topics/labor-migration/projects/reframe/WCMS_735795/lang--en/index.htm (accessed September 7, 2021)

ILO. (2020b). *Fair Recruitment Country Brief: Pakistan. April 20, 2020*. ILO, https://www.ilo.org/global/topics/fair-recruitment/publications/WCMS_741045/lang--en/index.htm (accessed September 7, 2021)

ILO. (2021). https://ilostat.ilo.org/who-are-the-women-on-the-move-a-portrait-of-female -migrant-workers/, Retrieved October 27. [https://worldpopulationreview.com/ countries/qatar-population; https://www.onlineqatar.com/visiting/tourist-information/ qatar-population-and-expat-nationalities (accessed September 7, 2021)

Jarallah, Y. (2009). "Domestic Labor in the Gulf Countries," *Journal of Immigrant & Refugee Studies*, 7 (1): 3–15.

Korinek, Anton and Joseph E. Stiglitz. (2021). *Artificial Intelligence, Globalization, and Strategies for Economic Development*. No. w28453. National Bureau of Economic Research.

Mathews, Gordon. (2020). "Destination China: Immigration to China in the Post-Reform Era. Edited by Angela Lehmann and Pauline Leonard," *Pacific Affairs*, 93 (2): 424–5.

McKinsey. (2021) *The Future of Work after COVID-19 February 18, 2021*. |Report. Assi and Marcait (2020).

Minaye, A. (2012). "Trafficked to the Gulf States: The Experiences of Ethiopian Returnee Women," *Journal of Community Practice*, 20 (1–2): 112–33.

Mughal, Abdul Ghaffar. (2021). "How did the Largest Overseas Scholarship Programme in History Narrow the Gender Capabilities Gap in Saudi Arabia?" *Higher Education in the Gulf*: 85–108.

Murray, H.E. (2013). "Hope for Reform Springs Eternal: How the Sponsorship System, Domestic Laws and Traditional Customs Fail to Protect Migrant Domestic Workers in GCC Countries," *Cornell International Law Journal*, 45: 461.

Naidu, Suresh, Yaw Nyarko and Shing-Yi Wang. (2016). "Monopsony Power in Migrant Labor Markets: Evidence from the United Arab Emirates," *Journal of Political Economy*, 124 (6): 1735–92.

Noh, Jae-Chul. (2014). "The Comparative Law Research on the Mandatory Control About Illegal Foreign Workers in China," *The Journal of the Korea Contents Association*, 14 (9): 236–46.

Peck, Jennifer R. (2017). "Can Hiring Quotas Work? The Effect of the Nitaqat Program on the Saudi Private Sector," *American Economic Journal: Economic Policy*, 9 (2): 316–47.

Piketty, Thomas. (2018). *Capital in the Twenty-First Century*. Cambridge, MA: Harvard University Press.

Pink, Daniel H. (2011). *Drive: The Surprising Truth About What Motivates US*. Penguin.

Qatar. (2020). "New Labour Law Ends Qatar's Exploitative Kafala System," *The Guardian*, September 1, https://bit.ly/3JoApeQ (accessed September 7, 2021)

Rani, Uma, R. Kumar Dhir, Maria Furrer, N. Gőbel, A. Moraiti and S. Cooney. (2021). *World Employment and Social Outlook: The Role of Digital Labor Platforms in Transforming the World of Work*. International Labor Organization, 16.

Ranju, K. "Pandemic Impact on Migrant Children and Youth in GCC."

Reinert, Erik S. (2019). *How Rich Countries Got Rich . . . And Why Poor Countries Stay Poor*. Hachette UK.

Sadiki, Larbi. (2020). "Middle of Where? East of What? Simulated Postcoloniality's Assemblages, Rhizomes and Simulacra," In Larbi Sadiki (ed.), *Routledge Handbook of Middle East Politics*, 21–69. London: Routledge.

Sadiki, Larbi and L. Saleh. (2020). "Reflexive Politics and Arab 'risk society'? COVID-19 and Issues of Public Health," *Orient*: 6–20.

Share of 'Knowledge Workers' in the Labor Force. *Competitive Knowledge Economy*, https://www.vision2021.ae/en/national-agenda-2021/list/card/share-of-knowledge -workers-in-the-labor-force (accessed January 21, 2022).

Sonmez, S., Y. Apostolopoulos, D. Tran, and S. Rentrope. (2011). "Human Rights and Health Disparities for Migrant Workers in the UAE," *Health and Human Rights*, 13: 17.

Soto, Raimundo and Rosalía Vásquez. (2011). *The Efficiency Cost of the Kafala in Dubai: A Stochastic Frontier Analysis*. No. 399.

Stark, Oded, Christian Helmenstein and Alexia Prskawetz. (1998). "Human Capital Depletion, Human Capital Formation, and Migration: A Blessing or a 'curse'?" *Economics Letters*, 60 (3): 363–7.

Stiglitz, J. (1999). "Public Policy for a Knowledge Economy," *Remarks at the Department for Trade and Industry and Center for Economic Policy Research*, 27: 79.

Trajtenberg, Manuel. (2019). "Artificial Intelligence as the Next GPT: A Political-Economy Perspective," 175–86.

Ulrichsen, K.C. (2014). *Insecure Gulf: The End of Certainty and the Transition to the Post-Oil Era*. Oxford University Press.

WEF. (2016). *The Future of Jobs: Employment, Skills and Workforce Strategy for the Fourth Industrial Revolution*. World Economic Forum, www3.weforum.org/docs/WEF_Future _of_Jobs.pdf (accessed July 9, 2021)

WEF. (2020). *The Future of Jobs Report 2020*. World Economic Forum, www3.weforum .org/docs/WEF_Future_of_Jobs_2020.pdf (accessed July 9, 2021)

World Bank. (2016). "World Development Report 2016: Digital Dividends," 154.

Vora, N. and N. Koch (2015). "Everyday Inclusions: Rethinking Ethnocracy, Kafala, and Belonging in the A rabian Peninsula," *Studies in Ethnicity and Nationalism*, 15 (3): 540–52.

World Bank. (2020). https://tcdata360.worldbank.org/indicators/00827cf1?country=BRA &indicator=40464&viz=line_chart&years=2013 (accessed January 21, 2022).

Zulfiqar, Fahd. (2019). "Hafeez A Pasha. Growth and Inequality in Pakistan, Volume-I. Islamabad: Friedrich Ebert Stiftung. 2018. v+ 218 pages," *The Pakistan Development Review*, 58 (2): 223–4.

4

Socioeconomic Effects of COVID-19 Pandemic on the GCC Countries

Threats and Opportunities

Héla Miniaoui[1] and Anis Khayati[2]

COVID-19 Epidemic: Origin and Spreading in the GCC Region

The emergence of the 2019 novel coronavirus disease (COVID-19) is considered to be an unexpected crisis derailing the global economy. COVID-19 started to expand in the Chinese district of Wuhan in December 2019. From there, it spreads to 196 countries around the world. COVID-19 was officially announced as a pandemic by the World Health Organization (WHO) on March 11, 2020. As of February 23, 2022, there have been 426, 624,859 confirmed cases of COVID-19, including 5.899.578 deaths.[3] The Gulf Cooperation Council (GCC) countries consisting of Bahrain, Kuwait, Oman, Qatar, the Kingdom of Saudi Arabia (KSA), and the United Arab Emirates (UAE) were, like all countries, affected by the COVID-19 pandemic. The first confirmed case in the UAE was announced on January 29, 2020. The virus was confirmed to have reached Bahrain on February 21, 2020, and Oman on February 24, 2020, when two citizens tested positive for coronavirus after returning from Iran. The first verified case of coronavirus in Kuwait was announced on February 24, 2020. Qatar's Health Ministry declared its first confirmed case in the country on February 29, 2020. The patient was returning from Iran. In KSA, the Ministry of Health reported the first case on March 2, 2020, in a traveler returning from Iran through Bahrain. In 2020, Saudi Arabia had the most deaths (2,733) among all the GCC countries followed by Kuwait with 433 deaths, Oman (384 deaths), UAE (344 deaths), Qatar (165 deaths), and Bahrain (140 deaths).[4]

Unprecedented global public isolation measures were taken, ranging from home lockdowns to social distancing. Businesses, restaurants, shops, and transportation services were shuttered. Cancellation of public and private events, closure of schools and universities as well as remote work led to border and airports shutdown, complete paralysis of tourism, and disruption of supply chains, and the volume of international trade. These pandemic preventive actions have caused tremendous damage to the

GCC's economic activity and they were the source of volatility in their capital markets, leading the GCC economies to a standstill.

This chapter addresses the following basic questions pertaining to the pandemic "risk society" in GCC countries: To what extent has COVID-19 underscored and deepened socioeconomic inequalities in the GCC countries? How has a "return of the state" manifested in the GCC region? And what were the main impacts on civic freedoms during the pandemic?

The remaining of the chapter is organized as follows. The second section analyses the economic threats that the COVID-19 pandemic posed to the GCC region mainly through three channels: tourism, energy, and retail, all considered key job-rich sectors. Section three examines the GCC states' response to this outbreak. Section four highlights the "risk society" effects of increasing state intervention, as well as regarding the role of the civil society. Section five presents the future prospects of this pandemic in the GCC region. Section six discusses the possible opportunities that the COVID-19 pandemic could offer to the GCC countries. Section seven concludes the chapter and suggests certain measures that could be taken into consideration in order to achieve a sustainable economic recovery. These policy prescriptions have the potential to lessen the impact of Beck's "risk society," in the direction of his "reflexive modernization."[5]

Economic Repercussions of COVID-19 Outbreak

The GCC countries were hit by a "dual shock" of the sharp plunge in oil prices coupled with the coronavirus epidemic, both having disproportionate repercussions on their economies. In 2020, the COVID-19 pandemic and the decline in global oil demand caused a GDP contraction of 4.8 percent Overall real GDP growth for the GCC is projected at 2.5 percent in 2021 and the real oil GDP for the region is expected to reach 5.3 percent in 2022.[6]

Even though the GCC economies are mostly driven by the energy sector, the COVID-19 pandemic has also affected these economies through the industry of tourism. In fact, in July 2020, S&P Global Ratings classified the effect of COVID-19 outbreak and low oil prices on the aviation, tourism and hospitality and oil and gas sectors in the GCC countries as "very high."[7] The COVID-19 crisis also has dramatically disrupted the retail sector in this region. Economic shocks have thus been the most obvious manifestation of pandemic-era MENA "risk society"[8] in the Gulf region.

The Tourism Sector

The implementation of stringent confinement measures to slow the diffusion of the COVID-19 disease has caused the tourism industry to slump. The United Nations World Tourism Organization (UNWTO) reported an 11 percent decline in arrivals in the first three months of 2020 in the Middle East region.

The GCC countries that have been the most afflicted are the KSA and the UAE. In effect, the KSA suspended Umrah and cancelled the Hajj pilgrimage season 2020 for visitors from outside the kingdom as a set of precautionary actions to contain the spread of the disease. Around two million pilgrims were supposed to visit the KSA to conduct the Hajj ritual in summer 2020. The loss of this expected huge revenue from religious tourism[9] in 2020 exacerbated the budget deficit of the kingdom, estimated at SR 187 billion, representing 6.4 percent of GDP for the fiscal year 2020.[10]

The UAE was supposed to host the Dubai Expo 2020 that was scheduled for October 2020 and was anticipated to be a major economic catalyst for the country. Expecting to attract 25 million visitors, this event was postponed by a year because of coronavirus.

Qatar took measures to boost its tourism industry, after facing a decline in arrivals from the blockading countries since the 2017 diplomatic crisis. The upcoming FIFA World Cup 2022 could boost the recovery from COVID-19.[11] To soften the economic effect of the pandemic on this sector, Oman launched a campaign encouraging local tourism and the sector has resumed under protective measures of COVID-19. Saudi Arabia is also working to promote domestic tourism and the development of heritage sites such as Al-Ula.

The Oil Sector

Between February and April 2020, oil prices fell by 60 percent and recorded negative prices plummeting to −$37 as the pandemic led to a collapse in global oil demand and concerns about storage capacity.[12] The GCC economies were differently affected by the oil crash. For instance, Bahrain and Oman are the most vulnerable economies compared to their GCC peers given that they face large balance of payments and fiscal gaps.[13] Besides, Qatar joins Bahrain and Oman in terms of high levels of gross debt. However, Qatar would manage to offset this debt through its substantial financial assets.[14]

The drop in oil demand as well as the disruption of global value chains due to the COVID-19 pandemic have shrunk the GCC countries' revenues and have instigated them to draw on their sovereign wealth funds for stimulus packages providing support for their citizens and residents and boosting key economic sectors. Indeed, GCC governments have put unrivaled policy responses in place (see Figure 4.1) in order to lessen the dual shock impact.

As the pandemic is not yet completely overcome, the uncertainty and ambiguity are still reigning on the oil market.[15] This decrease in the GCC income in the energy sector was reflected in the other economic sectors including the retail.

The Retail Sector

The economic stoppage brought about by this disease has sharply affected the retail sector in the GCC region, and rendered millions of workers, among them migrants, unemployed. The GCC countries are heavily reliant on foreign workers to build their infrastructure and grow their economies. These countries host 10 percent of global migrants mainly from low- and middle-income countries (LMICs). Indeed, the

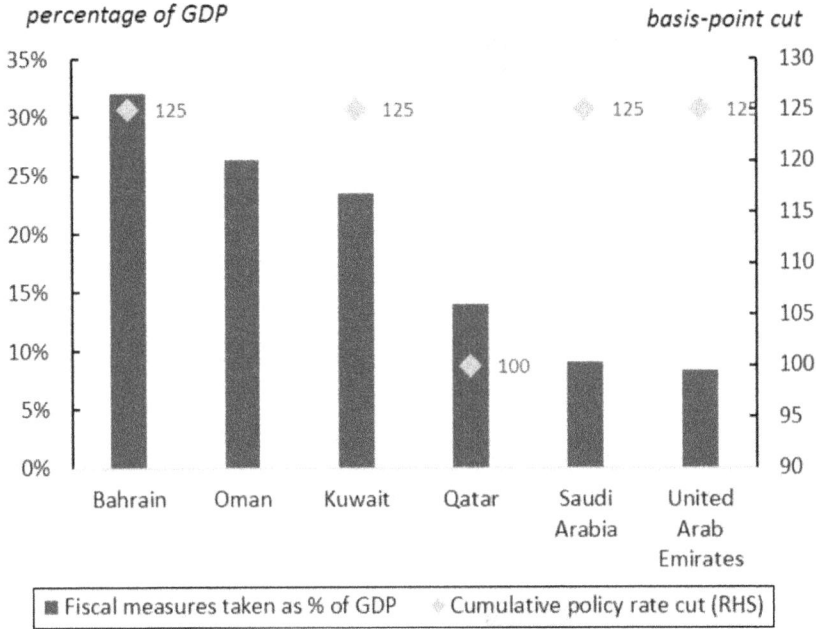

Figure 4.1 Fiscal and Monetary Measures Taken in GCC Countries. Note: The information is fluid as countries are adding measures to respond to the dual shock. *Source*: JP Morgan as of April 15, 2020. In Arezki, R., Yuting F. R., and Nguyen, H. "Covid-19 and Oil Price Collapse: Coping with a Dual Shock in the Gulf Cooperation Council," ERF Policy Brief No. 52, April 2020.

proportion of non-nationals in the GCC population exceeds an average of 50 percent ranging from around 40 percent in the KSA to 90 percent in Qatar (see Figure 4.2).

Retail, along with the tourism and oil sectors, is considered the most labor-intensive sector of the GCC economies and a source of high remittance flows of expatriates who represent a large proportion of most GCC states' workforce. As a results of the COVID-19 crisis, there is an ongoing repatriation of thousands of expats from the GCC region to their countries of origin. In fact, the uprooting of middle-class residents

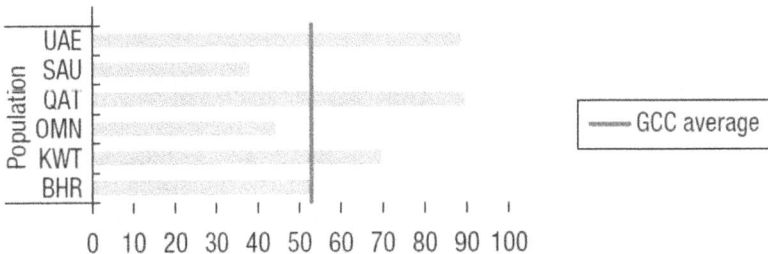

Figure 4.2 GCC Share of Expatriates in Population (Percentage of total). *Source*: IMF Regional Economic Outlook, October 2020.

and their families is liable to negatively impact (GCC) domestic economies, as sectors that relied on these customers such as restaurants, schools, clinics, and the retail sector, will suffer major losses.[16] In addition, job loss in this category of labor force often leads to immediate economic hardship, since they benefit from limited social protection and basic working conditions, which intensifies the high risk of disease exposure. This has reignited debates about workers' rights. The COVID-19 pandemic has a detrimental effect on employment in the GCC region, with more disproportional adverse impact, on some sectors more than others.

The COVID-19 pandemic has impelled the GCC governments to reduce the workforce mainly in these sectors in response to the financial impact. As a result, expatriate labor that used to remit a huge amount of money to workers' respective home countries annually has halted remitting money to their families, leading to a substantial drop in remittances. In 2020, due to the COVID-19 pandemic, remittance flows to LMICs were projected to decline by around 20 percent, marking the sharpest reduction in recent history, due to a fall in wages and the employment of migrant workers in the recipient countries.[17] However, defying predictions, remittance flows have proved to be resilient during the COVID-19 crisis and reached $540 billion, only 1.6 percent below the $548 billion seen in 2019.[18] The resilience of flows seen in 2020 was followed by a recovery in flows in 2021.[19] It may be that remittances are to an extent the most temporary dimensions of Gulf "risk society," but only time will tell.

GCC States' Intervention: Surveillance Measures and Securitizing Discourses

Since the beginning of the crisis, GCC states' intervention has taken many forms, covering various dimensions of public life, such as security, media, and the economy.

There was an early collective confrontation with the pandemic that was demonstrated during the extraordinary emergency meeting of the health ministers of the Gulf states in mid-February 2020. During the meeting, officials agreed to implement WHO regulations and to apply standard health procedures at the border crossings of the GCC countries. They also decided to assign committees to exchange information and follow-up developments of the epidemic.[20]

From the beginning of the pandemic, the Gulf countries have adopted a number of preventive measures such as the closure of schools in the beginning of March 2020. The precautionary measures also included early repatriation of most Gulf nationals from China and other Asian countries. All airports were sterilized and medical teams were deployed to examine arrivals from abroad with advanced devices. Some Gulf states appealed to their citizens not to travel to Iran and other risky countries, while requiring medical reports for arrivals from certain countries where the virus has spread.

Later, the GCC countries gradually isolated themselves. Kuwait and Saudi Arabia were the first to do so with the suspension of all international flights starting in mid-March 2020. Then, a rather strict confinement of the population was enacted at the end of March. This included suspension of cultural and entertainment activities. In the UAE, a "national disinfection program" of public spaces prevented residents from moving freely at night at first. This confinement became total from April 4, 2020.

To enforce compliance with these measures on their residents, Gulf countries have introduced heavy sanctions. In Kuwait, for example, anyone breaking the curfew was sentenced to up to three years in prison and a fine of 10,000 KWD (around US $ 33,000).

Many security measures were taken to confront the disease including the closure of a number of cities and commercial complexes, the prevention of gatherings and the imposition of curfews at specific hours.

The security forces of the various GCC states succeeded in extending their control over cities and their entrances, and in controlling the movement of the population as no major crimes, attacks, or thefts of property were recorded. They have shown what some consider professionalism in dealing with this unprecedented crisis, through firmness in law enforcement and the use of modern methods of tracking and monitoring, including drones and robots.[21]

The role of security personnel in GCC countries was not limited to maintaining security; it expanded to include meeting the basic needs of citizens and residents, and repatriating workers from different nationalities wishing to return to their home countries.

State intervention was also clear through the important role played by government media. This role included educating people about the danger of the virus and spreading social awareness about the seriousness of the disease, as well as the necessary precautions that should be taken. This significantly helped in limiting the spread of the epidemic.

Traditional media entered into competition with social media. Thus, the principal mission of the government media was to refute the rumors that could be a major cause in creating tension and other negative repercussions on the society. This has required the dissemination of transparent and timely information.

The media adopted two main types of discourses. The first one included the methods of prevention and treatment, and the second one was directed to support the medical and nursing staff working on the front lines and defending lives. The messages were diverse and broadcast in several languages to target the largest possible audience, and to ensure that all segments of society would be reached, including both citizens and foreign workers.

Regarding the use of technology in confronting the coronavirus, the GCC governments have made an important progress in terms of e-services, which gave them a strategic advantage during the period of the crisis. The e-government contributed to the regularity of work of GCC institutions without major effects on their performance. Many meetings took place remotely, whether within each state or between officials of the Gulf states. The educational institutions in the Gulf countries continued to provide their services to students and learners, and the educational process was at least not halted by the crisis.

All countries of the GCC have launched applications on smart phones that serve the population and provide them with appropriate medical advice and guidance. In Kuwait, the Central Agency for Information Technology launched the "Shlonik" application, to support the efforts of the Ministry of Health in organizing the process of monitoring. The application also allows quarantined people to enter their vital data, and to communicate with medical teams at the Ministry of Health in case any symptom appears.

In Qatar, the application "Ehteraz" was launched by the Qatar Supreme Committee for Crisis Management. The application contains a barcode in four colors, and is connected to a database linked to the Ministry of Public Health. In the event that a case of infection with the coronavirus is discovered, the application enables the competent authorities to track the areas in which the person appeared from the time he downloaded the application until the moment of infection.

The Saudi Ministry of Health also launched the "Tetamman" application. The application contains an icon for services that includes a library of educational content, test results, contact information updates, daily follow-up of health status, and links to support epidemiological investigation.

In Bahrain, the Supreme Council of Health and the Ministry of Health, in cooperation with the Information and e-Government Authority, launched, in mid-March 2020, the "BeAware" application. The application alerts residents in the event they come close to a case infected with the virus.

The UAE has launched two main applications in this regard that serve the same purpose of providing important information to the population about the virus. One of them is called "TraceCovid" and the other one is "StayHome." Similarly, the Omani Ministry of Health launched the "Tarassud" application. In a statement, the ministry said that the launch of this application came to follow-up coronavirus cases in the country.

Regarding the economic measures, the GCC countries announced important economic and financial packages in support for citizens and the private sector. The announced values for this package reached in Saudi Arabia, UAE, and Bahrain, respectively, SR 120 billion (US$31.9 billion), 126 billion AED (US$34.3 billion), and 4.3 billion BD (US$11.4 billion).

Economic actions also included paying part of the salaries of private sector employees, increasing banks' lending capacities and loan restructuring, exemptions from paying electricity and water bills as well as different municipal, industrial, and service fees.

GCC "Risk Society'": Increasing State Intervention

In times of crises, many governments tend to impose restrictions that can interfere with the basic freedoms of individuals. These "risk society" restrictions include those that governments may place on the media, people's rights to privacy, campaigns against human rights activists, and freedoms as well as an expansion of emergency measures.

Also, spending billions of dollars on economic stimulus programs and in the medical sector may create endless opportunities for corruption. Some governments may reach the point of withholding information about their actual performance in facing crises.

Fears of excessive government interference include granting the state too much legal powers in society. Generally, in responding to global crises, countries deploy important voluntary work through the concerted efforts mainly of governments and civil society acting via nongovernmental organizations (NGOs).

However, a problem associated with the rise of NGOs is the spread of GONGOs, namely, government-sponsored nongovernmental organizations, called also QUANGOs[22] for quasi-autonomous nongovernmental organizations. In fact, several governments have overseen and initiated the creation of NGOs which, either directly or through funding, work as a foreign policy tool and lack real agency.[23] Even so, the phenomenon of GONGOs should not be overgeneralized as some can be benign, some are irrelevant, but many can be dangerous by serving as a disguised tool controlled by states.[24] However, some have argued that even state-sponsored GONGOs, such as women's groups in the Gulf, can contribute to development and even serve to "reconfigure" governance within states.[25] In the case of the GCC countries, amid the pandemic, governments have rapidly reacted to contain the coronavirus by developing massive policy and institutional plans to support their societies. The Gulf region has also witnessed significant volunteer work, including from women's civil society associations in Kuwait.[26]

Increasing State Intervention

Governments around the world have imposed unprecedented control over the daily lives of their citizens in response to the coronavirus. Following the appearance of the pandemic, GCC countries, like other nations, imposed quarantines, shut down a large part of the economy, and implemented numerous systems for tracking and monitoring (people carrying or possibly carrying) the disease to contain infection.

From an economic perspective, there are real risks that can emerge from state interventionism. During the pandemic, industrial policies shifted in many countries following attempts from governments to intervene vigorously in the economic sphere after decades of free market policies. The interventionist policies include, for instance, the strengthening of trade administration through tariffs, licenses, supply quotas and quality standards, limiting exports notably for food and medical supplies, and injecting billions of dollars to save local companies. This implies that governments can determine the economic entities that would be saved, and those that would not receive support. These policies may represent just the beginning of an anticipated package of subsidies to domestic goods, tax exemptions, government procurement and storage, encouragement of local industries, and other plans that many countries would put in place to structure production and access to a wider range of goods and services considered to be essential to national security and basic well-being.

In the GCC countries, the biggest impact related to an increase in the role of governments seems to have taken place through a rise in public services and infrastructure investments. The move of GCC countries to promote infrastructure development, particularly in the case of Bahrain, is likely to help economic recovery,[27] but causes fears of state control over economic life.

From another perspective, the issue of digital surveillance to combat the emerging coronavirus epidemic has sparked a special controversy regarding the issue of human rights. In this regard, more than 100 groups of civil society organizations have signed a joint statement[28] specifying the conditions that must be met before using digital surveillance technology. They are of the view that governments cannot simply ignore the right to privacy and must ensure that any new measures should include strong human rights guarantees.

In the case of Gulf countries, Amnesty International considers Kuwait and Bahrain to have adopted the most privacy-violating smartphone applications for individuals. This makes the privacy and security of users vulnerable. The rights group found that the applications were tracking users' sites to a degree that could be described as an exaggerated violation of users' privacy. Some researchers link these applications with developments in the "Google Maps" application, which collect data from the personal phones of the application's users.

At times of crises, weak groups within society are likely to be more affected and to bear the biggest "risk society" burden. In light of the repercussions of the coronavirus crisis, it seemed to many observers that GCC countries took advantage of the crisis to carry out large-scale layoffs of foreign workers.[29] Millions of unskilled workers, from Asian and Arab countries as well, have been let go and given orders to leave the country, in a process that international labor and human rights organizations see as a violation of labor laws.

And what happened was not limited to the government sector in those countries, as GCC governments have given a green light to private sector companies to carry out large-scale layoffs of foreign workers, as well as making significant salary cuts. For instance, Saudi Arabia issued a decision that allows reducing the salaries of workers in the private sector by 40 percent, with the possibility of termination of work contracts on the pretext of facing the economic effects of the pandemic. Consequently, several major companies have laid off hundreds of thousands of migrant workers.[30]

Meanwhile, the most alarming development as monitored by international human rights organizations during the Gulf states' dealing with this crisis is the escalation of racist discourse in Gulf media and social media.[31] It has portrayed foreign workers as the main cause of the spread of the virus in the respective countries, and as beneficiaries of the country's bounties without demonstrating loyalty.

In light of the criticism faced by the Gulf countries following their dismissal of thousands of foreign workers, the GCC governments defended their decisions by arguing that their economic conditions can no longer bear the employment of a large number of foreign workers at a time when the number of unemployed citizens is increasing.

As a counterpoint, observers consider expatriates to have become an essential component in the labor market and the commercial life in the GCC countries by their contribution to the development process, the participation in construction work, the formation of commercial establishments, and the sustainability of many economic sectors such as transportation.

Besides, many economists question the possibility that the Gulf countries will completely dispense with their foreign workers. They consider the risk of the departure of the expatriates to be the possible reduction of the revenues of the GCC governments from fees and value-added taxes. Doing so may, therefore, slow down reform efforts notably through an expected reduction of demand for all goods and services. This risk can lead to deflationary effects.

The Role of Civil Society

During the coronavirus crisis, the Gulf countries witnessed a remarkable volunteer activity. In fact, in the Kingdom of Bahrain, the National Campaign to Combat the Coronavirus announced the opening of the door for volunteering to work and received, during the first hours of the announcement, thousands of citizens confirmed their willingness to volunteer work.

The Bahrain Red Crescent Society was at the forefront of Bahraini civil society organizations in the face of the pandemic, as it allocated fifteen members of its full-time cadres to work in Bahrain International Airport. The Society was at the forefront of the supporting national financial and voluntary activities, by continuing its awareness campaigns, developing volunteers' capacities, supporting medical staff, making home visits, and visiting the quarantine center in Hidd. It trained more than 900 Bahraini volunteers to deal with the pandemic and delivered in-kind aid to more than 4,500 families through small teams, according to a list of registered needy families. The distribution covered seventy-three areas throughout Bahrain.[32]

Saudi Arabia has witnessed the launch of an initiative by the Ministry of Health entitled "Ready Health Volunteers."[33] The initiative aims to qualify and train health practitioners and students at health colleges in all the regions of the country, in a move to involve specialized community members in combating the coronavirus. The initiative targets physicians of all categories, nursing and pharmacists, non-physician specialists and technicians in all their specialties, public health specialists, administrators and internship doctors, in addition to final year students in medical specialties.

The authority supervising the initiative launched virtual training programs that include sessions to qualify participants in volunteering and communication skills, sessions for basic infection control in health facilities (BICSL), in addition to qualification courses in dealing with the coronavirus.

Many private companies participated in financial support. For instance, the company Ma'aden contributed with 15 million riyals to support the Health Endowment Fund at the Ministry of Health.[34]

In the UAE,[35] the cabinet ministers approved the formation of the Higher National Committee for Regulating Volunteering during Crises, with the aim of developing an integrated and sustainable system for volunteer work in the country, and in cooperation with all parties concerned with volunteering, including individuals, private sector institutions and civil society organizations.

The Federal Youth Authority has also launched national initiatives with the aim of raising the readiness of the youth and enhancing their effective role in dealing with the pandemic and limiting its negative social impacts. Those initiatives included:

- Training courses in the basics of medical pandemic prevention.
- An initiative called "values for generations" that seeks to share with senior citizens advice for young people on prevention methods, as well as Emirati values in various circumstances.
- Launching a digital platform that enables youth, within the framework of civil society organizations, to access all opportunities to participate in pandemic prevention efforts.
- The Youth Endowment Initiative for Prevention. The initiative, in cooperation with the General Authority of Islamic Affairs and Endowments, aims to involve youth and institutions in allocating times to protect the society from the pandemic, by providing sterilizers and other tools and equipment for this purpose.

Among the most important institutions of the national community that provide programs and initiatives of volunteer work: the Emirates Red Crescent, the Emirates Voluntary Academy in Abu Dhabi, the National Volunteer Program for Emergencies, Crises and Disasters and the Dubai Volunteer Program named "Together We Are Good."[36] In the State of Kuwait, the Ministry of Interior announced the opening of training sessions on how to deal with emergency situations and potential risks.[37]

Kuwaiti civil society launched a donation campaign to support the Kuwaiti government's efforts to confront the coronavirus. An alliance of forty-one Kuwaiti charity organizations, under the supervision of the Ministry of Social Affairs, initiated a campaign that aims to support workers affected by the crisis, to help needy and affected families inside Kuwait, and to aid the ministries and government institutions in the establishment, management, and provision of logistical support to health and quarantine centers.

At the beginning of the pandemic, the first national campaign of the alliance of charitable societies in Kuwait collected more than KWD 9 million (around US$29,750,000) during the first week of March. In addition to this campaign, the Ministry of Social Affairs in Kuwait issued a report on the efforts of civil societies in combating the coronavirus, indicating that the associations contributed with about KWD 2.9 million (around US$9,500,000) during the month of March 2020.

The ministry stated that the associations provided 150,217 meals to workers in state ministries and health institutions and provided services to 90,000 affected Kuwaiti expatriates and workers, as well as financial support, food, and health baskets. It indicated that the associations provided 387,500 water bottles to a number of institutions and control sites, 154,200 hand sanitizers and protective bags, and equipped 32 quarantine locations serving 14,400 beneficiaries.[38]

In Oman, the National Youth Committee invited voluntary work to confront the coronavirus. Also, civil society institutions in Oman have contributed to supporting the efforts of the government in confronting the coronavirus by collecting donations and contributing to community awareness, in addition to supporting workers affected by the decisions relating to business closures in the country.[39]

Also, in Qatar, "Qatar Charity" in cooperation with the ministries of public health, labor, administrative development, and social affairs, implemented awareness campaigns for foreign workers in several languages on the importance of following preventive measures, and distributed hygiene supplies along with personal and preventive materials.[40]

The Future Prospects of Coronavirus in the GCC Countries

The GCC countries may be in a better position than other countries with limited financial revenues to withstand the repercussions of the pandemic. However, some effects might be negative in the medium and long run if appropriate measures are not taken. "Risk society" and its detrimental effects still loom in the horizon. Future prospects might include the following features of Gulf risk society:

Risk of erosion of financial reserves: The returns on foreign assets and investments, especially those with high risk, will be increasingly volatile. Estimates of the value of the assets of Gulf sovereign wealth funds (SWFs) have declined since 2019, and this decline may deepen if the economic recession prolongs due to the repercussions of the pandemic.[41] At a time when the need to increase government spending appeared to compensate for negative impacts of the pandemic, the risks of eroding financial reserves and increasing the accumulation of deficits in the coming years emerge. This risk is related to potential stock market losses and drawdowns taken by cash-squeezed governments.[42]

Rise in stalled projects: Various factors can make the GCC countries more vulnerable to the pandemic than other regions,[43] as "risk society" threatens to manifest in specific ways. These factors include the high dependence on undiversified trade, the volume of foreign workers and the establishment of big events such as the World Cup in Qatar and the Dubai World Expo in the UAE. The projects related to the last two events will eventually take place, albeit at a different pace. But other projects in Gulf countries remain threatened by a lack of funding due to changes in budget priorities of governments and private institutions. This is expected to lead to a slowdown in the pace of project implementation and a delay in the completion of other projects.

Acceleration of Reforms: The COVID-19 pandemic revealed weaknesses in the GCC countries that may affect their economic growth and induce social transformations in the medium and the long run. Some of the weaknesses include: (i) limited diversification of national revenues; (ii) lack of reliance on the national human capital; (iii) excessive dependence on the movement of foreign markets, and (iv) limited coordination, especially at the level of food and health security. The same factors that have helped to "modernize" the Gulf states, that is, become sources of socioeconomic problems, in their version of pandemic-heightened "risk society."

As reform may be the only way to ensure long-term stability, it is expected that the COVID-19 pandemic will accelerate the implementation of deep and fundamental reforms.[44] The reforms would include higher rationalization and diversification of national revenues, an increase in the application of governance, and a reduction of reliance on foreign labor. These reforms can be met with popular criticism and can affect the pattern of welfare in the GCC countries. However, they remain arguably the best and safest solutions to preserve prosperous development in the future.

New range of economic activities: The process of diversification is expected to accelerate. Even prior to the pandemic, and despite high costs, most countries in the region were already engaged in some form of diversification strategy.[45] Important progress has been made in this regard. For instance, the GCC governments have launched incentive packages to provide immediate economic assistance to individuals and firms, notably small- and medium-sized companies (SMEs). This was destined to encourage firms to take initiatives in various economic fields. Digital industries and remote servicing are likely to become the most important sources of inspiration for future projects within the GCC countries. However, many non-oil industries depend heavily on the flow of goods, investors, and foreign visitors. This would make the GCC economies more affected by the fluctuations of global markets.

Greater attention to fragile sectors: The GCC region suffers from a severe shortage of agricultural and water resources. Increased risks to food security and self-sufficiency will induce encouragement and stimulation of food, semi-food, and agricultural production, especially in the Kingdom of Saudi Arabia and Oman. Therefore, the agricultural sector should be subject to policies that enact reforms, encourage the growth of investments, and greater credit facilities in the future.

It is expected that the Gulf states will need to focus more intensely on maintaining their scarce supplies of water, as the growing population and wasteful use of water puts more and more pressure on supplies.[46] However, water shortages create opportunities to develop new technologies and industries for water production, including new and more energy-efficient desalination technologies.[47]

More mergers and board changes: The percentage of mergers between institutions, especially those in distress or threatened with bankruptcy, may increase to improve financial solvency and future growth.[48] This may also result in changes of directors. A wave of layoffs and replacement of decision-makers, managers, and leaders of institutions is expected.[49] This would increase the quality of management and the competence of the leaders.[50] These projections are based on the crisis management model that many governments and companies had followed after the global financial crisis.

Retreat of rentier mentality: Oil-based economies have affected the labor and consumption culture of the GCC citizens for many decades and have made a large proportion of the society dependent on the rentier state. This has hindered enterprise initiatives and private investment and left a large part of economic sectors fragile.[51] Consequently, modifying the economic model has become important to keep pace with accelerating changes, which can, in turn, gradually bring changes to the concept of the individual's role in the society and make the citizen more active and involved in building strong economies for future generations.[52]

Employee benefit reductions: Governments may accelerate reform measures such as imposing fees or restricting the process of promotions and privileges. Income tax may be an emergency option for Gulf governments. Governments may not feel hesitant to move forward with the gradual implementation of such austerity measure.[53]

However, it should be noted that the good solvency of Gulf governments may not push them to impose significant austerity on wages and basic services provided to citizens. Gulf governments may find themselves compelled to a minimum of necessary reforms that may not be popular. Therefore, they are expected to be imposed gradually. The urgent need for these reforms varies among GCC countries according to several variables such as population, the national deficit of each country, and the development of non-oil sectors.

Safety nets for vulnerable households: Despite the variation from one country to another, studying the tendency of GCC governments to manage the COVID-19 crisis highlights one trend that supports the middle-income and low-income classes. This is evidenced by the continuation of subsidy policies related to basic consumption goods, which has helped to stabilize prices and prevent the collapse of the purchasing power of various social groups. The Gulf states are among the most generous countries in providing various support services and aid to citizens, which makes them far from the spectrum of countries and groups falling into extreme poverty.

However, this does not prevent the existence of challenges that arise through the increase in the proportion of the population approaching the circle of poverty.[54] Concerns remain about the increasing suffering of some social groups from diminishing household income, especially in cases of deepening economic imbalances, prolonged implementation periods of austerity policies and shrinking job opportunities due to the repercussions of the pandemic.

Greater empowerment for youth: It seems that the repercussions of the pandemic, which will reduce revenues and resources, will inevitably push the search for new solutions. This type of "reflexive modernization," as Beck puts it, may be aimed at encouraging the digital economy and remote servicing. In this regard, the pace of competition among young entrepreneurs may increase for new projects adapted to future economic changes.

One of the features of the GCC countries is their human potential, characterized by a large proportion of educated youth. The youth represent catalysts of inclusive and resilient societies in periods of crises that countries might face (OECD 2020).[55] Thus, the priority of the GCC governments may become more oriented toward increasing investments in human development, enhancing youth capabilities and qualifying them to lead the major transformation phase toward economies that are less dependent on oil. This can be done by raising the quality of training and education, intensifying youth initiatives in innovative business fields, and increasing investments in non-oil sectors such as renewable energy, science, and trade. It is likely that the success of Gulf governments in raising the efficiency of human capabilities may quickly enable them to create new sources of wealth.

Enhancing self-reliance: It is possible that the Gulf states will be more exposed to foreign markets and their dependence may increase in different sectors such as food and water. This may represent a future threat. Dependency may be deepened by rising populations and higher demand for consumption goods.[56]

The risks of increased dependency on the outside may, however, reinforce policies of self-sufficiency. In effect, the issue of lack of self-sufficiency in different sectors such as food, education, and health is not new, but finding solutions has become more necessary today than ever. The Gulf countries need to move from the planning stage to serious implementation of programs to enhance self-sufficiency in various sectors and to resolve deficiencies and imbalances.[57]

Economic Drivers of COVID-19 Pandemic: What Opportunities?

Rounding off the mixed picture of its "risk society," the COVID-19 pandemic has benefited certain sectors in the GCC economies. This crisis has compelled public and private sectors institutions to convert to remote work that could accelerate the pace of digital transformation in these countries, already adopted in their national visions. In effect, the pandemic has forced people to use e-government services. For instance, in Qatar, the number of e-government transactions has increased after the COVID-19 shock as shown in Figure 4.3.

This crisis could be a catalyst that inspires a slew of robotics and triggers creativity contributing to nurturing the innovation ecosystem. As data and information are the

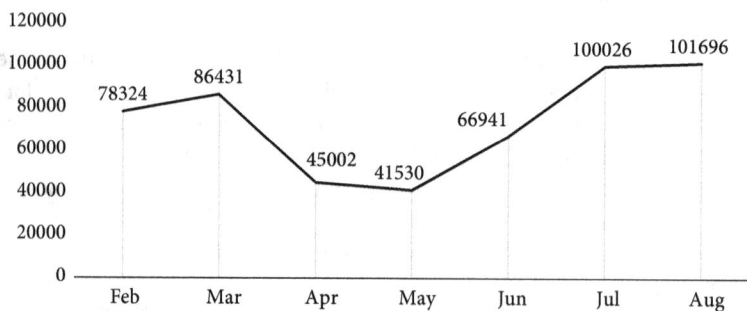

Figure 4.3 Qatar e-Government Services Use in 2020. *Source:* Planning and Statistics Authority, Monthly Reports, 2020

new basic resources representing the "new oil,"[58] the GCC policymakers should look at the COVID-19 pandemic as a development crisis-speeding up the transformation of the GCC countries toward knowledge-based economies.

The COVID-19 outbreak has altered the education sector and made a transition from conventional face-to-face education to the remote learning system. Diverse constituents were also explored to upgrade a suite for online education infrastructure and engage in several digital learning platforms. Many academic events were cancelled amid the pandemic. However, a virtual alternative was offered to conduct pre-scheduled international conferences. This crisis is an opportunity to reinvent education and research.

Having started their transition toward less oil-dependent economies, the desperate need for economic diversification amid this twin shock becomes more apparent in the GCC countries.

This crisis unveiled the vulnerability of these economies and reveals the importance of diversifying the economic base of these countries. This could be a tipping point to precipitate the economic diversification process and sustainable development in these countries.

In order to reach the required level of diversification, the GCC countries must be highly competitive and innovative. Specifically, more efforts should be made in the following aspects to "reflexively" transform "risk society" vulnerabilities into opportunities:

- Increasing the number of skilled workers, especially in engineering and management majors: This should help in developing promising sectors such as artificial intelligence. The epidemic crisis has shown how innovation and technology are the source of solutions to economic problems. Investing in science, innovation, and technological inventions to meet the needs of society and the economy is no longer a luxury, but an urgent necessity to achieve economic growth.
- Strengthening the incentive system to improve the dynamism of the private sector: In particular, priority should be given to the following measures: (1) increasing the number of industrial banks in order to facilitate long-term credit for productive industries; (2) reducing rents and taxes in industrial cities; (3) reducing energy, water, and government service prices for various productive sectors; (4) improving marketing facilities for local products; (5) providing better pre-investment incentives and detailed market studies; and (6) implementing questioners and feasibility studies on industrial sectors.
- Encouraging public and private sectors to invest in the production of capital goods. In fact, the high cost of imported intermediate equipment raises the average production cost and makes domestic products less competitive. The local production of these commodities can serve various industries and boost the growth of industrial exports.
- Achieving a greater degree of corporate vertical integration: The development of some projects requires less capital and energy, reduces production costs, and ensures long-term sustainability, especially in the manufacturing sectors.

- Promoting regional cooperation: This point is especially important. Since the manufacturing industries are export-oriented, joint marketing efforts among the GCC countries could overcome some of the expected difficulties to enter the global market. The Gulf countries share similar economic, social, and political characteristics. This encourages the Gulf states to adopt a comprehensive economic development strategy in order to coordinate their policies and direct the scarce natural resources, thus improving development prospects. Demand for petrochemical and aluminum products, for example, will only be expanded through this cooperation. The demand will expand further if this cooperation includes other Arab and Islamic countries. Local firms will increase their viability if they are able to penetrate the markets of populated and nearby countries such as Egypt, Iran, and Pakistan.

Implementing these measures will allow the GCC countries to improve the level of economic diversification and drive sustainable growth. GCC economies are open and dynamic, and these characteristics are ideal for making the countries achieve development goals. Therefore, policymakers must work to achieve greater economic diversification and promote more robust and resilient growth in the long term. Diversification measures are not limited to economic sectors, but include other dimensions such as labor markets, export activity, enterprise base, and investment capital concentration. This kind of comprehensive diversification is not easy to implement, but would yield significant profits in the form of more stable economies that are less vulnerable to the influence of external crises.

Paving the Way for an Efficacious Economic Recovery

The GCC countries have put in place mitigation measures to confront COVID-19 that has wreaked economic havoc across the world. For instance, the UAE reported a US$27 billion stimulus plan to help promote the economy. This includes subsidies to water and electricity for citizens and commercial and industrial activities. Qatar announced a package of US$23 billion to bolster and provide financial and economic impetus to the private sector. Saudi Arabia declared a US$13 billion package to assist businesses and small and medium enterprises.[59]

The COVID-19 pandemic has pinpointed the role of governments in response to the outbreak—the "return of the state"[60]—and the necessity of agile and adaptive governance in crisis response. In terms of policy responses to the pandemic, the GCC states have adopted major fiscal and monetary policies to mitigate the pandemic impact. These governments have announced certain monetary policy measures that include cutting interest rates and all GCC countries, except Kuwait and Oman, implemented some fiscal policy measures, such as strengthening and/or broadening unemployment benefits.[61]

The GCC countries are still dealing with the economic fallout of COVID-19 pandemic, while trying to glean salient benefits from this opportunity aiming to recovery of economic fundamentals. In particular, GCC policymakers should look at the COVID-19 pandemic as a development crisis speeding-up the "reflexive" transformation of the GCC countries toward knowledge-based economies. Moreover, this crisis has unveiled the vulnerability of these economies and reveals the importance of diversifying the economic base. This could be a tipping point to precipitate the economic diversification process, feeding into Gulf sustainable development.

The GCC states could not avoid the economic fallout from the "dual shock" of the coronavirus outbreak and the oil price collapse on their development trajectory. Nonetheless, the GCC governments have put in place a set of policy responses to soften the pandemic's economic effects. They should also take decisive steps and initiate targeted policies necessary for shaping a sustainable recovery from the COVID-19 outbreak, to build resilient economies against future shocks. Kristina Georgieva, managing director of the International Monetary Fund (IMF), stated that "Countries with stronger macroeconomic fundamentals, social cohesion, and safety nets are likely to experience faster and stronger recoveries."[62] To hasten the economic recovery, the GCC authorities should mainly prioritize spending on health in responding to this pandemic. They should also support the private sector to foster their economies which, except Oman, are expected to have positive growth in 2021 according to the IMF.[63] More actions should be taken after the recovery to cope with the low hydrocarbon prices.

Uncertainty and ambiguity remain regarding the coronavirus as vaccine roll-outs take effect. A durable recovery from the COVID-19 global crisis requires global cooperation to overcome its enduring effects. The Gulf region should take part in the coordinating policy responses within these monumental global transformations.

Conclusion

Amid the COVID-19 crisis, the concept of economic resilience is receiving increasing attention by economists, in an attempt to measure the ability of economic systems to rapidly regenerate from various external shocks. However, the notion of economic resilience is not new for the GCC policymakers. This region has achieved certain resilience through economies that encompass a range of sectors. Consequently, these countries were on relatively strong footing when the pandemic emerged. They had enough medical supplies and basic commodities for their people and healthcare workers due to their national stockpiles, which were supported by a diverse network of trading partners.

The speed and wisdom of "reflexively" adapting with the epidemic were prominent in many aspects, such as using time in modernizing infrastructure and strengthening e-learning. Moreover, civil society responses have been forthcoming. However, the pandemic has also revealed certain "risks society" vulnerabilities. In fact, like other countries, there was a shortage of some commodities and raw materials vital to industrial production as well as declining in labor supplies due to disruptions and travel bans. Consumption has also decreased in a number of industries.

Therefore, it is fundamental for the GCC policymakers to strengthen economic resilience for the future. To prepare for growth in the post-pandemic years, these countries need to increase domestic production of basic food and medical supplies, invest in and adopt energy-saving technologies, and seek to create new job opportunities in the growing green economy. These efforts will make GCC economies more resilient and sustainable, and thus give them a competitive advantage.

In practice, a number of basic commodities can be produced and eventually exported, such as some medical supplies and foodstuffs. GCC countries can invest in research on energy technologies and resources such as decentralized energy systems and low carbon energy. In this context, the demand is expected to increase even for services related to these sectors, such as engineering and legal consultations. Also, the impact of climate change and the loss of biodiversity must be confronted, as they can cause the spread of pandemics and lead to social and economic damages that may be greater than those caused by the epidemic. Therefore, for the economic recovery from the COVID-19 crisis to be durable and resilient, more must be done than restore the pre-pandemic pace of life and economic growth. Economic recovery packages should be designed to achieve what has become known by international organizations as Building Back Better (BBB).

Recovery policies also need to stimulate investment, increase supply chain circularity, and seek behavioral changes in individuals and institutions. These measures can reduce the risks of future shocks and increase resilience. This also includes the creation of more accountable institutions that will increase citizens' confidence, strengthen the social contract, and intensify efforts to support equality, by moving forward with more empowerment of women, youth, and social protection.

In short, for a more resilient Gulf economy and the minimization of its "risk society," the approach in the aftermath of COVID-19 should be a focus on diversity and inclusion, whether in productive sectors or in social and environmental structures and policies.

Notes

1 International Labour Organization. Email: miniaoui@ilo.org.
2 College of Business Administration, University of Bahrain. Email: aelkhayati@uob .edu.bh.
3 https://covid19.who.int/.
4 Ephrem, Appaadurai, and Dhanasekaran (2021).
5 See Sadiki and Saleh (2020).
6 International Monetary Fund, Economic Prospects and Policy Challenges for the GCC Countries - 2021.
7 Ministry of Finance, Budget Statement Fiscal Year (2020), p. 5.
8 Sadiki and Saleh (2020).
9 In 2019, there were more than 19 million pilgrims for Umrah and 2.6 million pilgrims for Hajj. Combined, they earn the Kingdom approximately $12 billion a year. Thomson Reuters, June 2020.
10 https://www.spglobal.com/ratings.

11 KPMG (2020).
12 International Monetary Fund, World Economic Outlook, October 2020, p. 43.
13 World Bank (2020).
14 International Monetary Fund, Regional Economic Outlook, MENAP, October 2020, p. 9.
15 International Monetary Fund, World Economic Outlook, October 2020, p. 43.
16 COVID-19-induced impact on oil, tourism sectors to have wide-ranging economic, social ramifications on GCC countries over coming months—GCC Analysis | MAX Security (max-security.com).
17 The World Bank (2020).
18 The World Bank (2021a).
19 The World Bank (2021b).
20 GCC Secretariat General (2020).
21 Aldroubi (2020).
22 Kleinschmit and Edwards (2017).
23 Szalai (2018).
24 Naím (2007).
25 Krause (2009).
26 Alkhoja and Abdullah (2020).
27 Augustine (2021).
28 Amnesty International (2020).
29 Barbuscia and Rashad (2020).
30 Naar (2020).
31 Migrant-Rights.Org. (2020).
32 http://www.akhbar-alkhaleej.com/news/article/1245314.
33 Al-Thamiri (2020).
34 Ma'aden: Our ongoing response to Covid-19 https://www.maaden.com.sa/en/covid/?
35 The official portal of the UAE government: "Handling the COVID-19 outbreak." https://u.ae/en/information-and-services/justice-safety-and-the-law/handling-the-covid-19-outbreak.
36 Ibid.
37 Keshk (2020).
38 Al-Khaleej (2020).
39 Sievers (2020).
40 http://khaleej.online/qm42Vv.
41 Bortolotti and Fotak (2020).
42 Reuters (2020).
43 https://www.arabianbusiness.com/politics-economics/454440-how-the-covid-19-crisis-is-impacting-the-gcc-countries.
44 UNSDG (2020).
45 Oxford Business Group (2020a).
46 Arabian Business magazine (2020).
47 Dawood (2011).
48 Oxford Business Group (2020b).
49 John (2020).
50 Sneader and Singhal (2020).
51 Herb and Lynch (2019).
52 Hertog (2020).
53 Khaleej Times (2020).

54 Bazoobandi and Alexander (2020).
55 OECD (2020).
56 Soubrier (2020).
57 Woertz (2020).
58 Schilirò (2020).
59 United Nations Development Program (2020).
60 Sadiki and Saleh (2020, 14–16).
61 International Monetary Fund, Regional Economic Outlook, MENAP, October 2020, p. 15.
62 Georgieva (2020).
63 International Monetary Fund, Regional Economic Outlook, MENAP, October 2020, p. 9.

References

Aldroubi Mina (2020). "Bahrain Deploys Robots to Combat Coronavirus," *The National*, May 20, https://www.thenationalnews.com/world/gcc/bahrain-deploys-robots-to -combat-coronavirus-1.1022343 (accessed April 20, 2021).

Al-Khaleej Online. (2020). "Kuwait Charitable Societies: An Effective Tool to Confront the Corona Crisis," April 6, http://khaleej.online/DwJEP3 (accessed July 10, 2021).

Alkhoja Ghassan and Abdullah Maryam (2020). "Women are Leading the Fight Against Coronavirus in Kuwait," *World Bank Blogs*, May 19, https://blogs.worldbank.org/ arabvoices/women-are-leading-fight-against-coronavirus-kuwait (accessed February 20, 2021).

Al-Thamiri Abdessalam (2020). "Ready Health Volunteers: An Initiative for Community Participation in the Fight against 'Covid-19,'" *Al-Iqtisadia*, March 20, https://www.aleqt .com/2020/03/20/article_1784976.html (accessed June 20, 2021).

Amnesty International. (2020). "Digital Surveillance to Fight COVID-19 can only be Justified if it Respects Human Rights," April 2, https://www.amnesty.org/en/latest/news /2020/04/covid19-digital-surveillance-ngo/ (accessed April 30, 2020).

Arabian Business Magazine. (2020). *Middle East Water Supplies will be under Pressure Post-Covid-19*, https://www.arabianbusiness.com/energy/446076-middle-east-water -supplies-will-be-under-pressure-post-covid-19 (accessed March 15, 2021).

Augustine Babu Das (2021). "How Gulf Countries are Recovering from the Economic Slump," *Gulf News*, Special Report, March 11, https://gulfnews.com/special-reports /how-gulf-countries-are-recovering-from-the-economic-slump-1.1615454572962 (accessed March 30, 2021).

Barbuscia Davide and Marwa Rashad (2020). "'What's the Point of Staying?' Gulf Faces Expatriate Exodus," *Reuters*, May 7, https://www.reuters.com/article/us-health -coronavirus-gulf-jobs-idUSKBN22J1WL (accessed August 25, 2021).

Bazoobandi Sara and RhiannonAlexander (2020). "GCC Oil Wealth: The Power and the People," in S. Bazoobandi (ed.), *The New Regional Order in the Middle East. International Political Economy Series*, 27–48. Cham: Palgrave Macmillan, https://doi .org/10.1007/978-3-030-27885-4_2.

Bortolotti Bernardo and Fotak Veljko (2020). "Sovereign Wealth Funds and the COVID-19 Shock: Economic and Financial Resilience in Resource-Rich Countries," BAFFI CAREFIN Centre Research Paper, (2020–147).

Dawood Mohamed (2011). "Water Import and Transfer Versus Desalination in Arid Regions: GCC Countries Case Study," *Desalination and Water Treatment*, 28 (1–3): 153–63.

Ephrem Ben, Appaadurai Samuel and Dhanasekaran Balaji (2021), "Analysis of COVID-19 infections in GCC Countries to Identify the Indicators Correlating the Number of Cases and Deaths," *PSU Research Review*, 5 (1): 54–67.

GCC Secretariat General. (2020). "Extraordinary Emergency Meeting at the General Secretariat Headquarters," February 19, https://www.gcc-sg.org/en-us/MediaCenter/NewsCooperation/News/Pages/news2020-2-19-6.aspx (accessed February 20, 2020).

Georgieva Kristalina (2020). "Beyond the Crisis," *Finance & Development, International Monetary Fund*, June, 11.

Herb Michael and Lynch Marc (2019). "Introduction: The Politics of Rentier States in the Gulf," in *The Politics of Rentier States in the Gulf, Middle East Political Science*. George Washington University, *POMEPS, Studies*, 33: 3–7.

Hertog Steffen (2020). "The 'rentier mentality,' 30 Years on: Evidence from Survey Data," *British Journal of Middle Eastern Studies*, 47 (1): 6–23.

John Issac (2020). "The Pandemic in the Gulf: What it Portends for NRIs in the Region," *The Viral World*, ORF Special Report No. 104, April, Observer Research Foundation.

Keshk Ashraf (2020). "The Coronavirus Crisis: Implications and Crisis Management Mechanisms Pursued by Countries," Bahrain Center for Strategic, International and Energy Studies, Report, April, 1–16.

Kleinschmit Stephen and Edwards Vickie (2017). "Examining the Ethics of Government-Organized Nongovernmental Organizations (GONGOs)," *Public Integrity*, 19 (5): 529–46.

KPMG. (2020). "Tourism and Hospitality," *Potential Impact of COVID-19 on the Qatar Economy*, May, 14.

Krause Wanda (2009). "Gender and Participation in the Arab Gulf," *LSE Centre for the Study of Global Governance*, Research Paper, No 4, September, 1–43.

Migrant-Rights.Org. (2020). "The COVID-19 Crisis is Fuelling More Racist Discourse Towards Migrant Workers in the Gulf." April 5, https://www.migrant-rights.org/2020/04/the-covid-19-crisis-is-fueling-more-racist-discourse-towards-migrant-workers-in-the-gulf/ (accessed December 25, 2020).

Miriam, Allam, Ader Moritz, and Igrioglu Gamze (2020). "Youth and COVID-19: Response, Recovery and Resilience," *OECD*: 1–36, June 15.

Naar Ismaeel (2020). "Coronavirus: Saudi Arabia Ministerial Decision to cut Private Sector Salaries by 40 percent," *Al Arabiya News*, May 5, https://english.alarabiya.net/coronavirus/2020/05/05/Coronavirus-Saudi-Arabia-cabinet-decision-to-cut-private-sector-salaries-by-40- (accessed May 20, 2020).

Naím Moisés (2007), "Missing Links: What is a Gongo?," *Foreign Policy*, 160 (May-Jun): 95–6.

Oxford Business Group. (2020a). *How will Covid-19 Affect Gulf Diversification Efforts?* November 18, https://oxfordbusinessgroup.com/news/how-will-covid-19-affect-gulf-diversification-efforts (accessed January 18, 2021).

Oxford Business Group (2020b). *Will Covid-19 Spur M&As in the GCC Banking Sector?*, May 19, https://oxfordbusinessgroup.com/news/will-covid-19-spur-mas-gcc-banking-sector (accessed September 10, 2021).

Sadiki Larbi and Layla Saleh (2020). "Reflexive Politics and Arab 'Risk Society'? COVID-19 and Issues of Public Health," *Orient: German Journal for Politics, Economics and Culture of the Middle East*, 61 (2): 6–20.

Schilirò Daniele (2020). "Towards Digital Globalization and the Covid-19 Challenge," *International Journal of Business Management and Economic Research*, 11 (2): 1710–16.

Sievers Marc (2020). "Oman's Handling of the Coronavirus," *Atlantic Council*, Middle East Programs, MENASource, April 3.

Sneader Kevin and Singhal Shubham (2020). *Beyond Coronavirus: The Path to the Next Normal.* McKinsey & Company Insights, March, https://www.mckinsey.com/industries /healthcare-systems-and-services/our-insights/beyond-coronavirus-the-path-to-the -next-normal.

Soubrier Emma (2020). "Covid-19, Diversification and the Future of Food Security in the Gulf," ISPI, Italian Institute for International Political Studies, July 9.

Szalai Máté (2018). "The International Ngo Triangle In The Mena Region," Middle East and North Africa Regional Architecture (MENARA), Working Papers No. 19, October, 1–26.

The World Bank. (2020). "COVID-19 Crisis Through a Migration Lens," Migration and Development Brief no. 32, April, 7.

The World Bank. (2021a). "Resilience COVID-19 Crisis Through a Migration Lens," Migration and Development Brief no. 34, May, 2.

The World Bank. (2021b). "Recovery COVID-19 Crisis Through a Migration Lens," Migration and Development Brief no. 35, November, 11.

Tom, Arnold (2020). "Oil-Rich Wealth Funds Seen Shedding upto $225 Billion in Stocks," *Reuters*, March 29, https://www.reuters.com/article/us-health-coronavirus-swf-analysis -idUSKBN21G05K (accessed February 25, 2021).

United Nations Economic and Social Commission for West Asia (2020). "COVID-19 Economic Cost to the Arab Region," E/ESCWA/CL3.SEP/2020/Policy Brief.1.

UNSDG. (2020). "Policy Brief: The Impact of COVID-19 on the Arab Region: An Opportunity to Build Back Better," sg_policy_brief_covid-19_and_arab_states_english _version_july_2020.pdf (un.org).

Waheed, Abbas (2020). "Which other GCC State Could Introduce Income Tax after Oman?" *Khaleej Times*, November 7, https://www.khaleejtimes.com/business/economy /which-other-gcc-state-could-introduce-income-tax-after-oman (accessed November 25, 2020).

Woertz Eckart (2020). "Wither the Self-Sufficiency Illusion? Food Security in Arab Gulf States and the Impact of COVID-19," *Food Security*, 12 (4): 757–60.

Arezki, Rabah, Yuting Fan Rachel, and Nguyen Ha, "Covid-19 and Oil Price Collapse: Coping with a Dual Shock in the Gulf Cooperation Council," ERF Policy Brief No. 52, April 2020.

Part II

The Maghreb (Western MENA)

5

North Africa and the Pandemic

Mohamed El Hachimi

Introduction

Despite the essential difference between democracy and authoritarianism, the context of the pandemic was, and continues to be, an occasion to see how political systems behave in a standardized manner when they face an existential threat. Nonetheless, while lockdown measures have triggered waves of social protest in some democracies, authoritarian systems did not face significant challenges from below. They seem to have found it much easier to further tighten their grip on their already controlled societies in the name of fighting the pandemic. This situation seems to have given a new momentum revising resetting the terms of the old global debate on the merits of authoritarianism versus democracy. To what extent can the exceptional conditions linked to the context of the pandemic, such as transforming the role of non-state actors, centralizing power, and closing the democratic space, call into question the very institutional and cultural foundations of democracy? How likely is pandemic-induced fear to roll back democracy and alter the post-2011 balance of power between state and society in North Africa?

This chapter seeks to answer these questions using the theoretical framework of risk society and reflexive modernity, coined by sociologists Urlech Beck and Anthony Giddens. In spite of the criticism directed against Beck for neglecting non-Western societies in his conceptualization, the notion of risk seems to apply to North African countries, as a side effect of their modernization. Indeed, although Algeria, Morocco, and Tunisia did not yet reach the same level of economic development as industrialized Western societies, they are nonetheless increasingly exposed to the same global risks of modernization that induce systematic and often irreversible harm while remaining generally invisible (Beck 1992, 22–3; see also Sadiki and Saleh 2020). The harm caused by COVID-19, including climate change-related risks, are, inter alia, clear signs that show that these North African societies are facing the same challenges pertaining to modern forms of life characterized increasingly by uncertainty, instability, and doubt. Their very existence is no longer ruled entirely by the logic of wealth distribution, but also by the logic of risk distribution (Sadiki and Saleh 2020).

The chapter engages with a preliminary assessment of different strategies North African states have been using to deal with the COVID-19 crisis. To this end, it conducts a comparative analysis of the way the pandemic has been dealt with so far, in Morocco, Algeria, and Tunisia, and the impact of the pandemic on the ongoing political transitions in the three countries.[1] It seeks to explore the extent to which the differences between these three polities were a determining factor in shaping the way this crisis was perceived and dealt with. Additionally, it will look at the effects such an existential threat has or is likely to have on the trajectories of political change in these cases (*Hirak* in Algeria, the third way of reform in Morocco, and democratic consolidation in Tunisia). The chapter starts with assessing the three countries' preparedness to manage the crisis in light of some of the main structural factors that hamper their development. Then it delves into the impacts of the restrictions imposed by the authorities on human rights and rule of law. Lastly, it sheds some light on the pandemic's effects on democracy and human rights activists, and the tactics they used to operate in the context of the pandemic.

Assessing crisis management preparedness in North Africa

Prior to the outbreak of coronavirus pandemic, the macroeconomic situation was far from identical in the three countries of the Maghreb. While Algeria and Tunisia were already experiencing one of the worst periods of economic turmoil in their history, Morocco was enjoying a more stable situation. Algeria's economy, suffering from a structural dependency on hydrocarbons, has been under intense pressure over the last five years. In a country that relies heavily on hydrocarbons for 75 percent of its national budget, the crash of oil prices deeply and severely affected its finances and trade balance, forcing the government to resort to some drastic and unusual measures, such as spending cuts and tax increases (Gonzalo Escribano 2016).

In Tunisia, the macroeconomic situation before the pandemic was marked by the political vicissitudes of a rather protracted democratic transition, and heavily dependent on the security situation (Atradius 2019). According to a World Bank report, after a growth rate of 2.5 percent in 2018 and 2 percent in 2017, Tunisia experienced weak growth of 1.1 during the first quarter of 2019. The Tunisian GDP in 2019 remained moderate and insufficient to reduce the high unemployment rate estimated at over 15 percent (Atradius 2019).

Contrary to Algeria and Tunisia, the pre-COVID-19 situation in Morocco was much more stable, in spite of the decline in the growth rate (2.5 percent in 2019 from 3.1 a year earlier). The macroeconomic outlook was overall positive, as the country was expecting to benefit from a rise in exports and measures to raise tax revenue and investments. Moreover, according to a paper published by the Organisation of Economic Cooperation and Development (OECD), domestic demand was projected to rise by 4 percent in 2020 from 2.4 percent in 2019, and improving global economic conditions were expected to lead to a growth in external demand to 5.4 percent from 4.2 percent (OECD 2020).

A mere few weeks later, the consequences of the pandemic lockdown started to deeply affect the economies of the three countries, blurring the nuances that differentiated them before the pandemic. The impact of COVID-19 crisis on almost every single aspect of economic activity in Morocco caused the local economy to enter its first recession since 1995 (World Bank 2019). The economic slowdown can easily be linked to the immediate effects of the worldwide restrictions caused by the pandemic. However, it can also be argued that COVID has only brought to light some of the common vulnerabilities usually hidden behind strategies of reform adopted by the three countries since independence. These common features can be analyzed as a "three-dimensional trap" that can be traced back to the political choices and development strategies adopted by postcolonial elites. The three-dimensional trap consists of the lack of a self-reliant economy, an unequal social system, and a very low level of regional integration. The next section argues that these three factors are features of "risk society" that caused Algeria, Morocco, and Tunisia, taken both individually and as a subregional system, to enter a vicious cycle that made them deeply vulnerable to the pandemic. At the same time, this "trap" undermined their very efforts to handle COVID.

Pandemic and Inequality: A Mutually Reinforcing Cycle

Unlike other types of diseases, pandemics, as public health issues, cannot be dealt with only as a medical problem. Their consequences are additionally shaped by socioeconomic and other extra-medical determinants, including culture and values. A sound understanding of the COVID-19 pandemic requires a context-specific analysis. From this perspective, the spread of Coronavirus in the already-unequal social systems of the Maghreb has caused the three countries to enter in a self-reinforcing cycle in which existing inequalities worsen the spread of the virus, while the pandemic is at the same time deepening inequalities. It should be noted however that vulnerability to COVID-19 in the cases compared here is "structural for the countries, regions and/ or segments of the populations within them" (Sadiki and Saleh 2020). Moreover these structural inequalities are often exacerbated by the fact that the distribution of burdens is unequal (Sadiki and Saleh 2020).

In spite of the exceptional efforts made by public authorities in North Africa, the virus put a huge amount of pressure on their health systems. Unsurprisingly, the deplorable condition of healthcare services in the region is symptomatic of deep social and territorial inequalities that had become a real threat to social cohesion in the three North African societies. Development policies that were implemented over the last five decades seem to have fallen short of overcoming these weaknesses.

The elites that ruled this part of North Africa set up highly concentrated political systems. Before the 2011 uprisings, representative and participatory institutions designed to achieve a distribution of power were used as a facade for autocratic regimes. As a matter of fact, this concentration of political power was only possible with a strong tendency to concentrate wealth and economic power in the hands of those elites. Since their early years of independence, the authoritarian regimes in Morocco, Algeria, and Tunisia privileged the interest of some affluent coastal areas at the expense of the rest of their countries, namely the interior areas that were left behind.

These territorial disparities became a real structural obstacle to development in the three countries. In Tunisia, the economic policies adopted since independence were mainly focused on tourism and low-cost manufacturing. This approach led to a concentration of infrastructure investments in coastal regions and was detrimental to agriculture communities (Meddeb 2020). This has resulted, over the last few decades, in a paradoxical situation in which inland provinces that hold 50 percent of the country's oil, gas, and water resources, 70 percent of wheat production, and 50 percent of olive and fruit production, are the most disadvantaged (Meddeb 2020). In Morocco, despite the hope brought by the launch of the National Initiative of Human Development (INDH) in 2005, regional inequalities are yet to be eradicated. A report of the Economic, Social and Environmental Council (ESEC) found that access to social services such as education, healthcare, and job markets, is marked by huge disparities among the twelve regions of the kingdom (ESEC 2019). In terms of the contribution of these territorial entities to the GDP, figures from the High Commission for Planning (HCP) show that only three regions out of the twelve monopolized more than half of the wealth of the country in 2016 (HCP 2018). In 2013, four regions shared 51.2 percent of the national GDP, which means that development policies have been deepening inequalities instead of bridging the gap between rich and poor regions.

The other facet through which regional disparities manifest themselves is inequality in terms of poverty rate and employment. In Tunisia, a big divide in poverty rates has accumulated over time between the traditionally disadvantaged *North West* and the Centre West regions whose poverty rates are almost twice the national average, and the coastal and more urbanized eastern regions (Tunis area, North East, and the Centre of Tunisia) (Macro Poverty Overlook World Bank 2019). In Algeria, statistics show that 5.5 percent of the population is considered poor, with large regional variations and higher concentration in the Sahara and steppe regions (MPO World Bank 2019). As for Morocco, the government has been spending heavily on poverty reduction programs, and millions of poor people were targeted by various projects in both rural and urban areas. However, recent figures show that only slight progress has been achieved and that poverty is declining at a much slower pace than spending (MPO World Bank 2019, 167).

These territorial and social inequalities are a breeding ground for the coronavirus pandemic to widen the gap between the rich and the poor. According to a study published in late 2020, COVID-19 is expected to push 45 million Arab and North Africans into poverty, while 1.7 million risk losing their jobs (Barkawi Ban 2020). In the countries compared here, education remains the most affected sector where the gap between rich and poor can be easily detected. A report published by the Higher Council for Education of Morocco in September 2021 shows that children of low-income families have been facing more difficulties during the pandemic. These conditions included the lack of the necessary equipment for distance learning, overcrowding homes, and unfavorable family environment. Moreover, girls were overloaded by more housework, at the expense of time dedicated to education. Reports assert that while these inequalities preexisted COVID-19, the pandemic has deepened them, especially among poor families in rural areas. For example, the report of the Higher Council for Education report shows that the number of students attending distance learning sessions in rural areas was much lower compared to students in urban areas (CSEFRS 2021).Likewise, in Tunisia 51 percent of students were not equipped with devices (smartphones or laptops) necessary for distance learning. This percentage rose to 70 percent in primary schools, according to a national survey held by the ministry of education (Housseini 2020). This gloomy perspective cannot be attributed solely to the impact of COVID-19. The root causes of the socioeconomic vulnerabilities can be explained in light of the structural drivers of inequality and marginalization, such as economic dependence and the lack of regional economic integration.

All in all, the pandemic has shown that inequality in North Africa is symptomatic of the difficulties faced by local elites in postcolonial state-building. In spite of looming post-pandemic uncertainties, COVID-19 can be seen as an opportunity not only to mitigate the impacts of inequality on social cohesion but also to prevent inequality-related risks in the future. These risks are preventable because they are produced by society (Baxter Jamie 2020).

The Lack of Economic Self-Reliance

Economic self-reliance can be defined as a situation in which the growth of a nation does not depend on other economies. This concept emerged out of the debate on development strategies in the Third World in 1970, and was widely seen as the recipe for overcoming underdevelopment in newly independent nations in Africa, Asia, and Latin America (Matthies 1979). Half a century later, the world economy has reached an unprecedented level of interdependence that makes the idea of complete self-reliance, as a strategy of development, both anachronistic and unrealistic. Even China seems to have progressively abandoned Mao Zedong's self-reliance policy following its market reform starting from late 1970(Friedrich 1981).

However, the evolution of economic liberalism shows that a market economy has always been consistent with some level of self-reliance even in some overtly freemarket economies. Beyond its implications for the political aspects of sovereignty, different types of crises experienced by humanity over the last century show that the very existence of a nation will depend in the future on its ability to rely on its own resources.

In North Africa, the impact of COVID-19 on the three countries can be easily attributed to the dependence of their economies on international financial institutions and global economic powers. As result of decades of poor investment in human capital, they found themselves limited in logistical capacity, infrastructure, expertise, and even decision-making protocols (Saleh and Sadiki 2020).

This common characteristic manifests itself in various ways in the three countries. In Morocco and Tunisia, where tourism represents a significant share of GDP, travel restrictions resulted in the collapse of the tourism industry. In Tunisia, a sharp decrease in the number of tourists caused an increase in unemployment rate by 3 percentage points (18 percent) between the first and second quarters of 2020 (OECD 2020). As a result, tourism companies were forced to resort to drastic measures in an endeavor to survive the pandemic. Thousands of workers in this vital sector were made redundant. Likewise in Morocco, unemployment rose to 12.7 percent at the end of 2020 from

9.2 percent at the end of 2019 (HCP 2020). This loss is partly due to Morocco's tourism crisis.

In addition, Morocco and Tunisia, both aid-dependent countries, had no alternative but to resort to borrowing from Bretton Woods institutions, hence deepening their dependence on the IMF and the World Bank. In May 2020, the World Bank agreed on a US$20 million scheme for Tunisia to support the country's healthcare sector, in addition to another US $15million made a month earlier for emergency expenditures (Gnan 2020). To face exceptional COVID-19 management expenditures, Morocco was obliged to use the precautionary and liquidity line (PLL) for the first time since it started to benefit from this financial arrangement with the IMF. In April 2020, Moroccan authorities drew on all resources available under the PLL (US$3billion) to cope with the social and economic impact of the crisis (OECD 2020). As for Algeria, it was reluctant to get loans from international institutions. President Abdelmajid Tebboune rejected such an option, arguing that

when a country turns to international loans, it loses its sovereignty. Algeria is a free country and debts to international actors compromise this freedom. You will no longer be able to defend causes like the Palestinian cause and the Western Sahara conflict. (Handaji 2020)

Such an option is consistent with the ideology embraced by the ruling class in Algeria and does not seem to be motivated by the need to improve economic self-reliance or to reduce foreign debt. In the view of President Tebboune, a good alternative would be to borrow from "friendly countries." According to some analysts, he was alluding to China. As one scholar argues, this option "has obvious advantages, as Chinese money will come with less string attached and they won't discuss how authorities handle protests or how they will implement reforms" (Handaji 2020). Obviously, such an option is unlikely to solve the issue of sovereignty inasmuch as it substitutes dependence on the West with dependence on China. Indeed, besides avoiding pressure to political and economic reform, the incumbent regime may also use the money to buy social peace as part of its tireless endeavor to end the *Hirak*.

Despite variation in policies, since independence all three countries have been experiencing a structural negative trade balance. In 2019, Tunisia, Morocco, and Algeria imported more than they were able to export. This persistent imbalance in the three countries has led to a negative trade balance of−6,629,759.34 in thousands of US$, −21,747,058.24 in thousands of US$, and −10,861,898.57 in thousands of US$, respectively. Due to the exceptional expenditures caused by the pandemic, this trade deficit is very likely to continue to hamper efforts to building self-reliant economies in this part of North Africa in the foreseeable future (The World Integrated Trade Solution WITS 2020).

The Pandemic and the Price of Non-Maghreb

One of the driving factors of economic dependence in the Maghreb lies in the lack of economic integration between member states of this region. More than three decades after the leaders of Morocco, Algeria, Tunisia, Mauritania, and Libya gathered in Marrakech in 1989 and signed the treaty establishing the Union of the Arab Maghreb, the project that was initially motivated by the need to meet people's aspirations for an integrated and prosperous Maghreb remained an ink on paper. To recall, the treaty had envisaged a progressive integration process, starting with a free-trade area before the end of 1992, a customs union before the end of 1995, and a custom market before 2000 (Hedi et al.2007).

Today, this part of the eastern Mediterranean remains one of the least integrated regions in the world. The root cause of this stalemate is undoubtedly Morocco and Algeria's long-lasting misunderstanding over the Western Sahara. The establishment of an authentic Maghreb integration would allow them to save over $2 billion per year, according to IMF estimates (El Hachimi 2015). The negative effects of the political tension between rival Algeria and Morocco are not limited to their economies. These tensions continue to waste time, rendering the Maghreb, according to various observers, a "non-region" on the economic level (Ghiles 2010).

The advent of COVID-19 made the effects of the Morocco Algerian rupture on intra-Maghreb trade more visible. Indeed, the closing of the borders between the two countries since 1994 not only handicaps their economies but also prevents the establishment of an authentic Maghreb economic integration that would have served as an ideal framework of regional collaboration to fight the pandemic. Risk society here thus takes on a regional dimension.

In this context, the strong potential of economic complementarity remains unexploited by the three main countries of the Maghreb. It is striking to notice that while Algeria is a leading producer and exporter of gas and oil, its neighbours, Morocco and Tunisia, are burdened with an energy bill that deepens their dependency and increase their trade deficit. On the other hand, while Morocco and Tunisia, known as agricultural-producing countries, export their products mainly to the European Union and the United States, their neighbor Algeria heavily relies on importing food, with more than $1.93 billion only in the first quarter of 2020.

This structural difference between the three economies has never been dealt with as an opportunity for regional development. In a study conducted in early 2000s, some researchers suggest that:

> It is very expensive and costly for Maghreb countries to maintain trade barriers and restrictions between them. One of the main results of the study shows that a simple elimination of tariffs can induce a US$ 350 million welfare increase and an increase in GDP of up to 2.5 percent in the case of Tunisia and 0.4 percent for Morocco, and more importantly that the realization of a common market leads to potentially significant growth in earnings, including a US$ 4.6 billion welfare increase and an increase in GDP of 10 percent for Tunisia and 8 percent for Morocco. Additionally, a free trade area is more favourable to the diversification of the North African economies, while favouring a certain diversification among Maghreb countries and improving their welfare. (Hedi et al. 2007)

Against all expectations that the pandemic could help ease the rivalries between Morocco and Algeria, their already tense relations deteriorated even more, following Morocco's decision to launch a military operation to reopen the blocked *Guerguerat*

Frontier Gate with Mauritania. While Morocco claimed that this operation was motivated by the need to end the blockade of trucks traveling between the Morocco-controlled area of the disputed territory and Mauritania, and to restore free circulation of civilian and commercial traffic, the *Polisario* front deemed this move an aggression and a violation of the ceasefire agreement. Since then, tensions between Morocco and Algeria, key backer of *Polisario*, have been escalating amid mutual accusations of allegedly hostile actions against each other. The escalation reached its climax in August 2021 when Algeria decided to break off its diplomatic ties with Morocco.

How can this move be explained? And to what extent was this decision instigated by the pandemic? The literature on diplomacy has often been preoccupied with analyzing procedures for establishing relations, and with little attention to their rupture. In this regard, some scholars distinguished four major reasons causing countries to break relations with outside powers. It is argued that the decision to break diplomatic relations with outside powers can be attributed to domestic, bilateral, regional, or global factors (Gitelson 1974).

In light of the ongoing economic crisis and legitimacy deficit in Algeria, it is very likely that its decision to cut diplomatic relations with Morocco is motivated by domestic factors. There are at least two indicators suggesting this decision intends to divert attention from the failure of the regime to cope adequately with the pandemic. First, that there were no real diplomatic relations between the two countries, beyond the formal exchange of ambassadors. Hence, such a decision is very unlikely to have an impact on an already frozen diplomatic relationship. The other reason this decision may have been motivated by domestic factors lies in the fact that the Algerian regime is still under pressure of the *Hirak*. It is in dire need to use the rhetoric of the priority of fighting against a foreign enemy as a pretext to crackdown on the *Hirak* activists, and to cover up the chaotic management of the pandemic. Moreover, Morocco's normalization with Israel, its unprecedented invocation of "the right to self-determination for the Kabyle people," along with what Morocco celebrates as diplomatic success culminating in US recognition of the Moroccan sovereignty over the Western Sahara, have all given strong momentum to hostility between the two countries, and altered the geopolitical balance of power in the Western Maghreb (Maichel2020).

All in all, the aforementioned three-dimensional trap has significantly limited the options of fighting the pandemic in the North African countries. The escalating tensions between Morocco and Algeria, the problems of the protracted transition in Tunisia, and the political crisis in Libya, reverberate on the whole region. In this context, the weak level of economic integration prevents the three countries from setting up a joint economic recovery.

Instrumentalizing the Pandemic in North Africa: A Tendency to Rule by Law?

The rule of law has become one of the key pillars of modern democracies. This principle that "focuses on limiting and independently reviewing the exercise of public powers" is of universal validity(Council of Europe 2016). However, as an analytical tool, its definition does not seem to be a simple one. Indeed, "rule of law" is being systematically invoked by people embracing contradictory ideologies to characterize various systems of governance, ranging from genuine democracies to outright autocracies.

In an attempt to deal with the impact of this general over-use of the concept, some scholars and institutions suggest operational definitions. In an article dedicated to the meaning of the rule of law, Robert Stein offered a definition based on five characteristics that a society governed by the rule of law should have. Similarly, the European Commission for Democracy through Law issued a rule of law checklist to evaluate states. The checklist consists of five principles, namely, the principle of legality, legal certainty, prevention of abuse of powers, equality before the law and nondiscrimination, and access to justice (Council of Europe 2016). Put this way, the rule of law is one of the parameters of risk society, based on which the risks of COVID-19 crisis can be assessed. Indeed, it is worth mentioning that the theorists of the risk society insisted that "it is not just health and the environment that are at risk, but in addition, the fundamental sociopolitical values of liberty, equality, justice, rights and democracy are now at risk" (Ekberg 2007).

Notwithstanding practice-based definitions, the rule of law remains one of the most ideologically abused concepts to the point that it has become chameleon-like (Stein 2009). In the Maghreb, the phrase has come to be a key part of official political discourse. In practice the lack of an enabling democratic environment make it difficult for the values of the rule of law to take root. Instead of reinforcing democracy through law, what the official narratives refer to as the rule of law appears to be degenerating into a rule by law. This practice consists in using law-making to legalize undemocratic governance, manifesting itself differently in each country during the pandemic. In Algeria, a new constitution was approved via a referendum held in the context of the pandemic. According to some scholars, behind the slogan of building a new Algeria, the ultimate goal of the regime was to seize the opportunity of the exceptional circumstances of COVID-19 to hijack the popular protest demanding radical change. In this regard, an expert on Algerian politics argues that:

> For the regime, the referendum and new constitution are designed to break the momentum of the popular movement by trying to appropriate its objectives. For instance, the preamble mentions that the constitution is a response to "the will of the people" expressed through its "authentic blessed *Hirak*," which "put an end to [past] errors . . ." In other words, the vote is the regime's solution to move on, so that a new Algeria can emerge and the Hirak can be ended. (Ghanem 2020)

Obviously, the circumstances under which the referendum was held were a clear sign of the intention to reduce the role of the constitution, from a key pillar of the rule *of* law in democracy to a tool of rule *by* law. Furthermore, given the low voter turnout in this referendum, it falls short of meeting one of the most important criteria of the rule of law. Indeed, in a society governed by the rule of law, "members of society have the right to participate in the creation of and refinement of law that regulate their behaviour"

(2009). And most important, the constitution is a political chart from which every single political action or behavior is supposed to derive its legitimacy.

Another example that shows how authorities in the three cases took advantage of the pandemic to make the rule of law becomes a rule by law is the attempt to adopt undemocratic laws. In Algeria, the parliament approved a very controversially amended criminal code without a genuine public debate in the context of the pandemic. In a joint report by Article 19 MENA and MENA Rights Group, the two NGOs drew the attention of the UN special rapporteurs on freedom of expression and on the right to freedom of peaceful assembly and association to several provisions that violate international standards in the amended law. Besides the fact that the amendment was approved without parliamentary and democratic debate, the report raised serious concerns about article 95 that "provides authorities with excessive power to prosecute activists and human rights defenders receiving foreign funding, if the authorities consider that their activities undermine the normal functioning of institutions or national unity." The provisions related to the "offense of contempt" and "fake news" were also deemed contradictory to intentional standards of human rights.

In Morocco, the government approved a draft law n. 22.20 regulating the use of social media, open broadcast networks and similar networks in the middle of the pandemic. The text that was allegedly leaked by a member of the government was widely denounced by civil society and human rights activists. Indeed, it was argued that enforcement of this law will task providers with restricting content as well as enforcing criminal penalties for users who post what the text considers false information online. One of the issues that triggered a strong wave of anger and indignation was the criminalization of online calls to boycott. According to the draft law, users of social media who call for the boycott of certain products could face fines and up to three years of jail. The government came under severe criticism even from within parties of the coalition. Interestingly enough, some ministers expressed reserves on the draft law. A member of the governmental coalition told the newspaper Tel Quel, "Even within the government, this draft was perceived with big reservations by several ministers. Because regulating a sector is a good thing, but undermining freedom of expression, guaranteed by the constitution, is not acceptable" (Oudrhiri 2020).

State-Society Interactions during the Pandemic: A Return of the State?

To what extent does the response of states in Morocco, Algeria, and Tunisia, in terms of the scope and style of state intervention, usher in a return of the state in the three countries? To answer this question, it should be noted first that the idea of the return of the state in polysemic. It is used by scholars to characterize various phenomena in different contexts. It was first employed by critics of globalization to argue against the idea according to which the latter has precipitated the crisis of the nation-state which has arguably lost control on its national economy and other symbols of sovereignty, as new centers of power (global market, transnational corporations, etc.) emerge

(Bresser-Pereira 2008). From this perspective, they suggest that nation-states are the principal agents of globalization.

The return of the state was also used to describe the efforts made by some Western states to contain the financial crisis of 2008, which resulted in what some commentators called a quasi-shadow nationalization (Delwaide 2011). More recently, the same idea is being used as a way to advocate for a restructuring of the nation-state, arguing for a strong state capable of leading a more equitable economic recovery post-pandemic (Patrick 2021).

For the purpose of this chapter, the return of the state serves a different meaning. It refers to any kind of action, initiative, behavior, law, or any other course of action through which North African sates attempted to reconquer public spaces wrested from their grasp in the context of Arab uprisings. But had the state in the three countries indeed lost control over public spaces they are presumably reclaiming under the pretext of fighting the pandemic? To answer this question, a twofold methodological precaution should be addressed. First, the idea of the return of the state in North Africa presupposes that the state and society operate in two different spheres, the contours of which can be clearly identified. Indeed, measuring the extent to which the state is returning is conditioned by the ability to locate the spaces it used to occupy before its withdrawal from after the uprising. Second, it also suggests that the Arab Spring and subsequent political and institutional reforms have changed the balance of power between state and society in the region. These two underlying assumptions of the return of the state remain debatable in the context of North Africa, thus they should be approached very cautiously.

Based on the above, it can be argued that while the return of the state remains a well-grounded assumption to apprehend some aspects of state's response related to the role of the security apparatus, or the invocation of public order, it may also incorporate some positive aspects of state's response to the crisis. Indeed, the role played by public authorities in mitigating the socioeconomic impact of the crisis can also be seen as the return of the state as a service provider, and may mark an end to what some scholars call the ideology of public powerlessness (Delwaide 2011). In Morocco, King Mohammed VI took the initiative to set up a special fund dedicated to managing the pandemic. The fund raised over 32 billion dirhams in donations ($3.2 billion) in what some observers have characterized as a genuine Marshall plan to support economy and protect populations (Benamour 2020). The committee in charge with taking the necessary measures to mitigate the impact of the pandemic started to provide financial aid to families that had lost their source of income. Employees affiliated with the social security system benefited from a 2000 dirhams monthly allocation (approximately US$202). They also benefited from a suspension of loans and consumption credits reimbursements, until June 30, 2020. Given the high levels of informality, authorities decided to provide financial relief to informal workers suffering from the economic impact of COVID-19. The financial support was calculated based on the number of people per households benefiting from the medical assistance plan RAMED and which no longer have an income due to compulsory confinement. The committee decided to allocate 800 DH per month for households of two people or less; 1,000 DH per month for households of three to four people; 1,200 DH per month for households of more than four people. Households without RAMED, operating in the informal sector and who have lost their income following compulsory confinement, will also benefit from this provision by filling out their requests in an electronic platform (OECD 2020). Likewise in Tunisia, the authorities created a national solidarity fund which collected more than $70 million by October 2020. Furthermore, in June 2020, Tunisia unveiled a nine-month Rescue and Recovery Plan in collaboration with the IMF (Fakir and Werenfels 2021). The plan included more than $526 million to public projects and allocated $35 million for unemployment payments as well as $245 million to struggling businesses (Fakir and Werenfels 2021). As for Algeria, although the government took the initiative to help vulnerable and poor families, it was mainly relying on support from civil society networks and on the Algerian diaspora to provide relief (Fakir and Werenfels 2021).

The next section will examine the texts that declared a state of emergency in the three countries, and the circumstances under which they were adopted. The aim is to detect any decisions or measures that could amount to democratic setbacks. It will also assess the extent to which they can be seen as instigated by COVID-19 measures. Moreover, the weight of regime type and state/society balance of power in shaping the ways and the scale of instrumentalizing emergency measures will be also measured (ASL 2020).

Algeria: Fighting the Virus and Legitimacy-Building Challenge

It can be argued that handling the pandemic in Algeria was the most challenging compared to Tunisia and Morocco. At the time when the virus erupted as a health crisis, the Algerian regime was already struggling with an unprecedented economic crisis, coupled with a political one. At the economic level, Algeria has witnessed a sharp drop in hydrocarbon revenue, which accounts for 60 percent of the state budget and 95 percent of its total revenue(Camporeale et al. 2021). At the political level, the continuing *Hirak* following the presidential election is a clear sign of a deep popular dissatisfaction with the reform agenda of the regime. In this context, the pandemic offers a suitable opportunity for the regime to achieve a twofold goal: using COVID-19 exceptional measures to end the protest and, at the same time, handling the pandemic in a way that could help the regime to rebuild trust and overcome its legitimacy deficit.

Contrary to Morocco and Tunisia, Algeria did not witness strong demand for change in 2011, during the so-called Arab Spring. The prominent role of the army in controlling political life, its capacity to use oil revenue in buying social peace and, most importantly, the psychological impact of the black decade of the 1990s(ZeraouliaFaouzia 2020) have contributed, among other factors, to stabilizing the regime at such a crucial time in the region. Nearly a decade later, the decision of former president Bouteflika to run for a fifth term in February 2019 triggered a nationwide protest movement demanding genuine democratic change. This protest movement known as *Hirak* was widely seen as part of the second wave of the Arab Spring (Fahmi 2020). This unprecedented movement was first ignored by the regime, before the latter ultimately decided to abandon Bouteflika who was asked to resign in application of article 101 of the Algerian constitution.

The Algerian army played a determinant role in the overthrow of Bouteflika and was also the key player in setting and implementing the political roadmap for the post Bouteflika era. In the following paragraphs, we will assess the extent to which the regime sought to take advantage of the pandemic to impose its political agenda of reforms referred to as the new Algeria. We will also explore the attitudes of the *Hirak* activists toward the army's roadmap and the strategies they used to circumvent the obstacles they faced in the context of the pandemic.

Given the nature and evolution of the Algerian political system since the country gained independence, no credible analysis of the Algerian politics is possible without shedding some light on the role of the army. Indeed, it can be argued that the decisive role of the then chief of staff Ahmed Gaid Salah in the removal of Bouteflika, and as the main interlocutor of the *Hirak* during the transitional period, along with the inability of the current president to disguise his dependence on the army leadership, are important indicators. They show that army leaders cannot be considered only as reliable arbiters of political crisis between Algerian protesters and the ruling civilian elites, but the real rulers of the country behind the scenes.

The hypothesis that best describes the way the army was involved in the transitional process, both before and during the pandemic, is the idea of ruling behind the scenes. In other words, the army's strategy has been and continues to be, to rule the country but not to govern it, to use the phrase of Steven Cook. In his book titled *Ruling but Not Governing: The Military and Political Development in Egypt, Algeria, and Turkey*, Cook argues that the character of the military's interest in both a facade of democracy and indirect control of key aspects of political control is complex and nuanced. The officers seek to control but not to govern (Cook 2007). The decision of Ahmed Gaid Salah to firmly support a fifth term of Bouteflika, the ease with which he abandoned him later on, and his rashness in holding presidential elections, all show where real power lies in Algeria. Although the decision to cancel the two planned elections in April and July 2019 appears to be motivated by the continuing pressure of the *Hirak*, it did not affect the balance of power between the army and the *Hirak*. The postponement of elections turned out to be a tactical move that allowed the army to kill two birds with one stone. Having justified its decision to abandon Bouteflika by proclaiming its duty to side with the people, the concealment of the elections, to which large majority of Algerians were opposed, was meant to give more credibility to this narrative as a source of legitimacy of the army. At the same time, it allowed the latter to dawdle so as to gain more time to make the necessary arrangements to tighten its grip on political institutions.

By the end of 2019, when the pandemic started in China and in some European countries, the new president was already in office. Hence, it is very hard to attribute the way this political agenda was imposed to the eruption of the pandemic in Algeria in early 2020. It appears that factors like the leaderless nature of the *Hirak*, and the inability of elites to come up with a commonly agreed alternative to the existing system, have undermined the protest movement, making the *Hirak* unable to change the balance of power. This does not mean the army did not seek to take advantage of the pandemic, but only to accelerate an already planned agenda, as part of its strategy to rule the country without governing it.

Adapting the *Hirak* to the Pandemic

Following the lockdown declared by governments around the world, millions of people found themselves deprived of their rights to occupy public space as a form of protest. However, this does not mean that the crisis is likely to put an end to protest, although it has curtailed it. A group of researchers collecting data on the various methods people have used to express solidarity and adapted to this crisis have identified nearly 100 distinct methods of non-violent action that include physical, virtual, and hybrid actions (Chenoweth et al. 2020). The restrictions on access to physical public space compelled the *Hirak* to adapt its modes of mobilization. Activists began to explore new forms of activisms such as web and balcony-based protest, dish-banging from windows, and doubling down on social media communiques.

In a report broadcasted by a TV channel,[2] an old Algerian man insists on keeping the *Hirak* alive by using a creative form of protest at home. While the man is exercising on his treadmill, we can hear him saying, "for me, I decided to do my *Hirak* at home. Behind closed doors." From the posters he stuck up on the front of his machine, we can understand that the video was filmed on March 27, 2020, which coincides with Friday 58 of the *Hirak*.

Interestingly enough, the Algerian diaspora also contributed in adapting to the crisis. The most common form used by Algerians abroad consists in posting videos to show their solidarity with detainees and encourage their fellow citizens to keep up with new circumstances. In a video filmed at home, Riad Kaced, an Algerian engineer living in San Francisco, urged Algerians to look on the bright side of the crisis:

> My aim is to say to the mafia that we are still here. The pandemic is a very good opportunity for a lot of people, especially students, to prepare initiatives that seek to translate the popular uprising into strong action, once the pandemic is over.[3]

One year after the outbreak of COVID-19 crisis, at the time of writing this chapter public space is largely closed, under the pretext of fighting against the pandemic. Protesters are no longer able to hold Friday marches and it is hard to assume whether or not the spirit of the Hirak will survive the repression and pandemic.

Pandemic Management and Risks of Authoritarian Drift in Morocco and Tunisia

Unlike Algeria, Morocco and Tunisia have rapidly responded by declaring a state of emergency. In both countries, the state of health emergency was meant to provide governments with exceptional powers enabling them to take decisions to protect public health. Obviously, this situation entails considerable risks of arbitrary and human rights violations. Therefore, handling such a complex situation in democratic societies is conditioned by the ability of public authorities to strike the right balance between two seemingly contradictory objectives: protecting the right to health and, the right to life on the one hand, in a way that does not sacrifice freedoms and public liberties on the other. To recall, in March 2020 in an endeavor to anticipate potential misuse of the derogation provided for by article 4 of the International Covenant on Civil and Political Rights (ICCPR), the Office of the United Nations High Commissioner for Human Rights issued detailed guidelines member states should consider in case they resort to this article. While state members were allowed to restrict some rights as part of their response to the pandemic, they were urged to make sure the restrictions are necessary, legal, proportional, and not discriminatory.[4] It is against these guidelines that the state of emergency declared in Morocco and Tunisia, and its impact on human rights and democracy, will be assessed in the following paragraphs.

In Tunisia, it was the president of the Republic who took the initiative to declare curfew, after consultation with the head of government and the president of Parliament, based on Article 80 of the Tunisian constitution. In the case of Morocco, in the absence of specific constitutional provisions regulating the state of emergency, the government issued a decree-law based on which it declared the state of health emergency. While the state of emergency was seen as necessary to fight the pandemic in both cases, the formula used was much more contested in Tunisia than in Morocco. Logically, President Saied was not obliged to invoke article 80 of the constitution for two reasons: firstly, the health crisis did not hamper the regular functioning of institutions. Secondly, the resort to this article is conditioned by the presence of the constitutional court, which is the only competent authority to monitor exceptional measures declared by the president. As far as the legality of the restrictions is concerned, the presidential decree raises serious issues of legality and predictability. Presidential Decree No. 2020/24 establishes, among other things, the prohibition of movement during the curfew, without giving more details as to the terms or the potential penalties. This lack of precision was the source of confusion and misunderstanding on the part of citizens and justice actors, giving rise, especially at the start of its implementation, to numerous arrests and legal proceedings.

In both countries the rapid decision to close the borders, declared and implemented without reasonable notice, has led to several incidents at the land borders. On April 20, 2020, 65,018 Tunisians stranded for several days in Libya forced the *Ras Jedir* border crossing in the governorate of *Medenine* and forcibly entered Tunisian territory. All those forced through their passage were arrested and subjected to administrative and health checks, and then directed to compulsory isolation centers (ASL 2020). Likewise, hundreds of Moroccan citizens were stuck abroad following the government decision to close the country's borders. In both cases, the way the authorities have responded to the crisis has two common characteristics. On the one hand, the quick emergency measures allowed both countries to contain the spread of the virus during the first wave. This enabled them to strike a balance between saving lives and mitigating the socioeconomic impact of the pandemic by reopening their economies in June 2020. On the other hand, their responses raised serious issues related to the protection of human rights in the context of the pandemic.

Beyond these similarities, the crisis management in the two cases diverged. Indeed, the situation in Morocco and Tunisia seems to be diverging both in terms of the performance of the health system and the resilience of the governance system. As far as the epidemiological situation is concerned, while the situation in Morocco remained overall under control, despite the exponential rise of infections and deaths, the new wave of contamination accelerated the collapse of the health system in Tunisia in July 2021 (Reuters 2021). At the political level the strategy led by the king and implemented by the government is, by and large, still on track. In Tunisia, the polarization between the three presidencies has significantly undermined the ability of these institutions to set up a coherent and efficient plan to face the pandemic. The tension reached its climax in July 2021 when President Kais Saied decided to resort one more time to article 80 of the constitution. The president suspended the parliament and lifted immunity on its members. He also fired the prime minister and concentrated executive power in his hands.

How can these divergences between the cases of Morocco and Tunisia be explained? Is there a link between the nature of the political systems prevailing in the two cases and their crisis management strategies?

It is premature to make a clear judgment on the efficacy and efficiency of different systems of governance in handling the ongoing crisis. Thus, it does not make sense, at this stage of the pandemic management, to attribute the success or the failure of anti-covid responses to a given country's political system. Nonetheless, a preliminary comparison between Morocco and Tunisia blows the lid off some factors that may explain differences between the two cases. Three factors call for consideration here, namely, the distribution of power between key political institutions, the decision-making model, and the role of political parties. First, power distribution in the two systems is very different. In Morocco, a centralized political system, much of the executive power is concentrated in the hands of the king. Although the 2011 constitution has empowered elected institutions, such as the parliament and the government, it did not affect the centrality of the monarchy in the policymaking process. Beyond the constitutional separation of powers, the balance of power between the monarchy and other institutions is governed by an unwritten rule according to which policies are made by the monarchy and implemented by the ministers. This monarchy-dominated power distribution is an emanation of the multifaceted legitimacy of the monarchy. It is deeply rooted in the history of the state in Morocco, and was enshrined in the 2011 constitution.

This power distribution was also embodied in the new development model (NDM) prepared by a special commission appointed by the king.[5]Based on a long-term vision, the NDM defines the strategic challenges the country needs to achieve by 2035. Hence, the governments to be elected from now on will be above all entrusted with the task of translating these strategic orientations into concrete public policies. Due to this political configuration, when the pandemic reached Morocco, the institutions did not experience any hesitation or disputes over power. The king took the initiative and other institutions followed.

By contrast, in Tunisia where power is less concentrated and more democratically distributed, the decision-making process was an obstacle that undermined the response to the crisis. This may be explained, among other factors, by the fact that the three presidencies took different stances regarding the nature of the Tunisian political system, and how the institutions should function. While President Kais Saied was from the outset behaving as a head of state in a presidential system, the prime minister and the Speaker of the Council of Representatives of the People were reluctant to accept such presidential interpretation of the constitution. Instead, they were advocating for a parliamentarian system (Thabeti 2021). This dispute over power slowed down efforts to fight the virus, and triggered a wave of protests against the parliament that was judged unable to meet the hopes and demands of the revolution. The protests that took place in July 2021 provided President Saied with an opportunity to tighten his grip on the system. Under the pretext of responding to people's demands for change, the president suspended the parliament and fired the prime minister. In so doing, he was actually concentrating all the powers in his hands.

The second difference between Morocco and Tunisia has to do with the decision-making model prevailing in each. In Tunisia, the consensus model has thrown the country into political turmoil, casting doubt on the fate of the first Arab democracy on the making. In Morocco, by contrast, the monarchy-dominated governance, known locally as the executive monarchy, seems to have allowed the country to navigate confidently through the crisis so far.

Interestingly enough, if consensus was crucial in helping Tunisia's political transition overcome difficult moments, especially from the collapse of Ben Ali regime to the adoption of the new constitution in 2014, the victory of Ennahda Party in the first democratic elections created an atmosphere of ideological polarization. Unlike Morocco, where the king has always been in a position to arbitrate between opposing views and conflicting interests in such a way that he has the last say in decision-making, the search for consensus in Tunisia delayed necessary reforms that were supposed to take place in the early years of the transition. The formation of the National Unity Government, through which political protagonists sought to institutionalize their political agreement, failed to put the country on the right track. This can be demonstrated by various shortcomings that marked this coalition. First, although this government inhibited ideological polarization, it does not seem to have succeeded in putting an end to it. In this regard, some scholars have argued that:

> Despite much fanfare of bringing together Islamists and secularists, as well as revolutionaries and the old regime, the national unity government continued to be plagued by these issues. Both in terms of levels of polarization and the issues of debate, power-sharing in Tunisia appears to have had little effect. (Kubinec and Grewal 2018).

Second, Tunisia's political protagonists did not capitalize on their consensus to make policies and decisions necessary to meet demands for change voiced during the 2011 uprising. As some scholars noted, "The policies that emanated from the power-sharing agreement blocked, postponed, or reversed core demands of the 2010–2011 uprising for change. While national unity governments are designed to make difficult policy decisions more feasible—as blame is shared between parties—in Tunisia, this did not occur"(Yerkes and Ben Yahmed 2019). Lastly, another side effect of the consensus model is manifested by the little importance granted to the establishment of the constitutional court, a key pillar of the new democratic system. Furthermore, the two main parties (Ennahda and Nidaa Tounes) seem to have preferred to preserve their popularity to the detriment of the necessary and much-needed economic reforms.

As a result, it can be argued that the National Unity Government was a missed opportunity of reform that would have paved the way for Tunisia's successive governments and made the crisis management a much easier task. In contrast, the situation in Morocco was quite different. With a centralized decision-making model, the king was able to control the political agenda. While the consensus has blocked the political machinery in Tunisia, with a political class feeling comfortable to adopt a wait-and-see position, the monarch has been able to remind the government of its duties, or to directly take the initiative to fill in the vacuum in case of its inaction.

Conclusion

The main thrust of this chapter is to analyze the effects of the pandemic on Algeria, Morocco, and Tunisia. Their "risk society" has been examined from the perspective of the ability of existing systems to respond to and mitigate the impact of the crisis, and the ways incumbent regimes tried to take advantage of the pandemic to tighten their grip on power.

The analysis of socioeconomic structures in the three countries paved the way for a preliminary assessment of their low level of preparedness to cope with such an existential threat. It was suggested that structural weaknesses, referred to in this chapter as a three-dimensional trap, in Morocco, Algeria, and Tunisia, have exacerbated their vulnerabilities. Indeed, long-standing structural socioeconomic inequalities seem to be compromising their efforts to mitigate the impact of the pandemic. In the same vein, the lack of economic self-reliance, along with the very weak level of regional integration, have deepened their dependence on foreign financial powers, as shown by the rise of their pandemic-related debt. This three-fold risk society has caused difficulties in pandemic response and deepened already difficult socioeconomic situations.

The crisis had resulted so far in a sharp reduction of the distribution capabilities of the state, and rendered public authorities more tempted to use the pandemic as a pretext to roll back some hard-won freedoms and to slow down democratization processes. In Algeria, the curfew imposed by authorities has clearly affected the *Hirak* and reduced the momentum it gained before the pandemic. In Morocco, the closure of public space has impacted, to some extent, the exercise of public liberties. The bitter defeat of the Islamist Justice and Development Party in the September2021 elections may be partly explained by some COVID-19-related restrictions that prevent political parties from using in-person activities such as rallies and door-to-door canvassing.

Ten years after the Arab uprising, unprecedented difficulties facing democracy in Tunisia seem to be putting its democratic achievements at risk. Morocco, where genuine democratic change was sacrificed for the sake of stability, appears to be more resilient both economically and politically. This raises the question of whether development strategies are likely to succeed outside the context of liberal democracy? That some development models (Turkey, Russia, for example) have relatively succeeded in achieving development goals by flouting aspects of conventional democratic legitimacy and liberal understandings of human rights, gives new momentum to the question of whether development can be transformed into an alternative ideology that puts the essentials of liberal democracy into question.

In sum, beyond its effects on economy and society in North Africa, the COVID-19 crisis is also an opportunity to reflect on the policies conducted in the three countries since they gained independence. In this regard, it is striking that the anti-COVID measures in the three cases have resulted, so far, in strengthening the state at the expense of society, thus damaging newly required democratic freedoms (Sadiki and Saleh 2020). Nonetheless, the post-pandemic era seems to offer another opportunity to capitalize on rethinking the role of the state in light of its governance institutions and processes and their efficacy.

Notes

1 This chapter is limited to the three cases of Algeria, Morocco, and Tunisia for a series of reasons. The factors that shaped the postcolonial state in the three countries are quite similar and make the comparison reasonable. Unlike Algeria, Morocco, and Tunisia, the state-building process under Al Gaddafi in Libya did not result in a kind of institutionalized political system; the state was essentially reduced to the personality of the leader of *Al Fateh* Revolution. Indeed, ten years after Al Gaddafi was overthrown, Libya is still trapped in a spiral of violence and chaos, which additionally makes data collection a very difficult task.
2 The link to the video is:https://www.arte.tv/fr/videos/097136-000-A/algerie-le-hirak-a -l-heure-du-covid-19/, accessed on March 2021.
3 The link to the video is: https://www.arte.tv/fr/videos/097136-000-A/algerie-le-hirak-a -l-heure-du-covid-19/ accessed on March 2021.
4 https://www.ohchr.org/Documents/Events/EmergencyMeasures_COVID19.pdf
5 In December 2019 King Mohamed VI appointed the Special Commission for the New Development Model. The Commission was entrusted with examining the political, economic, social situation of the country and submit a report of the reforms needed to give development a strong momentum. On May 2021 the commission presented its report to the King. The report suggest a vision that is expected to serve as plan of action for the country till 2035. The final report of the commission is accessible at:https://www.csmd.ma/documents/Summary.pdf

References

Alliance pour la Sécurité et La Liberté (ASL). (2020). "Deux mois de lutte contre le COVID19 en Tunisie Analyse en matière d'État de droit," https://www.asf.be/wp -content/uploads/2020/06/ASL-Covid-19-1.pdf (accessed May 2, 2021).

Atradius (2019), *Rapport Pays Tunisie*, https://atradius.fr/publications/rapport-pays -moyen-orient-tunisie-2019.html (accessed January 2021).

Barkawi, Ban. (2020). "How Coronavirus 'supercharged' Economic Inequality in the Middle East," *Thomson Reuters Foundation*. https://news.trust.org/item /20200826152149-9drp0 (accessed January 11, 2021).

Baxter, J. (2020). *Health and Environmental Risk. International Encyclopedia of Human Geography, International Encyclopedia of Human Geography*, 2nd ed., Vol. 6, 303–7. doi:10.1016/b978-0-08-102295-5.10440-8.

Beck, Ulrich. (1992). *Risk Society, Towards a New Modernity*. London and New York: Sage.

Benamour, Najib. (2020). "COVID-19: Comment Le Maroc Met En Œuvre Un Plan Massif Pour Soutenir L'Économie Et Protéger Les Populations," https://www.forbes.fr/politique/covid-19-comment-le-maroc-met-en-oeuvre-un-plan-massif-pour-soutenir -leconomie-et-proteger-les-populations/ (accessed September 2, 2021).

Cecilia, Camporeale et al. (2021), "Beyond the Hydrocarbon Economy: The Case of Algeria," *intechOpen*, https://www.intechopen.com/chapters/71015 (accessed February 20, 2021).

Conseil Economique Social et Environnemental. (2019). *Annual Report*, https://www.cese .ma/media/2020/11/RA-VF-2019-1.pdf (accessed May 3, 2021).

Conseil Supérieur de l'Education, de la Formation et de la Recherche Scientifique (CSEFRS). (2021). "Enseignement au Temps de Covid," https://www.csefrs.ma/atelier -de-presentation-des-resultats-dune-evaluation-enseignement-au-temps-de-covid/ ?lang=fr (accessed September 20, 2021).

Cook, A. Steven. (2007). *Ruling But Not Governing: The Military and Political Development in Egypt, Algeria, and Turkey*. Baltimore: The Johns Hopkins University Press.

Council of Europe. (2016). "The Rule of Law Checklist," https://www.venice.coe.int/images/ SITE%20IMAGES/Publications/Rule_of_Law_Check_List.pdf (accessed June 10, 2021).

Ekberg Merryn. (2007). "The Parameters of the Risk Society A Review and Exploration," *Current Sociology*, 55 (3): 343–66, International Sociological Association SAGE (Los Angeles, London, New Delhi and Singapore), doi:10.1177/0011392107076080.

El Hachimi Mohamed (2015), *The Maghreb: Common Challenges and Diverging Approaches to Transition*, Barcelona: IEMed Mediterranean Yearbook.

Erica, Chenoweth, AustinChoiFitzpatrick, JeremyPressman, Felipe G.Santos and JayUlfelder. (2020). *The Global Pandemic has Spawned New Forms of Activism-and they are Flourishing*, https://www.theguardian.com/commentisfree/2020/apr/20/the-global- pandemic-has-spawned-new-forms-of-activism-and-theyre-flourishing (accessed April 3, 2021).

Escribano, Gonzalo. (2016). *The Impact of low Oil Prices on Algeria*. Center for Global Energy Policy, New York: Columbia University.

Fahmi, George. (2020). "A New Wave of Arab Uprisings: What have Both Arab Protesters and European Policymakers Learned from the Arab Spring?," *IDEES*, 51: 1–6.

Fakir, Intissar and WerenfelsIsabelle (2021). "The Pandemic and Governance in the Maghreb: A Moment of Truth," SWP Comment N.15, https://www.swp-berlin.org /publications/products/comments/2021C15_PandemicMaghreb.pdf (accessed September 12, 2021).

Friedrich, W. Y. Wu. (1981). "From Self-Reliance to Interdependence?: Developmental Strategy and Foreign Economic Policy in Post-Mao China," *Modern China*, 7 (4): 445–82, http://www.jstor.org/stable/189055 (accessed August 30, 2021).

Ghanem, Dalia. (2020). "Tebboune's New Algeria Looks Like the Old Algeria," *Al Qantara*, https://en.qantara.de/content/democracy-in-the-maghreb-tebbounes-new-algeria -looks-a-lot-like-the-old-algeria (accessed April 12, 2021).

Ghiles,Francis. (2010). "Le « non-Maghreb » coute cher au Maghreb," *Le Monde Diplomatique*, https://www.monde-diplomatique.fr/2010/01/GHILES/18755 (accessed April 13, 2021).

Gitelson, Susan Aurelia. (1974). "Why do Small States Break Diplomatic Relations with Outside Powers?: Lessons from the African Experience," *International Studies Quarterly*, 18 (4): 451–84.

Handaji, Madeleine. (2020). "Algeria Slashes National Budget as Oil Prices Plummet," https://www.moroccoworldnews.com/2020/05/301708/algeria-slashes-national-budget-as-oil-prices-plummet (accessed April 13, 2021).

Haut Commissariat au Plan. (2018). "Note d'information Relative aux comptesrégionaux de l'année 2018," https://www.hcp.ma/Les-comptes-regionaux-de-l-annee 2018_a2585.html#:~:text=Il%20s'agit%20des%20r%C3%A9gions,Oriental%20(4%2C2%25) (accessed March 4, 2021).

Haut Commissariat au Plan. (2020). "Situation du Marché de Travail en 2020," https://www.hcp.ma/La-situation-du-marche-du-travail-en-2020_a2650.html (accessed February 20, 2021).

Hedi, Bchir et al. (2007). "The Cost of Non-Maghreb Achieving the Gains from Economic Integration," *Journal of Economic Integration*, 22 (3): 684–722.

Housseini, Lilya (2020). "Tunisia is Experiencing a Crisis in the Digital Education Space in the Time of Covid," https://www.skynewsarabia.com/middle-east/1386964-%D8%AA%D9%88%D9%86%D8%B3-%D8%AA%D8%B9%D9%8A%D8%B4-%D8%A7%D9%94%D8%B2%D9%85%D8%A9-%D9%81%D8%B6%D8%A7%D1%94-%D8%A7%D9%84%D8%AA%D8%B9%D9%84%D9%8A%D9%85-%D8%A7%D9%84%D8%B1%D9%82%D9%85%D9%8A-%D8%B2%D9%85%D9%86-%D9%83%D9%88%D8%B1%D9%88%D9%86%D8%A7, (accessed March 20, 2021).

Jacobus, Delwaide. (2011). "The Return of the State?," *European Review*, 19: 69–91. doi:10.1017/ S1062798710000311 (accessed May 13, 2021).

Jennifer, Gnan. (2020). "Coronavirus: World Bank Approves \$20m in Healthcare Assistance for Tunisia," *The National News*, https://www.thenationalnews.com/business/coronavirus-world-bank-approves-20m-in-healthcare-assistance-for-tunisia-1.1013555 (accessed May 13, 2021).

Kaouthar, Oudrhiri. (2020). "Projet de loi sur l'utilisation des réseaux sociaux, un nouveau boulet pour l'Exécutif?," *Tel Quel*, https://telquel.ma/2020/04/28/projet-de-loi-sur-lutilisation-des-reseaux-sociaux-un-nouveau-boulet-pour-lexecutif%E2%80%89_1681664 (accessed June 23, 2021).

Luiz Carlos, Bresser-Pereira. (2008). "Globalization, Nation State and Catching-up," *Brazilian Journal of Political Economy*, 28 (4): 557–76.

Macro Poverty Outlook World Bank (2019), Tunisia accessed at: https://thedocs.worldbank.org/en/doc/100591553672422574-0280022019/original/TunisiaMEUApril2019Eng.pdf.

Maichel,Tanchum. (2020). "The Post-COVID-19 Trajectory for Algeria, Morocco and the Western Sahara," *IAI Commentaries*, https://www.iai.it/sites/default/files/iaicom2103.pdf (accessed May 15, 2021).

Matthies, Volker. (1979). "Collective Self-Reliance: Concept and Reality," *Intereconomics*, 14: 75–9, https://doi.org/10.1007/BF02930201 (accessed March 12, 2021).

Meddeb, Hamza. (2020). *Tunisia's Geography of Anger: Regional Inequalities and the Rise of Populism*. Carnegie Endowment for International Peace, Bayreuth, Lebanon: Carnegie Middle Ease Center.

Organisation of Economic Cooperation and Development (OECD). (2020). "Impact of Covid-19 Crisis on Morocco," https://www.oecd.org/mena/competitiveness/The-Covid-19-Crisis-in-Morocco.pdf (accessed May 11, 2021).

OECD Economic Outlook. (2020). https ://www.oecd-ilibrary.org/economics/oecd
-economic-outlook/volume-2020/issue-2_39a88ab1-en (accessed February 3, 2021).

Patrick, Allen, Suzanne J. Konzelmann and JanToporowski, eds. (2021). *The Return of
the State: Restructuring Britain for the Common Good.* Agenda Publishing, United
Kingdom: Newcastle.

Reuters. (2021). "Tunisia Says Health Care System Collapsing Due to COVID-19," https://
www.reuters.com/business/healthcare-pharmaceuticals/tunisia-says-health-care
-system-collapsing-due-covid-19-2021-07-08/ (accessed April 24, 2021).

Robert, A. Stein.(2019). "What Exactly Is the Rule of Law?," *Houston Law Review,* 57: 185.

Robert, Kubinec and Grewal Sharan. (2018). "When National Unity Governments are
Neither National, United, Nor Governments: The Case of Tunisia," *SocArXiv,* 6–7,
11–14, 24–7.

Sadiki, Larbi and SalehLayla (2020). "Reflexive Politics and Arab 'risk society'? COVID-19
and Issues of Public Health," *Orient,* 61 (3): 6–20.

Saleh Layla, Sadiki Larbi. (2020). "The Arab World between a Formidable Virus and a
Repressive State," https://www.opendemocracy.net/en/north-africa-west-asia/arab
-world-between-formidable-virus-and-repressive-state/ (accessed March 10, 2021).

Stein, Robert. (2009). "Rule of Law: What Does It Mean," *Minnesota Journal of
International Law,* 250, https://scholarship.law.umn.edu/mjil/250 (accessed May 16,
2021).

Thabeti, Adil. (2021). "Tunisian Speaker Urges Move to Parliamentary System," https://
www.aa.com.tr/en/africa/tunisian-speaker-urges-move-to-parliamentary-system
/2129254 (accessed June 8, 2021).

World Bank (2019) *Morocco's Economic Update,*https://www.worldbank.org/en/country/
morocco/publication/economic-update-october-2019.

World Integrated Trade Solution WITS. (2020). https://wits.worldbank.org/about_wits
.html (accessed September 10, 2021).

Yerkes and Ben Yahmed. (2019). "Tunisia's Political System: From Stagnation to
Competition," Working paper, Carnegie Endowment for International Peace, https://
carnegieendowment.org/files/Yerkes_Yahmed_Tunisia_Stalemate_final.pdf (accessed
May 27, 2021).

Zeraoulia,Faouzia. (2020). "The Memory of the Civil War in Algeria: Lessons from the
Past with Reference to the Algerian Hirak," *Contemporary Review of the Middle East,* 7
(1): 25–53.

6

The Impact of COVID-19 on the Political and Social Frames in Morocco from a Democratic Perspective

Aisha Kadaoui

Introduction

In times of crisis, democratic functioning may be questioned, highlighting the importance of democracy. On such occasions, not only is democracy but the debate about its crisis also finds itself renewed. The crisis of democracy as a system, and the questioning about how democracy can meet popular needs especially in competitive authoritarian regimes, was problematic even before the emergence of the coronavirus crisis. If the challenges in democratic states were about protecting existing institutions and processes through reforms and adaptation, the challenges in competitive authoritarian states were different. For this latter category in which most MENA countries fall, the crisis has been about protecting the formal institutions and preserving stability. This has largely undermined movements toward democratization since the third wave of democratization.

Clearly, as the literature has shown, the crisis of democracy worldwide is a direct outcome of several endogenous and exogenous factors that are specific to states (Gagnon 2014). In other words, what may generate the crisis in one state may not cause it in another one. Yet, with the emergence of the COVID pandemic, it was clear that panic marked the political actions and reactions of states worldwide. Therefore, coronavirus has accentuated the crisis of democracy and global popular disenchantment, ultimately undermining human rights and freedoms.

Indubitably, some states have managed to control the pandemic and its social and economic repercussions, while many others could not manage the threats regardless of their democratic functioning. Morocco was one of the first countries to respond to the health crisis in the MENA region, by imposing drastic but preventive measures such as a national lockdown and many other restrictions. These policies directly affected the rights and freedom of citizens who were at first supportive of the state's actions.

Needless to say, state effectiveness and "strength" is being questioned following the pandemic's eruption, especially since it has been often linked to its security apparatus (Saleh and Sadiki 2020). At the same time, the lack of infrastructures, qualified personnel, and expertise has been highlighted. This shock has impacted decision-making processes and, therefore, the (potential for) democratization across states, particularly in MENA. Here it is important to state that *the pandemic is engendering Beck's "reflexive modernization"* (Saleh and Sadiki 2020). This means that COVID is forcing society and the individuals to change due to the many problems of "risk society." In Morocco's case, the change consists of a return to the social working site *Le chantier social*, crucial to stability and central to handling the instabilities of risk that the pandemic provokes. The notion of risk society (Beck 1992) and reflexive modernization (Beck and Giddens 1994) are significant to the study of the pandemic and its impact on Morocco. Political and social dynamics have changed following the pandemic, challenging power structures and consequently overall stability within the state.

This chapter will consider the repercussions of COVID responses and measures on democratization and human rights in Morocco. It draws on qualitative and quantitative sociological methods, observations of government decisions, media research, royal speeches and interviews with Moroccan human rights activists and journalists. We argue that while the state was concerned with an immediate response to preserve stability, it didn't attend to the urgent needs for long-term changes in strategy and governance. Moreover, the chapter will demonstrate that some citizens argue that the state response to COVID-19 largely contributed to restoring some authoritarian practices and in undermining the rights and freedoms of citizens. In addition, and the health emergency was instrumentalized to legitimate some "undemocratic" decisions as well as the refurbishment of the security apparatus through the exclusive empowerment of the Minister of Interior in managing the pandemic.

To be able to specify what precisely is at stake, we need to answer some fundamental questions in order to appreciate democratic functioning as well as the impact of the novel coronavirus on the human rights system in Morocco. *How has the state response to the pandemic affected democratization and "democratic learning" in Morocco? How have rights and liberties been undermined during the management of the pandemic, given the refurbishment of Morocco's coercive apparatus?*

These questions will draw attention to political institutions and decision-making process under COVID-19 and the response to it, within the context of the pandemic, paying close attention to democratic learning (Sadiki 2015) in Morocco. We stress in this chapter that socioeconomic situations tremendously affect political change in Morocco and elsewhere (Huber, Rueschemeyer, and Stephens 1993). Moreover, the socioeconomic setting has an impact on democracy and equality, which should be examined and analyzed within specific contexts (Rowe 2018). The impact of COVID-19 on economics and society are, therefore, challenging democratization and its implementation, since the pursuit of economic and social stability is viewed as a priority for the state even when it undermines democracy and freedoms.

The Moroccan Political Reality Pre-COVID-19: An Authoritarianism in the Disguise of Democra*cy*

Before analyzing the democratic and legal trends under COVID-19, it is important to question the nature of democracy in Morocco. The literature offers many definitions and some confusion about the meaning of this political ideal. This is to say that democracy should not be perceived as a single normative concept. It is rather a complicated ideal that embraces a variety of principles and above all a variety of democratic modalities to be implemented within the internal structures of the state.

Hence, these principles, pillars, and uses of democracy are necessary for democratic rule. However, the existence of a democratic showcase may serve to present a veneer democracy instead of consolidating it, especially in hybrid regimes such as Morocco.[1] From the foregoing, this chapter is mainly concerned with impact of the pandemic on democracy in Morocco while taking into consideration the notion of *reflexive modernization* (Beck and Giddens 1994).

A Shaken Status Quo

Analysis of the political sphere in Morocco demonstrates the absence of democracy and the persistence of the *status quo* prior to the emergence of the pandemic. It goes without saying that the Moroccan regime is known for its ability to withstand crises, by implementing countless survival strategies and control mechanisms (Francesco 2007). These range from dividing opponents—*divide and rule strategies*—to the creation of *ex-novo* actors in order to preserve the stability of the regime.

Such strategies are meant for the survival of the regime and may undermine democracy and freedoms in the country, such that the ultimate goal of stability vocation often justifies repressive means. Yet, the manipulation of institutional and constitutional reforms is one of the adopted strategies by the regime. Scholars stress that these reforms were mastered and controlled by the latter, attempting to manage reformist expectations and aims (Sadiki and Bouandel 2016).

Studying the impact of the pandemic on democratization in Morocco requires examining the processes of political reform that took place since the independence of the country. The uniqueness of this process in the MENA region have highlighted a major trend. The transition to democracy is adopted in regime discourses and is an important reference in Arab constitutions. However, if we assume that *the constitution reflects the politics of a state*, we can conclude that political rule is ambiguous, for the simple reason that the Moroccan constitution abounds with contradictions and inconsistencies with democratic principles and pillars (Kadaoui 2020).

Scholars argue that a constitution is required in a democracy, a major necessity (Dahl, Dilemmas of Pluralist Democracy 1982). Yet, it is not the only prerequisite in an analysis of the political system, even when it is full of references to democracy. Needless to say, the implementation of a constitution remains more relevant for the establishment and the consolidation of democracy and the rule of law. This means that an analysis of the Moroccan political sphere and its constitutionalism must take into consideration the implementation and selective application of the Moroccan constitution of 2011. Thus, democracy as well as the constitution are understood through their actual operation, which also means that a democratic façade or the existence of a constitution do not alone point to democratic functioning in a state. Thus, the analysis of the political situation in Morocco brings up many controversies that we will highlight in the following pages. These are crucial to understanding the real impact of the pandemic on democratization in Morocco.

The main controversy that arises relates to the aim of the constitution in Morocco: is it to rationalize and justify the regime or to merely respond to a crisis and ensure, therefore, political stability? A further question regarding this foggy configuration is whether the constitutional reform of 2011 changed this renewed competitive authoritarian political configuration? More particularly, did it set up a constitutional edifice allowing the establishment and consolidation of democracy in Morocco? The aim of this chapter is not the study and analysis of the Moroccan constitution and its democratic uses, but we argue that it is important for the analysis to take into consideration the constitutional set-up, especially that the state's crisis management, when taking into account the constitution, seems to send us back to an intellectual dead end.

All the more so since references to democracy, democratic principles, and implementations are commonly alluded to by the government, which can be interpreted as regime reminders of proceeding on a democratic path. According to many articles of the constitution of 2011, Morocco is committed to consolidating democracy and to establishing the rule of law. However, the emergence of the pandemic has shaken the core of the constitution itself.

The constitutional encumbrances of democratic benchmarks did not, however, prevent the regime from putting constitutionally mandated institutions on hold during the management of the pandemic in Morocco. It goes without saying that the constitutional clutter of democratic references does not prevent either the preservation of inherited constitutional stipulations such as, the subordination of the parliament, the powers of the monarchy, the dependence of the judiciary, and the weakness of provisions for fundamental rights. These are largely conditioned by the stability of the kingdom itself[2] even when there is no democratic rationale for these restrictions.

The question regarding the effectiveness of the Moroccan constitution has been highlighted by scholars even before the pandemic. Many observers have stressed that successive reforms only intend to preserve the *status quo* as we stated previously, and are unlikely to democratize the regime (see, for instance, Benchemsi 2012). It goes without saying that the situation of human rights and freedoms in Morocco has been marked since 2011 by a restoration of the authority of the regime as well as several human rights violations. These confirm early predictions[3] and display a clear diversion from democratic principles and pillars.

Hence, the constant authoritarian configuration has been reinforced following the occurrence of the pandemic in late 2019 and into 2020. The constitution's implementation was at stake and democracy and freedoms were put on hold. Moreover, the pandemic shook the health system in Morocco which constitutionally guarantees the right to health to its citizens. According to Article 31 of the constitution "The State, public establishments and local authorities work to mobilize all the means available to ease equal access for citizens to the conditions allowing them to have access to the health care . . ."[4] This article legally binds the state to facilitate citizens' equal access to healthcare. However, mismanagement has characterized the healthcare system and equal access to its facilities and services, especially in the first months of the pandemic. According to Professor Kamal Marhom El Filali, MD, the infection of the health care personnel as well as understaffing have affected the management of the CHU and *by* extension, crisis management in hospitals, he declared to J. Lefort of the European Investment Bank. "It's an enormous organizational problem."[5]

The mismanagement of the healthcare system was not the only problem Morocco faced during the first months of the pandemic. The sudden occurrence of the pandemic has also led to a parliamentary lockdown even when the constitution states clearly the parliament prerogatives in articles 70 and 71 according to which, the parliament exercises legislative powers under the law. Its powers extend to fundamental rights and freedoms as well as the health system: "The Parliament legislate the rules and principles of the health system."[6] Yet, the same parliament was locked down during the pandemic and the Minister of Interior and the Minister of Health were solely charged with managing the crisis.

We thus arrive at the following situation: the Moroccan political regime was, prior to the emergence of the pandemic, considered to be a hybrid regime, one that displays a façade democracy and preserves inherited authoritarian rule. It is thus important to recognize that in terms of democracy and freedoms, constitutional reform cannot be perceived as a breakthrough to democracy, nor an instrument to consolidate an already initiated process of democratization. The years that followed that reform were marked by a decline in political liberalization, and a decay of rights and freedoms. This was among the reasons for the emergence of protest movements in the Rif region, as well as the regime repression that accompanied it. Until 2020, the political scene was marked by the persistence of the *status quo*. The pandemic and its "risk society" seems to have intensified democratic decline, and to reinforce a security apparatus granted full authority to manage the pandemic.

Democracy and Rule of Law under COVID-19: A Critical Overview

In the aftermath of the spread of the novel coronavirus, the state's political control increased and many strategies were deployed in order to slow reformist trajectories. Await-and-see attitude has characterized the reaction of political actors and institutions following the outbreak, who clearly watched for the Sovereign's (monarch) directions and orientations before responding to political developments. The king being the real head of the state is constitutionally and politically empowered to define political strategies, in accordance with several constitutional prerogatives vested in him.

The authorities awaited the royal directions to declare a state of health emergency on March 19, 2020, when only seventy-seven COVID-19 cases were recorded. The declaration of the measures was viewed to be early, and the authorities were expected to help managing the crisis and its repercussions. A general lockdown was imposed, international and national flights were cancelled, and global trade frozen in order to restrict the spread of the novel coronavirus among citizens and to minimize the consequences of the pandemic on an emerging, already fragile economy.

It was clear worldwide that the pandemic also put democracy under lockdown. However, in Morocco, the lockdown seems to be more severe. It has taken a more significant turn when it comes to democratic governance, since many reactionary measures were put in place at the expense of the rights and freedoms of citizens.

Democratic Governance under COVID-19: Between Rhetoric and Reality

The management of the pandemic required appropriate legislation. Therefore, a state of health emergency was established in order to control the pandemic and to keep COVID-19 hotspots under control. It is important to state that the Moroccan constitution does not contain any provisions regarding health emergencies. Yet, special measures can be taken following the declaration of the state of exception and the declaration of the state of siege—according to articles 59, 49, and 74 of the constitution.

Both citizens and politicians requested at the beginning of the crisis, even before the declaration of the state health emergency, *exceptional* measures in order to control a virus that spreads fast and that is likely to threaten not only the economy but the entire sociopolitical system. Yet, even when measures were taken early, it was clear that the authorities did not really manage to stabilize the situation. The number of confirmed cases was getting higher by the day and the epidemiologic situation was spiraling out of control, especially in metropolises such as Casablanca, Tangier, and Rabat. The measures and policies enacted were not comprehensive enough. The state of health emergency was extended several times, allowing the state to take exceptional measures without really succeeding in managing the pandemic situation. In addition, the state of health emergency has had a direct impact on government decision-making process and the exception has become the new normal.

The following graph displays the evolution of the epidemical situation in Morocco starting from March 14, 2020, until December 2020.

	March 14	March 23	March 31	April	May	June	July	August	September	October	November	December
Number of cases per month	18	143	617	3806	7807	4726	11789	38268	58593	97901	137252	82857
Total number of deaths	0	3	36	134	205	228	353	1141	2152	3695	5846	6000
Total number of cases	18	143	617	4.423	7807	12533	24322	62590	121183	219084	356336	439193

---- Number of cases per month ―― Total number of deaths Total number of cases

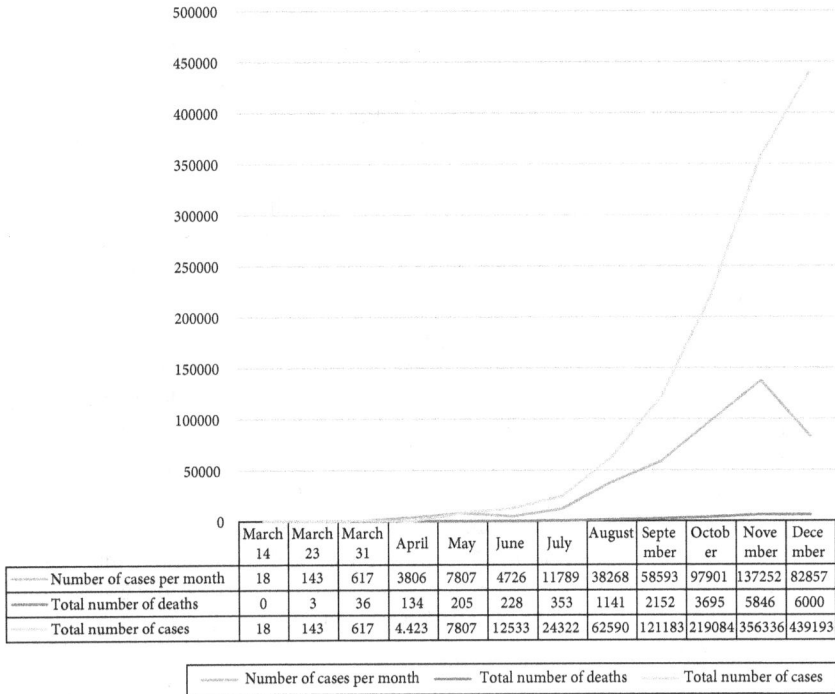

Figure 6.1 Evolution of COVID-19, 2020. *Source: Covid Daily Bulletin—The Moroccan Ministry of health* Data was retrieved from the official website of the ministry of health. http://www.covidmaroc.ma/Pages/AccueilAR.aspx

State responses could not stop virus contagion, as the numbers recorded were getting higher everyday even when parks, mosques, beaches, and gyms were closed. These measures required the adoption of two decrees, establishing therefore a legal frame meant to legitimize the government decisions and actions.

A Custom-Made Legal Framework

The Decree Law No. 2-20-292 and the Decree No. 2-20-293 were adopted, respectively, on March 23–24, 2020, when the number of active cases were still below 200. Besides offering a legal frame, the decrees also offered to the same authorities the means to take action against citizens for noncompliance, in accordance with the provisions of the second decree of March 24, 2020. Yet, from a democratic and legal perspective, this provision has been problematic in the sense that it largely undermines the rights and freedom of citizens.

In other words, the public authorities were given the regime's authorization to take the necessary measures to try and stop the spread of the epidemic. Hence, according to the second article of the Decree Law No. 2-20-293, "The public authorities can take the necessary measures to; ensure that citizens do not leave their homes, to ban the movement of people and to prohibit any gathering or reunion for any reason."[7] It is clear that legal formulations are enforceable. This, in turn, also means that "necessary measures" may undermine liberties and endanger democracy, in the process of enforcing the decree law.

The second article of the decree law is not the only article that seems to pose a problem from a democratic perspective. The third and fifth articles are furthermore interesting for our analysis: they legitimize the restoration of authoritarian practices in Morocco. Thus, according to the third article, "the regional Walis[8] and governors take by virtue of the attributions conferred to them all the necessary measures in order to maintain the public health order." The third article does not specify whether these measures must be aligned with democratic principles and restrictions, or can be implemented even when they undermine the latter.

Another limitation to democracy is apparent in the fifth article of the decree, which formally charges two ministries with its execution, namely the Ministry of Interior and the Ministry of Health. However, only the Ministry of Interior was effectively empowered to manage the crisis, according to one interviewee:[9] "The Ministry of Health wasn't really empowered or given prerogatives in order to help in the management of the crisis; this ministry's sole role was to receive instructions from the ministry of Interior and execute them." Another journalist[10] interviewed confirmed the previous statement and added that "the Ministry of health was largely subordinated to the Interior, and was limited to being a mere receiver of the Interior's instructions."

In fact, according to the Decree Law No. 2-20-292, which establishes the legal framework of the state of health emergency, the government is allowed to take any provisions necessary for the management of the epidemic through decrees, regulatory and administrative decisions, circulars, or notices. According to the fifth article of the same decree law, the government is empowered to take any urgent economic, financial, social, and environmental measures, which hampers legislative procedures and, therefore, popular representation. Yet, the precise role of the government as an institution in the management of the crisis remains unclear even in presence of these new provisions.

In light of this intentional vagueness, one question needs to be posed regarding the management of the crisis, specifically regarding the political actors empowered to manage the crisis. In other words, by hampering the parliament and putting the government on hold, who is actually managing the health crisis in Morocco? And does this management respond to democratic logic? After the decrees, the interior was empowered by the king as the head of state. In fact, a former 20 Février movement's member stated that "Global orientations and strategies [for policymaking] are constitutionally one of the exclusive jurisdictions of the king according to article 47 of the constitution, which also means that the monarchial institution is empowered in this matter by virtue of the supreme law of the state. This also means that the monarchial management of the crisis is in accordance with the constitution" (Interview, January 2021). Hence, the management of a crisis of such magnitude are technically within the prerogatives vested constitutionally in the monarch, who delegated management to the Interior, further legitimating monarchial management of the crisis.

To delve deeper into this matter, it is important to refer to the royal speeches addressed to Moroccan citizens since the beginning of the pandemic. In these speeches, it is clear that the sovereign explicitly appropriates ownership of pandemic crisis management. For instance, he stated, "During this period of crisis, we have succeeded, through our joint efforts, in mitigating the health impact and its economic and social consequences."[11] Yet, it was also clear that the king proclaimed himself in the same speech the godfather of mobilization against COVID-19, calling upon all political and social actors "to unanimously support the efforts deployed at the national level, in order to sensitize society [to the dangers of coronavirus], awaken its conscience and supervise it."

Another royal speech focused on the novel coronavirus and its economic and social implications. As discussed above, the king is authorized according to the constitution, to frame the strategic orientations of the legislative year, as he confirmed in a speech addressed to representatives in parliament. In that specific speech, the king mainly focused on the economic relaunch strategy, emphasizing the well-being of citizens. The king declared:

> This crisis revealed a set of dysfunctions and deficits and it has had a negative impact on the national economy and employment. This is why we have launched an ambitious economic recovery plan and a major universal social coverage project—Projet de couverture sociale. We also stress the imperative to apply the rules of good governance and the need to reform public sector establishments.[12]

In that speech, the king drew a roadmap for the parliament, which is constitutionally bound to execute it without discussion and debate. This means, in other words, that the king is empowered constitutionally to establish legislative guidelines.[13] In fact, this constitutional loophole clearly contradicts the proclaimed democratic orientation of the state's governing apparatus, which was under question even before the pandemic and has been only intensified since COVID's onset. In terms of management, according to a journalist, "It is clear that the measures taken emanated from the palace, which charged the Ministry of Interior, known to be a sovereign Ministry for the management of the crisis. Yet, the king drew the roadmap for the Interior and for the parliament, [the latter which] has been put on hold" (Interview, February 2021). When the king is empowered to act on behalf of all three branches of government, this does indeed undermine democratization, calling into question the constitution and its role in promoting and supervising political reform and transition.

Complicating matters, the majority of citizens seemed to encourage the palace's management of the crisis due to their growing mistrust in political actors and institutions. They view a monarchial management of state affairs as crucial, precisely because their trust in the government, parliament, and political parties has declined in recent years. Observations of debates and discussions on social media platforms, being new arenas of the traditional public sphere and, therefore, digitized arenas of political activism, confirms this trend. In addition, the belief that "the king is good, while political classes are rotten"[14] is widespread in Morocco since the independence of the country. The general tendency is to trust an institution known for its abilities for continuous self-renewal and for anticipating reforms, and to mistrust on the other hand all other political actors who are perceived as incompetent forces serving only their personal agendas instead of pursuing the general will and public interest.

It is clear that the crisis of trust in political actors has deepened since the pandemic. A civil society activist interviewed for this chapter stressed that mistrust of political parties in particular has grown during coronavirus: "Our trust in the political parties was non-existent before the pandemic, but parties they have proved once again [under COVID] that they are unable to manage a crisis of such magnitude and that they have no significant role in the political sphere." He added, "In light of the latest developments, why do we need to organize elections in the future since we have a wise king to govern us?"[15] (Interview, April 2021). This is to highlight that the implications of the pandemic on democracy goes beyond the establishment and the deepening of a trust crisis in political leaders. It underlines and emphasizes a crisis in political participation and a subsequent rejection of the electoral system itself—a central pillar of democracy!

As for legislative proceedings, the ratification of the decree laws by the parliament did not follow the conventional process. Moreover, the persisting subordination of the legislative to the executive throws into doubt the entire policymaking process and reveals the fragility of political representation in Morocco. It goes without saying that this subordination undermines the system of checks and balances, which may be more important to a democracy than a mere existence of the parliament (Dahl 1982). There is no doubt that the parliament has been given extended prerogatives by virtue of the constitution of 2011 (Kadaoui 2020), but it remains, years after the implementation of the latter, a body expected to carry out the wishes of the monarchical executive.

This is to say, the parliament as a representational body cannot reject a monarchial decision, order, or bill. Parliamentary votes usually favor the general orientations of the executive, which detracts from the legitimacy of the voting process within this branch of government. Moreover, passing bills that undermine rights and freedoms questions the putative role of parliament in consolidating democracy and in representing and legislating the people's will. In other words, even though the parliament's subordination to the executive is constitutionally mandated, the pandemic has brought to the fore the dysfunctions within the decision-making process and highlighted the insufficiencies that lie within the parliament itself.

In addition, empowering the government to take measures of any kind, according to the decree law, effectively shuts down the parliament as a legislative body. This in turn automatically excludes the people from the state's decision-making processes and jeopardizes all conventional democratic principles. If COVID-19 has fueled a democratic crisis all over the world (Repucci and Slipowitz 2020), in Morocco, considering the absence of a democratic configuration of power, matters are even worse. The pandemic has had a direct impact on political institutions that were shuttered, on the rights and freedoms that were weakened, and on the process of political reform that was halted. COVID-19 allowed for a strong comeback of authoritarian practices, and proved the insufficiency and the subordination of representation powers. This casts a dubious shadow over not only the entire process of reform in Morocco but also the regime's very will to implement it.

Rights and Freedoms in Morocco Amid COVID-19

Amid COVID-19 and the disruptions and shocks it brought, democracy has been put on hold and democratic pillars eroded, as argued previously. The public health crisis has threatened global democracy. Both democratic and competitive authoritarian states have used the emergency to supress rights and freedoms and to restore state power.

In Morocco, the pandemic has legalized the abuse of power, while the decrees adopted amid COVID-19 have eroded the democratic pillars. Another manifestation of the country's risk society is that these practices have undermined human rights. Since the parliament has been hamstrung and limited to an institution voting on instruction, the regime has granted itself unconstitutional prerogatives and extended powers. It is important to highlight that the public health emergency allows governments to also restrict some human rights in violation of international human rights law. According to the Siracusa principles: "Public health may be invoked as a ground for limiting certain rights in order to allow a State to take measures dealing with a serious threat to the health of the population or individual members of the population. These measures must be specifically aimed at preventing disease or injury or providing care for the sick and injured."[16] Yet, what is unethical democratically, is establishing restrictions that jeopardize basic and legitimate human rights in contradiction to democratic principles.

In fact, this fear of democratic decline, of the resurgence of authoritarianism and of the suppression of human rights, has been present since the beginning of the crisis. It prompted experts within the UN to urge states not to take advantage of the pandemic in order to supress rights or marginalize minorities.[17] Nevertheless, responses to the crisis within a context of generalized shock have served as grounds for states to restrict rights, threaten freedoms, and erode democratic pillars. If democracy is struggling in democratic states, it is curbed even more in fragile democracies and competitive authoritarian regimes. Democracy is henceforth in Morocco, a "luxury and less of a necessity, as it has always served as a façade for the international community," according to one human rights activist (Interview, January 2021).

Democracy and human rights in Morocco are struggling amid COVID-19, due to the absence of strong safeguards against the abuse of power. Of course, the freedoms in Morocco pre-COVID-19 were already shaky, as rights were conditional even when guaranteed by the supreme law. The Moroccan constitution of 2011, even when it subscribes to the guarantee of fundamental rights, conditions them under the monarchy. Hence, the constitutional encumbrance of fundamental rights does not necessitate their implementation, as explained earlier. However, with the declaration of the state health emergency, freedoms were even more restricted by the decree law that established a legal framework legalizing imprisonment and fines against anyone who opposes or does not abide by the health emergency bill.

In addition, freedoms, both civic and political, were already facing constitutional ambiguity. Political parties, representatives and human rights activists were not allowed prior to COVID-19 to utter statements that contradict constitutional "restrictions" and conditionalities. This also implies that these actors were not free to discuss topics and issues considered (by the authorities) red lines "not to be crossed." Amid COVID-19, the freedom of expression was further obstructed and journalists were subjected to many restrictions, leading to the imprisonment of some under *fake news* accusations (Reuters 2020).

The pandemic has allowed the regime to tighten restrictions already established, as one human rights activist stressed, "We are not talking about an increase in oppression. The regime has always been oppressive and has always repressed its opponents, but

COVID-19 has served as a legitimation grounds for existing authoritarian practices"
(Interview, January 2021). Both activists and representatives have criticized the return
of repression and human rights violations. One emphasized that "The measures taken as
well as the delegation of power to the interior have largely undermined the 'democratic
transition' in Morocco" (Interview, January 2021). It is important to state that there is
an established uncertainty in Morocco regarding democracy. Continuous political
liberalization is, therefore, viewed by politicians and activists as a democratic transition.
Thus, we stress that Morocco is engaged in a delayed political liberalization process that
has halted under COVID the democratic transition instead of proceeding with it.

Moreover, many representatives have also criticized the management of the
pandemic and how it negatively impacted human rights and freedoms in Morocco
and have increased poverty in the country, as well as impacting citizens' trust in
the government.[18] As mentioned previously, the state of health emergency allowed
the government to take exceptional measures to manage the epidemic in a manner
permitting violation of freedoms of expression, and assembly, as enabled by the
decree law. One interviewee described the law as "a concrete manifestation of
authoritarianism's return."[19]

Human rights violations have abounded. They have been severely criticized
by citizens following leaks about the adoption of a bill meant to restrict freedom
of expression on the net 2.0. The government approved in March 2020 a bill which
establishes severe restrictions on the freedom of expression on social media. The bill
N.22-20 was dubbed by some citizens as "the bib law—La loi bavette." It was meant
to prohibit the call for boycott against national products on social media, intending
to restrict the freedom of speech and expression and undermining at the same time
constitutional rights and freedoms. Though this bill is unconstitutional, according to
articles 25, 28 and 78 of the constitution, it was approved by the government in order
to codify clamping down on freedoms in social media networks, such as Facebook and
Twitter, since they are new arenas of "counter-power" in the country.

Both activists and a number of academics have criticized the bill and have agreed
that it exterminates and undermines human rights in Morocco. According to a civil
society activist, "The bib law is meant to criminalize any call for boycotts which has
became a new trend in Morocco. The purpose therefore is to prevent the integration
of the boycott culture in the collective unconsciousness in order to protect some well-
known [and powerful] individuals in the future" (Interview, April 2021).

In light of these developments under COVID-19, it became clear that rights and
freedoms are largely undermined and measures taken either by the government or
the Ministry of Interior[20] to silence critics. This has led to many instances of abuse
of power. By March 28, 2020, the prosecution had taken legal action against fifty-
six individuals for publishing false information on the Internet about the novel
coronavirus, as reported by the press.[21] According to the same source, "Around 450
people have also been arrested for violations of the state of health emergency since
the entry into force of the decree-law of March 24." The number of legal actions taken
against individuals two months later rose to 91,623, according to the prosecution: "As
part of the implementation of the repressive provisions provided for by Decree-Law
2.20.292 on the state of health emergency and the procedures for its declaration, some

91,623 individuals were prosecuted by public prosecutors in the courts of the Kingdom for violation of the state of emergency since the this went into effect, as of Friday, May 22 at 4 p.m." Hence, according to the annual report of the judicial police, 968,967 violations of the decree law of March 24 had been identified, 196,972 individuals of which have been subjected to judicial investigation.[22]

Moreover, freedom of the press was also obstructed under the pandemic. A journalist observes that the press was "largely undermined under COVID-19, and this is because of several restrictions journalists were subjected to, among others the requirement of the movement authorization granted by the authorities" (Interview, March 2021). This requirement violates the freedom of press that was enshrined in the constitution back in 2011. In other words, authorities during COVID-19 were empowered to limit and restrict press freedoms, through withholding the required authorization of movement from journalists. To provide the full picture, it is worth pointing out that freedom of press was in fact almost nonexistent even before the surge of COVID-19. As another journalist put it, "the freedom of press was already restricted in Morocco even before the pandemic, but subjecting journalists to the authority of the Ministry of Interior intensified violations of the freedom of press, simply because the ministry required journalists to violate professional secrecy and to report on the files they are working on" (Interview, February 2021). The Interior, in other words, did not allow journalists to fulfill their role as a "third party," a symbol of counter-power that citizens entrusted to keep them informed.

The violations were numerous, and have had varying impact on liberties and rights in Morocco, since the freedoms of press and expression are pivotal for democracy and the rule of law. A former journalist stressed that "there is a correlation between the suppression of the freedoms and the political reality in Morocco," which according to him "is no more than a disguised authoritarianism that was reveled under the health crisis" (Interview, April 2021). The regime was given the opportunity to implement and pass non-democratic laws, taking advantage of the epidemic and the shock that followed.

It is not difficult to say, then, that COVID-19 has permitted the establishment of new authoritarian practices, as well as the restoration of older ones. This may be explained by the fear of instability that the pandemic could provoke. Constitutional institutions have been disabled, the parliament ambushed, and democracy is put under lockdown in the sense that the response to the crisis has eroded central democratic pillars and principles. Our research in this chapter has found that the abuse of power has been one of the outcomes of COVID-19, more severe and aggressive than the worldwide trend in a country where democracy is wielded exclusively as a façade not as a horizon for prosperity, equality, and justice.

Economics, Inequalities, Aid and Dependencies

The decree law of March 24 has allowed the regime to enforce lockdown measures. Yet, these measures seem to be irrational and arbitrary and have not served to lower the number of active cases.[23] Instead, they have enabled the state to impose more severe restrictions on some deprived areas. This leading to the deepening of socioeconomic inequalities in Morocco and other MENA countries (Hoogeveen, Malaeb, and Phadera 2021).

The population has, therefore, faced severe constraints, but leaders urged citizens to adapt to the pandemic until "a vaccine is ready." Adopting the "new normal" rhetoric has served the state to implement measures undermined by human rights and eroded democracy. It has also exacerbated inequalities among the citizens. In addition, COVID-19 is considered to be the first pandemic in the last 100 years which has caused a great shock to the global economy, outperforming the global financial crisis in terms of impact and repercussions and even uncertainty (Brannen, Ahmed, and Newton 2020). Jerome Powell, the chair of the US Federal Reserve System stated: "The scope and speed of this downturn are without modern precedent, significantly worse that any recession since World War II."

Moreover, according to a World Bank report in June 2020, the global economy is witnessing a crisis worse than the Great Depression of 1920 and it is causing a recession worldwide, even in advanced economies. If the economic impact is tremendous in developed countries, it is even more serious in emerging economies. Morocco, hit so strongly and severely by the pandemic, has taken many macroeconomic measures in order to reduce the impact of the crisis. Yet, these measures failed to stabilize the fragile economy or minimize inequalities. At the time of writing, the impact is clear on the economy. Skyrocketing prices are threatening stability as citizen calls for revolts are multiplying.

In this regard, it is important to refer to one of the monarch's speeches during COVID-19, in which he urged political leaders to design a relaunch strategy whose contours were already outlined by the monarchial institution. It was also clear that the economy was considered by the monarchy to be a pillar of stability, and that the fear of eventual escalation in social unrest has motivated the regime to help the unfortunate during the first months of the lockdown. A fund called *the COVID-19 fund* was meant to manage the crisis along these lines. Yet, the efficacy of the plan seemed to be questioned by the citizens in the absence of transparency and in the presence of rampant corruption.

The importance of the economic relaunch and its hoped-for role in ensuring stability was clear in the monarch's speeches since the beginning of the crisis. Economic and social management was one of the prerogatives given to the king even prior to COVID-19. The creation of the COVID fund, which relied on a budget of 3 percent of the GDP, as well as the general directions for the economic strategy, were all set up by the king himself. Other political institutions and actors were only expected to execute monarchial instructions in a perpetuation of the wait-and-see attitude that has been the predominant mode of political behavior since Morocco's independence. Concerning transparency, ambiguity has surrounded the fund and many citizens did not benefit from state aid, which has heightened inequalities and contributed to aggravating poverty. Hence, according to a study led by collective researchers on the impact of the COVID-19 on inequalities in Morocco, the poverty rate has increased from 33.3 to 34.8 percent, and has reached values of 27.6 percent after granting the aid (Aazi et al. 2020). Basically, this means that COVID-19 contributed to increasing inequalities and poverty.

From an international perspective, and taking into consideration Morocco's links to the West and international financial structures, amid COVID-19 the country has benefited from an exceptional contribution of €450 million from the European Union,[24] a loan of $48 million from the World Bank,[25] as well as a contribution of $670,000 from the United States.[26] It is, therefore, important to state that these aids from Western countries mainly intends to increase "linkages" and may as well serve as a "leverage" tool (Levitsky and Way 2006). Morocco's links and ties with the European Union particularly are strong. The EU has granted to the country much development aid, but it is important to highlight in this regard that such assistance serve as a form of foreign policy and is not granted freely; it must be considered a significant instrument of influence (Candas, 2010).

This is to say, COVID-19 has increased the dependencies on Western states as well as on international financial institutions. The aid and loans dispensed will definitely be, per the inner-workings of international politics, means of exerting pressure on Morocco in the long run. This assistance aids may at first glance appear to be purely humanitarian aid, to help Morocco recover from the severe economic repercussions of the health crisis. However, pandemic aid is, in fact, an instrument of a more multifaceted strategy of influence over Morocco. Whether such pressure will work in the direction of democratic reform is unclear.

Conclusion

COVID-19 has indeed reshaped the future, through repercussions that have affected all areas of life around the world. Even now, no one knows for sure what will be the future of politics, international relations, societies, or economic and financial sectors. Both states and international organizations and structures are trying to come up with coping strategies and mechanisms to recover from a crisis that humanity was unprepared for.

This chapter has demonstrated what Morocco's risk society looks like from the vantage point of democratization. COVID-19 was indeed instrumentalized in order to restore the Moroccan state's power, further eroding pillars of democracy and undermining the human rights. The international context, marked by the shock and fear, was thus favorable for a restoration of authoritarianism which had already been carefully disguised within a merely façade democracy. Furthermore, inequalities have been accentuated and dependencies on Western states and international structures deepened. Together, these developments may, in the long run, endanger a democratic transition that is yet to be credibly initiated.

As of this writing, the COVID-19 pandemic is still sweeping through Morocco and the rest of the world. The pandemic, although caused by a virus with multiple variants, did not stop there. It endangered the economy, politics, and even rights and freedoms. The COVID-19 crisis was not only untimely and detrimental to life and health. It is also increasingly clear that it has suffocated economic, social, and political systems. Fears caused by the onset of the pandemic are not exclusively health-related. They also extend to democratization in societies struggling to establish democratic reforms.

Notes

1 Democratic index of 2021, *The Economist*.
2 According to the preamble of the constitution, the primacy of the International law, including treaties, pacts and agreements is conditioned by the existence of the Kingdom:

> "... grant to international conventions duly ratified by the state, within the framework of the provisions of the Constitution and the laws of the Kingdom, with respect for his immutable national identity, and upon publication of these conventions, primacy over the internal law of the country" Preamble of the constitution of 2011.

3 Several violations of human rights were recorded, especially violations of the freedom of speech and reunion.
4 The Moroccan Constitution of 2011, Article 31.
5 Statement of Professor Kamal Marhom El Filali, MD to J. Lefort.
   Janel Siemplenski Lefort (2020).
6 "Are of the domain of the law, in addition to the matters which are expressly devolved to it by other articles of the Constitution: ... the principles and rules of the health system" Article 71. Constitution of 2011.
7 Decree No. 2-20-293: http://www.sgg.gov.ma/Portals/0/BO/2020/BO_6870_Fr.pdf?ver=2020-04-09-094443-083
8 The governor of administrative divisions.
9 Y.y (January, 2021).
10 N. S (February, 2021).
11 Discours royal à l'occasion du 67ème anniversaire de la Révolution du roi et du peuple (Aout 21, 2020).
12 Discours au Parlement à l'occasion de l'ouverture de la 1ère session de la 5ème année législative de la 10ème législature (October 9, 2020).
13 According to the Art. 52 of the constitution of 2011, "The King can address messages to the Nation and to the Parliament. Messages are read in both Houses and may not be the subject of any debate."
14 https://core.ac.uk/download/pdf/226982817.pdf
15 Legislative, communal and regional elections were organized on September 8, 2021.
16 4672bc122.pdf.
17 "While we recognize the severity of the current health crisis and acknowledge that the use of emergency powers is allowed by international law in response to significant threats, we urgently remind States that any emergency responses to the coronavirus must be proportionate, necessary and non-discriminatory," the experts said, https://thewire.in/rights/un-experts-coronavirus-emergency
18 An intervention of the representative, Hicham El Mhajri of September 11, 2020.
   View the full intervention on: https://www.youtube.com/watch?v=MW5dJkPWBpc
19 A.T (January, 2021).
20 The management of the pandemic was mainly delegated to the Ministry of Interior, the government seemed to not be concerned and sometimes to not be informed of the development of the crisis. The chief of government could not answer basic questions during many interviews with the press, and praised the management led by the Interior.
21 https://www.lesiteinfo.com/maroc/etat-durgence-sanitaire-voici-le-nombre-darrestations-au-maroc/

22 https://www.infomediaire.net/le-bilan-2020-complet-de-la-police-marocaine/
23 View Graphic 1.
24 https://ec.europa.eu/commission/presscorner/detail/en/IP_20_2524
25 https://www.worldbank.org/en/country/morocco/overview
26 https://ma.usembassy.gov/u-s-provides-additional-assistance-to-morocco-to-respond
-to-novel-coronavirus-covid-19/#:~:text=RABAT%20%E2%80%93%20Today%2C
%20the%20U,for%20International%20Development%20(USAID).

References

Aazi, Fatima-Zahra, Martine Audibert, Youssef Bouazizi and Safia Fekkaklouhail (2020). *Crise sanitaire et répercussions économiques et sociales au Maroc.* Casablanca: Revue Réflexions Économiques.

Autexier, Christian (1997). "Chapitre 5: Les droits fondamentaux, Introduction au droit public allemand," *Revue générale du droit.*

Beck, Ulrich. (1992). *The Risk Society: Towards a New Modernity.* University of Munich, Germany: Sage Publications

Beck, Ulrich, et Anthony and Lash, Scott Giddens (1994). *Reflexive Modernization— Politics, Tradition and Aesthetics in the Modern Social Order.* Cambridge: Polity.

Benchemsi, Ahmed. (2012). "Morocco: Outfoxing the Opposition," *Journal of Democracy,* 23 (1): 57–69.

Bourricaud, François (1959). "Démocratie et polyarchie Une forme nouvelle du pouvoir," *Esprit,* 273 (5): 772–88.

Brannen, Samuel, HabibaAhmed and HenryNewton (2020). *Covid-19 Reshapes the Future.* Washington, DC: Center for Strategic and International Studies (CSIS), 25

Candas, Ulas, (2010). "L'influence normative de l'Union Européenne par le biais de liens conventionnels," *Ankara Avrupa Çalışmaları Dergisi,* 9 (2): 21–44.

Dahl, Robert. (1982). *Dilemmas of Pluralist Democracy.* New Haven: Yale University Press.

Ferrié, Jean-Noël and Baudouin Dupret. (2011). "La nouvelle architecture constitutionnelle et les trois désamorçages de la vie politique marocaine," *Confluences Méditerranée,* 78 (3): 25–34.

Francesco, Cavatorta. (2007). "More than Repression. The Significance of Divide & Impera, In the Middle East and North Africa. The Case of Morocco," *Journal of Contemporary African Studies,* 25 (2): 187–203.

Gagnon, Selen A. Ercan and Jean-Paul (Winter 2014). "The Crisis of Democracy, Which Crisis Which Democracy?" *Democratic Theory,* 1 (2): 1–10.

Gosepath, Stefan. (2007). "Equality," in Edward N. Zalta (ed.), *The Stanford Encyclopedia of Philosophy,* https://plato.stanford.edu/entries/equality/#Aca/> (accessed June 27, 2020).

Hoogeveen, Johannes, Bilal Malaeb and Lokendra Phadera. (2021). "COVID-19 Inequities in MENA: How Data and Evidence can Help us do Better," *World Bank Blogs,* September 2, https://bit.ly/3teVKBE (accessed October 14, 2021).

Huber, Evelyne, Dietrich Rueschemeyer, et John D. Stephens. (1993). "The Impact of Economic Development on Democracy," *The Journal of Economic Perspectives,* 7 (3): 71–86.

J.O. (2020). Personal interview. (A. Kadaoui, Intervieweur), December 4.

Janel Siemplenski Lefort, (2020). "Un Soulagement Rapide," December 2, EIB; https://www.eib.org/fr/stories/morocco-health-system-covid-19

Kadaoui, Aicha. (2020). *Etude sur le changement politique au Maroc à la lumière de la constitution de 2011: Réforme politique ou transition démocratique?* Casablanca: University Hassan II.

Levitsky, Steven and Lucan Way (2006). "Linkage versus Leverage. Rethinking the International Dimension of Regime Change," *Comparative Politics*, 379–400.

Markoff, John. (1999). "Globalization and the Future of Democracy," *Journal of Word Systems Research*, 5 (2): 207–309.

Mcelhenny, Shaun. (2004). *Minimalist Conception of Democracy: A Normative Analysi.* New York: New York University.

Moghadam, Valentine M. (2013). "What is Democracy, Promises and Perils of the Arab World," *Current Sociology*, , 61 (4): 393–408.

Moore, Barrington. (1966). *Social Origins of Dictatorship and Democracy: Lord and Peasant in the Making of the Modern World.* Boston: Beacon Press.

Moses, Adagbabiri. (2015). "Constitutionalism and Democracy: A Critical Perspective," *International Journal of Humanities and Social Science*, 5 (12): 108–14.

Naimi, Mohamed. (2016). "Mouvement du 20 février et appropriation de l'espace public au Maroc," *Les Cahiers d'EMAM, no. 28.*

Popper, Karl and E.H. Gombrich (2013). "The Open Society and Its Enemies: New One-Volume Edition," Paperback, Princeton University Press, 808.

Repucci, Sarah, et Amy Slipowitz (2020). "Democracy under Lockdown, The Impact of Covid on the Global Struggle for Freedom," *Freedom in the House*, October, 16.

Reuters. 2020. "Morocco Makes a Dozen Arrests over Coronavirus Fake News," March 19, https://www.reuters.com/article/us-health-coronavirus-morocco-idUSKBN2162DI (accessed February 23, 2021).

Rousseau, Jean Jacques. (2011). *Le contrat Social.* Nouvelle Edition. Flammarion, Collection GF.

Rowe, Christopher (2018). "Plato on Equality and Democracy," in Gerasimos Santas and Georgios Anagnostopoulos (eds.), *Democracy, Justice, and Equality in Ancient Greece: Historical and Philosophical Perspectives*, 63–82. Springer Verlag.

Sadiki, Larbi. (2015). "Towards a 'Democratic Knowledge' Turn? Knowledge Production in the age of the Arab Spring," *The Journal of North African Studies*, 20 (5): 702–21.

Sadiki, Larbi and Youcef Bouaandel. (2016). "The Post Arab Spring Reform; The Maghreb at a Crossroads," *DOMES, Digest of Middle East Studies*, 25 (1): 109–31.

Sadiki, Larbi and Leyla Saleh, (2020). "Reflexive Politics and Arab 'risk society'? Covid 19 and Issues of Public Health," *Deutsche Zeitschrift fü Politik und Wirtschaft des Orients*, 60 (3): 6–20.

Sadiki, Larbi and Saleh, Leyla L. Sadiki. (2020). "The Arab World between a Formidable Virus and a Repressive State, What Does the Coronavirus Pandemic Spell for Democracy in the Arab World?" *Récupéré sur Open Democracy*, April 6, https://www.opendemocracy.net/en/north-africa-west-asia/arab-world-between-formidable-virus-and-repressive-state/ (accessed February 4, 2022)

Schmitter, Philippe C. and Terry Lynn Karl. (1991). "What Democracy is and is Not," *Journal of Democracy*, 2 (3): 75–88.

Y.S. (2020). Personal interview. (A. KADAOUI, Intervieweur), December 10.

Part III

The Mashreq (Eastern MENA)

7

Risking Health Security

COVID-19, the WHO, and the Limits of the State in Egypt

Mohammed Moussa and Takayuki Yokota

Introduction

Global pandemics reveal the often taken-for-granted yet interdependent connections between different regions in the world. Although states demarcate ostensibly separate political, economic, social, and cultural spaces, the unchecked spread of the novel coronavirus (COVID-19) created the perception of a threat that goes beyond borders. Governments have found themselves cooperating with a variety of actors to hastily set up and maintain public health strategies. Fears about the coronavirus primarily revolve around its deadly symptoms and the efficacy of infectious disease control measures such as vaccines and quarantines. The agenda of public health, spearheaded by the World Health Organization (WHO) in the pre-coronavirus period, has witnessed renewed impetus within and among states. Uncertainty continues to shape the perceptions of both decision-makers and ordinary people. Scientific experts and the national body politic have participated in an uneven process of risking the pandemic—constructing the nature and boundaries of the public health threat. In this chapter, we analyze the impact of the global pandemic on Egypt as an uncertain risk. The Egyptian body politic is located, it will be argued, in a web of global, regional, and local actors, including politicians, experts, intergovernmental organizations, and pharmaceutical companies. During the pandemic, the continuity of the range of political power was not interrupted. On the contrary, the state's ability to create, monitor, and discipline the behavior of citizens and foreigners alike was justified by the perceived uncertainty of the virus and its contagious nature. A new risk presented an existential threat to public health and the security of citizens.

Our analysis of the process of risking the coronavirus by the Egyptian body politic is divided into two parts. Part one contains a theoretical discussion of Timothy Mitchell's poststructuralist account of the state as effect and Ulrich Beck's notion of risk as commonly perceived threat of modernity's radicalized consequences. Mitchell's arguments about the state provides one of the points of reference for this chapter's analysis. States are not structural organizations that simply dominate societies. Structural effects are engendered by the discipline, surveillance, and control of the body of the human subject and its subjectivity or "the individual mind."[1] Beck's contribution to the study of risk can be untidily unpacked into two components: first, the objective reality of the new consequences of a radicalized modernity; and second, the perception of threats that seemingly elude and render obsolete existing solutions. The risking of events in public discourses, both global and national, is also essentially intersubjective. Risk is, therefore, a species of knowledge. In part two, we analyze the process of risking the coronavirus by the Egyptian body politic in a global web of organizations and actors. The uncertainty of the global pandemic contributes to closer affinities between science and politics. Public health has become a commonly espoused agenda among global, regional, and national actors in the Middle East. Capacity development, good governance, and public health discourses do highlight the glaring inequalities of healthcare provision within and across Arab states in a global capitalist system.[2] Egyptian efforts at managing infectious diseases before and during the pandemic include extensive collaboration with intergovernmental organizations such as the WHO and UNICEF. A national strategy of infectious disease control, on the levels of perception and implementation, reproduces the body politic. Despite the publicized reassertion of the Egyptian state, the transfer of foreign expert authority and medical know-how betrays an unavoidable dependence on external actors.

State as Effect and Risk as Anticipation

Two aspects appear to characterize global discourses on health security. First, the need to protect human beings through disease control and the accompanying regulation of public health. Second, the role of states in managing health crises, both threats and actual effects. Thus, a rules-based international regime exists extending from the global to the local in the twenty-first century. Infectious diseases pose an evasive risk that crosses imagined borders and the complex apparatuses of security of states that aim to keep them from becoming porous—fixing the ever elusive inside and outside of the national body politic. To this end, we do not consider the state to be a structure that stands atop society or occupying an autonomous position above citizens. We adopt Mitchell's arguments about the disciplinary methods of states that occur at the level of "microphysical forms of power."[3] These disciplinary methods do not simply control actions of individuals but create them in a physical context.[4] What passes off as the structure of the modern state is "an effect of detailed processes of spatial organization, temporal arrangements, functional specification, and supervision and surveillance, which create the appearance of a world fundamentally divided into state and society."[5] The state strives to create, monitor, and discipline the behavior of subjects, citizens, immigrants, and foreigners, in a variety of spaces.

Beck's notion of risk provides an entry point to identify and explore the Egyptian state's attempt to reassert its control of a broad range of spheres. A "radicalized modernity," a culmination of the first stage of modernity, in which progress in technology and science, among other arenas, generates the "new risks" of "manufactured uncertainties and dangers."[6] Human actions cause problems outside of the previous horizon of the political and scientific management associated with the nation-state. For manufactured uncertainties

> are dependent on human decisions, created by society itself, immanent to society and thus externalizable, collectively imposed and thus individually unavoidable; their perceptions break with the past, break with experienced risks and institutionalized routines; they are incalculable, uncontrollable and in the final analysis no longer (privately) insurable (climate change, for example).[7]

Consequences generated by modernity are initially unforeseen by policymakers, scientists, companies, and ordinary people. However, risks are not simply actually existing events but acquire salience by the spectre of an "anticipated catastrophe."[8] Competing "realistic" and "constructivist" accounts present in Beck's work reveal the tensions of a physical risk that can be reproduced or changed and a subjective perception of risk.[9] Risk is no less than a species of knowledge.

Here Beck's notion appears to require experts, politicians, and the general public to imagine a threat or problem for it to become a global risk. Anticipated catastrophe runs through global and national discourses. Nonetheless, Beck questioned the assumption that risk is an ally of the nation-state espoused by Mary Douglas and Michel Foucault in a general critique of "methodological nationalism" and proposed it to be "an unreliable ally" or "a potential antagonist."[10] New forms of risk appear over and under the state. Global risks pose existential threats, to both citizens and nation-states, which put into jeopardy not only the legitimacy but also the possibility of the state.[11] In addition, side effects caused by progress move politics from the state or the formal sphere to a "sub-politics" located in society.[12] Although such an account of the destructive consequences of modernity uncritically reproduces the binary of state and society, the state is decentered in a vast complex of unpredictable relations. Threats such as terrorism may even lead to the revival of a Hobbesian preoccupation of security but ultimately reveal a "phantom state" and its inability to solve problems of a globalized or transnational nature.[13] When risks arise in national discourses, states struggle to define its identity, impact, and solution. However, the state stubbornly remains one of the principal referents for action among a set of competing actors ranging from intergovernmental organizations to experts to communities.

In the post–Cold War era, the concept of security among scholars has been expanded, beyond the conventional framework of security studies, to include non-military components such as the economy, environment, and infectious diseases.[14] The constructivist approach of the Copenhagen School proposes an intersubjective concept of security without any seeming universal pretensions. Repetitive "speech acts," described as a "securitizing move," by a "securitizing actor" that an object is a threat seek to persuade an "audience" of the validity of this claim.[15] Events or issues, perceived to be threats, in this process of securitization can become "politicized" and a policy concern for states to take action—at times justifying emergency measures or the suspension of "normal" politics. Nonetheless, security, including non-military factors, is continually redefined by actors other than the state with whom it has to and does compete to assert wavering claims of legitimacy and competence. Human security's appearance in the last three decades signals a shift from the exclusive focus on the state, without necessarily rejecting it, to the protection of people in a global context.[16] A people-centered approach to human security can also emphasize freedom from fear, want and indignity needed to realize complementary "basic goods."[17] States can potentially accommodate definitions of security agreed outside of the narrow confines of national decision-makers, backed by intergovernmental organizations. These intergovernmental organizations exercise authority for national elites to follow suit in the implementation of their guidelines, rules, and agendas. The definition of "health security" as a "duty" for states to protect citizens from "emergencies with health consequences" falls in the scope of the WHO's activity.[18]

Beck's discussion of Aihwa Ong's "global assemblage" focuses on the unexpected cooperation among "institutions, governments, experts and ethics across borders and great geographical distances" to contain SARS when "[t]ransnational intervention spaces arose where risk zones threatened to violate the prevailing safety norms."[19] No single center possesses a preponderant presence. Multiple actors simultaneously cooperate and compete in frequent public spectacles of authority, know-how, and control. Moreover, the application of the Deleuzian concept of assemblage to the Middle East reveals the web-like relations that bind together constantly moving bodies in a variety of spaces.[20] Dynamic interconnections characterize the milieu in which states find themselves while they struggle to name and manage events as risks. Control of contagious diseases frequently transforms the conception of national borders and territories and occasion the ceding of claims of state sovereignty. However, the sharing of expertise and disease control techniques between actors can greatly expand the possibilities for government control, surveillance, and monitoring. In addition, the public spectacle of cooperation can proffer much-needed legitimacy to state elites to justify the suspension of rights and liberties. Disease control measures recommended by intergovernmental organizations such as the WHO can justify or augment existing extraordinary acts curtailing the freedom of citizens or travelers.

The ubiquity of risk undermines previous forms of threat analysis and management associated with the national state. Beck argues that when "[e]veryone poses a risk for everyone else. The qualitative distinction either/or is replaced by the quantitative difference between more or less."[21] Citizens, immigrants, and foreigners are literally the embodiment of risk. An indiscriminate mass of human bodies, therefore, necessitates direct intrusion employing methods from detection to restriction to separate the healthy from the ill. Spaces subject to "new methods of power," policing, supervising, and instructing, were introduced in nineteenth-century Egypt with "a language of the body" for the promotion of "individual cleanliness and tidiness."[22] In the case of the coronavirus pandemic, notwithstanding the wide array of symptoms similar to illnesses from a common cold to pneumonia, the invisibility of the threat means it can only be properly gauged through mass testing and managed in specific places through hospital care and quarantines.

Expert committees, staffed by scientists and doctors, have been created by governments across the world for the express purpose to manage the threat of coronavirus. Although expert knowledge has been incorporated in public spectacles, the "non-knowledge" of risks is also evident when "the so-called 'unknown unknowns' (the knowledge we don't know that we lack)" is followed, sooner or later, by their discovery.[23] Politicians, doctors, and scientists, as well the general public, are stuck in a continuous process of catching up with developing, at times conflicting, research findings and public health advice. Nonetheless, the demise of the state and of the authority of experts has not yet arrived in what could be described as the current condition of ambiguity that has left uneven effects in both spheres.

COVID-19 and the Limits of the State in Egypt

A Public Health Strategy for a Pandemic

When the first reported cases of the novel coronavirus in China appeared in international news outlets and online in December 2019, countries around the world, with few exceptions, perceived a remote health crisis. The city of Wuhan and the province of Hubei experienced a lockdown that severely restricted the freedom of movement and stringent quarantine measures. However, the coronavirus rapidly spread from China to many other countries. A national or local public health threat was conceived to be a global risk. Exponential increases of infection cases and the death toll on different continents provided the justification for the WHO to finally declare that COVID-19 was a "pandemic" in March 2020.[24] Egypt was unable to escape the global spread of the virus. A foreign tourist at Cairo International Airport who tested positive for the virus in mid-February 2020 became the first recorded case in Africa and the second instance in the Arab world.[25] In early March, there was the first reported coronavirus diagnosis of an Egyptian. The Egyptian state soon recognized the dual threats of a deadly contagious disease to the health security of citizens and its political legitimacy for any apparent policy failures. While the conventional notion of security presumes threats to be military in nature, the global risk of an infectious disease was construed to challenge the capacity of the body politic to run the economy and avoid the collapse of health services. Political securitizing of the virus can be located in a process of risking. Ubiquity and uncertainty characterized the threat to citizens and foreigners.

President Abdel Fattah al-Sisi's speech, commemorating the "June 30 Revolution," identified "a new challenge in facing the Coronavirus pandemic that affects the whole humanity" among a group of threats that included the "evil force" of the Muslim Brotherhood and extremists.[26] Government officials exercise their authority in an attempt to define the nature and boundaries of risks in an unequal relationship with ordinary Egyptians. The Ministry of Health led by Hala Zayed has played a public role in managing the coronavirus in Egypt through various initiatives and policies. Al-Sisi sent Zayed to China in March 2020 to secure the transfer of Chinese and WHO policy practices on infectious disease control to contain the newly emerged virus in a climate of heightened caution.[27] In addition, the Health Ministry's coronavirus scientific committee fulfils the function of contributing to the promotion of a public health strategy in the areas of inspection, quarantine, and vaccination. While the government has appointed local medical and health experts to offer advice on infectious disease control, the Higher Committee for the Management of the Coronavirus Crisis, chaired by the prime minster, remains a key decision-making institution for increasing and decreasing restrictions.[28] Expert advice can also be found in the presidency's staff of special advisors such as Mohamed Awad Tag el-Deen, chairman of the largest pharmaceutical manufacturer Arab Company for Drug Industries and Medical Appliances (ACDIMA), for health affairs. Arab industry and the Egyptian state cooperate to acquire or further consolidate the scientific credentials of counter-coronavirus policies.

Two components are present in the Egyptian government's public health strategy to contain COVID-19. General restrictions on freedoms and mandatory rules, and the nationwide rollout of vaccinations. First, restrictive measures were implemented to contain the spread of the virus. Amid the uncertainty and lack of knowledge about the coronavirus, the state attempted to detect the unseen threat through polymerase chain reaction (PCR) and ID NOW tests. Scientific technology, however, could only offer limited glimpses about the extent of this infectious disease's transmission within Egypt and at its borders. In addition, disease control efforts have led to the restriction of movement, namely lockdowns, inspections, and quarantines, according to the demarcation of public and private spaces and within particular times.[29] Night curfews and restricted working hours for service industries from restaurants to shopping malls were tools for infectious disease management. Emergency measures were adopted for the imposition of masks and social distancing in public places and other spaces. Parliament approved a new law empowering the Health Minister to make face masks obligatory with responsibility falling to the Interior Ministry for the enforcement of this rule and fine violators.[30] The Egyptian government has employed various measures indicative of a global trend of containment, prevention, and treatment. It has been presented with the opportunity to develop its surveillance strategies to monitor citizens and foreigners suspected of carrying infectious diseases at its borders and airports. Despite the available means of implementing an extensive public health agenda, utilizing security personnel, laws and expert advice, the head of the health ministry's coronavirus scientific committee ruled out in May 2020 the need for a lockdown and instead urged social distancing to break the chains of transmission in a policy of sharing or delegating health security to Egyptian citizens.[31] International flights from mid-March to June were almost completely halted. Counter-discourses to the state's official narrative on the coronavirus were legally proscribed as fake news or rumours in contravention of "public security."[32] Popular health provision by Islamists of the past failed to materialize in COVID-19 disease control efforts amid the continued incarceration of Muslim Brotherhood leaders and activists.[33]

Second, a campaign of mass vaccination was adopted by the government. An Egyptian spokesperson for the government declared that coexistence with the coronavirus was a necessity, for economic considerations, till a vaccine appeared.[34] British, German, Russian, and Chinese pharmaceutical companies had developed effective COVID-19 Vaccines in the last stages of research trials by the end of 2020. Several vaccines by Pfizer-BioNtech, AstraZeneca-SK Bio, Serum Institute of India, Janssen, Moderna, Sinopharm, and Sinovac Biotech received the WHO's approval for emergency use. While several countries rolled out their mass vaccination campaigns in early 2021, Egypt regarded vaccinations as merely one component of an overall strategy to maintain health security. From international procurement to local vaccination, the state is present at every stage of conceiving and implementing an infectious disease control strategy in a shared process. Digital and physical spaces are simultaneously amenable to the organizing logic of the national body politic amid a global assemblage with changing relations among experts and politicians belonging to different institutions. WHO teams of experts have visited Egypt to implement technical and cooperation. External support for the state's strategy against the global pandemic shows and compensates for the inadequacies of the national body politic's infectious disease control capacity.

Risking the Coronavirus in a Global Context

The rapid movements of ideas through the Internet and of people through mass transportation have altered the connections among multiple sites occupied by experts, decision-makers, and the general public. Collective perceptions of public health events also betray traces of the swiftness of the creation, production, and reception of images. Egyptian efforts to manage the spread of the coronavirus within the local population have not exclusively relied on a national program of information, containment, and treatment. Blurred lines exist between the global and the local on the one hand and the public and the private on the other. The threat posed by the pandemic becomes a constructed reality in a process of risking the coronavirus that is both intersubjective and uneven in a global context. A shared understanding of public health is constantly redefined in what can be a haphazard sequence with the risk of the coronavirus shaped by the pronouncements of politicians and experts to a largely lay public. Risking health security involves global and local actors in an assemblage.

While the WHO expressed early reservations about attributing a seasonal sequence of waves to the coronavirus's impact,[35] it was soon considered as such with vertical rises and falls along a horizontal movement through time. In Egypt, the Central Agency for Public Mobilization and Statistics (CAPMAS), a government agency, has played a leading role in describing and presenting the spread of the virus as a wave.[36] Official information produced by this agency creates, organizes, and classifies data in a bid to lessen the uncertainty surrounding the coronavirus and its threat to Egyptian society. However, the Health Minister's acknowledgment of the official infection figures being merely one-tenth of the perceived reality in January 2021 reveals the limits of data collection, namely surveillance, and the ability to make policies informed by fairly accurate information.[37] Despite the increasing familiarity with the coronavirus's symptoms and the types of medical treatments, the lack of an effective national infrastructure of testing contributes to the persistence of the unknown about its transmission. The risking of the virus's impact in the language of waves by politicians and experts is constrained by the state's capacity to gather adequate knowledge from formal detection and medical practices.

A poll conducted by Baseera, an independent Egyptian research organization, involving telephone surveys estimated the number of infections at almost three million as of January 2021.[38] Conventional methods of data collection are used by actors, outside of the state, to record the effects of an extraordinary event for the purpose of generating knowledge to minimize uncertainty. Expectations of a third wave for April 2021 within the government were cognizant of the potential mass transmission of the virus during Ramadan, when families gather to break daily fasts and perform communal prayers, but precluded the imposition of a lockdown due to its potentially negative consequences on the economy.[39] Different concurrent threats appear to have been assessed in formulating policies that alternate between enabling economic activity and restricting freedom of movement. Public health during the pandemic is not the only consideration in the process of identifying and addressing risks to the national body politic. During Ramadan, before the festival of Sham al-Nessim that ushers in spring, the expected third wave of coronavirus inflections did not lead to a nationwide lockdown but witnessed individual governorates imposing restrictions on public parks and beaches.[40]

During the pandemic, inter-ministerial coordination continued apace with the Ministry of Health and Population brought to the forefront of managing the threat of the contagious disease. Different ministries in Egypt have worked with the WHO and applied its public health guidelines. Tobacco, namely waterpipe tobacco smoking, has been a target of the Ministry of Local Development's precautionary measures sent to governorates and the public health awareness campaigns organized by the Ministry of Health and Ministry of Social Solidarity in line with WHO's recommendations.[41] Human beings are the causes, if not the embodiment, of the threat to themselves. Multiple sites of management contribute to identify and control the contagious nature of coronavirus among the population in a variety of spaces ranging from domestic to leisure. Frequent and publicized coordination can create the appearance of a uniform state that obscures fragmented institutions and personnel with different, if not competing, areas of expertise and agendas. Online spaces were also transformed into nodes of increasing public health awareness. The WHO director general's tweets in the "#SafeHands" spring 2020 campaign, encouraging the hygienic cleaning of hands according to WHO advice, to high-profile politicians and ministers, included Hala Zayed who in turn tweeted a video in which she washed her hands. Such public spectacles do not simply use social media websites in an instrumental fashion. They insert images of prescribed cleanliness, through visual forms, into the daily habits of Internet users.

Direct coordination between the WHO director-general and the Egyptian Minister of Health subsumes not only support against the coronavirus but the supply of polio vaccines and expertise and recognition of the elimination of Hepatitis C.[42] National strategies against endemic contagious diseases continue to involve the transfer of expertise and medicine from the WHO to the Egyptian state. The coronavirus has spread in Egypt amid a Ministry of Health-led campaign, supported by the WHO and UNICEF, to prevent the reappearance of polio through medical teams carrying out mass vaccination among 16 million children.[43] Preventive efforts of this scale reinforce the perception of a national threat for which the state is responsible to monitor, manage, and avert. Immunization practices are a political concern without any discrimination between science and politics. Egyptian politicians, civil servants, doctors, and nurses form a web of decision-makers and implementers of the public health strategies against coronavirus, polio, and Hepatitis C influenced by intergovernmental organizations and international experts. Development, humanitarian activity, and public health have converged in Egypt during the coronavirus pandemic. United States Agency of Development (USAID) has supported the "large-scale community outreach programs" of the Egyptian Red Crescent (ERC), with its 30,000 staff, to promote public awareness of hygiene and detection of the virus.[44] For the ERC also simultaneously occupies a space within the state, not being a nongovernmental organization, and a local extension of the independent International Committee of the Red Cross. Public health strategies during the pandemic demonstrate the multiple, although by no means contradictory, institutionalizations cutting across global and national lines and state and civil society.

A central plank of the Egyptian government's declared coronavirus strategy in 2021 has relied on a national campaign of mass immunizations. Conventional strategies of disease detection through testing and quarantining diagnosed or suspected infected people were soon recognized by medical experts and doctors to have a limited impact. Strict measures by governments in Egypt and around the world, to curtail the freedom of movement such as lockdowns and curfews, could not effectively contain the spread of COVID-19. From lax implementation of these measures to public disregard of rules, the campaign of educating and convincing residents and foreigners about "social distancing" and wearing masks met with some resistance. Mass immunizations of populations have been considered to be a viable measure to manage the worst effects of the pandemic—principally the reduction of hospitalizations. Vaccine security in the interrelated areas of national campaigns to immunize residents and the development of vaccines appears to be an urgent concern. Since December 2020, the British government's efforts to inoculate citizens were followed by similar efforts in the United States, China, Russia, India, and other countries with varying degrees of success.

The Egyptian government was eager to join this growing trend and acquired vaccines through international vaccine alliances or bilateral ties with vaccine-producing countries discussed earlier. Invisibility of an extremely contagious virus added a sense of urgency to the task of carrying out mass vaccinations among medical workers and those considered to be the most vulnerable in Egypt. Successful procurement of various vaccines enabled the government to launch a national vaccination campaign in January 2021 followed by the creation of a Ministry of Health website for Egyptians to book appointments. Citizens have been urged to register on this website using a software that gives priority to individuals according to the severity of chronic illnesses, aged over 40 years and the elderly.[45] The state's health security policies classify and separate the population according to the danger posed by the virus to them. Different categories of people were to be vaccinated in stages. First, the initial priority group was about 207,000 doctors, nurses, administrators, and workers at quarantine, fever, chest, and screening hospitals. Second, citizens with chronic illnesses and the elderly were the next target group. Approximately 68,000 citizens registered on January 28, 2021, the first day of the online system, for vaccine appointments. Priority vaccinations began on March 5 with 1,141 citizens receiving the first shot.[46] Egyptian residents over 18 years old were permitted on February 28, 2021, to make appointments on the Ministry of Health's online registration system. Vaccine appointment registrations are designed to be completed using the online system.

Government policy on the rolling out of the vaccine to more social groups has levied a cost of 200 Egyptian pounds for 2 doses with needy families and persons, under the Takaful and Karama (Solidarity and Dignity) program, exempted from this charge.[47] Prime Minister Mustafa Madbouly announced 2.5 million citizens out of the total number of 6 million who had registered had received vaccines by early June 2021.[48] Health security is conceived by the state to include the expansion of its activities and recording of citizens' data in cyberspace. Physical and digital spaces reproduce the national body politic and its public health agenda. Baseera had carried out an opinion poll in late 2020 about attitudes among Egyptians toward vaccinations with respondent results of 67 percent strongly agreeing, 25 percent agreeing, 3 percent disagreeing, and 4 percent strong disagreeing.[49] According to this sample of Egyptians, it was inferred that a majority welcomed the state's push for its mass immunization campaign. Yet again, orthodox methods of data collection were employed to measure citizens' perception about the vaccines explicitly and the pandemic implicitly. Close state-religion relations contributed to the public health measure of vaccinations. Senior Muslim religious authorities supported the state's campaign to persuade people to receive the vaccine. Al-Azhar issued a *fatwā* (religious edict) about the permissibility of being vaccinated during the day-long fast, its continued validity, in the holy month of Ramadan, from April to May in 2021.[50]

However, the securing of vaccines for the Egyptian government's mass immunization campaign entails a dependence on external expertise and agreements with foreign governments and pharmaceutical companies. Insufficient know-how and technology within the national body politic creates intractable challenges that can only be ameliorated through the transfer of expertise, namely specialists, knowledge, technology, and medicine. Research into vaccine development in North America, Western Europe, and China has borne relatively successful, if not mixed, results. While many vaccines have been created, there is the absence of equitable global chains of manufacturing, supply, and deployment.[51] The Egyptian Drug Authority (EDA), affiliated with the Prime Ministry, has sought to manage the importing of vaccines and medicine rapidly developed without the usual pharmaceutical oversights. Citizen security, specifically health and life, falls within the EDA's responsibility through its powers of granting emergency licences for the Indian Serum Institute's Covishield, the Russian Sputnik 5, and AstraZeneca's AZD 1222 manufactured in South Korea.[52] Foreign know-how and medical treatments are subject to official bureaucratic procedures and urgently receive approval.

Global uncertainty surrounding the COVID-19 virus challenges the hitherto perceived security provided by the state to its citizens. Globalizing trends have paradoxically undermined and reinforced the Egyptian national body politic in the different arenas of development, surveillance, and discipline. Overt dependence on the import of vaccines created by foreign states and private organizations reveals the limits of the state's capacity in health technology in Egypt and other countries. Egypt has participated, if not been a pioneer, in this regional trend. National public health relies on the Egyptian state's ability to convincingly assert the scientific competence and authority of its institutions, personnel, and policies. The regulatory powers of the state and the EDA used to approve vaccines are supposed to shore up the image of an efficacious body politic in response to a global public threat.

Mohamed Tag El-Din, presidential adviser for health affairs, has tried to dispel reluctance about the newly created vaccines through highlighting the scientific dimensions of the state's process of their evaluation.[53] Political responsibility for the security of Egyptian citizens consists of employing scientific authority to allay fears generated from a lack of knowledge about vaccines for the virus and its side effects. Nonetheless, state institutions such as the EDA participate in a web of global, regional, and national actors to expand their scope of activities and enable the transfer of absent advanced medical practice and treatment. Multilateral cooperation among actors has led to the establishment of supply chains for vaccines to greatly expand access to countries around the world. States, pharmaceutical companies, and intergovernmental organizations have contributed to the COVAX Facility's vaccine supply mechanism. The United States, the European Union (EU), and Japan have worked with the WHO and UNICEF to gradually provide Egypt with 40 million AstraZeneca vaccines from the COVAX Facility.[54] While the EDA and the Ministry of Health perform parallel functions, the approval of vaccines and the campaign of mass vaccinations are located at different points in the same global process of projecting a legitimate national body politic.

Manufacturing Vaccine Security

Government attempts in Egypt to implement a vaccination program were complemented by talks with foreign governments and companies to secure rights to manufacture vaccines at local factories. Zayed announced in March 2021 negotiations were occurring between the Egyptian Health Ministry and the Chinese government for the local production of Sinovac Biotech's CoronaVac vaccine in the country.[55] VACSERA, an Egyptian state-owned pharmaceutical company, subsequently signed an agreement with the parent company of Sinovac to manufacture the vaccine at its factories. Business coordination between these two companies, closely affiliated to their governments, would see Sinovac provide the required know-how and technical assistance for vaccine production as well as granting a manufacturing and brand licence to VACSERA for CoronaVac.[56] The transfer of Chinese medical technology is another indication of the limits of the Egyptian state in the area of pharmaceutical innovation and research. In a global web of actors, foreign companies with research facilities develop vaccines which are later manufactured in Egyptian factories. Local actors, both the state and companies, in Egypt occupy a position of dependency of being producers, rather than innovators, in the international biopharmaceutical sector. Following the Sinovac-VACSERA agreement, the EDA approved CoronaVac for emergency use. The first batch of raw materials arrived from China in late May 2021 to manufacture two million doses. VACSERA's newly expanded factory complex, situated in Giza, is expected to have a daily production capacity of 3 million doses, 40 million to be made by the end of 2021, involving cooperation with other companies.[57]

Inter-ministerial coordination with EVA Pharma, a private sector company, has also recently aimed to create a vaccine.[58] Demand for vaccines has spurred on the growth of the local Egyptian pharmaceutical sector. In this sector of industrial production, the Egyptian state has taken the lead in creating new linkages through which it attempts to manufacture health security through the creation of vaccines for Egypt and the African continent. WHO experts inspected VACSERA factories in order to approve their industrial production lines in a display of their scientific authority and the local need for international recognition.[59] The Egyptian Ministry of Health's Facebook page reported on July 7, 2021, that VACSERA's first batch of vaccines was produced.[60] Self-sufficiency in the industrial capacity to manufacture vaccines was an objective declared by Egyptian decision-makers. In a speech given by Madbouly on July 2021, the production of vaccines in Egypt was addressed as a matter of national security.[61] Pharmaceutical capacity for research and production in response to a global pandemic of an infectious disease now formed a central component in achieving security, including health, in the face of the uncertain consequences from a global threat. Egyptian pharmaceutical factories have also agreed to manufacture the other vaccines of the Chinese state-owned Sinopharm and the Russian Sputnik V. Foreign imports of raw materials in the vaccine production process will enable the creation of vaccines for export.

Conclusion

Catastrophic events of a global nature possess the two dimensions of objective reality and subjective perception. Ulrich Beck's theory of risk combines "realistic" and "constructivist" accounts of generated dangers. Rapid transmission of infectious diseases from the local to the global has preoccupied intergovernmental organizations and experts working in public health. The process of risking the coronavirus has involved different actors. While the Egyptian state has had experience dealing with contagious illnesses such as Hepatitis C and polio, the coronavirus differs in being a pandemic and the apparent lack of effective medical treatments. Conventional methods of discipline and surveillance have been utilized to manage, if not contain, the worst effects of the virus within the Egyptian population. In this chapter, we have considered the Egyptian body politic to be a culmination of the practices of control, discipline, and surveillance aimed at creating both the behavior of human beings and the context in which they first arise and are ordered.[62] The body politic, in its national incarnation, has been merely one line of defence and agency in the risking of the coronavirus pandemic. Despite the neoliberal strictures imposed on Egypt, the duty of the state to guarantee health security of citizens and even refugees is constantly reiterated by global bodies from the WHO to the UNICEF.

Intergovernmental organizations and foreign governments, as well as international pharmaceutical companies, have proved to be not only useful but also indispensable allies in the coronavirus public health crisis. The legitimacy of the Egyptian state has been dependent on accruing much-needed external scientific authority for its measures, whether restrictive or not, aimed at managing the swift spread of the coronavirus among citizens and foreigners. National actors such as Egyptian decision-makers are, therefore, implicated in a web or assemblage connecting local, regional, and global actors in which the transfer of medical experts, knowledge, and treatment can justify and inform their disease control strategies. State officials concluded major agreements with Sinovac and Sinopharm to produce their vaccines in Egyptian pharmaceutical factories in order to make Egypt a major hub for vaccine manufacturing in the Middle East and Africa. Uncertainty surrounding the coronavirus and anti-viral effective treatments against it indicate the Egyptian state is unable to furnish ideological, scientific, and bureaucratic resources to cope with the pandemic's consequences. Systematic testing on a national scale has been absent in the implicit acknowledgment by the Egyptian Health Minister's admission about the true figure of infections being much higher than the official count. Limits to the image and capacities of the state demand allies of a different variety—namely the WHO and its public health agenda. From infectious disease guidelines to vaccines, the existence of the state's anti-coronavirus national strategy is indebted to external sources of authority, know-how, and resources. Risking health security has been an activity pursued by the Egyptian state, and other regional and global actors for the purpose of dispelling a common uncertainty about a common threat.

Notes

1 Mitchell (1988, 175–6).
2 Sadiki and Saleh, Layla, (2020: 7–10).
3 Mitchell (1988, ix–x).
4 Mitchell (1988, xi).
5 Mitchell (1991, 95).
6 Beck (2008, 5).
7 Beck (2009, 293).
8 Beck (2009, 292-3).
9 Sørensen (2018, 8–9).
10 Beck (2009, 294); Wimmer and Quandt (2006, 345–6).
11 Beck (2016, 99–100).
12 Beck (1992, 208).
13 Wimmer and Quandt (2006, 341–2).
14 Buzan, Wæver and Wilde (1988, 21–3).
15 Buzan, Wæver and Wilde (1988, 23–31).
16 Oberleitner(2005: 190–1).
17 Korany(2020, 80 1).
18 WHO (n.d).
19 Beck (2008, 15–17).
20 Sadiki (2020, 50–61).
21 Beck (2009a, 3).
22 Mitchell (1988, 98–9).
23 Sørensen 2018, 12).
24 WHO (2020).
25 ET (2020).

26 SIS (2020).
27 Abdel Salam (2020).
28 SIS (2021b).
29 El-Din and El-Gundy (2020).
30 EI (2021).
31 Daily News Egypt (2020).
32 Abdel Aty (2020).
33 Sadiki and Saleh (2020, 12–13).
34 AO (2020).
35 UN News (2020).
36 CAPMAS (2021).
37 Ramadan (2021).
38 Baseera (2021).
39 El-Gundy (2021).
40 AO (2021).
41 EMRO (n.d).
42 SIS (2021a).
43 Hatem (2021).
44 USAID (2021).
45 ElSharkawy (2021).
46 AO (2021, April 5).
47 ElSharkawy (2021).
48 EI (2021, June 2).
49 Baseera (2020).
50 al-Mahdi and Beheiri (2021).
51 UN (2021).
52 EDA (2021).
53 Mosry (2020).
54 EMRO (2021).
55 El-Gundy (2021).
56 AO (2021).
57 AO (2021).
58 Soliman (2021).
59 ET (2021).
60 Egyptian Ministry of Health and Population (2021).
61 AO (2021).
62 Moussa (2020, 304–16).

References

Abdel Aty, Mohamed. (2020). "*Majlis al-wuzarā᾽ yatawa᾽᾽ad murawijī al-shāi᾽āt ᾽an fayrūs kūrūnā: tafāṣīl* (The cabinet threatens promoters of rumours about the coronavirus: details)," *Al-Masry al-Youm*, March 10, https://www.almasryalyoum.com/news/details /1584573 (accessed July 7, 2021).

Abdel Salam, Walid. (2020). "*Riḥla wazīra al-ṣiḥa li-l-ṣīn bi-taklīf al-ra᾽īs.. al-rasā᾽il wa al-makāsib (fīdīyū)* (Health minister's trip to China by the president's assignment . . . messages and gains: video)," *Youm7*, March 4, https://www.youm7.com/story/2020/3

/4/%D8%B1%D8%AD%D9%84%D8%A9-%D9%88%D8%B2%D9%8A%D8%B1%D8
%A9-%D8%A7%D9%84%D8%B5%D8%AD%D8%A9-%D9%84%D9%84%D8%B5
%D9%8A%D9%86-%D8%A8%D8%AA%D9%83%D9%84%D9%8A%D9%81-%D8
%A7%D9%84%D8%B1%D8%A6%D9%8A%D8%B3-%D8%A7%D9%84%D8%B1%D8
%B3%D8%A7%D8%A6%D9%84-%D9%88%D8%A7%D9%84%D9%85%D9%83%D8
%A7%D8%B3%D8%A8-%D9%81%D9%8A%D8%AF%D9%8A%D9%88/4656745
(accessed July 11, 2021).

Alaa El-Din, Menna and Zeinab El-Gundy. (2020). "Egypt to Impose EGP 50 Fine for Not Wearing Masks in Public," *Ahramonline*, December 27, https://english.ahram.org.eg/NewsContent/1/0/397639/Egypt/0/Egypt-to-impose-EGP--fine-for-not-wearing-masks-in.aspx (accessed June 24, 2021).

AO. (2020). "Egypt Must 'coexist' with Coronavirus as Some Restrictions Begin Easing in June: Cabinet," *Ahramonline*, May 8, https://english.ahram.org.eg/NewsContent/1/64/368895/Egypt/Politics-/Egypt-must-coexist-with-coronavirus-as-some-restri.aspx (accessed June 25, 2021).

AO. (2021). "Egypt Signs Agreement to Produce Sinovac Vaccine Locally," *Ahramonline*, April 21, https://english.ahram.org.eg/NewsContent/1/64/409719/Egypt/Politics-/Egypt-signs-agreement-to-produce-Sinovac-vaccine-l.aspx (accessed June 25, 2021).

AO. (2021). "1,141 Egyptians receive COVID-19 shot on first day of vaccine rollout for priority groups: Ministry," *Ahramonline*, April 5, https://english.ahram.org.eg/NewsContent/1/64/405384/Egypt/Politics-/,-Egyptians-receive-COVID-shot-on-first-day-of-vac.aspx (accessed June 25, 2021).

AO. (2021). "Egyptian Governors Order Closing Parks, Beaches on Sham El-Nessim due to Pandemic," *Ahramonline*, April 30, https://english.ahram.org.eg/NewsContent/1/64/410336/Egypt/Politics-/Egyptian-governors-order-closing-parks,-beaches-on.aspx (accessed June 21, 2021).

AO. (2021). "Producing Vaccines Locally is a Matter of National Security: PM Madbouly," *Ahramonline*, June 5, https://english.ahram.org.eg/NewsContent/1/64/416601/Egypt/Politics-/Producing-vaccines-locally-is-a-matter-of-national.aspx (accessed June 25, 2021).

AO. (2021) "Egypt Designates New Production Lines to Produce 3 Million Doses of Coronavirus Vaccines Daily," *Ahramonline*, June 20, https://english.ahram.org.eg/NewsContent/1/64/414651/Egypt/Politics-/Egypt-designates-new-production-lines-to-produce--.aspx (accessed June 25, 2021).

Baseera. (2020). *"Tawaqquʿāt al-miṣrīyīn li-l-ʿāmm al-jadīd fī wujūd faīrūsū kūfīd-19* (Egyptians' expectations for the new year in the presence of the COVID-19 virus)," *Baseera*, December 29, http://baseera.com.eg/RecentPolls2.aspx?ID=181 (accessed June 30, 2021).

Baseera. (2021). *"Al-iṣāba bi-fayrūs kūrūnā:* COVID-19 (Coronavirus infection: COVID-19)," *Baseera*, March 9, http://baseera.com.eg/RecentPolls2.aspx?ID=182 (accessed June 27, 2021).

Beck, Ulrich. (1992). *Risk Society: Towards a New Modernity*. London: Sage Publications.

Beck, Ulrich. (2008). "World at Risk: The New Task of Critical Theory," *Development and Society*, 37 (1): 1–21.

Beck, Ulrich. (2009a). "Critical Theory of World Risk Society: A Cosmopolitan Vision," *Constellations*, 16: 3–22.

Beck, Ulrich. (2009b). "World Risk Society and Manufactured Uncertainties," *Iris*, 1 (2): 291–9.

Beck, Ulrich. (2016). *The Metamorphosis of the World*. Cambridge and Malden: Polity.

Buzan, Barry, Ole Wæver and Jaap de Wilde. (1988). *Security: A New Framework for Analysis.* Boulder: Lynne Rienner.

CAPMAS. (2021). *"Miṣr mā bayna al-mawja al-ūlā wa al-thānīya min kūrūnā: dirāsa istikshāfīya* (Egypt between the first and second waves from coronavirus: An exploratory study)," *CAPMAS*, February 1, 24, https://www.capmas.gov.eg/Pages/ Researchs.aspx?page_id=5031 (accessed June 27, 2021).

Daily News Egypt. (2020). "COVID-19 Committee Head: Egypt Needs Social Distancing Not Lockdown," *YouTube*, May 7, https://www.youtube.com/watch?v=JxJZcpXxVNU (accessed July 6, 2021).

EDA. (2021). *"Manaḥ al-tarkhīṣ al-ṭāriʾ li-istikhdām laqāḥ "kūfīshīld/astirāzīnīkā" al-muḍādd li-fayrūs kūrūnā al-mustajid* (Granting an emergency licence to use the Covishield/AstraZeneca vaccine against the emerging coronavirus)," *Egyptian Drug Authority*, January 31, https://www.edaegypt.gov.eg/ar/%D8%A7%D9%84%D9%85 %D8%B1%D9%83%D8%B2-%D8%A7%D9%84%D8%A7%D8%B9%D9%84%D8%A7 %D9%85%D9%89/%D8%A7%D9%84%D8%A7%D8%AE%D8%A8%D8%A7%D8 %B1/%D9%85%D9%86%D8%AD-%D8%A7%D9%84%D8%AA%D8%B1%D8%AE %D9%8A%D8%B5-%D8%A7%D9%84%D8%B7%D8%A7%D8%B1%D8%A6-%D9 %84%D8%A7%D8%B3%D8%AA%D8%AE%D8%AF%D8%A7%D9%85-%D9%84 %D9%82%D8%A7%D8%AD-%D9%83%D9%88%D9%81%D9%8A%D8%B4%D9 %8A%D9%84%D8%AF-%D8%A7%D8%B3%D8%AA%D8%B1%D8%A7%D8%B2 %D9%8A%D9%86%D9%8A%D9%83%D8%A7-%D8%A7%D9%84%D9%85%D8%B6 %D8%A7%D8%AF-%D9%84%D9%81%D9%8A%D8%B1%D9%88%D8%B3-%D9 %83%D9%88%D8%B1%D9%88%D9%86%D8%A7-%D8%A7%D9%84%D9%85%D8 %B3%D8%AA%D8%AC%D8%AF/ (accessed July 3, 2021).

EDA. (2021). *"Manaḥ al-tarkhīṣ al-ṭāriʾ li-istikhdām laqāḥī "sbūtnīk V" wa "astirāzīnīkā/ AZD* ١٢٢٢" (Granting an emergency licence to use Sputnik V and AstraZeneca/AZD 1222 vaccines)," *Egyptian Drug Authority*, April 24, https://www.edaegypt.gov.eg/ar/ %D8%A7%D9%84%D9%85%D8%B1%D9%83%D8%B2-%D8%A7%D9%84%D8%A7 %D8%B9%D9%84%D8%A7%D9%85%D9%89/%D8%A7%D9%84%D8%A7%D8%AE %D8%A8%D8%A7%D8%B1/%D9%85%D9%86%D8%AD-%D8%A7%D9%84%D8 %AA%D8%B1%D8%AE%D9%8A%D8%B5-%D8%A7%D9%84%D8%B7%D8%A7 %D8%B1%D8%A6-%D9%84%D8%A7%D8%B3%D8%AA%D8%AE%D8%AF%D8 %A7%D9%85-%D9%84%D9%82%D8%A7%D8%AD%D9%8A-%D8%B3%D8%A8 %D9%88%D8%AA%D9%86%D9%8A%D9%83-v-%D9%88-%D8%A7%D8%B3%D8 %AA%D8%B1%D8%A7%D8%B2%D9%8A%D9%86%D9%8A%D9%83%D8%A7-azd -1222/ (accessed July 3, 2021).

Egyptian Ministry of Health and Population. (2021). *"Taḥdī kabīr wa nuqla tārīkhīya li-miṣr* (A great challenge and a historic shift for Egypt)," *Facebook*, June 7, https:// www.facebook.com/egypt.mohp/posts/1231633799994885 (accessed June 25, 2021).

EI. (2021). "Egypt's Interior Ministry Fines 14,958 People for Failing to Wear a Mask," *Egypt Independent*, May 14, https://egyptindependent.com/egypts-interior-ministry -fines-14958-people-for-failing-to-wear-a-mask/ (accessed July 7, 2021).

EI. (2021). "Egyptian PM announces 2.5 million citizens are vaccinated against COVID- 19," *Egypt Independent*, June 2, https://egyptindependent.com/egyptian-pm-announces -2-5-million-citizens-are-vaccinated-against-covid-19/ (accessed June 25, 2021).

ElSharkawy, Lamis. (2021). "Egypt's Coronavirus Vaccination Campaign: A Timeline," *Ahramonline*, February 27, https://english.ahram.org.eg/NewsContent/1/64/404860/ Egypt/Politics-/Egypts-coronavirus-vaccination-campaign-A-timeline.aspx (accessed June 20, 2021).

EMRO. (2021). "Egypt Receives Second Shipment of 1.77 million COVID-19 Vaccines through the COVAX Facility," *WHO Regional Office for the Eastern Mediterranean*, May 14, http://www.emro.who.int/media/news/egypt-receives-second-shipment-of -177-million-covid-19-vaccines-through-the-covax-facility.html (accessed June 20, 2021).

EMRO. (n.d.). "Egypt bans Waterpipes and Ramps up Health Awareness during COVID- 19," *WHO Regional Office for the Eastern Mediterranean*, http://www.emro.who.int/ tfi/news/egypt-bans-waterpipes-and-ramps-up-health-awareness-during-covid-19 .html (accessed June 24, 2021).

El-Gundy, Zeinab. (2021). "FAQ: Third Wave of the Coronavirus in Egypt," *Ahramonline*, March 17, https://english.ahram.org.eg/NewsContent /1/64/406043/Egypt/Politics-/FAQ-Third-wave-of-the-coronavirus-in-Egypt .aspx (accessed June 20, 2021).

El-Gundy, Zeinab. (2021). "Egypt in Talks with Chinese Government to Manufacture Sinovac Coronavirus Vaccine: Health Minister," *Ahramonline*, March 22, https:// english.ahram.org.eg/NewsContentP/1/407548/Egypt/Egypt-in-talks-with-Chinese -government-to-manufact.aspx (accessed July 15, 2021).

ET. (2020). "Egypt Announces First Coronavirus Infection," *Egypt Today*, February 14, https://www.egypttoday.com/Article/1/81641/Egypt-announces-first-Coronavirus -infection (accessed July 8, 2021).

ET. (2021). "Egypt Seeks WHO's Approval to Locally-Made Sinovac Vaccine," *Egypt Today*, June 16, https://www.egypttoday.com/Article/1/105079/Egypt-seeks-WHO%E2 %80%99s-approval-to-locally-made-Sinovac-vaccine (accessed June 20, 2021).

Hatem, Mohamed. (2021) "In Photos: Egypt Vaccinated 52.9% of Children against polio on 1st day of Inoculation Campaign," *Ahramonline*, March 1, https://english.ahram .org.eg/NewsContent/1/64/405103/Egypt/Politics-/In-Photos-Egypt-vaccinated--of -children-against-po.aspx (accessed June 25, 2021).

Korany, Bahgat. (2020). "Travelling the Middle East without a Map: Three Main Debates," in Larbi Sadiki (ed.), *Routledge Handbook of Middle East Politics*, 70–87. Abingdon, Oxon and New York, Routledge.

Al-Mahdi, Usama and Ahmed Beheiri. (2021). "*Fatwā min al-Azhar al-sharīf bi-shaʾn taṭʿīm laqāḥ kūrūnā fī nahār ramaḍān* (A fatwa from the noble al-Azhar about the corona vaccine during the day in Ramadan)," *Al-Masry al-Youm*, March 6, https://www .almasryalyoum.com/news/details/2275822 (accessed July 15, 2021).

Mosry, Ahmed. (2020). "Egypt won't Administer any Coronavirus Vaccine until 100% Sure of Safety, Efficacy: Presidential Health Adviser," *Ahramonline*, December 16, https://english.ahram.org.eg/NewsContent/1/64/397002/Egypt/Politics-/Egypt-wont -administer-any-coronavirus-vaccine-unti.aspx (accessed June 20, 2021).

Moussa, Mohammed. (2020). "Patronage in Reverse and the Secular State in Egypt," in Larbi Sadiki (ed.), *Routledge Handbook of Middle East Politics: Interdisciplinary Inscriptions*, 304–16. London: Routledge.

Mitchell, Timothy. (1988). *Colonising Egypt*. Los Angeles and London: University of California Press.

Mitchell, Timothy. (1991). "The Limit of the State: Beyond Statist Approaches and their Critics," *American Political Science Review*, 85 (1): 77–96.

Oberleitner, Gerd. (2005). "Human Security: A Challenge to International Law?," *Global Governance*, 11 (2): 185–203.

Ramadan, Bassem. (2021) "*Wazīra al-ṣiḥa: iṣābāt "kūrūnā" al-muʿlana "ʿushr" al-raqm al-ḥaqīqī (fidīyū)* (The health minister: announced coronavirus infections are a tenth of the real number)," *Al-Masry al-Youm*, January 4, https://www.almasryalyoum.com/news/details/2226662 (accessed June 27, 2021).

Sadiki, Larbi. (2020). "Middle of Where? East of What?: Simulated Postcoloniality's Assemblages, Rhizomes, and Simulacra," in Larbi Sadiki (ed.), *Routledge Handbook of Middle East Politics*, 21–69. Abingdon, Oxon and New York, Routledge.

Sadiki, Larbi and Layla Saleh. (2020). "Reflexive Politics and Arab 'risk society'? COVID-19 and Issues of Public Health," *Orient: Deutsche Zeitschrift fü Politik und Wirtschaft des Orients*, 60 (3): 6–20.

SIS. (2020). "Statement by H.E. President Abdel Fattah El Sisi on the 7th Anniversary of June 30 Revolution," *State Information Service*, June 24, https://www.sis.gov.eg/Story/148932/Statement-by-H.E.-President-Abdel-Fattah-El-Sisi-on-the-7th-Anniversary-of-June-30-Revolution?lang=en-us (accessed June 25, 2021).

SIS. (2021a). "Health Minister Probes with WHO Director Issues of Mutual Concern," *State Information Service*, June 16, https://www.sis.gov.eg/Story/155880?lang=en-us (accessed June 21, 2021).

SIS. (2021b). *"Ra ʾis al-wuzarā ʾ yatar ʾas ijtimā ʿ al-lajna al- ʿulyā li-idāra azma fayrūs "kūrūnā"* (The prime minister chairs the meeting of the higher committer for the management of the coronavirus crisis)," *State Information Service*, July 4, https://www.sis.gov.eg/Story/220219/%D8%B1%D8%A6%D9%8A%D8%B3-%D8%A7%D9%84%D9%88%D8%B2%D8%B1%D8%A7%D8%A1-%D9%8A%D8%AA%D8%B1%D8%A3%D8%B3-%D8%A7%D8%AC%D8%AA%D9%85%D8%A7%D8%B9-%D8%A7%D9%84%D9%84%D8%AC%D9%86%D8%A9-%D8%A7%D9%84%D8%B9%D9%84%D9%8A%D8%A7-%D9%84%D8%A5%D8%AF%D8%A7%D8%B1%D8%A9-%D8%A3%D8%B2%D9%85%D8%A9-%D9%81%D9%8A%D8%B1%D9%88%D8%B3-%D9%83%D9%88%D8%B1%D9%88%D9%86%D8%A7-?lang=ar (accessed July 7, 2021).

Soliman, Mohamed. (2021). "Egypt's Drugmaker EVA Pharma to Manufacture Coronavirus Vaccine: Cabinet," *Ahramonline*, May 26, https://english.ahram.org.eg/NewsContent/1/64/412978/Egypt/Politics-/Egypts-drugmaker-EVA-Pharma-to-manufacture-coronav.aspx (accessed July 15, 2021).

Sørensen, Mads P. (2018). "Ulrich Beck: Exploring and Contesting Risk," *Journal of Risk Research*, 21 (1): 6–16.

UN. (2021). "Unequal Vaccine Distribution Self-Defeating, World Health Organization Chief Tells Economic and Social Council's Special Ministerial Meeting," *United Nations*, April 16, https://www.un.org/press/en/2021/ecosoc7039.doc.htm (accessed July 3, 2021).

UN News. (2020). "COVID-19 is not Just Seasonal, Cautions WHO, as 'first wave' Continues," *United Nations*, July 28, https://news.un.org/en/story/2020/07/1069111 (accessed June 27, 2021).

USAID. (2021). "Response Operations to Covid-19 Epidemic," *USAID*, June 23, https://www.usaid.gov/egypt/global-health/response-operations-covid-19-epidemic (accessed June 25, 2021).

WHO. (2020). "WHO Director-General's Opening Remarks at the Media Briefing on COVID-19—March 2020," *World Health Organization*, March 11, https://www.who.int/director-general/speeches/detail/who-director-general-s-opening-remarks-at-the-media-briefing-on-covid-19---11-march-2020 (accessed June 6, 2021).

WHO. (n.d.). "Health Security: WHO Response," *World Health Organization*, https://www.who.int/health-topics/health-security/#tab=tab_2 (accessed June 8, 2021).

Wimmer, Jeffrey and Thorsten Quandt. (2006). "Living in the Risk Society," *Journalism Studies*, 7 (2): 336–47.

8

Dual Combat

Resisting COVID-19 and the Israeli Occupation

Basem Ezbidi

Introduction

The ongoing COVID-19 pandemic is the most dramatic and far-reaching event in modern times in terms of the speed of its transmission and the scope of its response globally—even though its death toll pales compared to pandemics in history or major wars. Commentators contemplate the pandemic's effects on human lives and health, social and political orders, the planet, and international relations, even citing divine providence (Agamben 2020, Zreik 2020). Questions about COVID-19 consider the role of modernity's ills, reminding us of Rousseau's position on the morally corrupting effects of the arts and sciences, as he examines the influence of nature versus society on humans (Masters 1964). This perspective similarly questions the value of modernity's commitment to scientific advancement and scrutinizes its moral bearings. While progress has produced ecological degeneration, global warming, and technological over-control, thereby perpetuating economic inequality and alienation, it also provides tools to counteract the negative, brutal aspects of modernity.

The question thus becomes: what can be learned from COVID-19? It is not imprudent to consider the pandemic a moment of notable learning. After all, the imprisoned is the one who better understands freedom; industrial progress shapes the awareness of ecological deterioration; colonialism triggers the passion for freedom; and masculinity arouses feminist awareness (Sadiki and Saleh 2020). As we strive to minimize future risks, the concept of "risk society," developed by Ulrich Beck (1992) and Anthony Giddens (2013), proves useful (see also Sadiki and Saleh (2020)). It addresses "distributional conflicts" in competition over who must bear the "bads," and explains how risks are distributed and can be prevented, controlled, and legitimized (Sadiki and Saleh 2020). This concept considers most modern risks reflexive and socially induced, subjected to the self-conscious control of social actors. Furthermore, while medical and environmental concerns are growing, fears regarding crime, immigration, Internet security, financial markets, and social unrest are increasing as well. Risks relate to science because they induce technological advancement that may backlash, as with nuclear power and ozone-depleting chemicals in the Earth's atmosphere. But science is also present in both the diagnosis and the correction of problems (Yearley 2021), as evident in the COVID-19 pandemic.

Considering COVID-19 as engendering a kind of reflexive identity (Sadiki and Saleh 2020), this chapter chooses Palestine as a case to examine how such reflexivity may develop in its "pandemic condition." Its main assertion is that although COVID-19 has impacted both Palestinians and Israelis, the extent of both suffering and recovery has not been equal. A considerable gap exists between the options and responses available to each in dealing with the pandemic, due to serious differences in structural vulnerability. While Israel efficiently recruited its various resources to contain the virus, Palestinians were hampered by limited resources and policy ineffectiveness.

The analysis will also benefit from two other theoretical frameworks. The first is Agamben's (2004) notion of the "state of exception" that considers an emergency situation (such as the COVID-19 pandemic) an opportunity to override checks, balances, and the principle of legality, thereby deepening repression. Second, the discussion of time and its transformative quality during conflict as raised by Amal Jamal (2016), which shows how during the pandemic, time has been converted and employed as an effective tool of oppression.

The chapter's main body consists of three sections. The first outlines the manner in which Palestinians have encountered the pandemic while forced to cope with the restrictions imposed by the Israeli occupation. The second section examines how the Israeli occupation affects structural factors Palestinians must deal with, such as their captured economy, inefficient health sector, and administration of Gaza under blockade. Making matters worse, Israel is violating Palestinian rights by evading responsibility for the population that lives under occupation, suppressing prisoners, and discriminating against laborers. The third section outlines the Palestinian Authority (PA)'s disorganized and ineffective response to the pandemic, as it resorted to authoritarianism, suppressed civil liberties, and cracked down on civil society.

Chasing Two Calamities

In late February 2020, Palestinians in the West Bank and Gaza, beleaguered for fifty-three years by the occupation, were confronted with the COVID-19 pandemic. When the first coronavirus cases were recorded in Bethlehem, the city and neighboring towns were placed under lockdown immediately. This was soon followed by the declaration of a thirty-day countrywide state of emergency that was renewed monthly amid a debate about its constitutionality in the absence of the Palestinian Legislative Council (PLC). Israel and Jordan closed their borders and all crossings into the Palestinian territories, and Palestinian workers in Israel were either returned to their homes or told to remain in Israel. The Gaza Strip remained subject to the tight blockade imposed by Israel since 2007. While these closures limited the influx of infected persons to some extent, they did not prevent the spread of COVID-19. In the Gaza Strip, a few cases were recorded, which alarmed and prompted the Hamas government to establish quarantine facilities for quarantine, but without declaring a state of emergency until August 2020. At that point, the virus began to spread in Gaza, leading to a lockdown and suspension of public institutions for two weeks.

In November 2021, Israel outlawed the entry of its citizens and East Jerusalem residents into the Palestinian areas for one month. As the PA's financial crisis affected the financial sustainability of the six East Jerusalem hospitals that had accrued debts and payment arrears of US$68 million (OCHA 2020b), the operational capacity of these hospitals was affected.

In Gaza, the Hamas government announced that, as of November 15 and until further notice, all shops across Gaza Strip must close by 5 p.m. Additionally, indoor gatherings of more than fifteen people were prohibited, and the authorities designated twenty-three out of the ninety-four geographic areas in Gaza as red, where no movement was allowed (OCHA 2020b). By the time of writing in late August 2021, the number of deaths reached 5,235, the total number of reported cases amounted to 605,347 (319,514 in the West Bank, 230,058 in the Gaza Strip, and 55,775 in East Jerusalem and its suburbs), and the number of recoveries was estimated at 344,422 (MoH, Feb 2022).

With respect to the Palestinian citizens of Israel, COVID-19 has revealed the racist nature of the Israeli state and its policies. From the beginning, they faced different conditions from their Jewish counterparts, in addition to language barriers that made it difficult for them to implement instructions on how to deal with the virus's outbreak. They generally did not use online medical services; quite a few towns and villages lacked sufficient clinics; and many individuals flocked to hospital emergency rooms, which intensified the load there and increased exposure to diseases (Lavie et al. 2020). These asymmetries in healthcare access resulted in a three times higher death rate among Israeli Arabs than the Israeli population as a whole (Efrati 2021).

Through legal actions in Israeli courts, Adalah, an independent human rights group, has highlighted the discrimination faced by the Palestinians inside Israel. Adalah has pointed out several areas of clear racial discrimination against the Palestinians, including the inaccessibility of online distance learning; major gaps in access to emergency medical services, testing, and isolation facilities; unequal rollout of economic stimulus measures to assist workers, households, small businesses, and vulnerable communities; the failure to collect and publish comprehensive data on infected cases among the Palestinian citizens of Israel; the failure to provide updated public health information in Arabic; excessive reliance on emergency regulations during the first months of the pandemic, where many of these regulations led to human rights violations (World Justice Challenge 2021). This multifaceted discrimination has deepened the long-entrenched discrimination faced by the Palestinians inside Israel.

Through its occupation and racist policies, Israel directly contributed to the deteriorating health conditions of Palestinians during the pandemic and entrenched its occupation. The average testing rate of COVID-19 has been modest in Palestine, not exceeding 635 tests per million, whereas Israel carried out 9,800 tests per million. By July 2021, 988,226 vaccine doses had been administered among Palestinians and 11.09 million vaccine doses in Israel. By early April 2020, close to 90 percent of the 256 ventilators available in the West Bank and the 87 ventilators available in the Gaza Strip were being used. While Israel was worrying that 40 ventilators per 100,000 people was insufficient, the densely populated Gaza Strip had 3 ventilators per 100,000 individuals (Asi 2020).

Although the Israeli authorities provided the PA with training and equipment to control the spread of the virus, the same authorities stated that "the Palestinians' needs are greater than what Israel is able to provide" (Asi 2020). Meanwhile, countries (the Czech Republic, Hungary, Guatemala, Honduras, and other unnamed countries) willing to move their embassies to Jerusalem in defiance of UN resolution 478 were given free vaccines (Haaretz February 23, 2021). The limited Israeli assistance to Palestinians was not apolitical either. In responding to PA criticism about Israel's handling of COVID-19 within the Palestinian areas, Danny Danon, the Israeli ambassador to the UN, stated that Palestinians must prove that they deserve aid but may not criticize the Israeli government's behavior—or risk being accused of incitement and anti-Semitism. If they want to continue receiving coronavirus aid, they need to stop the incitement, he suggested (Asi 2020).

The territorial fragmentation of Palestine hampers a coordinated response to the pandemic, while the relegation of Palestinians lower class citizen status and lower priority in terms of care leads to neglect and reduces COVID-19 protection and treatment. Thus, any discussion of the challenges Palestinians are facing must account for Israel's policies in light of its transformation into an apartheid state. Several reports, the most recent by *Amnesty International* in February (2022), have described Israel's policy of segregation and institutional discrimination of Palestinians even inside Israel. In 2018, the apartheid status of Israel was given a legal label after the approval of a law stating that all of Israel (i.e., Mandatory Palestine) is the national state of solely the Jewish people (Hattis Rolef 2018). Palestinians in the West Bank are subjected to military law and a silent policy of annexation, and Jerusalem is subject to systematic policy of Judaization (Amnesty International 2022). Such repression explains the anger that erupted among Palestinians in May 2021 in historic Palestine. They protested repressive Israeli policies at Al-Aqsa Mosque and against the residents of Sheikh Jarrah, as well as the attack on the Gaza Strip.

Deepening Vulnerability

This section examines in more detail risk society under occupation. Specifically, two sets of Israeli coercive and discriminatory measures will be introduced, measures that affected the Palestinians negatively in responding to the coronavirus. The first set consists of three physical factors, namely the economy, the health sector, and the blockade of Gaza. The second set comprises of three violations of Palestinian rights: evading responsibility for the population living under occupation, suppressing prisoners, and discriminating against laborers.

A Strangled Economy

The pandemic has demonstrated the weakness of the Palestinian economic capacity and the absence of tools required to deal with its tremendous challenges. The economy is deteriorating and has moved from bad to worse since the outbreak of the pandemic (UNCTAD 2020b). In the years 2020 and 2021, the GDP per capita has decreased by 3–4.5 percent. The West Bank recorded its lowest growth rate since 2012 (1.15 percent), while the growth rate in Gaza remained at close to zero, which increased poverty and unemployment rates among a large segment of Palestinians (*UNCTAD* 2020a).

As the Palestinian economy is under siege, restrictions continue in line with the Paris protocols of the Oslo Accords. The leakage of fiscal resources undermines the Palestinian economy, with the annual leakage of Palestinian financial resources into Israel amounting to nearly 3.7 percent of the GDP or 17.8 percent of total tax revenues (UNCTAD 2020b). The situation worsened when at the start of the pandemic Israel decided on deducting, as a punitive measure, US$144 million from the proceeds of the Palestinian customs clearance—the value of the aid the PA provides to the families of Palestinian political prisoners and victims of occupation-related violence (considered martyrs by Palestinians) (Rasgon and Halbfinger 2020).

Even prior to the pandemic, the deterioration of the economic condition was exacerbated by a significant decline in donor support that fell from a high 32 percent of the GDP in 2008 to 3.5 percent in 2019 (UNCTAD 2020b). In 2020, donor support decreased to around US$266 million, and the decline was expected to continue in 2021. This has weakened the already difficult economic performance and led to a further deterioration of Palestinians' social and economic conditions.

Many estimates on the cost of the pandemic point to an economic loss in the range of 7 percent to 35 percent of the GDP (UNCTAD 2020b). The measures taken to encounter the pandemic entailed frequent closures that made the economic situation unbearable for many Palestinians. As the tourism sector has come to a standstill for the last year and a half, and trade was affected worldwide, the PA's revenues from trade, tourism, and remittances fell to their lowest levels in twenty years. This has destructively affected the rate of spending on health, social allocations, and support for the private sector that has also been hit hard by the repeated closures. Due to the pressures caused by the pandemic and a weak economy crippled by the occupation, the PA lacks the economic policy tools required to deal with the enormous challenge posed by COVID-19.

A Distressed Health Sector

The health system in Palestine consists of four bodies that provide health services, namely the Palestinian Ministry of Health, the United Nations Relief and Works Agency for Palestine Refugees in the Near East (UNRWA), the private sector, and NGOs. This system is characterized by occupation-imposed geographical fragmentation, such as the separation between East Jerusalem, Gaza, and the West Bank. Moreover, it features restrictions imposed on the freedom of movement of patients, medical equipment, and healthcare personnel, as well as by the poor performance of the healthcare system.

Israeli brutal measures against the Palestinians have targeted health workers and contributed to the destruction of health facilities. Since 2018, direct Israeli attacks have caused 48,246 injuries and 452 deaths (most of them in the Gaza Strip), increasing the burden and pressure on hospitals, as have attacks carried out by Israeli settlers (AlKhalidi 2020).

Moreover, the health system suffers from a chronic shortage of resources, which include equipment, devices, and medicines (Falah 2020). The sector also lacks effective governance and innovative policies to secure and guarantee the necessary financial resources, knowledge sharing, information, technologies, and coordination among health partners. Gaza's facilities are affected by frequent power cuts that decrease the capacity of hospitals to work. It is also ailed by poor water and sanitation systems, exacerbated by the lack of electric power. These multiple problems make it difficult for individuals and public utilities to abide by the protocols necessary to combat COVID-19.

The COVID-19 pandemic has placed additional pressures on UNRWA, as it is overburdened and chronically underfunded. On March 17, 2020, UNRWA launched its first Pandemic Flash Appeal, seeking to raise US$14.1 million to respond to the pandemic's immediate health impacts. This appeal was then expanded to respond to needs that arose in the areas of healthcare, hospitalization, water, sanitation and hygiene, and education. Thus, UNRWA needed US$93.4 million to cover its humanitarian operations that benefit 5.6 million refugees, including 871,000 in the West Bank and 1.4 million in Gaza, where US$5,453,529 were allocated to the former and US$13,981,413 to the latter (UNRWA Report May 2020).

UNRWA interventions included two main areas. In the health sector, the agency provided personal protective equipment and medication, furbished isolation and quarantine centers, ensured the supply of water, sanitation and hygiene, and provided cash and food assistance. In the education sector, it helped safeguard continuity through self and distance learning, gave psychosocial support, supplied health and hygiene equipment, supported technical and vocational education and training, and aided in monitoring and evaluation.

The COVID-19 outbreak in Palestine has highlighted the structural weakness of the Palestinian health system after years of occupation and blockade, compounded by limited financial allocations. This fragility and the modest capabilities of the sector have made it difficult not only to deal with the current pandemic but also with other preexisting health challenges. With the onset of the pandemic, many worried about the lack of adequate health infrastructure, including lacking healthcare equipment, testing capabilities, respiration devices, medicines, and disposable protective equipment (*WHO 2021*).

The Gaza Blockade and the Cutting of Aid

Upon the eruption of COVID-19, the Hamas government and Gaza's health and humanitarian workers focused their primary efforts on prevention. After a long siege and repeated Israeli military attacks, living conditions had become inadequate. With a dilapidated infrastructure and weak healthcare system, Gaza was certainly unprepared for dealing with a pandemic. Since the imposition of the blockade in 2007, the movement of people, goods, and equipment through the crossings has remained under tight control by the Israeli and Egyptian authorities, hindering the development of the infrastructure as a whole and affecting the availability of medicines and medical equipment. This blockade aspect of Gaza's risk society has progressively deepened poverty, as the poverty rate today is at least 80 percent, up from 39 percent in 2011 (Abdel Hadi 2021). Unemployment levels have drastically risen and now reach more than 50 percent of the labor force in general and over 70 percent among youth.

The freeze on the relationship between the PA and Israel that followed the latter's announcement of its intention to annex 50 percent of the so-called Area C in May 2020 (30 percent of the West Bank) severely affected Gazans. Procedures through which the Israeli side had allowed Gazan patients to leave for treatment in the West Bank or Israel were halted. Moreover, the PA rejected the transfer of tax revenues that had been collected on its behalf by Israel. This in turn had severe consequences for the Strip, as the PA could not pay Gaza's electricity fees or the salaries of an estimated 16,000 government employees. This came after the Trump administration had cut off US aid to the Palestinians in the West Bank, Gaza Strip, Jerusalem and stopped the US contribution to first USAID (February) and then UNRWA (August) in 2018. These steps had dire effects on Gazans, as food aid, basic medicines, a wide network of schools, water and sanitation operations, and other services were suspended entirely. It is important to remember here that more than 80 percent of Gaza's population depend on humanitarian aid (OCHA 2020a).

Israel's latest attack on Gaza from May 10 to 21, 2021, causing 254 deaths and 2,212 wounded and displacing about 120,000 according to Euro-Med Monitor's field count, has made matters worse in the fight against the coronavirus. The attack severely damaged twenty-four medical facilities, including hospitals, clinics, and the ministry of health headquarters (Euro-Med Monitor 2021).

Evasion of Responsibility

While keeping Palestinians under the grip of the occupation, Israel has failed to abide by the stipulations of international humanitarian law that oblige the occupying force to care for the population under occupation, acting in that population's best interest, as stipulated by Article 42 of the 1907 The Hague Regulations, the Fourth Geneva Convention of 1949, and the Additional Protocol I of 1977. This obligation includes caring for health-related needs. Israel, however, has not protected the health of Palestinians, before or during the pandemic. Not only has the occupation contributed to, if not caused, the remarkable fragility and weakness of the Palestinian health system, apparent before the outbreak of the pandemic. The occupation authorities furthermore restricted Palestinian initiatives in dealing with the new pandemic health situation.

Israel not only raided a COVID-19 testing center in Silwan, Jerusalem, it also arrested its organizers to prevent "any PA activity in the city." Meanwhile, it provided only limited services through Israeli government authorities. As well, Israeli authorities did not service areas such as Kufr Aqab that are technically within Israeli-drawn boundaries but lie beyond the separation wall, where Israel bans PA activity. This leaves the Palestinians who live there without any government services. In places where Israel severely limits PA operations, Israeli authorities have neglected to build and promote sufficient testing facilities or provide accurate data, and NGOs had to step in to ensure that updated COVID-19 information was available in Arabic (Asi 2020).

Israel's legal obligations toward the Palestinians, especially during this pandemic, are outlined in several documents. Article 55 of Geneva Convention IV, for example, stipulates that the occupying power secure food and medical supplies for the population under occupation, especially when "the resources of the occupied territories are modest." Article 56 calls for ensuring and maintaining public health and hygiene, while Article 59 calls on the occupying powers to facilitate humanitarian relief efforts. Article 60 explicitly states that the provision of humanitarian relief—from states, international organizations to private individuals—does not exempt the occupying power from any of its responsibilities. All this means that Israel has not fulfilled its obligation of securing the necessary preventive means to "combat the spread of infectious diseases and pandemics," which has contributed to the death and suffering of many Palestinians.

Suppressing Prisoners

Palestinian prisoners are among the groups most affected by the pandemic because they are directly subjected to the occupation's oppressive measures and to its policy of health negligence, having to face the deadly virus under severe limitations to protect themselves inside prison (Al Mezan 2020). More than 5,000 Palestinians are detained in Israeli prisons, most of them political prisoners, some under administrative detention. They are stripped of their most basic rights and frequently subjected to brutal treatment prohibited by the Geneva Convention. The conditions Palestinian prisoners face under normal conditions are harsh and frequently amount to crimes under international humanitarian law. Deliberate medical neglect, isolation in solitary confinement, beatings, abuse, and torture are common forms of abuse.

The Israeli authorities have used COVID-19 as a tool of repression and intimidation, including Israeli investigators threatening prisoners that they will expose them to the virus (Human Rights and Democracy Media Centers SHAMS 2020). This was accompanied by systematic medical negligence that came to the attention of human rights organizations, resulting in a request that Israel ensure the supply of Palestinian prisoners with the minimum preventive measures, such as disinfectants and masks (International Bar Association 2020).

The spread of infection among prisoners caused great concern for their lives. Yet, Israel refused to respond to calls by human rights organizations to reduce overcrowding and improve prison conditions. As Israel failed to provide the appropriate opportunities to follow the hygiene protocols required for protection from infection, the Israeli Supreme Court ruled that the Palestinian prisoners do not have the right to social distancing (Khalel 2020).

As Israel still does not provide safe conditions for Palestinian prisoners, refuses to implement basic precautionary procedures such as the facilitation of appropriate hygiene measures, and sustains a shortage of general cleaning materials amid high humidity and little ventilation, the coronavirus will continue to pose a serious threat to the lives of Palestinian prisoners (Kuttab 2020).

Discriminating against Laborers

The coronavirus crisis had grave, direct repercussions on Palestinian laborers.[1] For the first two months after the pandemic's outbreak, Israel requested that laborers not return to their places of residence in the West Bank. Nearly 40,000 Palestinian workers had to live in dire conditions, adding to the pressures of being separated from their families. Israel not only ignored their rights to safe working conditions but also exploited them. Israeli police threw them on the streets of the West Bank without recourse to any medical care in case of symptoms or infection (Arraf 2020).

These severe measures had a devastating effect on the workers and their families, particularly when workers suspected of illness had to return to their homes to be cared for. These workers subsequently exposed their families to the virus, increasing its spread in the areas under the PA. The PA responded by calling on all Palestinian laborers to return to the West Bank, requiring them to self-quarantine in their homes. But this measure was insufficient and ultimately unfeasible, given the PA's limited resources to support them during their absence from work. Israel picks and chooses when it wants to act as an occupying force that controls and when to refuse taking responsibility because it claims that the PA is "in control."

The PA's Dealing with the Pandemic

The PA's Ineffective Response to the Pandemic

Adding to Palestine's risk society under occupation is the ineptness of governance by the PA. When a number of East Asian tourists who had visited Bethlehem tested positive for SARS-CoV-2 in March 2020, the PA declared a state of emergency, closed all schools and public institutions, and started an information campaign about hygiene and social distancing to curb the spread of the virus. Soon, a special committee was established. Initially, these measures were met with criticism. Some considered the emergency decision as hasty and unjustified, but this view changed with the increasing number of infected cases. Although the government's early measures won the praise of the World Health Organization (Quran 2020), the overall approach drew criticism because the Gaza Strip, controlled by Hamas, was not included in the emergency committee (Abd al-Hameed 2020). This rendered cooperation with Gaza weak, especially on issues regarding health, e-education, and the support of families and individuals affected by quarantine and siege (Abd al-Hameed 2020). The formation of the special committee was questioned, because it lacked a legal basis, and stood accused of being unilateral. This was because it was not subject to consultation within the Palestine Liberation Organization (PLO). The committee was considered a reflection reflecting the Fatah movement's monopoly and control, implemented with the help of security agencies.

Although people's approval of the Palestinian government differed regarding the various measures that were implemented, their overall satisfaction with the cabinet's dealing with the pandemic was high, ranging from 57 to 80 percent (Palestinian Center for Policy and Survey Research 2020). Even the barriers set up by Palestinian police to reduce people's movement and monitor the return of laborers from Israel were colloquially called "checkpoints of love" to differentiate them from the Israeli checkpoints that dot Palestinian areas. Things changed, however, when the financial crisis worsened and the economy declined, as did foreign aid. These dips have all affected the PA's ability to implement anti-COVID measures.

Early on, the PA was unable to support poor people who lost their jobs, as apparent through the unsuccessful initiative of the Waqfet Izz Solidarity Fund. Established by Palestinian prime minister Mohammad Shtayyeh, it included thirty Palestinian businessmen and representatives of the private sector. But this segment of society lacks people's trust, and many refrained from donating to the fund. While the fund aimed to provide approximately US$250 to needy families during the pandemic, the targeted amount of US$28 million was not met; donations did not exceed US$15 million by the end of May 2020, and the project was discontinued (Ezz El Din Asaad 2020).

The situation deteriorated after the PA in April 2020 decided to halt security coordination with the Israeli authorities, following the formation of the Israeli right-wing unity government that pledged to move forward with annexing large parts of the West Bank. Israel responded by imposing severe restrictions on the movement and activities of the Palestinian security forces, including forces tasked with enforcing virus prevention measures. Thus, efforts to secure medical supplies and equipment to the occupied territories were blocked, and coronavirus testing and treatment were dangerously delayed (Abou Sittah 2020).

To make matters more difficult, the PA refused in June 2020 to accept the customs revenues collected by Israel on its behalf. This too was in response to Israel's threat of annexation. Instead, the PA relied on the private sector, the diaspora, and donor contributions. Thus, popular support for its handling of the pandemic decreased significantly, as public sector employees, including police officers and healthcare workers, did not receive their full salaries. Although the PA later on recovered its withheld tax revenues from the Israeli side, the damage to an effective response to the pandemic was difficult to undo. In Gaza, Hamas acted independently, perpetuating the gap with the West Bank. Israel was ready to exploit the rift between Ramallah and Gaza, for instance when it transferred health aid shipments from the United Arab Emirates to Gaza after Ramallah refused to accept them because they came through Tel Aviv without coordination with or the knowledge of the PA (Aljazeera May 2020).

The spread of the pandemic neither improved internal Palestinian relations nor reduced tensions between the West Bank and Gaza. Instead, the two sides exchanged accusations. Hamas accused the PA in Ramallah of not providing the Gaza Strip with sufficient health care and financial support to contain the coronavirus. From its end, the PA in Ramallah accused Hamas of coordinating with the Israelis on health protection matters, including allowing Gazan doctors to receive training from Israeli counterparts (Shehadeh 2020). The conflict has weakened both sides and prevented them from following a unified strategy.

Resorting to Authoritarianism

In the middle of these difficult times, poorly thought-out legal decisions regarding the law of retirement and bonuses were issued (Law by Decree No. 15 of 2020). The public considered these a gross abuse of the state of emergency (a la Agamben) and reacted with widespread discontent and rejection, as these measures exempt senior officials from paying their pension premiums and refund what they paid in the past, causing the pension fund to lose millions of US dollars. Simultaneously, the salaries of this category of employees were raised. Their retirement age was also increased from 62 to 65 years, allowing them to collect more benefits. When these two decisions lowered the PA's approval rate and caused widespread protests, they were cancelled. Still, the PA failed to regain public approval.

Another decision that aroused public discontent was the issuing of Law Number 5 on March 19, 2020 (Abd al-Hameed 2020, 197). It grants the president's office additional, new powers, assigning the president's office a head with the rank of a minister. Moreover, the measure allows its budget to be drawn up by its employees, approved by the president, and included as a separate item in the PA's budget. This office oversees all the president's work both locally and internationally, which ultimately marginalizes the work of the government. This situation is particularly worrisome because the power of the judiciary is already limited, as the Legislative Council has been more or less absent since 2007. Law Number 5 also assigns the Office of the President the right to own movable and immovable funds. Essentially, this converts it into an investment authority that can operate unconstrained by clear measures of transparency or accountability.

The fact that these decisions were issued during a period when Shtayyeh's government enjoyed significant popular support raises questions about the power dynamics and the centers of power within the ruling circle in Palestine. Many expressed concern were raised over the true intention behind these decisions, which might be interpreted as part of a corruption scheme and a power struggle. That these decisions were made while the public was preoccupied with COVID-19, the Israeli annexation plan, and the PA's financial crisis may reveal the influence of certain segments within the PA. Such a circle may place narrow interests of its members ahead of national interests. They could be part of the contest for power struggle taking place behind the scenes to succeed Abbas and reinforce the authoritarian order in Palestine.

While the people were facing off against the coronavirus, the PA exploited the exceptional circumstances to enforce the dominance of President Abbas over the judiciary. It issued a set of laws that were approved on January 1, 2021. These laws—basically presidential decrees, in the absence of a parliament—failed to revise the existing election law even though the political parties demanded such amendments, viewing them as necessary to ensure the integrity of the expected elections. Elections have been long overdue, as president Abbas rules on a mandate from the 2005 elections. On January 15, only days later, the elections decree was issued, announcing that legislative elections would be held in May, presidential elections in June, and PNC (PLO parliament) elections in August. On April 29, however, the elections were postponed indefinitely under the pretext that Israel refused to allow that elections be held in Jerusalem. As the postponement (or cancellation) of these long-overdue elections infringed on the civil rights and liberties of the Palestinian people, widespread protests arose, and stern criticism of the leadership was voiced. In response, protesters, opponents, and activists were arrested and tortured, on the grounds of incitement. This was a blatant infringement on the freedom of expression. Some of the protesters and critics had been candidates for the elections, such as Nizar Banat who was beaten to death during arrest in June 2021.

In early June 2021, the Pfizer vaccine scandal made headlines when the PA canceled an agreement of exchanging one million doses of the Pfizer vaccine from Israel after inspecting the first delivery and realizing that the doses did not conform to important technical specifications, particularly the expiration date (BBC 2021). This scandal was seen as part of a pervasive state of corruption in all institutions in addition to being an Israeli attempt at subterfuge and cheating the Palestinians. According to a public opinion poll, 84 percent of Palestinians believe that corruption is present in the PA's various civil, security, and economic institutions (Palestinian Center for Policy and Survey Research June 2021).

Suppressing Civil Liberties

The two dominant authorities in Ramallah and Gaza both carry out arbitrary arrests and restrict the freedom of expression and peaceful criticism of the authorities, especially on social media by journalists, university students, dissidents, and peaceful demonstrators (Amnesty International 2020). Recently, female journalists in Ramallah have been targeted and beaten, had their cameras smashed, and were even threatened with rape. The two authorities have taken advantage of the state of emergency (extended monthly, in violation of the constitution) and of the elastic laws that restrict protests and criticism and criminalize unwanted activity. This is frequently and traditionally justified by claims that oppositional activities cause strife, disturb security and order, and ultimately harm the aspirations of the Palestinians and their national project (Human Rights Watch 2018).

The harshest incident the PA ever faced was the killing of Palestinian activist Nizar Banat in June 2021. He was brutally killed in an area under the full control of the occupation authorities. Angry demonstrations and rallies ensued to condemn the killing, both in Palestinian cities and abroad. Protesters demanded that the leaders of the security forces be brought to justice, the PA regime be overthrown—particularly Abbas and his corrupt circle—and free and fair elections be held as the only means to bring about an accountable leadership. In commenting on Banat's killing one month later, the PA minister Hussein Al-Sheikh (Friedson 2021) described the appalling act as a mistake and asserted that such mistakes happen even in the United States or France.

In another recent development, the PA canceled Article 22 of the Cabinet Resolution No. 4 of 2020 regarding the Code of Conduct for civil servants that had granted "the employee . . . the right to express his opinion and publish it verbally, in writing, or by any other means of expression or art, subject to the provisions of the legislation." Thus, when expressing an opinion or comment on social media, employees now must explicitly stress that this opinion is personal and does not reflect the government's stand. This decision has been viewed as part of a worrisome trend in suppressing the freedom of expression. It comes at a time when Palestinians continue to voice their anger over the killing of political activist Nizar Banat by PA security forces and are protesting the widespread corruption and nepotism, the cancelation of elections, and the growing power of security forces.

Cracking Down on Civil Society

Palestinian civil society has not escaped the PA regime's authoritarian approach. In early March 2020, President Abbas issued a revision of Decree Law No. 7 regarding charitable societies and civil organizations, amending some articles of the original law in a manner that gives the PA increased power over civil society and its activities. Previously, this move had been rejected by the civil society groups (Palestinian Gazette Issue 167). The amendments include the stipulation that organizations must submit an estimated annual budget and publish plans that must be in line with the plans of the relevant ministries. The new rule furthermore determines that salaries and operating expenses should not exceed 25 percent of the total annual budget. In addition, the amendments give the Palestinian Ministry of Interior the power to liquidate the properties of dissolved organizations.

These amendments further narrow the space for and assert control over more than 4,600 organizations, impeding their activities, and subjecting them to the PA's total control. By having to submit annual work plans that are in accordance with PA policies, civil society organizations turn into quasi-governmental bodies that lack autonomy and must depend on the PA's projects and policies. This despite the fact that these organizations may not necessarily agree with the PA. For example, civil society organizations active in the field of agriculture will be expected to work together with the PA's inefficient ministry of agriculture. Thus, these organizations will be unable to criticize flawed PA policies in this sector. In another example, human rights organizations and women's associations will be asked to adjust their plans to the policies of the ministries of justice and interior. This raises serious questions about how these organizations can engage against, for example, the cybercrime law while their hands are tied behind their backs. They would be forced to coordinate their work with the two ministries responsible for issuing and applying this law.

On the other hand, the amendment that requires organizations to provide details about their activities and implementation plans is unclear. It may turn the government into a judge who adjudicates the organizations' activities, but without issuing clear criteria. This could expose organizations to blackmail, as their work could be evaluated on the basis of their loyalty or support for the PA rather than their actual performance.

By limiting the operating expenses and salaries to 25 percent of an organization's annual budget, the PA demands that most of civil society's revenues must be diverted to productive activities. This demand fails to acknowledge that most of the organizations provide intangible services. For example, human rights organizations produce periodic reports, document violations, conduct training, and provide pleadings in courts; health sector organizations provide healthcare and medical services; the services and activities of educational and training organizations are not financially profitable, and the same applies to cultural organizations. Therefore, in these NGOs, operating costs and salaries comprise the largest share of their budgets. Due to this amendment, a large proportion of the 40,000 employees of these organizations will lose their jobs. Oddly, the PA cannot apply what it is trying to forbid, as the percentage of PA-operating expenses and salaries reaches 95 percent of the total public budget (World Bank 2016). In private sector companies, operating costs exceed half of the budgets.

According to this amendment, the PA will be allowed to regulate the collection of donations and control whether organizations may accept or must reject them. It furthermore grants the Ministry of Interior the powers to liquidate and dissolve civil society organizations and to target the organizations that the PA perceives as unfavorable. These measures add to Israeli pressures against civil society organizations on the one hand. At the same time, the European Union is linking the funding of Palestinian organizations to these organizations "renouncing terrorism." This is considered a measure to suppress any political party that does not follow Fateh's practice of accommodating Israeli demands as much as possible, even at the expense of the Palestinian cause.

Conclusion

Through repressive and discriminatory measures, Israel has successfully exploited the pandemic to further consolidate the already existing asymmetrical power balance with the Palestinians. The measures discussed in the chapter make up risk society under occupation. They are part of a comprehensive policy of forced displacement and demographic control adopted by successive Israeli governments for the past seven decades. It aims to extend temporal measures and entrench permanent policies to strengthen the grip of the Israeli occupation, apartheid regime, and hegemony and control over Palestine in all aspects. The occupation, supposedly a temporary condition, has become permanent, speaking to Jamal's notion of transformative time. Moreover, Agamben's state of exception is continuously extended and expanded. Israel has entrenched its control over Palestine's physical space, time, aspirations, and narrative, while it capitalizes on the ongoing pandemic as an opportune development to strengthen its grip. The power imbalance converts the occupation from a temporary rupture into a permanent state of suffering.

The analysis of how Israel and the PA dealt with the pandemic has benefited from three theoretical expressions, namely Beck and Giddens's notion of risk society, Agamben's theory of the "state of exception" and the reflection on time and its transformative temporality. These approaches serve to illustrate that the pandemic has lowered people's faith in the institutions of modernity (precautionary measures, tests, vaccines, etc.) and has shaken trust not only in governments and world bodies such as the WHO, but also in science itself. Thus, people consider current "reflexive" modernity as part of the problem and not the solution, causing deep anxiety in the present and fear of the future. But, while the impact of the COVID-19 pandemic (or other ills such as pollution or ozone depletion) is democratic in its distribution, its negative consequences are hierarchical and not evenly distributed. Risk society is not experienced equally by everyone. Palestinians found themselves much more vulnerable than Israelis. These three approaches also served to illustrate how COVID-19 enabled both Israel and the PA to reinforce their versions of a state of exception. This enabled both authorities to expand their control. When it comes to governance, risk society under occupation has an internal (PA) element in addition to the problems of external (Israeli) occupation. Israel exerts hegemony over the PA, and Israel and the PA jointly applied measures to keep Palestinians under control. Israel entrenches its repressive policies to prolong its occupation, and the PA consolidates its authority to prolong its deficient rule.

Despite shared interests, vast differences characterize the respective perceptions of Israel and Palestine vis-à-vis the conflict, including what is permanent and what is temporary, and how it should be utilized. Each side seeks to prolong the permanent and shorten and derail the temporary. Both assign contradictory meaning to time, thus it has become part of the conflict itself; both utilize it to generate collective consciousness and harness the tools of its materialization. Thus, in moments of conflict and fear, time carries special relevance once it has been incorporated into the nation's grand narrative that is the source of various claims.

The COVID-19 calamity gave Israel the opportunity to emphasize its distinctiveness. For instance, it was among the most successful countries in testing and vaccination rates and in the ability to provide the devices and equipment necessary to confront SARS-CoV-2. Moreover, Israel consolidated its (inexpensive) occupation and deepened its apartheid regime, increasing the weakness of the Palestinians. Israel presents such measures as necessary to encounter the existential threat it claims to be facing, as it depicts itself on the righteous side in a battle with evil—the Palestinians.

Finally, the pandemic clearly revealed that the PA enjoys a "medium" level of power, which serves the Israeli occupation while partially serving the Palestinians. This raises serious questions about the PA's fitness to embody and achieve Palestinian aspirations for an independent state. As it stands today, the PA is incapable of influencing Israeli policies, nor can it survive without security coordination with Israel or without the funds collected as customs and taxes by Israel on its behalf. Consistent with Agamben's characterization of the state of exception, the conditions of emergency have prevailed in Palestine in the course of combating the pandemic. Part and parcel of its risk society, this fight has rendered it difficult to effectively encounter Israeli occupation. Even though these issues remained important, it took second place while combating the pandemic became the ultimate priority. The PA is strong enough to control Palestinians and suppress dissent through its numerous security forces, and prisons. It is brutal to the extent that it does not hesitate to kill opponents. In light of this power disparity between Israel and the Palestinians, the former is likely to continue to transform the exceptional (occupation) into the permanent and what the Palestinians wish to be permanent (the right to be free) into an exceptional matter. This enforces Israel's intransigence vis-à-vis solving the conflict with the Palestinians and leaves the PA weak and impotent with or without the calamity of COVID-19. Risk society grows deeper, leaving Palestinians under duress by policies of occupying and occupied power.

Note

1 The number of Palestinian workers who apply for work permits inside Israel has been rising continually. In 2020, 137,600 Palestinians worked in Israel and in settlements in the West Bank and Jerusalem, most of them crossing over to Israel on a daily basis (Palestinian Central Bureau of statistics 2020).

References

Abd al-Hameed, Muhannad. (2020). "Palestinian Responses and Transformations in the Time of Coronavirus" (in Arabic). *Majallat al-Dirasat al-Filastiniyya* 123, Special Issue: The Age of the Epidemic, Summer 2020: 191–201.

Abdel Hadi, Ismael. (2021). "Poverty Rates in the Gaza Strip are the Highest in the Palestinian Territory" (in Arabic). *Al-Quds Al-Arabi*, July 31, https://www.alquds.co .uk/%D9%85%D8%B9%D8%AF%D9%84%D8%A7%D8%AA-%D8%A7%D9%84%D9 %81%D9%82%D8%B1-%D9%81%D9%8A-%D9%82%D8%B7%D8%A7%D8%B9- %D8%BA%D8%B2%D8%A9-%D8%A7%D9%84%D8%A3%D8%B9%D9%84%D9 %89-%D9%81%D9%8A-%D8%A7%D9%84%D8%A3%D8%B1/ (accessed August 27, 2021).

Abou Sittah, Ghassan. (2020). "The Virus, the Settler and the Siege: Gaza in the Age of Corona" (in Arabic). *Majallat al-Dirasat al-Filastiniyya* 123, Special Issue: The Age of the Epidemic, Summer 2020: 109–34.

Agamben, Giorgio. (1998). *Homo Sacer*. Stanford, CA: Stanford University Press.

Agamben, Giorgio. (2004). *The State of Exception*. Chicago IL: University of Chicago Press.

Agamben, Giorgio. (2020). *The Kingdom and the Garden*. Translated by Kotsko. Seagull Books.

Agamben, Giorgio. (2021). "The Invention of an Epidemic," in M. Foucault, G. Agamben and S. Benvenuto (eds.), "Coronavirus and Philosophers." *European Journal of Psychoanalysis*, https://www.journal-psychoanalysis.eu/coronavirus-and-philosophers/ (accessed July 26, 2021).

Al Mezan. (2020). "Press Release: Urgent Action Needed to Protect Palestinian Detainees Amid Surge in COVID-19 Cases in Israeli Prisons," *Al Mezan Center for Human Rights*, https://reliefweb.int/report/occupied-palestinian-territory/urgent-action-needed -protect-palestinian-detainees-amid-surge (accessed August 27, 2021).

Aljazeera. (2020). "Palestinian Authority Rejects UAE aid sent via Israeli Airport: Palestinians Say Medical Aid through Tel Aviv is 'a Cover for Normalization' of Ties with Israel," *Aljazeera*, May 21.

AlKhalidi, Mohammed, Rasha Kaloti, Duha Shella, Aisha Al Basuoni and Hamza Meghari. (2020). "Health System's Response to the COVID-19 Pandemic in Conflict Settings: Policy Reflections from Palestine," *Global Public Health* 15 (8), https://www .tandfonline.com/doi/full/10.1080/17441692.2020.1781914 (accessed August 2, 2020).

Amnesty International. (2020). "Amnesty Slams Palestinians' Freedom of Expression Arrests," *TRT World*, May 7.

Amnesty International. (2022). *Israel's Apartheid against Palestinians: Cruel System of Domination and Crime Against Humanity*, file:///C:/Users/Admin/Downloads/MD E1551412022ENGLISH.pdf (accessed May 24, 2022).

Arraf, Suha. (2020). "The Moment a Worker is Sick, They Throw him to the Checkpoint Like a Dog," *+972 Magazine*, March 24.

Asaad, Ahmed Ezz El Din. (2020). "The Country Is Carrying its People: The Waqft Fund, Optimism of the Mind and Pessimism of the Will," *Institute for Palestine Studies*, May 18.

Asi, Yara. (2020). "Occupation in the Time of COVID-19: Holding Israel Accountable for Palestinian Health," *Al-Shabaka*, November 15.

BBC. (2021). "COVID: Palestinians Cancel Vaccine Swap Deal with Israel," *BBC News*, June 19.

Beck, Ulrich. (1992). *Risk Society: Towards a New Modernity (Published in Association with Theory, Culture & Society)*. London, Newbury Park and New Delhi: Sage Publications.

Berger, Peter and Thomas Luckmann. (1967). *The Social Construction of Reality*. New York: Irvington.

Efrati, Ido. (2021). "Israeli Arab Death Rate From COVID-19 Was Three Times Higher Than the General Population, Study Finds," *Haaretz*, June 24.

El Sakka, Abaher. (2021). "Between the Palestinian Authority's Social Policies and Israel's Occupation Policies: Palestinians during the Corona Pandemic," Chapter 3 in Rima Majed et al. (eds.), *Rethinking Social Transformations: Inequalities in the Arab Region in Light of COVID-19 Pandemic, Mohamed Elagati, ed*, 104–13. Beirut: Arab Forum for Alternatives.

Elias, Norbert. (1992). *Time: An Essay*. Oxford, Cambridge: B. Blackwell.

Euro-Mediterranean Human Rights Monitor. (September 2021). "Left in Tatters," https://euromedmonitor.org/uploads/reports/GazaReportEN.pdf.

Fabian, Johannes. (1983). *Time and the Other: How Anthropology Makes its Objects*. New York: Columbia University Press.

Falah, Belal, Jihad Meshal and Wafaa Betawi. (2020). "Palestinian Health Sector Assessment: Macro-Analytical Study," Palestine Economic Policy Research Institute MAS.

Field Team in Gaza. (2021). "Inescapable Hell: The Israeli Attack on the Gaza Strip," *The Euro-Mediterranean Human Rights Monitor*, May.

Friedson, Felice. (2021). "Exclusive: Palestinian Authority's Hussein Al-Sheikh Tells The Media Line PA Is Ready for Direct Talks With Israel (with Video)," *The Medialine*, July 25.

Giddens, Anthony. (2013). *The Consequences of Modernity*. John Wiley & Sons.

Harb, Imad K. (2021). "The Utter Failure of the Abraham Accords," *Aljazeera Opinion*, May 18, https://www.aljazeera.com/opinions/2021/5/18/the-utter-failure-of-the-abraham-accords (accessed May 12, 2021).

Hareuveni, Eyal and Dror Etkes. (2021). "This Is Ours—And This, Too: Israel's Settlement Policy in the West Bank," *B'Tselem*.

Hattis Rolef, Susan. (2018). "Basic Law: Israel-The Nation State of the Jewish People," Unofficial translation. *The Knesset*, https://main.knesset.gov.il/EN/activity/Documents/BasicLawsPDF/BasicLawNationState.pdf (accessed August 27, 2021).

Human Rights Watch. (2018). "Two Authorities, One Way, Zero Dissent: Arbitrary Arrest and Torture Under the Palestinian Authority and Hamas," *Middle East Eye*, October.

Human Rights Watch. (2021). "A Threshold Crossed: Israeli Authorities and the Crimes of Apartheid and Persecution," *Human Rights Watch*, April 27.

International Bar Association. (2020). "Issue 25: 3. Prisoners and Detainees, Israel/Palestine," *International Bar Association*, October 9.

Jamal, Amal. (2016). "Conflict Theory, Temporality, and Transformative Temporariness: Lessons from Israel and Palestine," *Constellations*, 23 (3): 365–77.

Jean-Jacques, Rousseau. (1964). *The First and Second Discourses*, ed. with introduction and notes by Roger D. Masters, trans. Roger D. Masters and Judith R. Masters. New York: St. Martin's Press.

Khalel, Sheren. (2020). "Coronavirus: Israeli Court Rules Palestinian Prisoners Have no Right to Social Distancing," *Middle East Eye*, July 24.

Kuttab, Daoud. (2020). "How the Coronavirus Exposed Israeli Occupation's Green Line," *Middle East Institute*, March 31.

Lavie et al. (2020). *Israel's Arab Society and the Coronavirus Challenge. The Institute for National Security Studies*, https://www.inss.org.il/publication/coronavirus-and-the -israeli-arabs/ (accessed June 20, 2021).

Maltz, Judy (2021). "Israel to Send Thousands of Vaccines to Countries Opening Embassies in Jerusalem," *Haaretz*, February 23.

MoH. (n.d.). "Coronavirus (COVID-19) in Palestine," *Palestinian Ministry of Health*, https://corona.ps (accessed August 27, 2021).

OCHA. (2020a). "End of Palestinian Authority Coordination with Israel in Response to Annexation Threat: Decision Already Impacting Medical Referrals," *United Nations Office for the Coordination of Humanitarian Affairs*, July 20.

OCHA. (2020b). "Occupied Palestinian Territory (oPt): COVID-19 Emergency: Situation Report No. 22, 3–17 November," *United Nations Office for the Coordination of Humanitarian Affairs*.

Office of Fatwa and Legislation. (2020). "Palestinian Gazette, Issue 167 (in Arabic)," *Palestinian National Authority*, https://www.lab.pna.ps/cached_uploads/download /2020/05/13/167-1589376271.pdf (accessed June 10, 2021).

Olsson, Stefan. (2009). "Defending the Rule of Law in Emergencies Through Checks and Balances," *Democracy and Security*, 5 (2): 103–26.

PCBS. (2020). "The Labor Force Survey Results 2020: The Impact of the Coronavirus Pandemic on the Labour Market," *Palestinian Central Bureau of Statistics*, https://www .pcbs.gov.ps/post.aspx?lang=en&ItemID=3924 (accessed May 15, 2021).

PSR. (2020). "Public Opinion Poll No. 76, June 17–20," *Center for Policy and Survey Research (PSR)*, http://pcpsr.org/en/node/813 (accessed July 25, 2021).

PSR. (2021). "Public Opinion Poll No. 80, June 9–12," *Palestinian Center for Policy and Survey Research (PSR)*, June 15, https://www.pcpsr.org/en/node/843 (accessed July 5, 2021).

Quran, Fadi and Mustafa Tahani. (2020). "Palestine and COVID-19: Lessons for Leadership During Times of Crisis," *Al-Shabaka*, September 10.

Rasgon, Adam and David M. Halbfinger (2020). "Seeking Restart With Biden, Palestinians Eye End to Prisoner Payments," *New York Times*, November 19.

Reychler, Luc. (2015). *Time for Peace: The Essential Role of Time in Conflict and Peace Processes*. Brisbane: University of Queensland Press.

Sadiki, Larbi and Layla Saleh (2020). "Reflexive Politics and Arab 'risk society'? COVID-19 and Issues of Public Health," *Orient - Deutsche Zeitschrift fü Politik* und *Wirtschaft des Orients*, 60 (3): 6–20, 6.

SHAMS. (2020). "Position Paper (3): Conditions of Palestinian Prisoners in Israeli Prisons - The Threat of Corona's Arrival," (in Arabic). *Human Rights and Democracy Media Center SHAMS*, April 8, https://www.achrs.org/wp-content/uploads/2020/04/%D9%88 %D8%B1%D9%82%D8%A9-%D9%85%D9%88%D9%82%D9%81-%D8%AD%D9%88 %D9%84-%D8%A7%D9%84%D8%A7%D8%B3%D8%B1%D9%89-%D8%A7%D9

%84%D9%81%D9%84%D8%B3%D8%B7%D9%8A%D9%86%D9%8A%D9%8A%D9%8A%D9
%86.pdf (accessed August 27, 2021).

Shehadeh, Amal (2020). "Will Corona Close an Account That Has Been Open for Years
between Israel and 'Hamas'?" (in Arabic). *The Independent Files, Arabia*, https://www
.independentarabia.com/node/111471/%D8%A7%D9%84%D8%A3%D8%AE%D8
%A8%D8%A7%D8%B1/%D8%A7%D9%84%D8%B4%D8%B1%D9%82-%D8%A7
%D9%84%D8%A3%D9%88%D8%B3%D8%B7/%D9%87%D9%84-%D9%8A%D8
%BA%D9%84%D9%82-%D9%83%D9%88%D8%B1%D9%88%D9%86%D8%A7-%D8
%AD%D8%B3%D8%A7%D8%A8%D8%A7-%D9%85%D9%81%D8%AA%D9%88
%D8%AD%D8%A7-%D9%85%D9%86%D8%B0-%D8%B3%D9%86%D9%88%D8
%A7%D8%AA-%D8%A8%D9%8A%D9%86-%D8%A5%D8%B3%D8%B1%D8%A7
%D8%A6%D9%8A%D9%84-%D9%88%D8%AD%D9%85%D8%A7%D8%B3%D8
%9F (accessed May 24, 2021).

The Law by Decree No. 4 of 2020 Amending the Law on the Honoraria and Salaries of
Members of the Legislative Council, Members of the Government and Governors No.
11 of 2004 as Amended. For full text see alwaqayie alfilastinia or the Palestine Gazette
issues number 155 and 166, https://www.lab.pna.ps/cached_uploads/download/2020
/05/13/167-1589376271.pdf?fbclid=IwAR2ENARrmgZsyRW2TojM2FgOcC_vX
_WC5hxR-ScydWWQhTUpR-x89tuBhpM (accessed 7, 2021).

Thompson, Jack. (2018). *Trump's Middle East Policy*. Center for Security Studies, Analyses,
233, October, http://www.css.ethz.ch/content/dam/ethz/special-interest/gess/cis/center
-for-securities-studies/pdfs/CSSAnalyse233-EN.pdf (accessed May 11, 2021).

UNCTAD. (2020a). "Report on Assistance to the Palestinian People: Developments in the
Economy of the Occupied Palestinian Territory," *United Nations Conference on Trade
and Development*, August 5.

UNCTAD. (2020b). "Covid-19 Devastates the Shattered Economy of the oPt," *United
Nations Conference on Trade and Development*, September 8.

UNRWA Report. (2020). Updated Unrwa Flash Appeal for the Covid-19 Response March-
July 2020, May, https://www.unrwa.org/sites/default/files/content/resources/covid-19
_flash_appeal_may_update_final_eng_v2.pdf (accessed June 1, 2021).

WHO (2021). "Occupied Palestinian Territory: Coronavirus Disease (COVID-19)
Situation Report 58," *World Health Organization*, January 6.

World Bank (2016). *West Bank and Gaza–Public Expenditure Review of the Palestinian
Authority: Towards Enhanced Public Finance Management and Improved Fiscal
Sustainability*. International Bank for Construction and Development/The World
Bank, https://documents1.worldbanWk.org/curated/en/320891473688227759/pdf/
ACS18454-REVISED-FINAL-PER-SEPTEMBER-2016-FOR-PUBLIC-DISCLOSURE
-PDF.pdf (accessed August 26, 2021).

World Justice Challenge (2021). *Adalah's Emergency COVID-19 Project: Demanding Equal
Treatment and Non-Discrimination for the Arab Minority Through the Israeli Legal
System*. World Justice Project.

Yearley, Steven (2001), "Risk, Sociology and Politics of," in Neil J. Smelser and Paul B.
Baltes (eds.), *International Encyclopedia of the Social & Behavioral Sciences*, 13360–64.
Pergamon, https://www.sciencedirect.com/science/article/pii/B0080430767032022.

Zreik, Raef. (2020). "Wuhan, Bergamo, Milan: Intellectual Implications in the Time of
Coronavirus," (in Arabic) *Majallat al-Dirasat al-Filastiniyya*, 123: 68–74.

9

Crisis and Ceding of State Sovereignty

The Case of Lebanon and the COVID-19 Pandemic

Assem Dandashly

Introduction

As it spread across the globe, the COVID-19 (coronavirus) pandemic posed a problem not only for weak and fragile states but also for Western countries (Jones and Hameiri 2021). COVID-19 has seriously challenged many countries in the Western world including the United States, and the European Union (EU) member states. The EU "has implemented numerous strategies to face emerging issues. EU Member States have adopted measures such as the closure of borders and significant limitations on the mobility of people to mitigate the spread of the virus" (Goniewicz et al. 2020, 3838). In the Arab world – a risk society with perennial problems ranging from unemployment to marginalization - COVID 19 has increased the magnitude of such societal challenges and the need of adequate response. (Sadiki and Saleh 2020). So while the COVID-19 pandemic did not create already existing problems of inequality, exclusion, marginalization, etc., it has made these problems more noticeable in the Arab societies (Sadiki and Saleh 2020, 6–7).

When the pandemic reached Lebanon officially in February/March 2020, this small country—already suffering from a serious economic and financial crisis, an extended refugee crisis, and ongoing protests—had one more thing to deal with. According to the United Nations Resident Coordinator in Lebanon and Acting Humanitarian Coordinator Claudio Cordone, "this health crisis comes at a difficult time for Lebanon economically, financially and socially" (United Nations 2021). The pandemic arrives to a country already suffering from several crises that had seen continuous spending cuts to many policy sectors including the healthcare system (Peri 2020; Chehayeb 2020)—thus rendering it unequipped to deal with such a global pandemic. Against this background, this chapter seeks to study the effect of the crisis and reassertion of the state in the case of Lebanon by asking: to what extent has the crisis revealed the vulnerability of the state structures? And what impact has the crisis had in strengthening the role of hybrid groups and civil society organizations to compensate for the state's role and responsibilities?

In answering these questions, the chapter uses interviews conducted from 2020 to 2021 and primary documents such as official statements, documents of the Ministry of Health and the United Nations, in addition to secondary sources and newspapers' articles. The chapter builds on crisis response scholarship that focuses on certain indicators to evaluate how a massive crisis is managed by the authorities in a specific context. These indicators are decision-making, communication and use of (social) media, collaboration and coordination, and control (Blondin and Boin 2020; Boin and Hart 2003; Comfort 2007; Kapucu et al. 2011; Kapucu and Moynihan 2021; Li, Chandra and Kapucu 2020; Van Wart and Kapucu 2011), in addition to the level of trust in the government/political elites.

The chapter shows that the handling of the crisis was in sharp contrast to the vulnerability of the state, given the severe economic and financial crisis that the country is going through. This economic and financial crisis pushed the World Bank to state that it can be ranked among the three most severe crisis since the mid-1800s (Al-Jazeera 2021). So despite the failure of the state institutions at all levels—based on the very low expectations for competence and effective governance, given the levels of governmental corruption, nepotism, and incompetence impact all levels of daily life from electricity to water to trash collection—Lebanon managed to handle the repercussions of the COVID-19 pandemic with the support of the United Nations (UN) and the international community. However, the pandemic also revealed significant weaknesses in the system such as the inequality and injustice in the Lebanese context in regard to "who gets what, when and how" (using Harold Laswell's definition of politics). This inequality was revealed in the way the refugees (Palestinians and Syrians) were treated (Yassine 2020), for example, or how the vaccinations were distributed in the early phases according to favouritism, that is, prioritizing certain groups based on sect or closeness to the political elites, as we will see later. This goes against the idea that access to health care and good health are among the main rights of individuals, and shows how this "human and development right [is] far from fully realized [in Lebanon and] across the region" (Sadiki and Saleh 2020: 7). In addition, it conflicts with the "leaving no one behind" strategy of the United Nations, the World Bank, and other international organizations (IOs) in supporting Lebanon's handling of the pandemic (United Nations 2021). This poor health system, especially in terms of access to good health, in Lebanon as well as in the Middle East and North Africa (MENA) region more generally, is the result of high levels of corruption, weak civil society organizations, lack of good governance, and a clientelist mentality that still persist since the colonization period (and even prior).

Following this introduction, the next section provides the analytical framework for how to understand the choices made by the government and the success of these choices. This is followed by a contextual background on the situation in Lebanon before turning to the outcome of the policies taken. The final section concludes with some findings and observations.

Analytical framework

Crises and disasters such as the COVID-19 pandemic often test and affect the abilities of political leadership and bureaucracies as well as the structure of the state. This is a good example of examining the concept of "risk society" that confirms Beck's concept of risk and the emergence of unprecedented catastrophic events that serve to undermine the nation-state (see Beck, Giddens and Lash 1994). In that sense, Beck argues that "the nation state's scope of jurisdiction is overtaxed by historical developments—internationally interlocked markets and concentrations of capital—but also by the global exchange of pollutants and toxins and the accompanying universal health threats and natural destruction" (Beck 1992:189). The speed with which COVID-19 "has spread around the globe has been unanimously interpreted as a consequence of the dense interconnection that binds national societies to each other. This is just another manifestation of the dark side of modernity" (Arias-Maldonado 2020, 5).

During a time of crisis, bureaucracies are bombarded with new tasks that go beyond what they are accustomed to handling. Understandably, they struggle with these new tasks, "especially ones that do not fit neatly into the responsibility of any single unit or level of government. Therefore, this raises the importance of investigating whether conventional decision-making processes in Lebanon are no longer effective. In these situations, the importance of political leadership is magnified" (Kapucu et al. 2011: 2). Research on the topic has highlighted the importance of leadership, capabilities, and readiness to cope with sudden disasters, communication methods, and usage of media, in addition to the importance of cooperation with other countries and IOs (Boin and Hart 2003; Comfort 2007; Coombs 1995; Kapucu et al. 2011; Li, Chandra, and Kapucu 2020; Palenchar and Heath 2007; Waugh and Streib 2006).

All these aspects have been highlighted by the scholarship as important steps to cope with disasters/crises. Scholars such as Oh (1997), Oh and Rich (1996), and Walgrave and Dejaeghere (2017) have highlighted the importance of information and how elites are bombarded with it, especially during times of crisis—and how they have to be selective in what information to convey and make sense of. So when a major crisis breaks out, such as the COVID-19 pandemic, "different levels of government have access to different types and amount of information at the ground level (e.g., local governments access local situations better than the central government), and this creates the problem of information asymmetry among public administrators and prevents them from making timely decisions and taking appropriate actions" (Li, Chandra and Kapucu 2020). What concerns us in the time of crisis and increased risk is "the type of dialogic rationality, which mediates mutuality and agreement (and inevitably disagreement, too) via speech acts (language, meaning, signs, values, worldviews)" (Sadiki and Saleh 2020, 18). The communication tools used, through dialogue, deliberations, and argumentation, are necessary for reaching common ground and understanding when it comes to taking certain decisions. This is the Habermasian communicative rationality that drives society toward values and patterns of solidarity and pluralist social change. Habermas emphasizes that "the lifeworld, which is itself articulated in the medium of language, opens up for its members an interpretive horizon for everything that they experience in the world, about which they

Table 9.1 Key Indicators and Explanations

Key Indicators	Explanation
Decision-making	Consistent and clear decisions that have rational and logical bases in accordance with experts' opinions.
Communication and use of (social) media	The use of various channels and means of communication to raise awareness and spread information that is based on scientific research and evidence.
Collaboration and coordination	Involvement of international organizations/players and local stakeholders in the most appropriate decisions and implementation of policies.
Trust and public acceptance	Level of public trust in the government's decision.

Source: Author's compilation based on Kapucu et al. (2011).

reach understanding, and from which they can learn" (Habermas 1998, 335). Therefore, without communication and collaboration among the different stakeholders, reaching common ground and understanding in regard to the measures needed to address certain risks and crises becomes impossible.

In light of what is discussed previously, communication and dialogue in the Arab world to handle risks and crises has to be bidirectional: "global-local" and "local-global." The local dimension is based on internal dialogue to process international and professional expertise (such as WHO recommendations in the COVID-19 situation). Yet, "it will not be sufficient to 'think globally and act locally,' but also 'think locally and act globally,' as it were. Bidirectional dialogue and deliberation are key" (Sadiki and Saleh 2020, 18). This dialogue among the various local stakeholders (bureaucracies, experts, law enforcements, healthcare businesses, various segments of the society, elites, etc.) is necessary. "The idea centres on how to bring together all of these various groups within society to create some sort of consensus on how to best respond to the inequalities [and risks due to COVID-19], and persuade people to accept the new measures taken without violations" (Sadiki and Saleh 2020, 18).

Against this reality, how do political elites handle major crises? To answer this question, the chapter engages with the current research on crisis response and focuses on key indicators such as decision-making, communication, and use of (social) media, collaboration, and coordination (Kapucu et al. 2011, 2–3), and finally public trust and acceptance of the decisions (Table 9.1).

The Situation in Lebanon

The deterioration of the economic situation in Lebanon as of 2009 was escalated with the Syrian refugee crisis and the involvement of Hezbullah in the Syrian war. Starting on October 17, 2019, thousands of Lebanese took to the streets all over the country, requesting reforms and a total change of the political elites and parties who have been ruling the country since the end of the civil war. The protest against government/

traditional sectarian parties, or what is called the October Protest/Revolution, is considered the largest anti-government movement in almost fifteen years.

The country's political leaders failed to slow the economic meltdown and did not take any of the serious measures for reforms requested by the International Monetary Fund (IMF) and the international community. By the end of 2019, no funds had been disbursed to the Lebanese government (via the CEDRE Conference that promised around 11 billion euros) due to its delay in taking serious reforms for structural adjustments, fighting the high levels of corruption, and restoring failing public services and institutions. This structural problem and the delayed reforms are due to the consociational political system, created in the 1940s and updated in 1990, which is based on a difficult cooperation among the various heterogeneous sectarian groups who are in continuous disagreement and conflict even within the so-called consecutive unity governments (since the end of the civil war in the early 1990s). This sectarian system has proved to be a failure. It has resulted in high levels of corruption, inefficiency, political deadlock, and compromise that end up providing rents, dividing the benefits and shares of whatever project is being discussed at that moment (Adwan 2005).

The deterioration of the economic situation in Lebanon has reached unprecedented levels. Since October 2019, the Lebanese lira has lost around 90 percent of its value, and the annual inflation rate hit 84.9 percent in 2020 and continues to rise. According to government data, since the end of 2019, prices of consumer goods and basic needs have nearly quadrupled. With the outbreak of the COVID-19 pandemic, lockdowns added to the misery and collapse of the economy. In addition, the huge port explosion on August 4, 2020, which injured and killed hundreds of people, destroyed hundreds of houses, and had negative influence on the economy (as the port is the main export/import hub for Lebanon), only added to the frustration of the people (Malsin and Osseiran 2021; McCaffrey and Todman 2021). The increasingly dreadful situation "has likely dragged more than half the population below the poverty line, as unemployment soars and the price of basic goods surges" (Gharizi and Yacoubian 2021).

Moreover, the Syrian refugee crisis put more pressure on the weak economy. Lebanon hosts "the largest number of refugees per capita, with the Government estimation of 1.5 M Syrian refugees + some 14,815 refugees of other nationalities" (UNHCR 2021). The socioeconomic depression in Lebanon along with the COVID-19 pandemic and Beirut blast have contributed to "nine out of ten Syrian refugee families in Lebanon are now living in extreme poverty"—that is, "less than half the minimum wage in Lebanon" (ReliefWeb 2020). This situation resulted in depriving Syrian refugees from "basic human needs, including food, safe drinking water, sanitation, health, shelter, and education" (Karasapan and Shah 2021; see also Dagher 2021).

This economic slump, steep inflation, the Beirut port blast, and the COVID-19 pandemic "have pushed vulnerable communities in Lebanon—including Syrian refugees—to the brink, with thousands of families sinking further into poverty and vulnerability" (ReliefWeb 2020).

As can be noticed, the current crisis has already done significant damage to what made Lebanon stand out as a unique country in the Arab world: "In a country once billed as the Switzerland of the Middle East, the banks are largely insolvent. Education has suffered a blow as teachers and professors seek better opportunities abroad. And health care has deteriorated as reduced salaries have caused an exodus of doctors and nurses" (Hubbard and Denton 2021). These sectors and others have pushed highly skilled and educated labor to leave the country. "They were driven out by waves of COVID-19, declining salaries and the explosion in the Beirut port last year, which flooded the ward with casualties" (Hubbard and Denton 2021). According to the World Bank Lebanon Economic Monitor, the Lebanese economic and financial crisis is most probably sufficient to rank the country in the top three "most severe crises episodes globally since the mid-nineteenth century" (World Bank 2021c).

So with such a severe economic crisis and institutional collapse rendering Lebanon a failed state, how did the Lebanese government manage the COVID-19 pandemic? Before discussing the measures taken in the country, it will be useful to provide a brief background on the evolution of the virus in Lebanon.

COVID-19 in Lebanon

The Lebanese management of the pandemic went through different cycles of early containment, from a spread of the virus that put extreme pressure on the medical services and then to a sudden decrease in the curve to a moderate increase at the time of writing. Despite the decrease in numbers in the second half of 2021, this cannot hide the reality that coronavirus chaos significantly increased Lebanon's suffering (Abi-Nassif 2021), due to continuous closure and lockdown in a bankrupt country. Some criticized the government's measures, arguing that the

> Lebanese Corona crisis is tragic not only because of its human toll, but because of how unnecessary and avoidable it was. By learning from Italy's failed response to the pandemic, adopting a firmer stance vis-à-vis public disregard of safety measures, and engaging in more aggressive vaccine procurement efforts, Lebanese authorities could have more aptly prevented and contained the crisis. (Abi-Nassif 2021)

Some believe that the true numbers cannot really be known due to the lack of government resources, insufficient testing, and mistrust of the government which might be using the numbers to avoid protests against the current political elites (various interviews in Beirut, 2019–21). This finding is also reflected in Sadiki and Saleh (2020, 16) who use risk society analysis to discuss how the Arab states used the pandemic to become more "repressive" than "distributive"—shutting down and shutting out "Arab peoples, but without being an equaliser in a social, economic or political sense."

Even prior to the pandemic, under high levels of corruption that weakened the state's economic, institutional and financial resources, access to healthcare was limited to those with private insurance or sufficient means—which is in sharp contrast to basic human rights. As for public health care, it has faced a long struggle due to these high levels of corruption. The doors were, therefore, open for groups such as Hezbollah to provide services and security within the suburbs of Beirut and in the southern part of Lebanon. This situation of a fragile state that lacks the means to adopt and implement policies has led to a legitimacy gap, a security gap, and a capacity and effectiveness gap (Khalaf 2015). With the pandemic, Lebanon found itself challenged by weak health capacity and limited access to healthcare. This was partly the result of "postcolonial risks (oppression, poverty, inequality, conflict and varying degrees of dependency)" (Sadiki and Saleh 2020, 14). Thus, COVID-19 exposed the problems of postcolonial Arab development strategies and the subsequent neoliberal turn toward a market economy. These policies have "had profound implications for public health. Medical care has been commodified and privatised, yielding tiers of health systems and the shrinkage of coverage and services" (Sadiki and Saleh 2020, 15).

What complicates the situation even further is the existence of Palestinian refugee camps with very limited access to resources, and more recently the Syrian refugee crisis. This has further weakened the state's governance capacity, increased polarization and put more pressure on the government. To add to the miseries of the country, the Beirut port explosion resulted in further worsening of the economic situation, rendering the state incapable of attending to the day-to-day needs of its citizens. The crisis the country is going through has increased poverty to unprecedented levels which in turn has weakened the resilience of individuals and families in face of the pandemic (Sadiki and Saleh 2020, 10). These "challenges make Lebanon one of the most difficult places in the world to manage a Covid-19 response and vaccination effort, and the country is in dire need of additional support" (McCaffrey and Todman 2021).

The Management of COVID-19 Pandemic in Lebanon: Return of the State in a Failed State?

For nearly three years now, Lebanon has been facing continuous crises ranging from economic and financial to political and social followed by COVID-19 and the Beirut Port blast on August 4, 2020. The authorities have been incapable of managing the crises due to lack of responsibility, high levels of corruption, and lack of trust between the people and the political elites, and among the various political parties themselves. However, the situation concerning COVID-19 management does not look as gloomy as the other crises the country is facing. The COVID-19 Committee has dealt with the pandemic by taking restrictive measures, airport closure, increased PCR testing, and lockdowns, launch of the vaccination programme, in addition to other measures that lower the negative impacts on the people and ease the pressure on the suffering health system.

Since the start of the pandemic, there have been around 650,000 infections and 8500 COVID-related deaths in Lebanon as of November 3, 2021 (Lebanese Ministry of Information 2021; Reuters 2021). The number of infections reached a peak in January/February 2021 (highest reported on January 16, 2021) before slowing to an average of around 600 new infections per day. With regard to deaths, the number was very low at the beginning of the pandemic before peaking in January 2021 only to decrease again afterwards with a daily average between zero and eight cases (Worldometer 2021).

In order to assess the role of the government in handling the pandemic, we should look at the specific policies and measures taken by the central authorities. Despite the collapse of all institutions in Lebanon, rendering it a failed state, this was not the case in the handling of the pandemic. In what follows, this section looks into four factors that are considered necessary to assess the effect of the pandemic on governance and the return of the state: decision-making, communication, collaboration, and coordination, and finally public trust in the central authority.

Decision-Making

With the detection of the novel coronavirus in China and international fear about the spread of COVID-19, Prime Minister Hassan Diab's government set up a National Committee for COVID-19 (NCC) on January 31, 2021. The committee was headed and staffed by experts such as medical doctors, academics, scientists, and professionals. The main task of the NCC has been to manage the preparedness of Lebanon to deal with the virus and later to handle and recommend measures to the government. The government was quick to react to the first case of COVID-19 on February 21, 2020. It "initiated a 'whole government response' through a public-private partnership, with the NCC directing the strategy and the Ministry of Health (MoH)—alongside other ministries—overseeing the implementation" (Khoury et al. 2020, 548).

Thus, Lebanon's early measures were aggressive and responsible, given the weak infrastructure to deal with pandemics in comparison to other countries. South Korea and Taiwan, for example, had advanced technology that allowed them to use "unified health registries with mobile phone tracking and messaging as well as computerized tracking of travel. Also, while these countries had extensive preparedness expertise and experience from prior epidemics, including unified health response command, Lebanon had to build these capabilities as part of this current response" (Khoury, Azar and Hitti 2020, 548).

Given the weak infrastructure and failing state capacities at all levels, Lebanon had no choice but to implement conservative measures to (1) curb any possible increase in COVID-19 numbers, (2) buy itself some time to get ready with the support of the international community, and (3) avoid pressure on the limited health facilities.

Since the first confirmed case in Lebanon on February 21, 2020, a number of measures were taken by the Lebanese government as advised by the NCC. Following the rest of the world's measures, the government started with implementing social distancing (1.5–2.0 meters). All educational activities were suspended as of March 1, 2020. Moreover, public gathering, religious ceremonies, and weddings were banned soon after on March 22, 2020. The government proceeded with the closure of all shopping centers, restaurants, cafes, and so on. These measures were succeeded by even stricter ones that included curfews, restricting the movement of cars and all vehicles (sometimes alternating between odd and even numbers), and creating a webpage for getting permits to go to the supermarket. These measures proved to be successful in limiting the number of COVID-19 cases until they were relaxed as of May 10, 2020.

These strict measures, in addition to "testing all people possibly exposed by travel-related affairs or showing symptoms as per World Health Organization (WHO) recommendations . . . helped limit the people's mobility and the disease's spread. And add to that the scarcity of public spaces and public transportation services in Lebanon, one can understand how the spread of the disease in Lebanon was more contained than in other countries" (Bizri et al. 2021, 489). With the opening of the country and especially the airport (at one-fifth of its normal capacity) on July 1, 2020, number of cases started to slightly increase as of August 2020 to reach a peak after the Christmas and New Year holidays (December 2020–January 2021).

With the increase in the number of cases, the government was torn between imposing further restrictive measures (as per the NCC recommendations) or keeping measures loose due to the sharp economic crisis in the country. In the end, the government decided to impose a sort of curfew with certain exceptions that could be expanded or limited depending on the number of positive cases. The Ministry of Interior "launched an e-portal for citizens seeking transport permits for emergencies and a list of imperative chores such as doctor, hospital, pharmacy or bakery visits and money transfers" (Zaazaa 2021). Despite the campaign and raised awareness regarding the dangers of COVID-19, people kept trying to violate the boundaries set by the government. For example, they would fill out a permit stating they were going to get groceries, while actually going for a walk or visiting friends (interviews with various officials and citizens in Beirut, February–April 2021).

According to one officer of the Internal Security Forces, many violations have been recorded where applicants state fake reasons for getting a transport permit in order to go hang out and have fun. Internal Security Officers have been employing extra caution, increasing their patrols and ramping up efforts to ensure that the laws and measures regarding COVID-19 restrictions and curfew are respected. In his address to the Lebanese, the officer adds that "amid this state of nationwide health emergency, we call on the applicants to be cautious and ethical for their own sake and that of their beloved ones. Covid-19 isn't a joke" (Zaazaa 2021). The efforts by the security forces have been remarkable in that sense, and despite the violations and limited resources, the situation has remained under control. The weak resources are not the result of the recent crisis alone but stem from a long period of corruption and limited support that has shaped the institutions in Lebanon. Moreover, the people's attitude and tendency to cheat the system reflects the widespread mentality of corruption that has developed since independence in the 1940s alongside the overarching failure to build functioning institutions and respect of the rule of law in the post-colonization period.

Overall, and despite the violations and the weak infrastructure, one can conclude that the government's decisions were necessary to combat the spread of the pandemic. Due to the economic crisis, however, the government could not keep up strict measures for a prolonged period. While the NCC was in favor of stricter rules, the government was also taking the economic situation into consideration. Therefore, on a number of occasions the government did not implement all the NCC recommendations.

Communication and Use of (Social) Media to Raise Awareness

Since the detection of the first case, Lebanon was on alert. In February 2020, the government launched a national strategic communication campaign. "The main strategy centered around flooding media outlets with information by health care professionals: talk shows hosted physicians and public health experts, and public service messages featuring physicians were streamed through social media and television outlets, in addition to governmental directives around 'stay home' orders and prevention" (Khoury, Azar and Hitti 2020, 549).

To raise awareness among the population, the World Health Organization, the United Nations Children's Fund (UNICEF), and the United Nations Development Program helped the Lebanese Ministry of Information to launch educational campaigns on various media outlets including television, radio, and social media. The main aim of these campaigns, beyond raising awareness, was to clarify misconceptions and rumours: "to combat fake and misleading news and hate speech, and reduce the stigmatization of people due to their infection with the Coronavirus" (United Nations 2021).

In cooperation with the Ministry of Health, several campaigns hosted by NGOs and religious communities were launched on social media to alert people about the virus. "Mosques and other places of worship have used sermons to instruct people on ways to protect themselves against the virus" (Arab News 2020).

Moreover, campaigns such as #SafeHands4Lebanon were launched on social media sites "to provide practical advice on how to take preventive measures against the virus and other measures to recover from it"; these campaigns successfully "reached more than three million people on television and 2.9 million on social media" (United Nations 2021).

Among the communication and awareness programmes, the Lebanese Ministry of Health, through the National Mental Health Programme, UNICEF, UNDP, the World Health Organization and the NGO Abaad joined forces to correct the image of those who are infected. They sought to "break the stigma associated with the novel corona virus ... Under the slogan '#TheRealTest,' the national campaign was launched on several TV outlets with a synchronized introduction of primetime news" (Lebanese Ministry of Public Health 2021a). Furthermore, short videos were developed and broadcast by the Ministry of Public Health along with messages of hope from local celebrities such as the Lebanese singer Assi el Halani. In addition, several campaigns were launched to clarify many of the misconceptions regarding the vaccine and its side effects.

According to Dr. Iman Shankiti, WHO Representative to Lebanon, "the battle against the COVID-19 outbreak is a double-fold struggle with the spread of misinformation." This is also supported by the statement of Yuki Muko, UNICEF Lebanon Representative, that "this is a time for science and solidarity" (United Nations 2021).

Collaboration and Coordination

From the detection of the first COVID-19 case, the government created the NCC both to centralize decision-making and to have access to expert opinion. Collaboration and coordination have been strong between the Ministry of Public Health, the Ministry of Interior, the Ministry of Information, and the NCC. This coordination was necessary to ensure that a cohesive message was spread regarding the virus and vaccination. Also the Ministry of Interior ensured that the decisions taken were implemented, especially during the lockdowns and curfews. Certain decisions regarding the closure/opening of schools by the Ministry of Education were not well coordinated and at times criticized by the NCC. For example, following the discovery of a fourth case of COVID-19, the Minister of Education ordered all educational facilities to close for a week as a precaution. This decision was ignored by some schools/universities such as the American University of Beirut. It was also criticized by Dr. Abdul Rahman Bizri, an infectious disease specialist and member of the emergency committee on coronavirus, who said the decision "was taken due to the confusion of the ministries of health and education, and it was taken for political reasons" (Arab News 2020).

Collaboration with international organizations, especially the World Bank and the United Nations, was crucial and very helpful to ensure the ability of hospitals to cope with the spread of the pandemic. The World Bank mobilized its resources and provided funds for supporting the infrastructure needed to fight COVID-19. Also the World Bank provided the necessary funds for the first batches of vaccine. The World Bank's Lebanon Health Resilience Project (USD 120 million) was restructured to help the Lebanese authorities deal with the pandemic. The funds generated in this project aided in the "training of health workers and frontline responders, covering the cost of hospital care for COVID-19 patients, and supporting the urgent procurement of goods and equipment to strengthen the capacity of public hospitals and the purchase and deployment of COVID-19 vaccines" (World Bank 2021b).

In addition, the World Bank funded several projects such as the Innovative Small and Medium Enterprises project (USD 30 million) to help Lebanese firms and research centers to produce COVID-19-related medical supplies. US$200 million was granted to support small farmers in dealing with the effects of the pandemic. At the same time, the World Bank provided US$246 million through its New Emergency Crisis and COVID-19 Response Social Safety Net to provide "emergency cash transfers and access to social services for extremely poor and vulnerable households, in addition to top-up cash transfer to children between the ages of 13 and 18 years, who may be at risk of dropping out of school" (World Bank 2021b).

In preparing for vaccine distribution, the Lebanese government, the World Bank and others performed a COVID-19 "vaccine readiness assessment, established a National COVID-19 Vaccine Committee, and prepared a National COVID-19 Deployment and Vaccination Plan (NDVP). The NDVP has all the key elements recommended by the World Health Organization (WHO) and represents a central part of Lebanon's vaccination readiness" (World Bank 2021a). During the vaccination campaign, the World Bank was also involved with the government and local and international NGOs. However, due to the weak infrastructure and history of favoritism and corruption, the World Bank and the International Federation of Red Cross and Red Crescent Societies (IFRC) signed "an agreement for the independent monitoring of Lebanon's COVID-19 vaccination campaign. Under this agreement, IFRC acting as the Third Party Monitoring Agency (TPMA), will be in charge of independently monitoring the compliance of the vaccination deployment with national plans, international standards and World Bank requirements in order to ensure safe handling of the vaccines, as well as fair and equitable access to all" (World Bank 2021a).

With the launch of the vaccination programme on February 14, 2021, with the support of the World Health Organization and other IOs such as the World Bank, things got slightly better. The program, which is financed by the World Bank, is succeeding according to the NDVP. The main aim of the COVID-19 Committee is "to vaccinate 70% of the total population, citizens and non-citizens in a multi-phase rollout by the end of 2022. Efforts are underway to speed up the campaign through the procurement of vaccines via additional sources, including the private sector" (World Bank 2021b). However, at the beginning of the vaccination program, the high level of corruption pushed the World Bank to threaten the Lebanese government to suspend financing the vaccines. Political elites aimed to distribute the vaccines on their supporters and the sects they belong to. While these first doses were supposed to go to at-risk groups such as healthcare providers, some officials were vaccinated in the parliament in addition to sometimes using sectarianism and favoritism to distribute the vaccines (Francis and Bassam 2021). Lebanese politicians even tried to use the COVID-19 vaccine to attract more voters for the next elections in spring 2022, which is considered "the latest variant on an old corruption trick" (France24 2021). This "vaccine for vote" method "builds on decades-old patronage practices that have seen leaders buy their way into office by offering voters money or public sector employment" (France24 2021).

Without the World Bank's reallocation of $34 million, Lebanon would not have been able to obtain around 60,000 Pfizer-BioNtech doses—the first doses received by Lebanon. So far, Lebanon has administered over three million doses of COVID-19 vaccine. If we consider that every person has taken two doses, then around one quarter of the country's population has been fully vaccinated (Reuters 2021). The majority of the vaccinated people are under 75 years old. Moreover, we see a balance between males and females (slightly higher for females). Most of the vaccinated are Lebanese with a slim minority of Syrian refugees and Palestinians (Lebanese Ministry of Public Health 2021b). This could be due to the prioritization of Lebanese at the expense of Syrian and Palestinian refugees—an issue raised by many activists and the international community.

As we can see, internal coordination was not always maintained. NCC recommendations along with those of the Ministry of Health were not always fully taken due to political reasons and the economic crisis. Collaboration with the international community such as the United Nations, the World Health Organization, and the World Bank has been strong and well developed.

Public Trust and Acceptance of Central Authorities' Decisions

While trust in the government is very low due to the history of corruption and favoritism that destroyed the economy and rendered Lebanon a failed state, people trusted the information they received regarding COVID-19. The majority "agree that media coverage of COVID-19 was comprehensive, and only a few say it was contradictory and exaggerated" (Melki et al. 2020). In the same study, those with higher education have more knowledge about the virus and do not believe false information.

When it comes to the government's decision, the level of trust declines significantly, reaching 95 percent in some regions such as Akkar or 84 percent in Beirut who do not trust the government. Overall, the lack of trust in the government is 59 percent and those who have partial trust are 32 percent (UNDP 2020a). Some respondents stated that "we don't trust the government. There is no government anyway, and we don't know what will come next. I have a very dark image in my head" (UNDP 2020a). People were also critical of the government's lack of justification for the measures taken. This crisis comes at a time when trust in politicians is already low and people believe that the system has failed, which pushes them to "turn to their natural state of doubt and go to the easy option of not adhering and not listening" (UNDP 2020a).

According to the UNDP and based on personal interviews conducted with a random sample of people, some doubt everything that the government says. People accuse the government of exaggerating the number of cases "so that they isolate the villages and stop the people from participating in the demonstrations. They [people] have also been saying that the Government is giving money to each reported positive case" (UNDP 2020b).

Conclusion

While the government, relatively speaking, managed to cope with COVID-19 and limit its negative effects, the pandemic certainly added to the woes of the failing state. The crisis also exposed the high level of inequality and corruption the system suffers from. It further showed that the once-flourishing healthcare system is mostly privatized and a limited number of people are able to obtain full and good healthcare. This reflects the postcolonialism liberal reforms, along with high levels of corruption, that have created high levels of inequality.

According to the International Labor Organization, the COVID-19 pandemic comes at a critical time for Lebanon which is suffering from a severe economic and financial crisis, "with lockdown measures hampering economic activities and leading to increased unemployment, under-employment and working poverty, among other things. In addition, while the economic crisis had mainly hit tradable sectors, the coronavirus epidemic led to the collapse of other sectors, including tourism and transport" (International Labour Organization 2020).

Looking at the effect of the pandemic on governance and the role of the state, it can be noted that the state was present, and the government dealt with the pandemic in a relatively acceptable manner—given the deep economic and financial crisis the country is going through. In terms of decision-making, the government acted quickly in creating a committee for COVID-19 and taking restrictive measures. This was not without problems and violations, as stated previously. The government used a variety of means of communication to convey its message and clarify misconceptions regarding the virus. Collaboration with NGOs and IOs has been crucial to deal with the crisis. Finally, the level of trust in the political elites has been significantly low due to the crisis

Table 9.2 Main Findings per Category

Key Indicators	Explanation
Decision-making	Conflict between economic well-being and COVID-19 restrictions. The economic difficulty the country is going through influenced the decisions of the government, which did not always abide by the COVID-19 Committee.
Communication and use of (social) media	Various channels such as social media, media, Ministry of Information/ Health Policy ads, street ads, speeches by religious sheikhs and leaders, etc., were used to raise awareness, spread information and clarify misconceptions regarding both the virus and the vaccine.
Collaboration and coordination	Internal coordination was established but at times the government ignored the recommendations of the NCC. Cooperation with IOs such as the World Bank, the UN, international players such as the EU and other Western countries was crucial to aid the measures, support the implementation of policies, provide financial aid, support the infrastructure, hospitals, vaccines, etc.
Trust and public acceptance	Level of public trust in government decisions has been low and uncertain.

the country is going through—which is blamed entirely on the political elites who have ruled the country for the past thirty years. This lack of trust affected public compliance with the decisions taken. Table 9.2 summarizes the main findings.

All in all, the pandemic added to the collapse of the state and the failing modes of governance over the past thirty years (post-civil war). Despite this, the handling of the crisis, given all the facts, has been overall acceptable and the COVID-19 Committee acted responsibly. The government's policies and strategies helped in coping with the pandemic with the fewest repercussions.

References

Abi-Nassif, Christophe. (2021). *COVID chaos Magnifies Lebanon's Suffering*. Middle East Institute, January 19, https://www.mei.edu/blog/weekly-briefing-why-world-watches-january-20 (accessed August 9, 2021).

Adwan, Charles. (2005). "Corruption in Reconstruction: The Cost of 'National Consensus,' in Post-War Lebanon,'" in Daniel Large (ed.), *Corruption in Post-War Reconstruction: Confronting the Vicious Circle*, 1–17. Beirut, Lebanon: Lebanese Transparency Association, https://www.anti-corruption.org/wp-content/uploads/2016/11/ Corruption in reconstruction TIRI Adwan.pdf.

Al Jazeera (2021) *Lebanon Crisis Could Rank Among World's Three Worst in 150 Years*, https://www.aljazeera.com/economy/2021/6/1/lebanon-crisis-could-rank-among-worlds-three-worst-in-150-years (accessed May 28, 2022)

Arab News. (2020). "Lebanon Shuts Schools after Fourth Coronavirus Case," *Arab News*, February 2, https://arab.news/vc9w3 (accessed August 21, 2021).

Arias-Maldonado, Manuel (2020). "COVID-19 as a Global Risk: Confronting the Ambivalences of a Socionatural Threat," *Societies*, 10 (4): 92, https://doi.org/10.3390/soc10040092.

Beck, Ulrich (1992). *Risk Society: Towards a New Modernity*. London: Sage.

Beck, U., A. Giddens and S. Lash (1994). *Reflexive Modernization Politics, Tradition and Aesthetics in the modern Social Order*. Stanford: Stanford University Press.

Bizri, Abdul Rahman, Hussein H. Khachfe, Mohamad Y. Fares and Umayya Musharrafieh. (2021). "COVID-19 Pandemic: An Insult Over Injury for Lebanon," *Journal of Community Health*, 46 (3): 487–93, https://doi.org/10.1007/s10900-020 -00884-y.

Blondin, Donald and Arjen Boin. (2020). "Cooperation in the Face of Transboundary Crisis: A Framework for Analysis," *Perspectives on Public Management and Governance*, 3 (3): 197–209, https://doi.org/10.1093/ppmgov/gvz031.

Boin, Arjen and Paul't Hart. (2003). "Public Leadership in Times of Crisis: Mission Impossible?," *Public Administration Review*, 63 (5): 544–53, https://doi.org/10.1111 /1540-6210.00318.

Chehayeb, Kareem (2020). "For Lebanon, Coronavirus is a Crisis in a Crisis," *Middle East Eye*, March 14, http://www.middleeasteye.net/news/coronavirus-lebanon-financial -crisis-turmoil-protests (accessed March 8, 2021).

Comfort, Louise K. (2007). "Crisis Management in Hindsight: Cognition, Communication, Coordination, and Control," *Public Administration Review*, 67 (s1): 189–97, https://doi.org/10.1111/j.1540-6210.2007.00827.x.

Coombs, Timothy W. (1995). "Choosing the Right Words: The Development of Guidelines for the Selection of the 'Appropriate' Crisis-Response Strategies," *Management Communication Quarterly*, 8 (4): 447–76, https://doi.org/10.1177 /0893318995008004003.

Dagher, Sam (2021). "'Death by a thousand cuts': Syrian Refugees Face Dire Conditions as Lebanon Unravels," *Middle East Institute*, May 3, https://www.mei.edu/publications/ death-thousand-cuts-syrian-refugees-face-dire-conditions-lebanon-unravels (accessed March 8, 2021).

France 24. (2021). "Jabs for Votes: Lebanon's Oligarchs Turn to Covid Bribery," *France 24*, June 10, https://www.france24.com/en/live-news/20210610-jabs-for-votes-lebanon-s -oligarchs-turn-to-covid-bribery (accessed March 8, 2021).

Francis, Ellen and Laila Bassam. (2021). "World Bank Threatens to cut Lebanon's Vaccine aid Over Line-jumping," *Reuters*, February 23, https://www.reuters.com/article/us -health-coronavirus-lebanon-vaccines-idUSKBN2AN15D (accessed August 21, 2021).

Gharizi, Osama and Mona Yacoubian. (2021). *Lebanon on the Brink of Historic Breakdown*. United States Institute of Peace, https://www.usip.org/publications/2021 /06/lebanon-brink-historic-breakdown (accessed August 11, 2021).

Goniewicz, Krzysztof, Amir Khorram-Manesh, Attila J. Hertelendy, Mariusz Goniewicz, Katarzyna Naylor and Frederick M. Burkle. (2020). "Current Response and Management Decisions of the European Union to the COVID-19 Outbreak: A Review," *Sustainability*, 12 (9): 3838, https://doi.org/10.3390/su12093838.

Habermas, J. (1998). *On the Pragmatics of Communication*, ed. M. Cooke. Cambridge, MA: MIT Press.

Hubbard, Ben and Brian S. (2021). "Collapse: Inside Lebanon's Worst Economic Meltdown in More Than a Century," *The New York Times*, August 4, https://www.nytimes.com /2021/08/04/world/lebanon-crisis.html (accessed August 11, 2021).

International Labour Organization. (2020). *Rapid Diagnostic Assessment of Employment Impacts under Covid-19 in Lebanon*. International Labour Organization, https://www .ilo.org/wcmsp5/groups/public/---ed_emp/documents/publication/wcms_754666.pdf (accessed August 21, 2021).

Jones, Lee and Shahar Hameiri. (2021). "COVID-19 and the Failure of the Neoliberal Regulatory State," *Review of International Political Economy*, doi:10.1080/09692290.2021.1892798.

Kapucu, Naim and Donald Moynihan. (2021). "Trump's (mis)management of the COVID-19 Pandemic in the US," *Policy Studies*, 1–19, https://doi.org/10.1080/01442872.2021.1931671.

Kapucu, Naim, Montgomery Van Wart, Richard Sylves and Farhod Yuldashev. (2011). "U.S. Presidents and Their Roles in Emergency Management and Disaster Policy 1950–2009," *Risk, Hazards & Crisis in Public Policy*, 2 (3): 1–34, https://doi.org/10.2202/1944-4079.1065.

Karasapan, Omer and Sajjad Shah. (2021). "Why Syrian Refugees in Lebanon are a Crisis within a Crisis," *Brookings*, April 15, https://www.brookings.edu/blog/future-development/2021/04/15/why-syrian-refugees-in-lebanon-are-a-crisis-within-a-crisis/ (accessed March 8, 2022).

Khalaf, Rana (2015). "Beyond Arms and Beards: Local Governance of ISIS in Syria," *E-International Relations*, http://www.e-ir.info/2015/01/07/beyond-arms-and-beards-local-governance-of-isis-in-syria/ (accessed March 18, 2022).

Khoury, Petra, Eid Azar and Eveline Hitti. (2020). "COVID-19 Response in Lebanon: Current Experience and Challenges in a Low-Resource Setting," *JAMA*, 324 (6): 548–9, https://doi.org/10.1001/jama.2020.12695.

Lebanese Ministry of Information. (2021). *Corona Virus in Lebanon* [in Arabic]. كورونا في لبنان, August 19, https://corona.ministryinfo.gov.lb (accessed August 19, 2022).

Lebanese Ministry of Public Health. (2021a). *National Campaign to Address Stigma Related to Covid19*, https://www.moph.gov.lb/en/Pages/0/34106/national-campaign-stigma-covid19 (accessed August 22, 2022).

Lebanese Ministry of Public Health. (2021b). *COVID-19 Coronavirus Lebanon Cases.* August 18, https://moph.gov.lb/maps/covid19.php (accessed August 22, 2022).

Li, Yiran, Yanto Chandra and Naim Kapucu. (2020). "Crisis Coordination and the Role of Social Media in Response to COVID-19 in Wuhan, China," *The American Review of Public Administration*, 50 (6–7): 698–705, https://doi.org/10.1177/0275074020942105.

Malsin, Jared and Nazih Osseiran. (2021). "Beirut Port Explosion Fuels Lebanon's Collapse: 'May God Save the Country,'" *The Wall Street Journal*, August 8, https://www.wsj.com/articles/lebanons-economy-still-reeling-from-beirut-port-explosion-falls-off-a-cliff-11628089525 (accessed August 12, 2022).

McCaffrey, Anna and Will Todman. (2021). *Navigating Collapse in Lebanon's Covid-19 Response*. Center for Strategic and International Studies, https://www.csis.org/analysis/navigating-collapse-lebanons-covid-19-response (accessed August 9, 2022).

Melki, Jad, Eveline Hitti, Mirna Abou Zeid and Ali El Takach. (2020). *Media Uses During Pandemics (Spring 2020)*. Lebanese American University, https://soas.lau.edu.lb/news/2020/03/media-uses-during-pandemics-sp.php (accessed August 21, 2022).

Oh, Cheol H. (1997). "Issues for the New Thinking of Knowledge Utilization: Introductory Remarks," *Knowledge and Policy*, 10 (3): 3–10, https://doi.org/10.1007/BF02912503.

Oh, Cheol H. and Robert F. Rich. (1996). "Explaining use of Information in Public Policymaking," *Knowledge and Policy*, 9 (1): 3–35, https://doi.org/10.1007/BF02832231.

Palenchar, Michael J. and Robert L. Heath. (2007). "Strategic Risk Communication: Adding Value to Society," *Public Relations Review*, 33 (2): 120–9, https://doi.org/10.1016/j.pubrev.2006.11.014.

Peri, Rosita Di (2020). *A Sectarianised Pandemic: COVID-19 in Lebanon* [Text]. IAI, https://www.iai.it/en/pubblicazioni/sectarianised-pandemic-covid-19-lebanon (accessed March 8, 2022).

ReliefWeb. (2020). *Nine out of ten Syrian Refugee Families in Lebanon are Now Living in Extreme Poverty, UN Study Says—Lebanon*. ReliefWeb, December 18, https://reliefweb .int/report/lebanon/nine-out-ten-syrian-refugee-families-lebanon-are-now-living -extreme-poverty-un-study (accessed March 8, 2022).

Reuters. (2021). "Lebanon: The Latest Coronavirus Counts, Charts and Maps," *Reuters*, August 19, https://graphics.reuters.com/world-coronavirus-tracker-and-maps/ countries-and-territories/lebanon/ (accessed August 19, 2021).

Sadiki, Larbi and Layla Saleh. (2020). "Reflexive Politics and Arab 'risk society'? COVID-19 and Issues of Public Health," *German Journal for Politics, Economics and Culture of the Middle East (ORIENT)*, 3: 6–20.

The World Bank. (2021a). *World Bank and IFRC Support Independent Monitoring of COVID-19 Vaccine Campaign in Lebanon*, https://www.worldbank.org/en/news/press -release/2021/02/12/world-bank-and-ifrc-support-independent-monitoring-of-covid -19-vaccine-campaign-in-lebanon (accessed August 22, 2022).

The World Bank. (2021b). *The World Bank in Lebanon*. The World Bank, https://www .worldbank.org/en/country/lebanon/overview (accessed August 15, 2022).

The World Bank. (2021c). *Lebanon Sinking into One of the Most Severe Global Crises Episodes, Amidst Deliberate Inaction*, https://www.worldbank.org/en/news/press -release/2021/05/01/lebanon-sinking-into-one-of-the-most-severe-global-crises -episodes (accessed August 12, 2022).

UNDP. (2020). *COVID-19 Information Landscape in Lebanon: Initial Insights*, www.undp .org (accessed August 22, 2022).

UNDP. (2021). *COVID-19 in Lebanon: Perceptions and Behaviors*, www.lb.undp.org (accessed August 22, 2022).

UNHCR. (2021). *UNHCR Lebanon: Fact Sheet*. ReliefWeb, November 26, https://reliefweb .int/report/lebanon/unhcr-lebanon-fact-sheet-september-2021 (accessed March 8, 2022).

United Nations. (2021). *Fighting the Covid-19 Virus on All Fronts: Lebanon Continues Not to Neglect Anyone* [in Arabic]. United Nations, https://www.un.org/ar/coronavirus/ un-agencies-provide-comprehensive-protection-lebanese-during-covid-19 (accessed August 22, 2022).

Van Wart, Montgomery and Naim Kapucu. (2011). "Crisis Management Competencies," *Public Management Review*, 13 (4): 489–511, https://doi.org/10.1080/14719037.2010 .525034.

Walgrave, Stefaab and Yves Dejaeghere. (2017). "Surviving Information Overload: How Elite Politicians Select Information," *Governance*, 30 (2): 229–44, https://doi.org/10 .1111/gove.12209.

Waugh, William L. and Gregory Streib. (2006). "Collaboration and Leadership for Effective Emergency Management," *Public Administration Review*, 66 (s1): 131–40, https://doi.org/10.1111/j.1540-6210.2006.00673.x.

Worldometer. (2021). *Lebanon COVID.* , August 18, https://www.worldometers.info/ coronavirus/country/lebanon/ (accessed August 18, 2022).

Yassine, D. (2020). "Clamping Down on Refugees will Not Save Lebanon from the Pandemic | Refugees | Al Jazeera," *Al-Jazeera*, April 11, https://www.aljazeera.com/opinions/2020/4 /11/clamping-down-on-refugees-will-not-save-lebanon-from-the-pandemic (accessed March 8, 2021).

Zaazaa, Bassam (2021). "Lebanon Clamps Down on COVID-19 Curfew Violators," *Al Arabiya English*, January 26, https://english.alarabiya.net/News/middle-east/2021/01 /26/Lebanon-crisis-Lebanon-clamps-down-on-COVID-19-curfew-violators (accessed August 21, 2022).

Part IV

Wider MENA

10

Gendering Security

The Impact of COVID-19 on Refugee Women in Turkey

Ravza Altuntaş-Çakır, Ayşegül Gökalp Kutlu, and Fatmanur Delioğlu

Introduction

Based on the assumption that modernity generates unintended risks and threats, Ulrich Beck's "risk society" can provide an insightful explanation of the impact of COVID-19 on societies. Although Beck's theory does not specifically focus on the risks posed by viruses, the COVID-19 pandemic, with its local origin and global consequences, can be considered an outcome of modernity. Larbi Sadiki and Layla Saleh highlight the challenges presented by the structural vulnerability of states and unequal public health systems in the Arab world. This observation of the uneven and diverse experiences of the consequences of the pandemic can be applied to the wider Middle East. Risk society gives rise to a reflexive modernization which entail an unavoidable engagement with its effects that have rendered previous modes of problem-solving ineffective.[1] Beck also focuses on inequality and how disadvantaged groups in the society have no choice but to bear a greater burden of the challenges of the "world risk society."[2] Given their marginal status and their limited access to resources, these groups will be excluded from the decision-making processes when governments manage such risks. The most disadvantaged groups in society will disproportionately face the outcomes of the decisions made by the power-holders. Recent risk events "give rise to a dramatic radicalization of social inequality both inter-nationally and intra-nationally [. . .]," and what we argue in this chapter is that COVID-19 is no exception.

COVID-19 demonstrates a concurrent set of vulnerabilities that lie at the heart of the global system: vulnerability of individuals to complex risks, the vulnerability of states in responding to health needs and the vulnerability of the international system in dealing with the global pandemic. Individuals may die in vast numbers or be in need of medical equipment to survive; states may desperately need the assistance of state and non-state actors (such as IMF and UNICEF), all of which indicate that the international system is based on the interconnected vulnerability of states, communities, and individuals at risk events. Instead of the "the autonomous and independent subject asserted in the liberal tradition," the pandemic has exposed "the vulnerable subject"[3] as the main agent in international theory and politics. Vulnerability describes "a universal, inevitable, enduring aspect of the human condition that must be at the heart of our concept of social and state responsibility" and can "define an obligation for the state to ensure a richer and more robust guarantee of equality" than currently exists.[4] Similar to Beck's understanding of inequality, vulnerability is greatly influenced by the quality and quantity of resources people possess or control.

Vulnerability can be critically studied from an intersectional perspective. Due to the diverse social, economic, and institutional relationships, people experience different vulnerabilities. Formulated by Kimberlé Crenshaw, intersectionality refers to the multiple social inequalities and the power relations that adversely affect individuals, resulting in their marginalization.[5] Accordingly, the pandemic has not affected populations equally and exacerbates existing inequalities and creates new forms of exclusion and poverty within certain groups.[6] Thus, inequalities should be factored into the analysis of the impact of the COVID-19 pandemic has on populations incorporating variables such as class and gender for understanding vulnerability in a holistic sense.

Those at the margins of each society are rendered more insecure by the pandemic as "the lower the social class, the higher the financial burden of the pandemic."[7] Perceived as "outsiders" and the "other," refugees are at the bottom end of the social hierarchy. Their already fragile and "precarious lives" and preexisting socioeconomic imbalances are exacerbated by the pandemic.[8] The COVID-19 pandemic has created "a double emergency" for refugees in obtaining sanitary assistance and health security on the one hand and accessing basic economic, social, educational, and political resources on the other.[9] Gender, bringing an additional risk factor to socioeconomic class, has been an important factor affecting the way refugees experience the effects of COVID-19. Women and girls have been at particular risk experiencing increased gender-based vulnerabilities. They are likely to experience the following issues: domestic violence, forced or early marriages, dropping out of the formal education system, no opportunity for online education, unemployment, and inaccessible healthcare facilitates.[10] Due to the intersectional nature of risks and vulnerabilities posed to women in general and women in disadvantaged groups in particular, we adopt a broader definition of security to analyze the refugee women in Turkey.

In this chapter, we will apply a gender-based analysis to study the notions of security and insecurity within the context of COVID-19 through the case study of refugee women in Turkey. We will examine the inequalities in the intersection of being both refugees and women while facing the pandemic. These inequalities are not created by the COVID-19, but they have been exacerbated by it. Turkey hosts 3.7 million Syrians, the highest number globally, with "temporary protection" status.[11] Our analysis of gendering security is divided into two parts. Part one contains a theoretical discussion of feminist IR theory. IR feminists critically reexamine the concept of security, defining it in "multidimensional and multilevel terms."[12] They broaden the notion of security to incorporate bottom-up factors instead of top-down. Security threats involve "domestic violence, rape, poverty, gender subordination, and ecological destruction, as well as war."[13] Feminist IR Theory also emphasizes the interdependence of states as well as "human connectedness, dialogue, and cooperation" in insecurities and risks.[14] The second part will evaluate the experiences of refugee women in Turkey with an emphasis on intersectionalities of the vulnerabilities experienced during the COVID-19 pandemic. We will argue that when forced migration, global pandemic and gender intersects, women are likely to experience "double or even triple burden" indicating greater insecurities within the spheres of health, family, work, and education.

Toward a Gender Perspective on Security in International Relations

Traditional IR theories define security in terms of state security. States are perceived to be unitary, rational, self-serving actors whose power-seeking behavior and military capabilities are invested in their survival.[15] The state-centric notion of security has come under greater scrutiny with the COVID-19. The pandemic revealed the complex, multifaceted, and interdependent nature of security, forcefully displaying the "global risk society" we live under. Beck defines global risks as new threats and uncertainties that are by-products of modernity's radicalized outcomes.[16] Threats like COVID-19 "break with experienced risks and institutionalized routines; they are incalculable, uncontrollable and in the final analysis no longer (privately) insurable (climate change, for example)."[17] Such omnipresence of risks destabilizes preceding forms of security management that fell within the scope of the state, necessitating broader conceptions of security analysis.

Among other critical approaches to security, Feminist International Relations Theory and Feminist Security Studies question conventional IR's logic on security for its failure to account for real-world risks and insecurities that individuals, communities, and the global environment experience.[18] Feminist theorists have articulated that "'real world' events are not adequately addressed by androcentric accounts that render women and gender relations invisible."[19] As opposed to a "generalized rationalist explanation of asocial state's behavior," feminist scholarship articulates how gender influences the way that IR works by focusing on social relations.[20] A feminist perspective "bring[s] to light gender hierarchies embedded in the theories and practices of world politics and allow us to see the extent to which all these systems of domination are interrelated."[21]

Feminist IR theorists use "a gender-sensitive lens" to theorize security that identifies how gender influences, structures, and informs international relations.[22] Gender is "a structural, pervasive feature of how we 'order' social life,"[23] which "is a property of collectives, institutions, and historical processes" and even states and nations.[24] Recognition of gender roles in security studies is imperative because "ignoring gender means not recognizing the ways key actors are defined and differentiated by their relationship to norms of masculinity and femininity."[25] The international system is constituted by socially constructed and historically contingent gender hierarchies that subordinate "women, nature, and all who are constructed as 'other'" including non-elite men and other disadvantaged groups. Through the processes by which identities, interests, and institutions are shaped at the global level, masculine values are generated and reinforced with attention to how they "marginalize and often make invisible women's roles and women's concerns in the international arena."[26]

Feminist IR provides "a better understanding of the interrelationship between all forms of violence and the extent to which unjust social relations, including gender hierarchies, contribute to insecurity, broadly defined."[27] Introducing gender analysis to security studies, Feminist International Relations scholars have demonstrated the degree to which mainstream concepts of security have been utilized in a masculinist practice that fails to include security issues women face on a daily basis. The gendering of security is seen in areas such as forced prostitution, interpersonal and domestic violence, human trafficking, refuge flows, militarization, development, rape, poverty, environmental degradation, forced migration, health epidemics, and other such crises.[28]

Feminist International Relations scholars view security through a multilevel and multidimensional lens where individuals' security is linked to domestic and international politics. Mainstream conceptions of security are broadened beyond interstate and intrastate military conflicts, showing how international politics affect the security of individuals. The notion of security is moved from a top-down (starting with the state) approach to a bottom-up (starting with the individual or community) one.[29] In Feminist IR, there is a robust recognition of "the close and complex relations between 'the intimate' and 'the global'":[30] "the personal is international [and] the international is personal."[31]

As a way of addressing gendered security, feminist theorists look at both the interrelationship between securities and risks, and the interrelationship between actors in addressing the global risk community we are living under. They award greater importance to the non-state actors in the international arena as well as their interdependence with the states. Feminist scholars reject the state as the sole guarantor of security in global politics. They advocate "the diminution of all forms of violence, including physical, structural, and ecological."[32] In the globalized world, successful risk management, even under national and local levels, would necessitate "transnational cooperation."[33] Organizations and institutions are not only significant in this cooperation for security management but also "human connectedness, dialogue and cooperation."[34] Essentially, "the sum of capabilities" of state, non-state, and human actors can be mobilized for providing solutions for the risks modernity brings.[35]

Existing structural and societal vulnerabilities continue to be intensified by the global health crisis with direct effects on gender insecurities. Gender-based vulnerabilities have been exacerbated in COVID-19 settings as such crises have much greater political, economic, and social repercussions on women.[36] Women's chances of experiencing additional patterns of discrimination and insecurities are higher just because of their gender.[37] Given the sociocultural and structural inequalities, it is usually difficult for women to access capital, social goods, or necessary legal means to protect themselves when crises arise.[38] Crisis and humanitarian emergencies worsen women's already marginalized access to educational options and safe employment, increase the burden of unpaid domestic work and family care responsibilities, limit access to legal protection, reproductive health, and other social services.[39] Thus, women are more likely than men to lose their capacity in accessing education, health facilitates, and decent work opportunities.[40] Crises also increase the prevalence of and ineffective response to various forms of gender-based violence and gender-based discrimination.[41]

Feminist perspectives on security claim that women identify themselves, their needs, and their relations with others and the state through their personal experiences of insecurity.[42] In studying the insecurities of refugee women, a major goal must be to understand how insecurity is experienced by women in daily lives. An approach to security with a gender-inclusive lens would enable the comprehension of refugee women's experiences of insecurity. Refugee women constitute a "minority within a minority" as they are "foreigners" in another country and because of their status in a patriarchal system. This chapter will now focus on gendering security within the context of refugee women in a Turkish context. We will argue that when forced migration, global pandemic, and gender inequalities have intersected, the COVID-19 has resulted in a triple crisis exacerbating gender vulnerabilities. A gender-sensitive lens will be applied to analyze the health, work, education, and domestic risks and insecurities generated by the COVID-19 pandemic among refugee women in Turkey.

The Impact of COVID-19 on Refugee Women in Turkey

Turkey currently hosts the world's greatest Syrian refugee population, 3.7 million in total, who are dispersed all around the country. Almost half of the Syrian refugees are women and less than 2 percent live in refugee camps.[43] Their "temporary protection" status entitles them to a range of free public services, including education and health care. However, they are prone to complex structural and societal vulnerabilities, which have become more pronounced during the pandemic. Living in densely populated quarters, crowded households, poor hygiene environments, unemployment, or in low-wage jobs, refugees have been hit especially hard by the pandemic and government responses to it. Food and rent inflation, distance learning, and limited access to healthcare are some of the issues with which they struggle.[44] Both documented and undocumented refugees face challenges at the workplace, where longer work hours, low earnings and unregulated work practices pose greater health risks.[45] Socioeconomic hardships have also brought worsening public attitudes toward refugees in public and gender-based violence at home.[46] The spheres of work, health, education, and family have been the main areas where refugees have experienced greater insecurity during the pandemic. This chapter focuses on these areas through a gendered-perspective in articulating how security and insecurity are gendered within the global context of COVID-19.

Work Securities and Insecurities

The work routines of refugees have been adversely affected, intensifying the insecurities they experience in their workplaces. Although refugees under temporary protection have the right to work in Turkey, they are usually employed to do precarious work that the locals often prefer not to do.[47] Turkish government regulates refugees' right to work via the Regulation on Work Permit for Refugees under Temporary Protection enacted in January 2016. This regulation obliges employers to apply for work permits for refugees they wish to employ and ensure that at least the minimum wage will be paid to them. As of 2019, 4,383 Syrian women and 59,406 men under temporary protection are working in Turkey with working permits.[48] The Regional Refugee and Resilience Plan (3RP)[49] Turkey Country Chapter 2020–2021 indicates that many Syrian refugees have gradually been able to find work; nevertheless, just 3 percent of working refugees are doing so being formally registered, with social security and a minimum wage.[50] The vast majority, around one million refugees, however, work illegally and are exposed to exploitation, working longer hours without occupational safety and below the minimum wage.[51]

In an attempt to slow down the spread of the COVID-19 virus within the population, the Turkish government announced the reduction of the weekly working hours in workplaces and also give the option to initiate short-time working allowances for insured employees. However, this policy covers only registered employees and excludes all refugees working informally.[52] The crowded and inadequately ventilated unhygienic workspaces preclude social distancing and clean sanitation to avoid the spread of COVID-19 among illegally working refugees.[53] In addition, refugees working in the informal sector were negatively impacted when many small- and medium-sized businesses ceased their activities due to government-imposed quarantine precautions. Refugees were dismissed without compensation and notice, and the lack of work permits made it impossible for them to apply for legal remedies. A research study in Istanbul indicates that deprived of their livelihood, refugees were more concerned about not being able to pay rent than catching the coronavirus.[54] For instance, refugees, for fear of losing their jobs in case of a positive diagnosis, prefer not to use the official health system unless their situation is serious.[55]

Refugee women faced economic insecurity before COVID-19 linked to the preexisting socioeconomic inequalities and gender pay gap in employment. They are likely to receive lower wages for the same job with less secure job profiles and face more discrimination in the labor market than either refugee men or the female citizens of the host country.[56] Refugee women usually work in precarious jobs in the host country's informal labor markets related to services and domestic work. Women are overrepresented in the host country's informal economy and overrepresented in sectors that have been highly impacted by lockdowns. The International Labour Organization (ILO) estimates that 42 percent of women are working in highly affected sectors worldwide, compared to 32 percent of men.[57] Refugee women have been affected by global employment loss to a greater extent than men, and they are more vulnerable to the economic downturn brought about by the pandemic. An Economic Policy Research Foundation of Turkey's (TEPAV) research study indicates that 93 percent of the women participants in Turkey were impacted by the pandemic due to unpaid leave, closure of businesses, reduction of work, and dismissals.[58] Evidence from previous health crises also shows that men's economic activity recovers faster compared to women's; hence, women are forced to accept more exploitative working conditions to earn a living,[59] rendering them more vulnerable to economic as well as sexual abuse.

Loss of income is directly related to food insecurity. In research conducted with 500 households by the International Federation of the Red Cross and Red Crescent Societies and the Turkish Red Crescent (IFRC, 2020)[60] highlights that 69 percent of refugee families suffered from loss of employment, 78 percent faced increased expenditure on food and hygiene items, and 82 percent had increased household debt. Accompanied by the loss of livelihood, food is identified as a priority need. Families indicate that they must borrow money to cover food, rent, and bills. Similarly, Care International's study in South-Eastern Turkey found 77 percent, 63 percent, and 75 percent of respondents believed that their abilities to meet basic food security, basic healthcare needs, and basic rental payments, respectively, worsened.[61]

The report also identified the entrenchment of preexisting gender inequalities. Women's workloads have become heavier during the COVID-19 pandemic period. Conventional gender roles of motherhood, housewife, and caregiver continue to influence the boundaries of the agency of women in social settings. Unpaid domestic labor such as shopping for food, cooking, cleaning, and caring for the disabled, elderly, and children have intensified.[62] While the stress level of overburdened women rises, they are going through the pandemic process under very difficult conditions with the absence of friends and extended family support networks due to quarantine and isolation.[63] Thus, as Feminist IR Theory points out, once emergencies and crises intersect with the traditional sexist gender roles, women experience a "double or even triple burden."[64]

Moreover, since the majority of the world's refugees are hosted in developing countries, their presence puts pressure on host communities' limited or strained resources. The numbers of refugees in need of economic assistance have unpredictably grown in 2020 and 2021 due to significant loss of income and struggle to cover basic needs due to the pandemic. In general, the national safety measures to manage the pandemic usually prioritize the host community and marginalizes the needs of refugees. Thus, the availability of help from NGOs and humanitarian organizations are critical to their survival. In order to provide cash assistance for Syrian refugees in Turkey, an Emergency Social Safety Net (ESSN) was created in 2016, financed by the European Union (EU) and implemented in partnership with the International Federation of Red Cross and Red Crescent Societies (IFRC), the Turkish Red Crescent (TRC), and Ministry of Labor and Social Security. In the case of Turkey, the 3RP partners could manage to mobilize US$695 million, which covered 53 percent of total protection, resilience, and humanitarian requirements for 2020.[65] Overall, the pandemic-related interruption of services by nongovernmental organizations (NGOs) and charities worsens the uncertainties and risks refugees face.[66]

The shutting down or reducing of essential social protection services makes it even harder for young women and girls to overcome economic insecurity. Food insecurity leaves refugee women and girls exposed to sexual violence and commercial sexual exploitation.[67] Refugee women face an increased risk of contracting HIV/AIDS and other sexually transmitted infections, as well as an increased number of unwanted pregnancies. While lockdowns are essential to reduce the spread of the virus, they obstruct refugee women and children's access to crucial health services such as reproductive, maternal, newborn, and child healthcare and psychosocial support.[68] Essentially, economic insecurities accelerate health insecurities.

Health Securities and Insecurities

Turkey has provided an inclusive health policy during the pandemic. With the advent of the pandemic, presidential decrees were issued to ensure "that everyone, regardless of whether the person has health insurance or not, will have access to personal protective equipment and testing for the diagnosis of the disease and treatment."[69] Hospitals were opened to immigrants, refugees, and unregistered people regardless of their legal status in Turkey.[70] Although given legal rights, refugees have not been able to effectively access to health institutions. Undocumented refugees, for fear of being deported, were hesitant to benefit from health services despite their newly introduced right to them.[71] Undocumented people tend to choose secret clinics opened by refugees or resort to other methods such as providing fake IDs and addresses. Fake information makes it impossible for the medical personnel traces them if they have a positive diagnosis.[72]

A major factor that prevents refugees from benefiting from the available health services has been the language barrier. Before the start of the pandemic, Refugee Health Centers were formed by the close cooperation of WHO and Turkish Ministry of Health. The Turkish Ministry of Health trains Syrian health workers to provide services to Syrian patients and employs Turkish-Arabic interpreters to assist these patients in hospitals. These centers operate in Ankara, Gaziantep, Hatay, Istanbul, Izmir, Mersin, and Şanlıurfa provinces.[73] Even though these centers are fundamental for refugees to access primary healthcare and health information, there was a sharp decline in patients visits after the onset of the pandemic. According to the research conducted by Budak and Bostan (2020), "30% of the Syrian refugees living in Turkey do not have enough information about the pandemic, and approximately 45% do not have access to or have limited access to personal protective equipment."[74] Although the Ministry of Health and Directorate General of Migration Management (DGMM) provided information about the pandemic in different languages and Istanbul Metropolitan Municipality prepared informative animations in foreign languages, people who live in underprivileged areas have not been able to benefit from these services.[75] Language barriers undermined a rapid response to slow the spread of the virus within the refugee community. Moreover, the NGOs that usually assisted the refugees with translation could not accompany them to hospitals during the lockdowns.[76]

Language barriers and the fears of deportation may explain the reason why a starkly low rate of vaccination is present among refugees. A Turkish Red Crescent Society's report (2021) shows a higher vaccination rate for refugee men than refugee women.[77] The report states that many refugees do not know how to get a vaccine appointment. The vaccination appointments are often made via the electronic e-government system that requires valid IDs. E-Devlet Kapısı (the e-Government Gateway) is necessary to access most, if not all, government services in Turkey and IT literary is a must. Many refugees do not have access to the Internet or are unable to book vaccine appointments due to a language barrier. However, online registration is not the sole option. Anyone with an ID starting with 99 (registered refugees under temporary protection) can be vaccinated, while those who are undocumented can apply to the immigration offices and report their requests to be vaccinated. The main problem seems to be the difficulty in accessing information about which community health centers are working actively in the field with refugees in Istanbul informed us about.

Refugees with non-COVID-19-related health issues are also negatively affected by the pandemic. Refugees with chronic diseases delayed their routine health checks, assuming that the hospitals would not provide services.[78] Women have suffered the most during the pandemic process as maternal, sexual, and reproductive health services have been severely interrupted or even stopped.[79] Almost half of the Syrian women participants in Care International's research in South-Eastern Turkey stated that their female hygiene needs are not met and 34 percent of women said that they had decreased access to sexual reproductive health services due to COVID-19.[80]

The health of refugees is closely related to their homes and places of accommodation. Most of the refugees in Turkey live outside refugee camps, usually in urban slums, with no reliable income. Many of these refugees cannot access official support and rely on charities or NGOs for livelihoods. They also work in temporary jobs in the informal market economy, many of which were closed due to government-ordered lockdowns.[81] Low-income and unemployment force urban refugees to reduce expenditure on food, medicine, and essential health services.[82] High rents and reluctance among local people to rent to refugees combine to force them to live in crowded houses.[83] In Turkey, 40 percent of Syrian refugee houses are shared by more than one family, and nearly half of the households live in accommodation with more than seven people.[84] Crowded houses strictly limit social distancing and hygiene standards. These limitations also increase the risk of gender-based violence, sexual abuse, and child marriage faced by women.

Domestic Securities and Insecurities

The pandemic worsened sexual, domestic, and intimate partner violence against women. UN Women relates increased security, health and economic pressures, and risks to the growing violence within households.[85] UN Women (2021) estimated in the early months of the pandemic that "for every three months of lockdown measures around the world, an additional 15 million women and girls would be exposed to gender-based violence" worldwide.[86] Lockdowns isolate women with violent partners where a coordinated response to domestic violence between police, health, and social services often proved ineffective or completely lacking. UN Women (2021) points out that when their movement is restricted (as women could not leave their house for help, reach networks of support or shelter) and counseling provided by phone, emails or digital platforms, women find it difficult to ask for help or escape situations of violence. Combined with economic insecurity, women have to stay in violent relationships and households.

There are serious limitations in acquiring data on gender-based violence during a pandemic.[87] Several secondary resources used in this study point out the difficulty of accessing violence victims through phone calls or online interviews (see, e.g., SGDD-ASAM 2020, Care International 2020). Even though there is no official report on the prevalence of sexual abuse or domestic violence in Syrian households in Turkey, our correspondence with KADAV (Kadınlarla Dayanışma Vakfı/Women's Solidarity Foundation) revealed that the numbers of Syrian applicants reaching the organization are quite high. KADAV also suggests that there is a significant increase in applications throughout the pandemic (from 47,8 percent in January–February 2021[88] to 67 percent in July–August[89]). The foundation stated that women mostly sought legal help, cash assistance, immediate protection from violence, shelter, employment, and educational support. International studies on COVID-19 maintain that stress, economic strains, and lockdowns tend to increase violence toward women.[90] Forced migration alters power relationships within households, escalating the instances of domestic violence. Though not particularly addressing domestic violence, IFRC-Red Crescent study[91] indicates that women were more likely than men to mention the negative psychological impact of staying at home and the heavy burden of caring for children full time. UNHCR (2020) reveals that one in five refugee women have witnessed sexual violence before the pandemic. Lack of privacy in refugee camps and socially isolated overcrowded households of the urban refugees, combined with economic strains, usually lead to domestic and intimate partner violence.[92] While the living conditions created by the pandemic increase the possibility of women being forced into abusive relationships or exploitative situations, forced migrant women have been especially vulnerable to intimate partner violence.[93] Once there is no state financial support or aid to refugee women and they are economically dependent on their partners for survival, it is harder for them to leave abusive relationships.[94] Indeed, "male violence continues to threaten lives as much as the virus."[95]

Educational Securities and Insecurities

The pandemic has dealt a great blow to educational provision for refugee children. Refugees' existing disadvantages in accessing education are exacerbated with the closure of schools due to COVID-19. As of the start of the 2020–1 school year, 774,257 Syrian refugee children were enrolled in Turkish public schools, 379,432 of them were girls.[96] Turkish Ministry of National Education introduced distance education through the Education Information Network (EBA) via TV broadcasting and Internet sources. IFRC-Red-Crescent study reveals, however, that 31 percent of refugee children enrolled in school cannot access online have no opportunity for distance learning.[97] Common barriers in accessing distance education are the lack of information regarding distance education services, the language barrier, the shortage of technological equipment (television, Internet, smartphone, computer, tablet, etc.), and the lack of a separate study room within crowded households.[98]

Refugee children have been disadvantaged in accessing and continuing education even before the pandemic. With the pandemic, UNHCR (2020) points out that in comparison to non-refugee children, refugee children are twice as likely to leave school. With no access to education, many refugee boys have to work and earn money to support their families, whereas girls have to do household work and take care of their siblings.[99] A decrease is expected in the rate of returning to school after the pandemic for boys, but this carries the risk of a higher rate for girls.[100] The UNHCR

(2020) expects that around 50 percent of refugee girls in secondary education might not return to school. School closures have impacts beyond the direct loss of education; the absence of formal education leaves girls out of the protection of a safe and supportive environment, health monitoring, and psychosocial support.

Suspension of education heightens the risk of child labor, sexual abuse, and forced marriage. According to the research conducted by TEPAV, refugee girls are forced to drop out of school and be forced into marriage at an early age due to economic hardships.[101] In cases of forced migration, families believe arranging a marriage for their daughters will protect them from sexual violence and "save family honor" within the vulnerable circumstances they lie.[102] The UN expects that due to economic circumstances, lack of education and isolation from support networks brought by the consequences of the COVID-19, an additional thirteen million girls, many of whom are refugees, are under the risk of early or forced marriage.[103] Thus, after the pandemic, a considerable portion of refuge girls are likely to lose the chance to return to school due to economic hardship or child marriage.[104] In order to support the education of refugee children, 682,882 pupils (335,978 girls) received Conditional Cash Transfers for Education through the cooperation of Turkish Ministry of National Education and UNICEF by February 2021.[105]

Conclusion

Interdependence of the sources and forms of insecurities are more evident in the phenomena of global risks such as COVID-19, challenging the narrow perception of IR that depicts the world in interstate terms. The global pandemic has manifested how security interacts with multiple actors and spheres of life such as individuals, communities, organizations, states, as well as economics, health, science, ecology, and culture. The most vulnerable groups in societies have suffered the most, refugees being one of the worst affected. Their already "precarious lives" and preexisting socioeconomic imbalances were exacerbated by the pandemic.[106] The COVID-19 pandemic has created "a double emergency" for refugees—in obtaining sanitary assistance and health security on the one hand and accessing basic economic, social, educational, and political resources on the other.[107] However, not all refugees experienced the same levels of pandemic-driven insecurities. The COVID-19 pandemic also has gendered consequences.

This chapter has shed light on many types of insecurities created when gender intersects with forced migration and a global pandemic. We argued that it is necessary to analyze global risks holistically to go beyond the scope of traditional IR theories. We chose to focus on the Feminist IR Theory because of its refusal of the limited definition of security and its focus on the security of the individual. Feminist theory accepts that for most people, security is about daily life, concerning access to secure housing, food and clean water, safe and secure jobs, basic human rights, or avoiding domestic, sexual or physical violence. Feminism does not abstract theory from the real world. Rather it endorses an emancipatory approach "improving the lives of the whole humankind."[108] Feminist IR aims to "enhance social justice, gender equity, and sustainable peace"[109] by "investigating the often disadvantaged lives of women within states or international institutions and structures to change them."[110] Therefore, Feminist IR brings a novel perspective for writing about the pandemic-related insecurities experienced by refugee women challenging the masculine, state-centric, realpolitik view of world politics.

The intersection of structural gender inequalities with the limited resources and constrained institutional capacity of the crises results in disproportionate impacts for women and girls. The pandemic and the following measures have exacerbated and reinforced existing inequalities and insecurity among women refugees. In times of crisis, women are more likely than men to experience gender-based violence and lack access to healthcare, the workplace, and education.[111] Introducing gender analysis to COVID-19, our analysis on refugee women in Turkey has demonstrated that gender "is an intersecting component of wider structural inequalities."[112] At the bottom of the social hierarchy, refugee women have endured the pandemic, both by facing insecurities due to their gender and as "foreigners" in the host society. Working in informal and precarious jobs, they were the first to be dismissed. Economic insecurity, coupled with food insecurity, led to further health and domestic insecurities. Job loss and lockdowns, associated with increasing care burden for women and domestic violence, resulted in refugee women's further marginalization. These issues demonstrate how a gendered-perspective is needed in approaching the insecurities generated or accelerated by the COVID-19, as gender is vital in understating the double or even triple risks and vulnerabilities women face in global crises.

Notes

1 Sadiki and Saleh (2020, 6–20).
2 Beck (2009a, 3–22).
3 Albertson Fineman (2008, 1).
4 Albertson Fineman (2008, 8).
5 Crenshaw (1991).
6 Akcapar and Çalışan (2021, 223–41).
7 Elçi, Kirisçioglu, and Üstübici (2021).
8 Tekin Koru (2020).
9 Dempster et al. (2020).
10 Abwola and Michelis (2020).
11 Temporary Protection." (2021).
12 Tickner and Sjoberg (2013, 51–67).
13 Tickner and Sjoberg(2013, 187).
14 Steans (1998).
15 Mearsheimer (2013, 51–67).
16 Beck (2008, 1–21).
17 Beck (2009b, 293).
18 Bilgin (2014, 9–24).
19 Peterson (1992, 183–206).
20 Tickner and Sjoberg (2013, 51–67).
21 Tickner (1992).

22 Peterson and Runyan (1999).
23 Peterson (2000, 11–29)
24 Hooper (2001: 35).
25 Sjoberg and Wadley (2010).
26 Hooper (2001), 1.
27 Tickner (2001, 49).
28 Tripp (2013, 3–32).
29 Tickner (2001).
30 Marchand and Runyan (2011).
31 Enloe (1990).
32 Tickner (2001).
33 Beck (2008, 1–21).
34 Steans (1998).
35 Beck (2008, 16–17).
36 Al-Ali (2020, 333–47)
37 OHCHR (2021).
38 Aolain (2011, 1).
39 UN Women (2020).
40 Gardam and Jarvis (2001).
41 UN Women (2020).
42 Jacoby (2006, 153–73).
43 "Temporary Protection. (2021)"
44 Kirişçi and Erdoğan (2020).
45 ILO (2020).
46 Kirişçi and Erdoğan (2020).
47 Yılmaz, Karatepe, and Tören (2019).
48 "Work Permits of Foreigners" (2019).
49 Under the leadership of UNHCR and UNDP, The Regional Response and Resilience Plan (3RP) was initiated to meet the obstacles faced by countries hosting Syrian refugees. 270 UN agencies, international and national NGOs and other partners work together to support the host countries. For further information, see UNHCR Global Compact on Refugees Digital Platform, https://globalcompactrefugees.org/article/syrian-refugee-regional-resilience-plan.
50 "3RP Turkey Chapter" (2020).
51 ILO (2020).
52 Doğanay et al. (2020).
53 ILO (2020).
54 SGDD-ASAM (2020).
55 Karadağ and Üstübici (2021).
56 Dempster et al. (2020).
57 "ILO Monitor" (2020).
58 Doğanay et al. (2020).
59 Dempster et al. (2020).
60 IFRC and Türk Kızılay (2020).
61 Care International (2020).
62 Care International (2020).
63 Al-Ali (2020, 333–47).
64 Tickner and Sjoberg (2013, 51–67).
65 "3RP Turkey Chapter 2020: Outcome Monitoring Report - Turkey."

66 Al-Ali (2020, 333–47).
67 UN Women (2020).
68 Bukuluki et al. (2020)
69 Mardin (2020).
70 Karadağ and Üstübici (2021).
71 Kocaoğulları, Avcı, and İnanç (2020).
72 Karadağ and Üstübici (2021).
73 World Health Organization (2021).
74 Budak and Bostan (2020, 579–89).
75 Jadoo et al. (2020, 278–85).
76 Karadağ and Üstübici (2021).
77 "Vaccination Status of Refugees in Turkey: Survey Results II - March 2021 - Turkey."
     (2021).
78 Akcapar and Çalışan (2021, 223–41).
79 Al-Ali (2020, 333–47).
80 Care International (2020).
81 Mbiyozo (2020).
82 Bukuluki et al. (2020).
83 Akay Ertürk (2020).
84 UN Women (2018).
85 UN Women (2021).
86 UN Women (2021).
87 Fraser (2020).
88 KADAV (2021, 6).
89 KADAV (2021, 5).
90 John et al. (2020, 65–8).
91 IFRC & Kızılay (2020).
92 Zaatari (2014).
93 Al-Ali (2020, 333–47).
94 Freedman, Crankshaw, and Mutambara.
95 Aygüneş and Ok (2020).
96 UNHCR (2021).
97 IFRC and Kızılay (2020).
98 SGDD-ASAM (2020).
99 UN Women (2021).
100 Aygüneş and Ok (2020).
101 Doğanay et al. (2020).
102 Charles and Denman (2013, 96–111).
103 UNFPA (2020).
104 Plan International (2020).
105 UNHCR (2021).
106 Koru (2020).
107 Abwola and Michelis (2020).
108 Peterson (1992).
109 Enloe (1990).
110 Tickner (2005, 2173–88).
111 Gardam and Jarvis (2001).
112 Hankivsky and Kapilashrami (2020).

References

"3RP Turkey Chapter 2020: Outcome Monitoring Report - Turkey," *ReliefWeb*, 2020, https://reliefweb.int/report/turkey/3rp-turkey-chapter-2020-outcome-monitoring -report (accessed Septemeber 15, 2021).

Abwola, Nancy and Ilaria Michelis. (2020). *What Happened? How the Humanitarian Response to COVID-19 Failed to Protect Women and Girls*. International Rescue Committee.

Akay Ertürk, Selma. (2020). "The Effects of COVID-19 on Syrian Refugees in Turkey," *Southern Responses to Displacement*, April 24, https://southernresponses.org/2020/04/24 /the-effects-of-covid-19-on-syrian-refugees- in-turkey/ (accessed September 10, 2021).

Akcapar, Sebnem Koser and Aysima Çalışan. (2021). "Neoliberal Düzende Artan Kırılganlıklar: Pandemi Döneminde Mülteci Sağlığı," *Göç Dergisi*, 8 (2): 223–41, https://doi.org/10.33182/ gd.v8i2.768.

Al-Ali, Nadje. (2020). "COVID-19 and Feminism in the Global South: Challenges, Initiatives and Dilemmas," *European Journal of Women's Studies*, 27 (4): 333–47, https://doi.org/10.1177/1350506820943617.

Albertson Fineman, Martha. (2008). "The Vulnerable Subject: Anchoring Equality in the Human Condition," *Yale JL & Feminism*, 20: 1.

Aoláin, Fionnuala Ní. (2011). "Women, Vulnerability, and Humanitarian Emergencies," *Michigan Journal of Gender & Law*, 18: 1.

Aygüneş, Aslı and Oğuz Can Ok. (2020). *Covid-19 Pandemisi Sürecinde Toplumsal Cinsiyet Çalışmaları İzleme Raporu*. İstanbul: Sabancı Üniversitesi Toplumsal Cinsiyet ve Kadın Çalışmaları Mükemmeliyet Merkezi.

Beck, Ulrich. (2008). "World at Risk: The New Task of Critical Theory," *Development and Society*, 37 (1): 1–21.

Beck, Ulrich. (2009a). "World Risk Society and Manufactured Uncertainties," *World Risk Society and Manufactured Uncertainties*: Iris, 1 (2): 291–9.

Beck, Ulrich. (2009b). "Critical Theory of World Risk Society: A Cosmopolitan Vision," *Constellations*, 16 (1): 3–22, https://doi.org/10.1111/j.1467-8675.2009.00534.x.

Beck, Ulrich. (2013). "Risk, Class, Crisis, Hazards and Cosmopolitan Solidarity/Risk Community-Conceptual and Methodological Clarifications," Foundation maison des sciences de l'homme Working Papers Series 31, https://halshs.archives-ouvertes.fr/ halshs-00820297/document (accessed September 23, 2021).

Bilgin, Pınar. (2014). "Dialogue of Civilisations: A Critical Security Studies Perspective," *Perceptions: Journal of International Affairs*, 19 (1): 9–24.

Budak, Fatih and Sedat Bostan. (2020). "The Effects of COVID-19 Pandemic on Syrian Refugees in Turkey: The Case of Kilis," *Social Work in Public Health*, 35 (7): 579–89, https://doi.org/10.1080/19371918.2020.1806984.

Bukuluki, Paul, Hadijah Mwenyango, Simon Peter Katongole, Dina Sidhva and George Palattiyil. (2020). "The Socio- Economic and Psychosocial Impact of COVID-19 Pandemic on Urban Refugees in Uganda," *Social Sciences & Humanities Open*, 2 (1), https://doi.org/10.1016/j.ssaho.2020.100045.

Care International. (2020). "COVID-19 Impact Assessment South East Turkey," May, https://reliefweb.int/sites/ reliefweb.int/files/resources/76662.pdf.

Charles, Lorraine and Kate Denman. (2013). "Syrian and Palestinian Syrian Refugees in Lebanon: The Plight of Women and Children," *Journal of International Women's Studies*, 14 (5): 96–111.

Crenshaw, Kimberle. (1991). "Mapping the Margins: Intersectionality, Identity Politics, and Violence against Women of Color," *Stanford Law Review*, 43 (6), https://doi.org/10 .2307/1229039.

Dempster, Helen, Thomas Ginn, Jimmy Graham, Martha Guerrero Ble, Daphne Jayasinghe and Barri Shorey. (2020). *Locked Down and Left Behind: The Impact of COVID-19 on Refugees' Economic Inclusion.* Center for Global Development, Refugees International, and International Rescue Committee.

Doğanay, Cansu, İlderya Avşar Koyuncu, Murat Kenanoğlu, Omar Kadkoy and Sibel Güven. (2020). "Zorunlu Göçmenler İçin Sosyal Eşitlik: Pandemi Sürecinde Yerel Yönetimlerin Ve STK'Ların Rolü," *TEPAV*, https://www.tepav.org.tr/tr/yayin/s/1582 (accessed September 25, 2021).

Elçi, Ezgi, Eda Kirisçioglu and Aysen Üstübici. (2021). "How COVID-19 Financially Hit Urban Refugees: Evidence from Mixed-Method Research with Citizens and Syrian Refugees in Turkey," *Disasters*, https://doi.org/10.1111/disa.12498.

Enloe, Cynthia H. (1990). *Bananas, Beaches and Bases: Making Feminist Sense of International Politics.* London: University of California Press.

Fraser, Erika. (2020). "Impact of COVID-19 Pandemic on Violence against Women and Girls," *UKAid VAWG Helpdesk Research Report*, 284.

Freedman, Jane, Tamaryn L. Crankshaw, and Victoria M. Mutambara. (2020). "Sexual and Reproductive Health of Asylum Seeking and Refugee Women in South Africa: Understanding the Determinants of Vulnerability," *Sexual and Reproductive Health Matters*, 28 (1), doi:10.1080/26410397.2020.1758440.

Gardam, Judith Gail and Michelle J. Jarvis. (2001). *Women, Armed Conflict and International Law.* The Hague: Kluwer Law International.

Hankivsky, Olena and Anuj Kapilashrami. (2020). *Beyond Sex and Gender Analysis: An Intersectional View of the COVID-19 Pandemic Outbreak and Response.* Global Policy Institute, https://www.qmul.ac.uk/media/global-policy-institute/Policy-brief-COVID-19-and-intersectionality.pdf (accessed October 10, 2021).

Hooper, Charlotte. (2001). *Manly States: Masculinities, International Relations, and Gender Politics.* New York: Columbia University Press, 35.

IFRC & Türk Kızılay. (2020). "Impact of COVID-19 on Daily Life of Refugees in Turkey," https://reliefweb.int/sites/reliefweb.int/files/resources/Impact-of-COVID-19-on-Daily-Life-of-Refugees-in-Turkey_.pdf.

ILO. (2017). "ILO's Support to Refugees and Host Communities in Turkey," *Refugees: ILO's Support to Refugees and Host Communities in Turkey*, April 5, https://www.ilo.org/ankara/projects/WCMS_379375/lang--en/index.htm (accessed October 5, 2021).

ILO. (2020). "COVID-19 Küresel Salgınında Göçmen İşçileri Korumak," *Politika Bilgi Notu: COVID-19 küresel salgınında göçmen işçileri korumak*, April 30, https://www.ilo.org/ankara/areas-of-work/covid-19/WCMS_745357/ lang--tr/index.htm (accessed October 7, 2021).

ILO Monitor. (2020). "ILO Monitor: COVID-19 and the World of Work. Third Edition Updated Estimates and Analysis," April 29, https://www.ilo.org/wcmsp5/groups/public/@dgreports/@dcomm/documents/briefingnote/wcms_743146.pdf (accessed October 7, 2021).

Jacoby, Tami. (2006). "From the Trenches: Dilemmas of Feminist IR Fieldwork," *Feminist Methodologies for International Relations*: 153–73, https://doi.org/10.1017/cbo9780511617690.010.

Jadoo, Ali, Saad Ahmed, Ilker Dastan, Mustafa Ali Al-Samarrai, Shukur Mahmood Yaseen, Assiyeh Abbasi, Hassan Alkhdar, Mohammed Al Saad and Omar Mohamed Danfour. (2020). "Knowledge, Attitude, and Practice towards COVID-19 among Syrian People Resident in Turkey," *Journal of Ideas in Health*, 3 (Special2): 278–85, https://doi.org/10.47108/ jidhealth.vol3.issspecial2.61.

John, Neetu, Sara E Casey, Giselle Carino and Terry McGovern. (2020). "Lessons Never Learned: Crisis and Gender- Based Violence," *Developing World Bioethics*, 20 (2): 65–8, https://doi.org/10.1111/dewb.12261.

KADAV. (2021a). "Kadına Yönelik Şiddet Ocak ve Şubat Ayı Raporu," https://kadav.org.tr /wp-content/uploads/2022/03/1-kadavrapor_ocaks%CC%A7ubat2021.pdf (accessed October 10, 2021).

KADAV. (2021b). "Kadına Yönelik Şiddet Temmuz ve Ağustos Ayı Raporu," https://kadav .org.tr/wp-content/uploads/2022/03/4-kadavrapor_temmuzag%CC%86ustos2021.pdf (accessed October 10, 2021).

Karadağ, Sibel and Ayşen Üstübici. (2021). *Protection during Pre-pandemic and COVID-19 Periods in Turkey*. Istanbul: Koc University (AdMiGov Deliverable 4.2), http://admigov .eu/upload/Deliverable_42_Protection_COVID19_Turkey_Karadag_Ustu bici.pdf (accessed October 8, 2021)

Kirişçi, Kemal and Murat M. Erdoğan. (2020). *Order from Chaos, Turkey and COVID-19: Don't Forget Refugees*. Washington, DC: The Brookings Institution, https://www .brookings.edu/blog/order-from-chaos/2020/04/20/turkey-and-covid-19-dont-forget -refugees/ (accessed September 12, 2021).

Kocaoğulları, Anıl, Elif Avcı, and Simten Birsöz İnanç. "Kentsel Hizmetlere Göç Perspektifinden Bakmak: Pandemi Döneminde İstanbul Örneği Ulusal Düzeyde Karar Alıcılar İçin Politika Önerileri," *Heinrich Böll Stiftung Derneği Türkiye Temsilciliği 2020*, http://yereliz.org/wp-content/uploads/2020/12/ Ulusal_Duzeyde_Karar_Alicilar_ Yonetici_Ozeti_TR_son-2.pdf (accessed September 19, 2021).

Marchand, Marianne H. and Anne Sisson Runyan. (2011). *Gender and Global Restructuring: Sightings, Sites, and Resistances*. London: Routledge.

Mardin, Deniz. (2020). "Salgın Sürecinde Sağlık Hakkı Ve Mülteciler," *Sosyal Demokrat Dergi*, June 6, http://www.sosyaldemokratdergi.org/f-deniz-mardin-salgin-surecinde- saglik-hakki-ve-multeciler/ (accessed September 27, 2021).

Mbiyozo, Aimée-Noël. (2020). "COVID-19 Responses in Africa Must Include Migrants and Refugees," *ISS Africa*, April 8, https://issafrica.org/iss-today/covid-19-responses-in -africa-must-include-migrants-and-refugees? utm_source=BenchmarkEmail&utm_ campaign=ISS_Today&utm_medium=email (accessed October 1, 2021).

Mearsheimer, John. (2013). "Structural Realism," Essay, in *International Relations Theories: Discipline and Diversity*, 51–67. Oxford: Oxford University Press.

OHCHR. "Special Rapporteur on Violence against Women, Its Causes and Consequences," https://www.ohchr.org/en/issues/women/srwomen/pages/srwomenindex.aspx (accessed October 1, 2021).

Peterson, V. Spike. (1992). "Transgressing Boundaries: Theories of Knowledge, Gender and International Relations," *Millennium: Journal of International Studies*, 21 (2): 183–206. doi.org/10.1177/03058298920210020401.

Peterson, V. Spike. (2000). "Rereading Public and Private: The Dichotomy That Is Not One," *SAIS Review*, 20 (2): 11–29, https://doi.org/10.1353/sais.2000.0048.

Peterson, V. Spike and Anne Sisson Runyan. (1999). *Global Gender Issues*. Boulder, CO: Westview Press.

Plan International. (2020). "Living under Lockdown: Girls and COVID-19," April 30, https:// plan- international.org/ publications/living-under-lockdown (accessed August 26, 2021).

Sadiki, Larbi and Layla Saleh. (2020). "Reflexive Politics and Arab 'risk society'? COVID-19 and Issues of Public Health," *Orient*, 61 (3): 6–20.

SGDD-ASAM. (2020). "COVID-19 Salgınının Türkiye'de Mülteciler Üzerindeki Etkilerinin Sektörel Analizi," *STGM*, September 18, https://www.stgm.org.tr/e

-kutuphane/covid-19-salgininin-turkiyede-multeciler-uzerindeki- etkilerinin-sektorel-analizi (accessed August 8, 2021).

Sjoberg, Laura and Jonathan Wadley. (2010). "Gendering the State: Performativity and Protection in International Security," Essay, in *Gender and International Security: Feminist Perspectives*, 38. London: Routledge.

Steans, Jill. (1998). *Gender and International Relations: An Introduction*. Cambridge: Polity Press .

Tekin Koru, Ayca. (2020). "Precarious Lives: Syrian Refugees in Turkey in Corona Times," https://voxeu.org/article/precarious-lives-syrian-refugees-turkey-corona-times (accessed October 10, 2021).

"Temporary Protection," (2021). Republic of Turkey Ministry of Interior Directorate General of Migration Management. Directorate General Of Migration Management, September 30, https://en.goc.gov.tr/temporary-protection27 (accessed August 23, 2021).

Tickner, J. Ann. (1992). *Gender in International Relations: Feminist Perspectives on Achieving Global Security*. New York: Columbia University Press.

Tickner, J. Ann. (2001). *Gendering World Politics: Issues and Approaches in the Post-Cold War Era*. New York: Columbia University Press.

Tickner, J. Ann. (2005). "Gendering a Discipline: Some Feminist Methodological Contributions to International Relations," *Signs: Journal of Women in Culture and Society*, 30 (4): 2173–88, https://doi.org/ 10.1086/428416.

Tickner, J. Ann and Laura Sjoberg. (2013). "Feminism," Essay, in *International Relations Theories: Discipline and Diversity*, 51–67. Oxford: Oxford University Press.

Tripp, Aili Mari. (2013). "Toward a Gender Perspective on Human Security," *Gender, Violence, and Human Security*, New York University Press: 1–32.

UNFPA. (2020). "Impact of the COVID-19 Pandemic on Family Planning and Ending Gender-Based Violence, Female Genital Mutilation and Child Marriage," April 27, https://www.unfpa.org/sites/default/files/resource-pdf/COVID-19_impact_brief_for _UNFPA_24_April_2020_1.pdf (accessed September 13, 2021)

UNHCR. (2021). "UNICEF Education Case Study, Turkey, Inclusion of Syrian Refugee Children into the National Education System," June 16, https://www.unicef.org/ media/102111/file/ Inclusion%20of%20Syrian%20refugee%20children%20into%20t he%20national%20education%20system%20(Turkey).pdf (accessed September 6, 2021)

UN Women. "COVID-19 and Ending Violence against Women and Girls," https://www .unwomen.org/-~/media/headquarters/attachments/sections/library/publications /2020/issue-brief-covid-19- and-ending-violence-against-women-and-girls-en.pdf? la=en&vs=5006 (accessed October 1, 2021).

UN Women. (2018). "Needs Assessment of Syrian Women and Girls under Temporary Protection Status in Turkey," https://eca.unwomen.org/en/digital-library/publications /2018/08/needs-assessment-of-syrian-women-and-girls-under-temporary-protection -status-in-turkey (accessed August 12, 2021)

UN Women. (2020a). "The Economic and Social Impact of COVID-19 on Women and Men: Rapid Gender Assessment of COVID-19 Implications in Turkey," https:www2 .unwomen.org/-/media/field%20office%20eca/attachments/publications/2020/06/ rapid%20gender%20assessment%20report%20turkey.pdf?la=en&vs=438 (accessed September 17, 2021)

UN Women. (2020b). *Policy Brief: The Impact of COVID-19 on Women*. New York: United Nations (accessed September 17, 2021)

UN Women. (2021). "COVID-19 Deepens Threats for Displaced Women and Children," *UNHCR*, August 5, https://storymaps.arcgis.com/stories/5bf55a1112144d7dafa58fb 4ecc8f9a7 (accessed September 30, 2021).

"Vaccination Status of Refugees in Turkey: Survey Results II - March 2021 - Turkey," *ReliefWeb*, March 2021, https://reliefweb.int/report/turkey/vaccination-status-refugees -turkey-survey-results-ii-march-2021 (accessed September 14, 2021).

"Work Permits of Foreigners," (2019), https://www.csgb.gov.tr/media/63117/ yabanciizin2019.pdf (accessed September 30, 2021).

World Health Organization, "Health Services for Syrian Refugees in Turkey," https://www .euro.who.int/en/health-topics/health-emergencies/syrian-crisis/health-services-for -syrian-refugees-in-turkey (accessed October 5, 2021).

Yılmaz, Gaye, İsmail Doğa Karatepe and Tolga Tören. (2019). "Integration through Exploitation: Syrians in Turkey." Augsburg: Rainer Hamp Verlag, https://kobra.uni -kassel.de/bitstream/handle/123456789/11330/LaborAndGlobalizationVol17.pdf (accessed October 25, 2021).

Zaatari, Zeina. (2014). "Unpacking Gender The Humanitarian Response to the Syrian Refugee Crisis in Jordan," *Women's Refugee Commission*, https://www.womensrefug eecommission.org/wp-content/uploads/2020/04/ Unpacking-Gender-The-Humanitar ian-Reponse-to-the-Syrian-Refugee-Crisis-in-Jordan-03-2014.pdf (accessed October 10, 2021)

11

Risky Pedagogies

Macro- and Micro-Politics of the Virus in the Times of COVID-19 Epidemic

Maziyar Ghiabi

The world of knowledge takes a crazy turn
When teachers themselves are taught to learn.

—Bertolt Brecht, *Life of Galileo*: 37

Pandemic in a Village

At the end of March 2020, in a remote village in central Iran, a man in his seventies fell sick and, after a few days, died. A witty and well-known figure in the otherwise isolated plateau located around 80 km south of Qom, he was a peasant and the owner of a mid-sized sheep cattle and a keen trader in rural commodities; despite the outbreak of the news about the virus in mid-February of that year, the man used to travel in his Zamyad pickup car—the Iran-produced equivalent of the more expensive Nissan pickup—from town to town in furtherance of his businesses. He had "pre-existing cardiovascular problems and was overweight," but people in the community whispered that "it was coronavirus [*korona*] that had taken away his life."

Fewer people than usual showed up at his funeral, which was held in the village where there is an adjacent cemetery on the slope overseeing the *Haftad Qolleh* valley. The entourage, including his closest kin, sat over 3 meters or more apart from each other and wore masks and gloves "out of the fear that the virus had reached this forgotten land." There was minimal physical interaction, few hugs and kisses and a certain concern over the wind blowing in the direction of participants further away. Some kept moving from place to place while awaiting the rituals of the burial, "because they feared that the wind could blow the virus towards them" bearing the virus from the dead to the alive. The dead man's nephew recalled later: "I've never seen a funeral like this. It was so civilized, *engar farhang budim*, it seemed we were in the West."[1] It also seemed that the ensemble of societal practices, communal judgments, and the system of assigned values to events and occurrences—in other words, the moral grammar—had shifted with the looming epidemic.

That event somehow sanctioned the coming of the COVID-19 epidemic into the imaginative world of the village. The material presence of the virus, instead, never manifested itself in that context, at least not with full force as it had occurred in nearby cities, such as Qom and Arak; health workers had later confirmed that he had not been infected with COVID-19 and that his death was caused by a heart attack due to an ongoing hypertension disorder. By then, the actual diagnosis of the disease had little or no importance because villagers had organized themselves in such a way to ward off "the intrusion" of the virus.

By mid-April, they had created sui-generis "check points" at the entrance of the village to monitor the movement of people, denying entry to "all those coming from the outside." This move, which propped up in numerous villages across Iran, was organized "from below," through kinship and grassroots community networks. However, it was later seconded and enfranchised by the Iranian government which gave village councils the right to manage the movement of people inside/outside their area of competence (Eghtesad Online 2020). In June 2020, the government put an end to this ordinance, but wariness toward urban visitors remains alive and in force throughout that year, but especially during Iranian festivities such as Nowruz. In autumn 2021, the great majority of the people living in village described above have received at least one dose of their COVID-19 vaccine, including people under the age of 30.

This vignette on the life of a village in the times of the most severe epidemic in contemporary history is an unusual place where to start laying the ground for broader meditations on the transformation of social and political processes in Iran. But this micro-dimension has its own advantages: what we observe in a small village is testimony to the penetration of transnational forces—that is, public perception of the pandemic, conflict and negotiations between local and national authorities, scientific advice and governmental decrees, local mobilizations informed and/or instigated by access to global information sources (e.g., social media, satellite TV, disinformation campaigns), and international sanction regimes—in an empirical setting that for structural and environmental reasons may well have stood isolated from them. The fact that these transnational forces reach far and deep in the public life of people living in the distant rural world shows how the village is a microcosm from where to start an analysis of health, life, and politics amid tectonic shifts generated by the COVID-19 epidemic in the life of Iranians (and humans overall).

To do so, the chapter explores the effect of the COVID-19 epidemic on politics in Iran, by mobilizing macro- and micro-analysis. It asks how people's organization and transformative experiences can counter forces and phenomena, such as the current epidemic; and how the epidemic shapes and is shaped by geopolitics. The chapter reflects upon the extant and emergent potentialities of the current situation, depicting trajectories from the contemporary and the coming life in the post-epidemic future. Rather than reaching definitive conclusions on the question of solidarity in times of crisis, the chapter's objective is to reflect upon the possibilities of studying disruptive events such as the epidemic across the macro–micro divide, and amid transformative events.

The chapter is organized in the following sections: first, it provides an overview of the unfolding epidemic crisis in Iran to familiarize readers with the existing conditions and structures, including the effect of geopolitical constraints such as US-led sanctions and domestic models of crisis management. It then moves to look at how crises and health crises in particular destabilize the framework of interaction between power and people, and how this can be remodeled through the technologies of trust (such as vaccines and medical practice) that become essential to the continuation of political and social life. Within this frame, the chapter analyses how the epidemic has produced and continues to transform forms of social organization and cultural praxis, which occur through the mobilization of solidarity and mutual help networks. These include an array of categories that have the potential to set the ground for a new sense of community amid impeding crisis, counterpoising the high-tech, authoritarian vision of grand solutions to the crisis with a low-tech mobilization and human-centered vision. Finally, the objective is to inquire into the potentialities of a politics of solidarity and hope, and their counter-values of demoralization, fear, and desperation. This is what the chapter elaborates as the pedagogy of the virus, a cognitive and practical journey which acquires the forms of an "ontological journey [made] of transformative cultural practices, international borders, policy regimes and public ethics" (Ghiabi 2021). At each stage, the notion and the perception of "risk" inform and deflect the making of political formulas and practices—reviving the category of "risk society" as re-elaborated by Sadiki and Saleh (2020). This risky pedagogy is produced by the concurrence of crises in health/politics, whereby ordinary people learn to (re)enact organization and community to change everyday life amid societal and political disruption. The pedagogy of the virus is a matter-of-experience rather than theory, it is cumulative rather than impatient and instantaneous; it is "risky" because it responds to the many faces and masks of "risk"; and it is "risky" in as much people exercising their agency work and learn together to overcome crisis, rather than following preset models of engagement. The chapter meditates upon the pedagogy of the virus, its potentialities and its pitfalls, and its future in the aftermath of the epidemic.

Biological versus Social Times of the Epidemic

Epidemics suspend the flow of ordinary life. Daily occurrences and rituals change in such a dramatic way that life itself appears under a different light, even when—from negligence or necessity—the acts of the everyday carry on as usual. As events with a broad lifeworld, epidemics have a health and a social life. The historian of science and medicine Charles Rosenberg hints at this double nature when he writes that "as a social phenomenon an epidemic has a dramaturgic form. Epidemics start at a moment in time, proceed on a stage limited in space and duration, following a plot line of increasing and revelatory tension, move to a crisis of individual and collective character, then drift towards closure" (Rosenberg 1989, 2). The timing of these stages is unpredictable and not always unidirectional. The social ending of an epidemic may not coincide with its biological closure, but rather with the conclusion of it being a public concern, even a media crisis. This is the case for previous epidemics, such as polio, and for current ones, such as HIV/AIDS. The height of concern for them were respectively the 1960s and 1980s–1990s, when the public and the governments considered these diseases a threat to the social, economic, and political order. Neither polio nor HIV/AIDS have been eradicated in the contemporary world. Polio is endemic in part of South Asia and sub-Saharan Africa, whereas HIV/AIDS exists across the world from the South America to Southern Africa, Russia and South East Asia. However, the social choreography that these epidemics generated in the past is no longer recognizable in the public eye today, because media and governmental focus have shifted to other matters of concern (Greene and Vargha 2020).

So, epidemics exist as biological as much as social phenomena and, because of their nature, they perform as part of a web of actions toward and response to them. They have a biological rhythm and a social rhythm, which rarely overlap. Fear governs the social time of the epidemic. It reveals what we previously ignored, a hidden enemy, and it triggers a war with an invisible force that may hide in every other human. Within the logic of fear, biological life (*zöe*) trumps civic and political life (*bios*), dislodging those rituals of support—such as in a community's practices of mourning—and the vicinity to fellow others in times of hardship—as it occurs in conflict and war. If in a crisis, the logic of fear prevails over all other instincts and rationalities, the very substrate of society defaults, reducing politics and community to the impulse of individual survival (against the virus or, for that matter, any other enemy: the Muslim, the migrant, the communist, the foreigner). Yet, it is under those conditions of disruption that human society expresses vital forces such as solidarity, the expression and practice of altruistic support aimed not solely at others as humans, but aimed at them as part of a union of you-and-me, of us-and-you, in a shared fluid vitality. The logic of solidarity is what enables "individuals who were *submerged* in reality, merely *feeling* their needs, to *emerge* from reality and perceive the *causes* of their needs" (Freire 2018, 90), where they can find a sense of totality. That is perhaps where the word *solidarity* holds its Latin original meaning, "the act of becoming solid, full, complete."

Seen through the prism of tensions between biological life and political and social life, the current epidemic is a historical moment to reclaim the power of humanity and of humanization. This is where the pedagogy of the virus should manifest itself: this can occur, in line with the argument put forward by Paulo Freire in *Pedagogy of the Oppressed*, that there cannot be a revolutionary process (understood as a fundamental change in the organization of life and politics) without a critical awareness of people's role "as Subjects of the transformation," rather than as mere objects in the plans of revolutionaries (Freire 2018, 100). Without this dialogical relation, any process of transformation subsequent to a crisis will trigger the logics of fear and myth-making (e.g., conspiracies about the virus, those bringing it), which are the driving force of reactionary politics (Brownlee and Ghiabi 2021).

Before discussing the emerging practice of solidarity that have appeared in Iran, let us take a look at the biological, social, and political times of the epidemic and how these have shaped people's experience of the crisis.

The Biological Time of the Epidemic

On February 19, 2020, the Iranian Ministry of Health informed the public that two individuals had tested positive for COVID-19 in Qom. It remained unclear how the virus had reached the holy city. Several sources referred to Chinese Muslim scholars returning from Wuhan or Chinese laborers on infrastructure projects; others identified Iranian merchants trading with China. By the end of February, Iran's deputy health minister and several high-profile political figures, including several members of parliament who had won seats on the February 21, 2020, parliamentary elections tested positive for the virus. It appeared that the government had been caught utterly unprepared.

By December 2020, Iran was going through its third wave of infection. The capital Tehran was put on full lockdown to avoid the overwhelming of the medical facilities, which were running at full capacity. The government declared that 95 percent of the country was in an alarming state (4 out of 5 in the degree of severity).[2] Iran's Ministry of Health, grappling with the fluid biological nature of the virus, used an eloquent metaphor to describe it. It said that COVID-19 was a *shotor-e gav-palang*, which is an obsolete Persian expression to define "giraffe." Literally *shotor-e gav-palang* means "a camel-bull-leopard" (like a giraffe which has a camel's hump, a bull's snout, and a leopard's coat). An ambiguous biological being, which is hard to know how it affects people's lives, the virus could bite (like a leopard); it could kick (like a camel); and it could gore with its horns (like a bull). This fluid existence of the virus is determined by the biological time of the epidemic, which by April 2021 was in its fourth wave—post-Nowruz—and by August 2021 in its fifth wave in Iran. The latter was also the deadliest round of the epidemic, which brought an official total of 120,000 deaths. While the virus underwent biological changes, becoming either more contagious, less aggressive, or changing in symptomatology, the epidemic transformed the social organization, cultural praxis and people's ideas of politics in a cumulative way, a process that is determined by the social time of the epidemic.

The Social Time of the Epidemic

On March 16, 2020, angry crowds defied the government's closure of the shrines of Fatemeh Masumeh in Qom and Imam Reza in Mashhad, the two holiest sites in Iran. The Qom crowd, led by a cleric, shouted that "Tehran did a damned thing [*ghalat karde*]; the Minister of Health did a damned thing, the President did a damned thing [to close the shrine]," for shrines are places of intercession and healing (VOA News 2020). Little mattered that Ayatollah Alam-ol-Hoda, the Supreme Leader's representative in Khorasan-e Rajavi, had spelled out that "Imam Reza is not in his tomb, neither he is in the golden shrine . . . Imam Reza heals, gold and silver don't heal!"

The social time of the epidemic, much like its biological time, is disputed and nebulous, in its outset as much as in the prospect of its closure. Measures of containment are the public signs measuring the social time; shifts in contagion rate and viral spread are markers of the biological time. For both, there are competing starts and possible ends; but it is the most contentious manifestations that mark the historical record, concomitant and connected to other events, in this case the series of public scandals and tragedies in 2019–2020 (i.e., clampdown in December 2019 protests, assassination of General Qasem Soleimani, downing of the P752 passenger flight).

Disruptive events, such as epidemics, rearrange culture and ethics and the understanding of larger historical time. Restrictions on social gatherings and public life unsettle the rituals of mourning, malady, pilgrimage, and celebration, but not without causing opposition and resentment. All over the world, a tension has arisen between those demanding a pause of social rituals to ensure the preservation of life and those deeming such rituals essential to life itself. Angry protesters seeking emotional comfort in the sacred spaces of Qom's Fatemeh Ma'sumeh shrine, like Orthodox Jews in Jerusalem or in New York and Christians in Orthodox churches in Greece, clashed with the rationale of prevention measures such as lockdowns. In Italy, far-right politicians such as Matteo Salvini "begged" the government to allow Easter celebrations to go ahead, affirming that "science is not enough" (Zapperi 04/04/2020). In spring 2021, in spite of now clear evidence of high infection rate, he reiterated his stance against lockdowns. These examples could be interpreted as the embodiment of a clash of irrationality versus rationality, religion versus secular science, or of political cynicism in electoral calculi. Yet, people attending non-religious rituals, such as football matches, new year celebrations, rave parties or, for that matter, US White House fundraising events, have equally opposed the bans and restrictions instructed by public health experts. In Iran, for instance, large crowds gathered in the parks of Tehran's Ekbatan neighborhood during the Nowruz festival of *chaharshanbeh suri*—a secularized folk event—or decided to depart for long-distance travels during the New Year holidays of 2020 and 2021, in spite of the Ministry of Health's advice to stay at home. On October 8, 2020, the death of Mohammad Reza Shajarian, Iran's foremost classical singer, brought thousands of people in the street chanting in front of the Qods Hospital where he passed away. The totality of those attending wore masks, but they sang loudly—therefore, increasing the chances of transmission, and maintained no physical distance. However, there was no public outcry against those mourning Shajarian, whereas there was much public opposition for (more or less religious) mourners during Muharram, which contributed to the Manichean portrayal of superstition versus science, religious zeal against secular rationality. In reality, both events represented moments of religious, emotional expressions amid the widespread disruption caused by the virus. In oxymoronic ways, it is rational to find comfort beyond reason.

Religious rituals characterizing the flow of everyday life faced a major transformation. In Catholic countries, the clergy gave up its historical and liturgical duty of providing the sacraments to dying people and to give comfort to the sick. Science in the form of medicine trumped the secular role of religion and those practicing its liturgies, the priests. This is perhaps the most important eclipse of the role of religion in our societies as an organized cultural practice (Agamben 2020), but not as an emotional desire. In Iran, this event was mitigated, not so much by the prompting of the higher echelon of the Islamic Republic—who similar to their Catholic counterparts upheld the exigency of public health isolation—but rather by the grassroots organizations of clerics and volunteers. Low-level clerical cadres mobilized to guarantee the performing of the rituals of dying and burial, while the highest cadres of the clergy agreed to limiting the public role of religious events to prevent the spread of the virus. A tension arises between cultural practice such as the rituals of everyday life that give meaning to the existence of people, in their spiritual and collective form, and the imperatives of public health as informed by scientific assessment. And as burials and mourning are governing principles in the social life of humans, the attending of these events shaped the social time of the epidemic which would have otherwise disrupted it by imposing a biological rhythm onto it. Hence, the significance of shrines in punctuating the social rhythm of the epidemic.

The Politico-Economic Time of the Epidemic

Caught between domestic pressure to intervene and the external challenges of geopolitical and economic isolation and US sanctions, the Rouhani government initially adopted a policy of wait and see. Commentators have pointed out that the economic cost of an interventionist approach involving a large-scale lockdown and public assistance to the unemployed would fall beyond the government's financial capabilities. State-led strong interventions were at odds with the government's political persuasion: Rouhani had been elected on a platform promising a retraction of the state from the economy, something that would be impractical under a lockdown where state presence is vital to avoid large-scale disruption and disorder. A draconian lockdown risked to uproot the livelihoods of the working class and large numbers of the self-employed in the informal sector, a scenario that could be conducive to bread riots and mass discontent on an even larger scale than the 2019 protests.

The US-imposed sanction regime has had a profound effect on the political management of the epidemic. The domestic pharmaceutical industry, which produces more than 90 percent of all drugs inside Iran, has been under heavy pressure, with medicine shortages affecting people's general health. In turn, this has a profound impact on the biological capacity to respond with a strong immune system to the virus (Ameli 2020). Thus, Iran is faced with a crisis that, in many ways, is larger than that faced by most other states, because it faces a geopolitical crisis coupled with an economic sanction regime among the harshest in history. Faced with these crises, the country lacked the means adopted by countries in the Global North, which have introduced fiscal measures, long-term lockdowns, and other protective welfare measures. Iran's Ministry of Health declared that the medical sector should take into account the economic and regional as well as cultural conditions and produce a protocol that can correspond to these necessities: "We are searching for an indigenous model [*model-e bumi*]" (Behdasht 2020), an idea reiterated by the head of the National Security Council, Ali Shamkhani. In other words, *following the science*—the recurrent claim of governments across much of the world—is a context-specific model, which follows the political times of the epidemic in space, that is, Iran's geopolitical and security place in the world.

Rouhani's government found the inspiration for this localized model in what has become the paradigm of crisis intervention in the post-revolutionary era: the Iran-Iraq War (1980–8) (Ghiabi 2019). In this way, the political time of the epidemic overlapped with the timing of the war, which in 2020 had its fortieth anniversary. What seemed a haphazard initial response and a reluctant strategy turned into a mass mobilization across the state apparatus. From a rhetorical standpoint, the Iranian state has mobilized its art and visual culture machinery to make sure those fighting on the frontlines against the epidemic—the health workers—were given the due prominence and were acknowledged as heroes of the contemporary nation. The decision to label health workers as martyrs on the line of duty—*shahid khedmat*—enables the state rhetoric to temper the hardships—mental and physical—these categories are going through, equating them with those heroes who suffered through the war. The use of the term *modāfeān-e Salāmat* ("defenders of health") is similar to the *modāfeān-e haram* ("defenders of the sacred shrine," i.e., the Shi'a shrines in Syria and Iraq) or to *modāfeān-e vatan* ("the country's defenders"). Tragedy is part of this choreography, which is one aspect of the epidemic's social and political time/life—one that had its proper dimension in Iran's history of public mobilization through sacrifice, especially in the post-revolutionary period.

But the political time of the epidemic lacked the authoritarian, top-down impetus that distinguished the response of other countries, where the state is strong and highly centralized. Countries such as China, Vietnam, South Korea, and Italy, put in place a powerful response with strict measures and mechanisms of control of the epidemic introducing far-reaching limits to civil liberties and the deployment of police and army to enforce a control regime. Iran did not fall under this category even though the Iranian state, by all definitions, is a powerful machine in economic, enforcement, and sociological terms; and limiting civic liberties would have posed, in principle, a less problematic step than in more democratic countries. Instead, the epidemic did not halt the parliamentary process—including the elections—and a lively and confrontational political debate carried on amid the emergency, undermining in several instances the governmental plan of intervention. Criticism against the government, the ministries, law enforcement, and other state apparatuses remained vibrant. Rather than a democratic impulse, however, this sporadic and reluctant governance was itself a product of the *infra*-elite tensions and negotiations that had been at the core of Iran's state management and crisis response. Reluctant governance may have avoided hyper-policing, but it had also given priority to state prerogatives such as smooth electoral process (which otherwise would have exposed the political order to accusation of dictatorial behavior). All of this had put the health sector under severe pressures costing lives to frontline workers, hence self-reproducing the post-revolutionary culture of sacrifice.

Technologies of Trust in Health and Politics

The logic of fear prospers upon a crisis in knowledge production. Likewise, the epidemic exists in epidemiological crisis, but also as an epistemological crisis, a crisis in the way people know and understand the world. Doubts about the origins of the virus and the politics behind it have been a powerful means which can shape people's minds about the epidemic and national and global politics. Different sources of authority both in the scientific world and in policymaking have expressed doubts about the viral origin of the epidemic, undermining the efforts to contain the virus through physical distancing measures and lockdowns. Even prominent global scientists and thinkers such as Giorgio Agamben strongly criticized the way governments around the world created a state of emergency built upon panic and fear (Agamben 2020). This is not unlike what happened, again, with HIV in South Africa, where heads of states at different turns and prominent intellectuals embraced conspiracies about the HIV/AIDS health treatment and prevention measures, for instance, on the value of anti-retroviral drugs. In the Iranian case, the authorities have maintained a relative clarity on the seriousness of the epidemic and its risks, even though there were attempts at covering it up in the initial weeks of the outbreak. After faltering in the first weeks of the epidemic when he conceded to conspiracy theories about the origin of the virus, the Supreme Leader, Ali Khamenei, has been straightforward in his compliance with the social distancing measures even during the religious ceremonies of Muharram where he attended a recital session on his own and maintained a safe distance from the pulpit of the *maddah*, the eulogist singing the tragedy of Imam Hussein and his companions in Karbala. But trust in public institutions is a key element in epidemic solutions. In Iran, the lack of trust in official discourses is endemic and caused by a historical experience of plots and conspiracies that effectively took place and were covered by the narratives of those in charge or foreign powers (Alimardani and Elswah 2020). So the epidemic occurred in a setting when people and governments lived in a state of suspicion and mistrust toward "news" and "events."

Moreover, the relentless disinformation campaigns that have targeted knowledge production and information-making in Iran exacerbated the game of perception of the epidemic. Trust in public institutions and in the state-owned media reached its nadir after the tragic event of the Ukrainian airplane accident in early January. Without an effective public information machine, conflicting instructions circulated on Iranians' social media, involving conspiracy theories from East and West (e.g., *it's the work of the Chinese*; *it's an American plot*; *it's a Russian weapon*), the number of deaths, the access to vaccines to the political elite, the experimental trial of domestic vaccines on vulnerable and marginal social groups. The spread of fake news is not peculiar to Iran, but its reach and potency there is on a different scale because of the enmity of the United States, Israel, and Saudi Arabia which have mobilized large sums to wage a propaganda war (Mortazavi and Hussein 2020).

A paradigmatic case occurred when, at the end of February, large numbers of people—including numerous contacts in the author's Telegram and WhatsApp contact lists—started to share videos that hinted at a coming apocalypse. The video showed raining eggplants [*sic*!] in different parts of Tehran, with those portrayed in the video shocked by the event. The event was reported in different settings of the capital, involving different people, who were all taken by utter surprise while posing for a picture or talking on a video call. A few days following the event, Iran's Fatah Policy for Cyber Crime declared that it had scaled up its monitoring program of fake news on COVID-19, arresting two dozen people involved in the prank. But in a condition of heightened domestic and geopolitical security, extraordinary signs have the potency to unsettle an already crumbling public trust and morale, unveiling the fragility of Iran's public institutions and their shrinking capacity to project trust to the people, as well as engendering fear in people.[3] As epidemics reconfigure public life, the need of mitigating the fear of epoch-making events compels people to cope through their own repertoire of cultural practices with supernatural forces such as the virus.

In the context of the village described in the first part of the chapter, local workers praised the curative power of a pill which a wealthy landlord had brought back from a trip to China. When one of his workers had caught the virus, the landlord asked him to quarantine in a room before giving him the pill. Locals swore that within two days the middle-aged man was back in full force. Fantasies about modern science (often coming from advanced capitalist unknowns, such as China and Israel) parallel the superstitious claims of traditional healers. Establishing public trust is not a minor and temporary issue. It will influence the forms and capacity of Iranian society as the epidemic will move to a new stage, with the creation of a vaccine or other forms of treatment or governmental interventions. As technologies of trust, vaccines and other forms of epidemic management require high levels of public trust, lest they be undermined in the objective to eradicate contagious spread (Vargha 2018). The process of reclaiming public trust in Iran is now outside the realm of the state. Instead, public trust—a key technology of government crisis—is remerging as part of the integration of biomedical approaches foregrounded by the biomedical workers, grassroots organizations active in social and socialized medicine and in the infrastructure of support and intervention of solidarity and mutual help among ordinary people. This triggers an imperfect balance between vertical technocratic interventions—leading to biomedical responses, for example, pharmaceuticals and vaccines—together with horizontal infrastructures of mutual care and health provision (Greene and Vargha 2020). It is an essential part of the pedagogy of the virus, of learning from the epidemic in the middle of risk, the fear of it, its management, and dismissal.

Although, the development of an effective vaccine gives rise to optimism across the world (but especially in the Global North), Iranians face hurdles in accessing significant doses of it due to the economic effects and the shortage of foreign currency caused by the US sanction regime. Ali Khamenei's veto on US and UK vaccines—but his tacit acceptance of UK vaccines produced in India and other countries—have cast doubts on the readiness of the state to prioritize public health over geopolitical calculi and public relations. By April 2021, Iran had received ca. 700,000 doses of the AstraZeneca vaccine through COVAX, the international initiative to promote equitable distribution of the vaccine. But doubts on the AZ efficacy and its side effects had then coupled with a slowing down in COVAX distribution plans. So, Iran has relied on its geopolitical allies. Geopolitics matters in health security. By late August, Iranian authorities had administered "18 million doses . . . 12 million were from China's Sinopharm; 4 million were the Oxford–AstraZeneca vaccine [through COVAX]; and one million were COVIran Barekat, developed by the Iranian state-owned Shifa Pharmed Industrial Group in Tehran. The remainder include doses of Russia's Sputnik V and India's Covaxin. More than half a million doses are being administered a day, and some 17%

of Iran's population of 85 million have received their first dose of a COVID-19 vaccine" (Mallapaty 2021). By October 2021, Iranian authorities had escalated the vaccination program, administering an average of one million vaccines per day, with an equitable focus on rural areas and cities (Tehran Daily 2021). The newly elected president, Ebrahim Raisi, made sure to take the merits for this escalation of the vaccination program, compared to the slow and faltering plan under former president Hassan Rouhani.

While Iranian scientists have successfully completed the first and second stages of an indigenous vaccine, full-scale trials will delay its potential distribution at least to the latter part of 2021, all things going well (MEHR News Agency 2020). Even then, a vaccination program on a countrywide scale puts Iran at a crossroads. On the one hand, people lack trust in official narratives and, consequently, are reluctant to follow impromptu guidance from the state; on the other, observation of recent historical processes show that Iranians have expressed a high level of confidence in scientific and, especially, medical guidance and protocols and have supported the directives emanating from the Ministry of Health. Policies on polio vaccination, treatment and prevention of HIV/AIDS, treatment and maintenance programs for "addiction" to opiates, and more recently social distancing measures, are all good examples of how trust and cooperation have worked in building and promoting health-oriented policies (Moussavi et al. 2012) (Ghiabi 2019). In particular, people are responding to the rapid changes in public life with new forms of social organization and grassroots mutual aid. The multiple crises—in public health, employment, governance, and the economy—brought about by the pandemic, and the resulting practices of solidarity, are the workshop where Iran's post-epidemic futures will take shape.

A New Sense of Community

The way social forces and ordinary people have acted upon their plight is a sign of what is there to remain as the crisis intensifies and moves to break down the world as we know it. Within the struggles of today around access to health, prevention of infection, support for livelihoods and the maintenance of education and the creation of economic opportunities and social dignity lies the future of politics and the politics of life (Fassin 2018). This struggle is a walk on a very thin, sharp, and long edge along which the risks of failure could lead to fanaticism and reactionary politics, to the reification of a cultural-and-political counterrevolution, which is part of a longer trend predating the epidemic (e.g., Brexit, Trump, Bolsonaro, Modi). To gauge the spirit of the post-epidemic futures, I suggest taking a look at the experience of solidarity and mutual aid, which have emerged in Iran over the last eighteen months. On the one hand, the experiences reported below take form in an exceptional time—as discussed earlier, that is, the times of the epidemic. On the other, these experiences of solidarity and social activism are not disjointed from the context of people's mobilization in the post-1979. The difference is in that the epidemic is not a political event *stricto sensu*, whereas the acts of participation and solidarity amid the revolution were all political *in nuce*. Yet, forms of solidarity in contemporary epidemic times revitalize latent forms of solidarity, which in times of disruption (war, protest, revolution, disaster) have manifested themselves overtly.

Healthcare and Social Workers

On the frontlines, healthcare workers—surgeons, anaesthesiologists, nurses—have volunteered to work around the clock to compensate the many shortcomings of the health system in Iran—which finds itself in the crossfire of US sanctions, domestic economic crisis, and the limits of slow government response. This is not simply another case of doctors and nurses being on the frontlines and being called "heroes" or "martyrs." What occurred in Iran is on a broader scale and it regards specialists in different health sectors who, during lockdown and amid the crisis, volunteered to carry out research and consultation with all those in need, free of charge. This has included pharmacists and other cadres essential in the maintenance of the health system and the provision of basic health responses in addition to COVID-19. Physicians and specialist consultants created WhatsApp and Telegram groups where they could be contacted for consultation in case people in need of medical referral could not attend hospitals or were in urgent need, or simply needed reassurance on their status and/or treatment. The Iranian Scientific Association of Social Workers (ISASW) activated a hotline and a website to reach out to those seeking support amid the crisis. The hotline redirects the calls to specific task forces staffed by one of three professionals: a social worker, a psychologist, or a psychiatrist. Based on a first assessment, those who call in are forwarded to specialists who provide both individual and group therapy (ISASW 2020a). The medical cadre involved in the program do so on a *pro bono* basis, dispelling the negative aura surrounding the private medical profession over the last decade.

The ISASW mobilization targets specifically groups at the margins of epidemic governance, such as children and the homeless. As across the globe, children must adjust to new life conditions under lockdown. For many working-class families, school closures and the lack of physical space and the mounting emotional and economic pressure turns the household environment into a disturbing space for children's daily life and their psychophysical development. Iran's director for social harms at the Welfare Organization declared that "although there are no precise statistics . . . calls to the social emergency number on the 123 line have gone up, which means there is an increase in child abuse and spousal abuse" (Shahrvand Online 2020).

To facilitate a safe environment at home, the ISASW created a number of free booklets with games and activities for children of different age groups, with the objective of decreasing pressure on families (ISASW 2020b). Public officials made clear that welfare provision and healthcare is free of charge and also available to peddlers, refugees, and those working in the informal economy. In this setting, the use of digital infrastructures to reach otherwise marginalized populations makes interventions faster and more flexible, limiting the risks of viral infection amid rising cases related to COVID-19. Where direct action is necessary, outreach social workers have intervened in impoverished neighborhoods. Large numbers of homeless people and child workers gather in the streets and alleys or under the highway bridges, heightening the risk of mass contagion (Ghiabi 2020).

The highly mobile urban population of homeless people is doubly at risk from the COVID-19 pandemic. Many of them do not have proper identification cards and risk being left out of the public health system. Exposed and hustling to earn money, many also have comorbidities and weakened immune systems, which means that they suffer from other health conditions such as tuberculosis or HIV/AIDS that increase their risk of serious illness from COVID-19. They often do not have access to the Internet so they lack basic information regarding the virus and proper preventive measures— or changing policy interventions, for that matter. Charities and local associations— based in mosques, congregation centers and in neighborhoods—are coordinating with social workers to provide hand sanitizers, masks, and gloves. They are also working to disseminate information on preventive practices, either by passing out brochures or by reading the brochure's text aloud in squares and public parks. These associations maintain regular contact with local personalities to guarantee swift intervention and referral to hospitals in case vulnerable people manifest COVID-19 symptoms. Therapeutic communities and rehabilitation centers—also known as "camps" (*kamp*) in Iran—have taken up the duty of quarantining homeless or "risky" drug users, hence acting as a non-state mechanism to manage the pandemic (Ghiabi 2019) (Majles Showra-ye Eslami-ye Iran 2020).

Another case is represented by Afghan Iranians who have resided in the country for decades, but that in a majority of cases hold only temporary documents or no documents at all. At the margins of public health interventions, Afghan Iranians were guaranteed access to health through both governmental and localized interventions, the latter including the mobilization of Afghan doctors residing in Iran. For instance, a 38-year-old Afghan refugee became the head of the COVID-19 public outreach program in the Isfahan province. She carried out remote and in-patient consultations with Afghan families infected by the virus or who feared being infected. With more than 100,000 Afghan refugees in the Isfahan province alone, the doctor had a team of five medical personnel which carried out over 200 referrals every evening, free of charge (Bhoyroo 2020). Solidarity toward Afghan Iranians is also justified in public health terms as it guarantees screening coverage and the monitoring of potential pockets of infection among a population that has been neglected by public institutions. That said, the question remains that far more Afghan Iranians should access the medical profession.

The epidemic also affects life through the fear that it engenders and through the organizational effects on people's lives, with very high levels of anxiety, manifesting panic attacks, stress, and suicidal reactions. In response to this, the ISASW has mobilized its network of support to guarantee care for all those facing the challenge of living in a state of epidemic, a condition of unsettledness and heightened psychological pressure to which many—especially among the younger generations—had not been exposed before. The mobilization of volunteer groups, such as professional associations and grassroots charities, occurred autonomously from state-led initiative and through mutual help groups.

Clerics and Mosques

Even the clergy mobilized through mutual aid groups to fulfil the duty of rituals and liturgies that have been disrupted by the epidemic. Receiving support from religious foundations, armed with personal protective equipment (PPE), clerics guaranteed that the dead could be cleansed before burial according to the Islamic rituals. In this way, the clerics could perform *ghosl* (ritual purification) for the dead, reclaiming their role as those who oversee the rituals, which define key moments in people's lives, rather than as the ruling class. This is no minor service for all those families for whom the dead must bid farewell to the world according to conventions and traditions and who could not do so given the health crisis disrupting them.

Likewise, mosques mobilized to collect food and basic goods to redistribute them to the many families that found themselves in dire need amid the lockdown and the economic crisis heightened by the epidemic. In some instances, mosques were transformed into production factories for PPEs as well as for the relocation of key equipment. An effective network of centers throughout the country, the mosques reclaimed a public space that they had lost since the 1980s, during the Iran-Iraq War, when they operated as recruitment centers for the front and redistribution agencies for the local communities. So, in the times of the epidemic, the mosques were reclaimed as centers of mutuality and solidarity support rather than as centers for ideological propaganda and bastion of clerical power. At the same time, mosques did not turn into a bastion of opposition to the scientific advice on social distancing and prevention measures, as it had occurred in the cholera epidemics of the nineteenth century. Even though there were instances of opposition to epidemic prevention measures, religious representatives embraced the guidelines sponsored by the governmental disposition, even when it came at the cost of limiting or cancelling ritual events with large followings.

There are also multifarious instances of local organization of solidarity. Independent women's associations in working-class neighborhoods have set up local factories to produce masks after receiving training through the mediation of NGOs (IRNA 2020). In the town of Divandarreh, in Iranian Kurdistan, local families raised more than $23,000 (a very large sum for such a small town, especially considering the devaluation of the Iranian rial) to purchase intensive care unit equipment when the hospital lacked the means to treat one of their fellow citizens who had fallen ill with COVID-19 (IRNA 2020). In the city of Bushehr, university students set up workshops to produce disinfectant liquid and distribute it to the community, while community organizations set up small factories to produce masks and other PPEs (IRIB NEWS 2020). Examples like this are innumerable and range from the work of philanthropy and altruistic gest to organized efforts to minimize—or at least manage—the epidemic and its effect on livelihoods (Soureh 2020; Batmanghelidj 2020).

These practices of solidarity are not simply cases of volunteering, self-help or civil society activism and are not merely compensating for gaps in the state's response. They are a pedagogy of struggle amid disruption and of community organizing primarily within the popular classes. Educators, social workers, and professionals are displaying mutual aid and solidarity *with* the popular classes, not *on behalf of* them. They are enabling communities to organize in settings where people have been accustomed to demobilization (and demoralization) for several decades. This mutual aid or "mutualism" creates spaces of encounter over real-life problems, which are common to the majority and move beyond single-issue activism (Je so' Pazzo Ex-OPG 2019). In its praxis, it works as a school for learning how to manage the commons. It creates inroads into new ways of imagining politics and the state, as emanation of human organization rather than as exogenous impositions. It has the potential for moving ordinary workers from a skeptical or naïve view of political life to a critical one, which is potentially creative (Freire 2018, 9).

The Pedagogy of the Virus

Will political life in Iran be changed by COVID-19? And if so, how? More than any sanctions regime or threat of war from the United States or Israel, the epidemic is reshaping the way people interact with the state and its rhizomes of formal and informal power projection, in the field of public institutions of welfare and health, in community organization, ethical legitimacy and care provision, education and economic development. It is transforming people's understanding of the state responsibilities and the public authorities' capabilities, as well as their right to healthcare and social welfare. A pandemic has the potential to reshape people's perspectives on life and death and reconfigure the place of religion, of power, and of community, and of those performing public duties. The forces that determine the post-epidemic future are made of the encounter between human agency, emotional and ideological tensions, scientific and technological politics, all of which is shaped and shapes social organization and solidarity. Once COVID-19 is no longer a large-scale threat, whether a vaccine becomes widely available or the virus turns into an endemic disease—the question of what constitutes a mutual society and a community of support around which life can prosper and state power is regulated may become all the more central to political mobilization and people's ideas. Here is where the seeds of the emerging political culture will be sowed, forming the struggles that determine the outcomes of state formation in the decades to come.

In epidemics—and in crisis in general—fear becomes the sentiment of the present and of the coming future. Carlo Levi, an intellectual and physician exiled during Italy's Fascist government (1922–43), writes that "fear of freedom is the sentiment that generated fascism" (Levi 2018). If the fear of losing one's biological life dominates all human relations, there remains no space for community. And it is undeniable that the current epidemic has given space and legitimacy to authoritarian propensity, because of the need of rapid, drastic, and centralized action. But fear and authority are not conducive to the return to the pre-epidemic "freedom," or to the bourgeois status quo of peaceful cohabitation with dispossession and injustice. Nor they can guarantee a life freed from the virus. It is through the concerted and organic mobilization of people that it is possible to create space for social life to prosper beyond the status quo ante, a condition that is neither possible nor equitable. It leads, instead, to a generalized lack of morale, to demoralization toward the possibility of change. It is through community organizations and existing solidarity practices, such as the ones exemplified above—and the ones extant in conditions of disruption—that the tensions between hope and despair are positively resolved. There people *realize* the vital importance of organization and of acting collectively. This may imply reclaiming the state as an important organizing tool for community building against the grain of decades of the state being perceived as hostile or as an obstacle to the thriving of people's lives. Shifts of this type could lead to a new imagination of the Iranian state, beyond the factional politics that it has characterized it since the 1980s. And as the value of life as matter of biology progresses over life as a social and political phenomenon, people's priority becomes to preserve *zöe* over *bios*, to keep our bare life in place, while abandoning—or better, distancing ourselves—from our civic life, our life as part of a human society. This shift in the ethics of life also has profound effects on everyday existence, if not in the present, it risks exacerbating inequalities in the near future, especially in the Global South where high-tech and high-capital solutions will further inequalities between the majority and the elites. The only response to this is to organize collectively, through networks of solidarity, which are the workshop of the post-epidemic futures. This very grassroots makes a politics of life real.

Acknowledgments

Research and writing for this chapter were made possible by a Wellcome Trust grant no. 219771/Z/19/Z, "Living 'addiction' in states of disruption" at the University of Exeter. My gratitude also goes to Professor Masoomeh Maarefvand from the University of Social Welfare and Rehabilitation Sciences in Tehran, for her comments on earlier versions of this chapter, and to the ISASW for sharing their field experiences. A previous shorter version of this chapter appeared in the Special Issue edited by Paola Rivetti and Francesco Cavatorta, *Partecipazione e Conflitto* 14 (2, 2021), available at http://siba-ese.unisalento.it/index.php/paco/issue/view/1832. This chapter and its previous versions are all published under Open Access Creative Commons (CC BY).

Notes

1 Phone interviews with two members of the deceased man's family, Markazi region, March 2020. The village is a field site where I have carried out research on Internet use in rural life since 2017.

2 By mid-October, Iran had ca. 30,000 deaths and almost half a million cases, of which ca. 400,000 had recovered. However, the government itself and public health officials within the country have openly acknowledged that the numbers were lower than the real scope of the epidemic. In a report published by the Parliament's Research Center (*markaz-e tahqiqati-ye majles*), the government estimated that the numbers were probably double or triple the official data.

3 In the United States, the QAnon conspiracy believes that lockdowns are used as a measure to cover up the arrest of an international cabal of pedophiles who are fighting against US president Donald J. Trump. According to this group, Trump is leading

a behind-the-scene operation against this cabal which involves thousands of very high-profile figures in American society and economy, some holding that they worship Satan. The "ideas" of QAnon have now spread in the United Kingdom under the group Save Our Children (SAC). They equally oppose epidemic prevention measures and mask-wearing.

References

Agamben, Giorgio (2020). *Una voce*, https://www.quodlibet.it/una-voce-giorgio-agamben (accessed May 10, 2022).

Alimardani, Mahsa and Mona Elswah. (2020). "Trust, Religion, and Politics: Coronavirus Misinformation in Iran," in *Meedan 2020. 2020 Misinfodemic Report: COVID-19 in Emerging Economies*, https://papers.ssrn.com/sol3/papers.cfm?abstract _id=3634677.

Ameli, Vira. (2020). "Sanctions and Sickness," *New Left Review*, 122: 49–57.

Batmangheldj, Esfadyar. (2020). "The Photos by @nkazeminava are Like Scenes out of a @ JOSH_BENNY or @NicolasWR Movie," in @YARBATMAN (ed.), *Twitter*.

BEHDASHT. (2020). مدل بومی ایران برای ارزیابی کیفیت خدمات بهداشتی دارای 40 شاخص است. https://behdasht.gov.ir/%D8%A7%D8%AE%D8%A8%D8%A7%D8%B1/%D9%85 %D8%AF%D9%84-%D8%A8%D9%88%D9%85%DB%8C-%D8%A7%DB%8C%D8 %B1%D8%A7%D9%86-%D8%A8%D8%B1%D8%A7%DB%8C-%D8%A7%D8%B1 %D8%B2%DB%8C%D8%A7%D8%A8%DB%8C-%DA%A9%DB%8C%D9%81%DB %8C%D8%AA-%D8%AE%D8%AF%D9%85%D8%A7%D8%AA-%D8%A8%D9%87 %D8%AF%D8%A7%D8%B4%D8%AA%DB%8C-%D8%AF%D8%A7%D8%B1%D8 %A7%DB%8C-40-%D8%B4%D8%A7%D8%AE%D8%B5-%D8%A7%D8%B3%D8 %AA (accessed April 20, 2022).

Bhoyroo, Farha. (2020). *Afghan Doctor Helps Refugees Fight COVID-19, One Phone Call at a Time*. UNHCR, https://www.unhcr.org/uk/news/stories/2020/7/5f155edc4/ afghan-doctor-helps-refugees-fight-covid-19-phone-call-time.html (accessed May 10, 2022).

Brecht, Bertolt. (2015). *Life of Galileo*. London: Bloomsbury Publishing.

Brownlee, Billie Jeanne and Maziyar Ghiabi. (2021). "The Mythological Machine in the Great Civil War (2001–2021): Oikos and Polis in Nation-Making," *Middle East Critique*, 30 (2): 127–48.

Eghtesad Online. (2020). روستاها دور از کرونا.

Fassin, D. (2018). *Life: A Critical User's Manual*. London: John Wiley & Sons.

Freire, P. (2018). *Pedagogy of the Oppressed*. New Jersey: Bloomsbury Publishing USA.

Ghiabi, M. (2019). *Drugs Politics: Managing Disorder in the Islamic Republic of Iran*. London: Cambridge University Press.

Ghiabi, M. (2020). "Under the Bridge in Tehran: Addiction, Poverty and Capital," *Ethnography*, 21 (2): 151–75.

Ghiabi, M. (2021). "Ontological Journeys: The Lifeworld of Opium across the Afghan-Iranian Border in/out of the Pharmacy," *International Journal of Drug Policy*, 89: 103116.

Ghiabi, M., M. Maarefvand, H. Bahari and Z. Alavi. (2018). "Islam and Cannabis: Legalisation and Religious Debate in Iran," *International Journal of Drug Policy*, 56: 121–7.

Greene, J.A. and D. Vargha. (2020). "Ends of Epidemics," in H. Brands and F.J. Gavin (eds.), *COVID-19 and World Order: The Future of Conflict, Competition, and Cooperation*, 23–39. Baltimore, MD: Johns Hopkins University Press.

IRIB NEWS. (2020). گزارش مکتوب ...... مقابله با کرونا جلوه ای از ایثارو همدلی مردم بوشهر, //:https www.iribnews.ir/fa/news/2671295/%DA%AF%D8%B2%D8%A7%D8%B1%D8%B4-%D9%85%DA%A9%D8%AA%D9%88%D8%A8-%D9%85%D9%82%D8%A7%D8 %A8%D9%84%D9%87-%D8%A8%D8%A7-%DA%A9%D8%B1%D9%88%D9%86 %D8%A7-%D8%AC%D9%84%D9%88%D9%87-%D8%A7%DB%8C-%D8%A7%D8 %B2-%D8%A7%DB%8C%D8%AB%D8%A7%D8%B1%D9%88-%D9%87%D9%85 %D8%AF%D9%84%DB%8C-%D9%85%D8%B1%D8%AF%D9%85-%D8%A8%D9 %88%D8%B4%D9%87%D8%B1 (accessed April 1, 2022).

IRNA. (2020). تولید روزانه ۳۰۰ ماسک توسط دختران موسسه خیریه همدم مشهد, https://www.irna.ir/ news/83696831/%D8%AA%D9%88%D9%84%DB%8C%D8%AF-%D8%B1%D9%88 %D8%B2%D8%A7%D9%86%D9%87-%DB%B3%DB%B0%DB%B0-%D9%85%D8 %A7%D8%B3%DA%A9-%D8%AA%D9%88%D8%B3%D8%B7-%D8%AF%D8%AE %D8%AA%D8%B1%D8%A7%D9%86-%D9%85%D9%88%D8%B3%D8%B3%D9 %87-%D8%AE%DB%8C%D8%B1%DB%8C%D9%87-%D9%87%D9%85%D8%AF %D9%85-%D9%85%D8%B4%D9%87%D8%AF (accessed April 1, 2022).

ISASW. (2020a). مداخلات حمایت روانی اجتماعی از راه دور راه اندازی شد, https://swi.ir/%d8%ae %d8%b7%d9%88%d8%b7-%d8%a2%d9%86%d9%84%d8%a7%db%8c%d9%86-%d8 %ad%d9%85%d8%a7%db%8c%d8%aa-%d8%b1%d9%88%d8%a7%d9%86%db%8c- %d8%a7%d8%ac%d8%aa%d9%85%d8%a7%d8%b9%db%8c-%d8%af%d8%b1-%d8 %ad%d9%88%d8%b2/ (accessed April 1, 2022).

ISASW. (2020b). مراقبت از کودکان (کروناویروس), https://swi.ir/%d9%85%d8%b1%d8%a7%d9 %82%d8%a8%d8%aa-%d8%a7%d8%b2-%da%a9%d9%88%d8%af%da%a9%d8%a7 %d9%86-%da%a9%d8%b1%d9%88%d9%86%d8%a7%d9%88%db%8c%d8%b1%d9 %88%d8%b3/ (accessed April 1, 2022).

JE SO' PAZZO EX-OPG. (2019). *Manuale del Mutualismo*. ROSA-LUXEMBURG-STIFTUNG.

LaFrance, A. (2020). "The Prophecies of Q," *The Atlantic*.

Levi, C. (2018 [1946]). *Paura della libertà*. Vicenza: Neri Pozza Editore.

MAJLES SHOWRA-YE ESLAMI-YE IRAN. (2020).
درباره مقابله با شیوع ویروس کرونا چگونگی حمایت و مراقبت از معتادین متجاهر در برابر ویروس کرونا.

Mallapaty, Smriti. (2021). "Iran Hopes to Defeat Covid with Home-Grown Crop of Vaccines," *Nature*, August 17, https://www.nature.com/articles/d41586-021-02216-z (accessed April 1, 2022).

MEHR NEWS AGENCY. (2020). "3 Iranian COVID-19 Vaccines to Receive Human Test License," https://en.mehrnews.com/news/166793/3-Iranian-COVID-19-vaccines-to -receive-human-test-license (accessed April 1, 2022).

Mortazavi, N. and M. Hussein. (2020). *State Department Cut Funding for Controversial 'Iran Disinfo' Project — But Kept Working With its Creators*. The Intercept, https:// theintercept.com/2020/09/22/iran-disinfo-trump-state-department/.

Moussavi, T., B. Sadrizadeh, M. Zahraei, R. Nategh and A. Nadim. (2012). Polio Eradication In Iran, Report, 107–9.

Rosenberg, C.E. (Spring 1989). "Living with AIDS ," *Daedalus*, 118 (2): 1–17., https:// theintercept.com/2020/09/22/iran-disinfo-trump-state-department/.

Sadiki, L. and L. Saleh. (2020). "Reflexive Politics and Arab 'risk society'? Covid19 and Issues of Public Health," *Orient*, III: 6–20.

Salami, I., H. Seddeghi and M. Nikfard. (2020). "Access to Health Care Services for Afghan Refugees in Iran in the COVID-19 Pandemic," *Disaster Medicine and Public Health Preparedness*, 14 (2): 1–2.

SHAHRVAND ONLINE. (2020). .افزایش خشونت خانگی علیه زنان و کودکان در قرنطینه

Tehran Times. (2021). "COVID Vaccination to Complete in 48 Days," September 15, tehra ntimes.com/news/465098/COVID-vaccination-to-complete-in-48-daysCS (accessed April 3, 2022).

Vargha, D. (2018). *Polio across the Iron Curtain: Hungary's Cold War with an Epidemic.* London: Cambridge University Press.

VOA NEWS. (2020). "Hardline Iranian Shiites Storm Shrines Shut By Coronavirus," YouTube at https://www.youtube.com/watch?v=ZVID5NHOT_g (accessed May 3, 2022).

Zapperi, C. (2020). "Coronavirus, Salvini: riapriamo subito le chiese per Pasqua, la scienza non basta," *Corriere della Sera*.

آفتابنیوز.(2020). 200 سؤال بلاتکلیف نمایندگان از وزرا, https://aftabnews.ir/fa/news/63997/200-%D8%B3%D8%A4%D8%A7%D9%84-%D8%A8%D9%84%D8%A7%D8%AA%DA%A9%D9%84%DB%8C%D9%81-%D9%86%D9%85%D8%A7%DB%8C%D9%86%D8%AF%DA%AF%D8%A7%D9%86-%D8%A7%D8%B2-%D9%88%D8%B2%D8%B1%D8%A7 (accessed March 20, 2022).

Part V

Regional Perspectives

12

EU-MENA Relations amid COVID-19 Pandemic. Between Economic Issues, Migration Challenges and Authoritarian Risk

Pietro Marzo[1] and Renata Pepicelli[2]

Introduction

The COVID-19 pandemic has had a strong impact not only on individual states but also on the relations between them. It is contributing to reshaping international agreements and partnerships, and it is generating new alliances and rivalries among states. For instance, the pandemic has affected relations between European Union (EU) and the Middle East and North Africa (MENA) countries. In particular, the virus spillovers have forced the EU—and EU member states—to focus on their domestic response to the pandemic. As a result, the EU is devoting less attention to foreign policy toward the southern neighborhood, despite the health emergency increasing the need for greater EU involvement in MENA countries. This chapter analyses how the spread of the virus has influenced EU foreign policy toward the MENA region. Retracing the long history of relations between the two shores of the Mediterranean, the chapter suggests that the pandemic is leading to the deterioration of an already fragile and controversial framework of cooperation.

The Onslaught of COVID

In early 2020, before the COVID-19 virus turned into a worldwide pandemic, the MENA region was living one of the most tumultuous times since the 2011 revolts. Some analysts warned that the region was on the edge of economic collapse, and a second wave of regional protest was gaining traction. The legacy of the 2010–1 revolt, which led to the demise of long-serving autocrats in Tunisia, Egypt, Yemen, and Libya, was disastrous in political and socioeconomic terms. Libya, Yemen, and Syria were mired in endless wars that had devastated entire cities, displaced communities, and deteriorated people's living conditions. Egypt seemed to slowly recovering economically,[3] but these improvements were only cosmetic, signaled by dubious indicators, even as domestic inequalities and socioeconomic struggles were ramping up. In addition, Sisi's military regime tightened its repressive hand on gender minorities[4] and the political opposition (Islamists as well as leftists). Algerians' nationwide 2019–20 mobilization brought a "deluge" of people to gather weekly in the street and to voice their discontent against *le pouvoir*, and its decision to keep wheelchaired and extremely sick Bouteflika as the presidential candidate. Lebanon was facing an acute political crisis, accelerated by economic fallout and growing inequalities.

Turkey's president Erdoğan was carrying out an unprecedented wave of arrests of non-aligned citizens or alleged dissidents, including scholars, journalists, and political activists. In the Levant, Iraq was seeing only little improvement in its twenty-year struggle. Protests and demands for political change raged across its national territory, which looked more than ever like a chessboard in the hands of regional and international powers. Tunisia's fragile democracy was the only country offering a glimmer of hope across in the region. Its fragile democratization, however, was showing clues of regression, demonstrating that the establishment of a procedural and minimalist democracy has neither addressed nor solved the majority of issues that ignited the 2011 revolution (Allan and Geisser 2018).[5]

Against this gloomy background, in March 2020, a deadly coronavirus (COVID-19) began to spread in Europe and across the Mediterranean, hitting MENA countries to different extents and at different paces. Initially, while some European countries were facing the ferocious speed of contagion, countries across the MENA, with the notable exception of Iran, seemed to be coping with a milder impact from the virus. It is not clear whether the slower progression of the contagion hinged on the lower rate of daily testing performed by MENA region authorities, or if it was simply due to less intense international connections with China—and the Asian continent as a whole—where the virus allegedly originated.

In any case, although MENA countries were not among the initial hotspots for COVID-19, by the beginning of the summer 2020, the virus spread ferociously. In order to deal with the first wave of contagion, MENA countries followed procedures taken by Western and Asian states, imposing general lockdowns and restrictions on people's movement, including overnight curfews and border closures. These measures slightly mitigated the virus diffusion. While health measures were taken everywhere across the region, little has been done to coordinate economic support or plan financial recovery, both at the country and (sub)regional level. Unfortunately, with the exception of rich Gulf states, MENA countries lacked the economic, institutional and organizational resources of their European counterparts. As a consequence, during the second spike of contagion that started in fall 2020, the strong and proactive measures taken early on have been limited, in favor of policies aiming toward the recovery of local economies. MENA-ruling elites claimed that another "season" of generalized lockdown was simply not sustainable and would generate fatal consequences for national economies.

Currently, a deep sense of uncertainty looms large on how regional authorities will address the enormous economic backlash that COVID-19 has unleashed. MENA economies foresee a dramatically dark future, precisely because the consequences of a pandemic were set in motion on an already depressed economic framework and a general trend of authoritarian regression. Against this backdrop, this chapter turns to the cross-regional dimensions of MENA risk society (Sadiki and Saleh 2020) in the wake of the pandemic, in the form of weakening ties between the EU and MENA.

Indeed, the global diffusion of the pandemic has also diminished international attention to MENA politics. Indeed, the pandemic has triggered inward-looking behavior among states worldwide, whose institutional focus and financial capacities have been fully shifted to the domestic response to the COVID-19. As a result, rich Western states and International Organizations have decreased funding devoted to international cooperation and democracy promotion.

European countries, significantly impacted by the pandemic, are no exception. Their attention has been overwhelmingly on the domestic response to the pandemic. Following the initial shock, representatives of European countries gathered within EU institutions and began to cooperate. A plan of economic recovery—Recovery Fund Next Generation the EU—was approved relatively quickly to provide relief to depressed economies, although division on fair distribution among beneficiaries' states still provoke debate. As Wolff and Ladi (2020, 1027) point out, "existing tools for crisis management and preparedness were mobilized quickly. The EU adopted decisions on Protective Equipment (PPE) which helped to buy equipment through funds coordinated by the European Commission. To that end, the EU Solidarity Fund was revised (Regulation 2020/461)." Quick decisions were also taken in the field of vaccine research and "green lanes" were put in place to allow essential workers and patients to move around Europe despite the suspension of Schengen.

Yet, EU member states have poorly collaborated to deliver a common response to COVID-19 outside of Europe. In the immediate aftermath of COVID-19 outbreak, while EU member states were fully focused on their domestic troubles, policymakers devoted some attention there to neighboring regions, realizing that these regions' socioeconomic performance and security dynamics have a symbiotic relation with EU stability. In tune with these concerns, the EU launched the "TEAM Europe" initiative, a financial plan aimed to provide immediate relief to the poorest countries in the Global South.[6] Allocation of money followed, but the initiative has been short-lived and implementation has not gone beyond slim financial support.

Regarding the MENA region, the EU has not promoted any multilateral talks to implement a Euro-Mediterranean plan of recovery. As a result, the EU has so far lacked a comprehensive plan of support that considers the direct and indirect implications of pandemic across the MENA region. While this is not surprising, given the poor record of EU support to its southern neighbors, the approach is highly problematic. We argue that it comprises a cross-regional dimension of "MENA risk society" precisely because, without an adequate and onward-looking response, the impact of COVID-19 across MENA will sharpen existing challenges for the EU itself.

Building on the idea that an adequate handling of the pandemic in the MENA region responds to both domestic priorities and geopolitical trends, this chapter analyzes the EU response to the pandemic outbreak in MENA region. It suggests that the EU's inward-looking approach epitomizes the decade-long, ineffective ENP toward the MENA region. The chapter suggests that the absence of a strategy is harming relations between EU and MENA countries. This cross-regional MENA risk society intensifies issues that have long undermined stability in the region.

The chapter is organized as following: first, it provides a brief outline of the EU–MENA relations since the launch of Euro-Mediterranean partnership, the so-called Barcelona Process. It argues that despite the EU's repeated efforts to craft a comprehensive neighborhood policy to foster prosperity, democracy, and stability in the MENA region, the EU approach to the Mediterranean neighbors has failed to attain the desired outcome. The EU response to the COVID-19 pandemic in the region epitomizes this failure. Second, the chapter explains how the deterioration of existing issues in the MENA—socioeconomic struggle, migration pressure, terrorism, and the return of authoritarianism—will affect the EU–MENA relations and will pose enormous challenges to EU institutions and member states, as MENA risk society spills outside the region's borders. Third, the chapter offers some reflections on potential building blocks through which the EU might deliver a proper post-pandemic neighboring policy, and manage to turn challenges into opportunities.

EU–MENA Relations from Barcelona Process to the COVID-19

In order to understand the impact of COVID-19 on the relations between the EU and the MENA region, it is necessary to retrace the history of these relations from at least the Barcelona Process of 1995 until today. In fact, the pandemic has been grafted onto national and regional histories, often exacerbating limits and problems already evident before the epidemic.

With the launch of the Euro-Mediterranean partnership (EMP) in 1995, the EU ushered in a coordinated foreign policy action toward the region, which was previously dealt with through states' bilateral agreements.

Eight years later, in 2003, the EU launched the European Neighborhood Policy (ENP). ENP was conceived to foster regional stability through economic integration, democratization, and multilateralism. In order to achieve this general goal, ENP strategy has revolved around three main components: the creation of a free-trade area, cultural exchanges, and political cooperation (Cavatorta and Rivetti 2014). In this respect, Ian Manner conceptualized "normative power Europe," suggesting that "conceptions of the EU as either a civilian power or a military power, both located in discussions of capabilities, need to be augmented with a focus on normative power of an ideational nature characterized by common principles and a willingness to disregard Westphalian conventions" (2002, 239). Manner put emphasis on the fact the EU had an inherent ability to be "changer of norms" in the international system, an actor who could be able to shape conception of "normal," projecting its basic principles worldwide.

However, beginning in the early 2000s, security issues emerged from the MENA region. In particular, the rise of jihadi terrorism became a serious threat that concerned EU policymakers. Therefore, academic debate focuses on the role and the strategy of the EU to contain threats at home and to help individuals across MENA countries (Hyde-Price 2006). On the one hand, some scholars suggested that, similar to its action in Eastern Europe after the Soviet Union collapse, EU normative power and political conditionality could have a democratizing and stabilizing effect across the southern neighbors. For example, some scholars argued that the liberalization of Turkey in early 2000s was a direct result of the EU conditionality mechanism and advantages (Aydin and Acikmese 2007). However, more recently scholars have pointed out the failure of EU political conditionality in Turkey (Süleymanoğlu-Kürüm 2018). Besides the controversial EU-Turkey case, in 2000s, scholars suggested that a single country could eventually embrace democratic procedures and promote liberal reforms at home, if a process of association with the EU had been implemented (Sadiki and Powell 2010). On the other hand, scholars argued that EU democracy promotion was harmless to authoritarian regimes, and in some cases also counterproductive (Van Hüllen 2015). Scholars also demonstrated that the large amount of EU money allocated to MENA countries to enhance liberalization and democratic reforms was failing to bring about the desired outcome, because authoritarian elites managed to "tame" EU democracy promotion (Bush 2015). Others pointed out that aid programs often target procedural components of democracy that do not generate real change, while neglecting support for social justice and economic rights (Teti 2015). EU political conditionality, aimed at fostering democratization, social-political inclusiveness, and liberal reforms, clashed with its realpolitik that gives priority to security and stability over democracy.

In the context of EU–MENA relations, besides the penetration of jihadi terrorism onto European soil, two prominent elements that have increased security concern have been the rise of Islamism and the increase in migration flows, both perceived as destabilizing factors for European countries (Lelb 2014; Lazaridis 2016; Fakhoury 2016). Historically, the EU has been reluctant to engage with Islamist actors, while showing a strong preference for anti-Islamist regimes (see European support to Ben Ali in Tunisia and Mubarak in Egypt). Europeans perceived Islam as one of the main sources of instability for the region. In the 1980s, 1990s, and early 2000s, the fear of political Islam made European policymakers support anti-Islamist regimes and marginalize any unfamiliar voices, such as Islamist civil society organizations.

Overall, in the last decade, despite a series of intercultural dialogues addressing Islam and democracy, the EU did little to factually support those Islamists who refused violence and were instead engaged in pro-democracy campaigns. Political frameworks such as the EMP and later ENP left Islamist actors, both politicians and civil society actors, completely out of the picture. In late 2000s and, most importantly, after the 2011 revolution, US and EU policymakers engage in a more dialogic cooperation with Islamist groups in Tunisia and Morocco—and to a lesser extent in Egypt. They realize these forces represented a large strata of Muslim population and could eventually participate in competitive politics without undermining regional and country stability. However, in most cases, EU support for the inclusion of political Islam movements has been short-lived and mild. Particularly, in the last years we witnessed that the initial "cooperative security" strategy of the Euro-Mediterranean partnership quickly shifted toward "policies of security cooperation." The initial European priority of promoting democracy in the region was replaced by a focus on guaranteeing the stability of regimes which presented themselves as bulwarks against international terrorism, gatekeepers against irregular migrants or simply as security providers that simultaneously engaged in "cosmetic reforms" to disguise their authoritarian grip on power.

The threat of terrorism has also raised concerns among EU policymakers, disempowering EU strategy to promote political and economic liberalization in the MENA. Indeed, in order to counter terrorism, the EU has preferred a certain degree of collaboration with secular authoritarian regimes across the region, whose strong-handed domestic policy secures border control and hampers any "anti-Western" political parties that might gain power.

Against this background, the majority of individuals across the MENA region generally perceive the European Union to be a distant and bureaucratic actor that despite pro-civilian narrative and democratic agendas in its foreign policy, prioritizes stability and security when it comes to relations with the region.

The unexpected outbreak of the Arab revolts in early 2011 pushed EU policymakers to change their foreign policy priorities. In May 2011, the EU reviewed its European Neighborhood Policy (ENP) as a response to the fast-evolving and unstable southern neighborhood. The elaboration of ENP revolved around the idea to compound democracy promotion activities with "conflict resolution actors, that could stabilize the Southern neighborhood" (Bouris and Schumacher 2017, 3). Yet, the main ENP shortcoming remained: the EU aspires to become a more assertive power abroad without having either the instruments or the resources to be assertive. Furthermore, according to Lehne (2014, 7), ENP was not adequate to deal with the Mediterranean geopolitical challenges, as it originated from a Eurocentric perspective that did not consider the strength of emerging competing actors in the region. Indeed, beginning in the aftermaths of Arab uprisings, authoritarian states such as Russia, Turkey, and GCC countries have increased their activism in the Southern Mediterranean. This activism poses a direct threat to EU ambitions to promote stability and democracy.

As a result, despite the European Union's attempt to seize the democratizing momentum of the MENA, it has been progressively engulfed, more than before, in a security-democracy dilemma (Dandashly 2018). As Kadher (2020, 28) noted, "From 2010 until 2020, Euro-Mediterranean and Euro-Arab relations were put on the back burner: financial aid was disbursed but there has been no significant innovative initiative. The question of democracy promotion, regional cooperation, and security arrangements were eclipsed by more urgent challenges as migration, terrorism, and internal security." Scholars and analysts continue to highlight the contradiction between ENP principle and narrative and the results on the ground. The call for a more effective ENP has been the mantra of policy analysts and commentators (Ait Ali et al. 2019; Otte 2021).

Particularly between 2017 and 2019, Brussel policymakers and pro-European political leaders mainly focused on rescuing the European Union project, threatened by internal disaggregating forces. These factors include internal issues, such as the Brexit referendum and the rise of Eurosceptic and Europhobic parties across Europe, as well as external threats such as aggressive Putin and Trump foreign policies against the EU and its multilateralism. The foreign policy of European member states complicates the implementation of the EU neighborhood policy in the MENA region. It also exacerbates the contradiction between the EU narrative driving programs of assistance and the real implementation on the ground. For instance, European countries' leading companies sealed billionaire trade deals with autocrats in the region, entrenching economic interests with their regimes, de facto disempowering any genuine change in European Union assistance programs. As an example, in 2018, the Italian oil company ENI signed a multimillionaire deal with Al-Sisi to exploit gas reserve basin in Egypt water.[7]

In addition, some member states (i.e., France) continue arms sales to MENA countries,[8] a trade that some EU member states[9] and transnational advocacy networks[10] have widely criticized for fueling regional conflict and endangering human rights. In short, divisions and competing interests among EU member states have hindered the European Union's ability to act in a constructive manner. As a result of the fragmentation of its member states, the European Union has dealt with crucial foreign policy dossiers such as the Syrian refugee crisis and the Libya war merely through palliative solutions.

The outbreak of COVID-19 in 2020 complicated the matter. With the EU countries mired in fratricide skirmishes (e.g., distribution of vaccines, allocation of recovery funding), the COVID-19 crisis has worsened EU–MENA relations by accentuating nationalism, closures, and authoritarian governance. We suggest this is a cross-regional form of MENA risk society. Such deterioration is occurring within an already widening distance between EU and MENA policymakers, with a shortage of talks and strategic approaches on the most challenging issue across the Mediterranean. As Tobias Borck (2020) stated:

> Just before the pandemic swept Europe, policymakers in London, Paris, Berlin and elsewhere worried about simmering tensions between the US and Iran, escalating conflicts in Syria, Yemen and Libya, and unfolding economic and governance crises in Lebanon, Iraq and Israel. None of these challenges have gone away. If anything, the pandemic gives them another, complicating dimension.

The EU dealt with the spread of coronavirus through an inward-looking response similar to that of most of industrialized and semi-industrialized countries, especially the United States. As Hokeman and his colleagues (2020, 77) pointed out, in the immediate aftermaths of the virus outbreak "many countries have restricted exports of medical products as part of their response to the COVID-19 pandemic with the aim to allocate domestic supplies to national healthcare systems and citizens." Data from Global Trade Alert reveal that as of mid-April 2020, most of the European member states, the United Kingdom, and the United States—but also industrializing countries such as China and India—had implemented some type of export curb on medical supplies and medicines or implemented measures to direct supplies to domestic needs.

Needless to say, countries from the Global South have borne the brunt of such inward-looking approaches. They have endured harsh and direct consequences of export bans, such as spiking prices of basic goods and, most importantly, shortage of medical supplies. In this respect, EU member states' policies to cope with the pandemic have damaged the European project and its cohesion by eroding trust among European partners themselves, *and between* EU and MENA countries.

The inward-looking responses to the health crisis have widened the gulf between narrative and actions characterizing the EU neighboring policy toward the Mena region for the last twenty-five years. On the one hand, EU policymakers' leaders are cognizant that solidarity and assistance toward their southern neighbors is key. Indeed, the 2016 global strategy emphasizes that "Instability in the neighborhood, if not addressed, will in one way or another continue to threaten the European way of life at home." On the other hand, the EU is struggling to craft a foreign policy approach that enhances resilience and fosters political liberalization across the MENA region, without jeopardizing EU security.

Although EU institutions are more and more involved in security matters—and have recently developed some important capacities, notably in policing, border management, and maritime security—they are not yet seen as natural partners for conflict prevention or resolution by many MENA governments, especially those with powerful military establishments and intelligence services. This is somewhat puzzling considering the fact that Europe has extended its policies of prevention of violent extremism (PVE) radicalization and terrorist recruitment into North Africa, the Middle East, and South Asia. In the broader context of the EU Counter-Terrorism Strategy (EU-CT) created in 2005, Europe developed a specific plan of counter-terrorism cooperation with the southern neighborhood that focuses on four main fields: building state capacities, strengthening rule of law and respect for human rights, fostering regional cooperation, and preventing and combating terrorism (Council of the European Union, 2015). Several analysts underline that in the last few years, the EU has given priority to a security approach that encourages cooperation with the Third Mediterranean Countries in order to ensure stability and the status quo, rather than focusing on long-term political and economic reforms that strengthen processes of social justice and democratization (Kaunert and Léonard 2011, 289; Simoncini 2020)

COVID-19 Implications for EU–MENA Relations: Cross-Regional "Risk Society"

The socioeconomic and political consequences of COVID-19 are leading most MENA countries' economies into uncharted territory. It is not easy to predict the exact scale of the damages that the pandemic will bring about in each regional setting. Yet, it is relatively easy to identify four main issues that the COVID-19 will exacerbate. This four-pronged "risk society" will generate spillover that will negatively affect EU-MENA relations.

First, the socioeconomic effects of the pandemic. International organizations, such as the World Bank and the United National Development Program (UNDP), portray a steep downturn in MENA economies, warning about the inability of these countries to use structural economic instruments available in the Western world. Indeed, while an economic downturn is expected to occur globally, MENA countries will likely be hit harder as their economies were already on the edge of collapse. The economic decline affecting MENA is compounded by conflicts, endemic corruption, and political instability, all of which makes it more difficult to implement recovery plans. On the EU side, socioeconomic struggles are reverberating to MENA economies, some of which heavily depend on exports to EU countries. For instance, Algeria has witnessed a sharp decline of oil revenues, and others such as Tunisia and Morocco that rely on receding tourism. European lockdowns have heavily affected the Maghreb region, which trades 65 percent of its goods with the EU. In addition, MENA migrants in Europe are facing severe unemployment and their remittances to their home countries have diminished considerably. All these elements contribute to a sharp decline of GDP in all Maghreb countries, which will cause increased unemployment and higher poverty rates in the years to come. Charities and humanitarian organizations operating in the region are already witnessing a rapid increase of poverty, and demand for basic livelihood sources such as water and food.[11]

Second, the rise of human rights violations perpetrated by the tightening of authoritarian regimes will prompt new waves of protests and clashes between MENA authorities and publics. As mentioned earlier, the lockdown that the pandemic imposed has silenced, at least temporarily, thousands of protesters, ultimately rescuing authoritarian and semi-authoritarian regimes. However, while autocrats managed to disempower demands for accountability, responsiveness and social justice, the resurgence of ferocious upheavals is foreseen in the near future. As Khader (2020, 17) notes, "In Algeria, Iraq and Lebanon, fear of the virus and the social distancing measures introduced to slow its spread has brought a temporary end to months-long protest movements. The political and economic problems that brought people into the streets, however, remain and are sure to be compounded by the looming public health and concurrent economic crises." Failure to address human rights and individual and collective freedoms in the MENA will increase the level of instability across the region, leading to security repercussions on the EU itself.

The third issue is associated with the migration challenge. Following the crisis triggered by the Arab uprisings, the EU has seen an unprecedented surge in incoming economic migrants and refugees. Yet, instead of turning the challenge into opportunities, European Union has preferred to ask regional political actors such as Erdoğan, or tribal leaders in Libya, to stop migration flows in exchange of money. As Moran (2020) noted, the "EU has retreated to the European trenches as the perceived twin threats of irregular migration have come to dominate its stance."[12] As an example, when millions of individuals were fleeing war-torn MENA countries, especially from Syria and from sub-Saharan Africa via porous North African borders, a number of European countries, including Sweden, Germany, France, Denmark, and Austria suspended Schengen temporarily.

It is common wisdom that the EU migration policy has largely failed to cope with the migration challenge. The EU appears unable to deliver a comprehensive integration plan and highly fragmented in decision-making. As Fakhoury (2016, 74) noted, "Overarching strategies revolve around externalizing migration governance and cloaking it in 'human security' and 'conflict resolution' dimensions. In this context, the EU has drawn on a variety of transnational tools such as enhancing regional dialogue on migration, delegating border control to Southern neighbors, and increasing humanitarian and refugee facilities to keep migrants in third countries."

In short, the EU has undergone an acute securitization turn, transforming migration from an issue to a threat, a move that helps the EU justify exceptional measures to contain flows of migrants (Fakhoury 2016, 69). This strategy has contributed to increasing the death toll among individuals from MENA. Between 2011 and 2021, the Mediterranean Sea has been the home of heart-breaking tragedies, with thousands of people, including children and pregnant women, losing their life. While scientific evidence and indicators show the significant contribution that new migrants could play to boost European countries' economies (Ferragina, Iandolo, and Taymaz 2021) and demography (Livi Bacci 2018), migration is increasingly seen as a threat to European identity and socioeconomic components. The growth of anti-migrant sentiment, however, is not the root of the problem. Yet, it is the result of flawed integration policy, both at EU and national level, that left incoming migrants at the edge of society, forcing most of them—especially youth—to join the European informal job market or to fall into European criminal networks in order to make a living.

Migration is a key issue for EU–MENA relations, which COVID-19 pandemic is likely to aggravate. The EU, however, is once again demonstrating a short-sighted understanding of challenges ahead and has frozen debates on migration policy, not considering it an urgent priority. In the last year, the limitation of movement as a result of COVID-19 reduced migrant flows and, thus, migration discussions have been sidelined in EU institutions. Yet, this standstill is based on a wrong perception. Indeed, there is no doubt that migration pressure from Africa and MENA region will restart soon, given worsening socioeconomic conditions.

During the writing of this chapter in summer 2021, migrant departures from the Libya and Tunisian shores toward Europe have increased and human tragedies have started to occur once again in the Mediterranean Sea, as demonstrated by the events of May 2021.[13] If the EU does not address the issue immediately, offering serious and feasible, yet comprehensive, solutions, the upcoming flow of migrants will find the EU stuck in inaction, forced to implement last-minute, likely inhumane solutions that do not align with European values, traditions, or history.

In this respect, the EU needs to review its migration and social integration policy, and avoid brokering deals with bordering countries' dictators to deter migration flows. Besides indirectly placing the humanitarian responsibility on the EU, this approach has generated unintended geopolitical consequences that have weakened the EU's negotiating power in the Mediterranean. The most glaring example is the result of the 3 + 3 billion deal EU made with Turkey's president Erdoğan to halt Syrian refugee flows entering Europe via Turkey.[14] While Erdoğan has kept Syrian migrants in full-fledged camps in Eastern Turkey, Turkey is using migrants as a threat to leverage the EU on many negotiating tables.[15]

A fourth issue stemming from COVID-19 pandemic has an inherent geopolitical dimension. Without coordinating a solid and comprehensive plan of assistance, the EU will not only contribute to the impoverishment and destabilization of MENA but will also inadvertently open doors to geopolitical shifts in the international relations of the region. As aforementioned, the MENA countries' economic recovery plan is weak or non-existing. Many regional countries will rely on loans from international organizations, which will impose severe conditionalities and geopolitical demands in exchange for financial aid.

In this respect, it is worth noting that the dynamics surrounding COVID-19 may accelerate an ongoing rebalancing of influences and hierarchy among foreign actors involved in MENA affairs. In the last ten years, narrowing EU engagement in MENA economic and political affairs, coupled with US disengagement from the region, has opened space for other international players, notably Russia and China, to expand their influence. MENA countries with moribund national economies will be compelled to increase demands for economic and logistic assistance from authoritarian actors such as China, Russia, and the Gulf states. In turn, these non-democratic countries will likely seize the opportunity to further advance their geopolitical influence and interest in the region, diminishing EU influence and shrinking EU–MENA cultural exchanges and market agreements.

This risk is also evident if we look at the management of vaccination campaigns in the MENA region. We can observe the emergence of so-called vaccine diplomacy (Woertz and Yellinek 2021). In this perspective, the use of vaccine supplies is a tool of soft-power projection and the EU has proved to be absent and unprepared in this field. The management of vaccines during the pandemic has become an instrument of domestic and foreign policy. While Europe has concentrated on addressing the vaccine issue only within its own territories (with differences from country to country), China and Russia have sought to enhance their influence in the Middle East and North Africa (MENA) region with a number of high-profile vaccine deals. The Chinese Sinopharm vaccine forms the cornerstone of vaccination campaigns in the UAE and Morocco, and that of Chinese Sinovac in Turkey. Sinopharm has also made inroads in Egypt, Bahrain, Iraq, and Algeria. The Russian Sputnik vaccine has been distributed in the Palestinian territories, Syria, Iran, the UAE, and Egypt (Woertz and Yellinek 2021.) As it has been observed, "the presence of Chinese and Russian vaccines in the Gulf reflects wider debates about the changing security role of traditional Western allies in the Gulf" (Ispi 2021). And, more generally, it reflects the emergence of new geopolitical trends where Europe and the United States are marginalized. Although the president of the European Council, Charles Michel, criticized Chinese and Russian initiatives as "highly limited but widely publicized," labeling them as operations of "regimes with less desirable values than ours" (Woertz Yellinek 2021), the weakness of Europe in handling the vaccine campaigns in North Africa and the Middle East is notable. It will result in a loss of influence in the region.

Enhancing MENA Resilience to Crisis: The Way Forward to Review ENP?

Arab societies are showing their fragility and unpreparedness to deal with the greatest threats characterizing the contemporary time, above all health and environmental risks. In recent decades, Arab political and economic elites have focused on lucrative projects and seem to have neglected institutional reinforcement and socioeconomic empowerment of their citizens. They have done little to strengthen their society's ability to manage crisis and deal with risks. As Sadiki and Saleh explained, "It is time for Arab political leaders to realize that state-building involves more than Dubai skyscrapers, US arms deals, or EU trade agreements. It requires developing the infrastructure tools, and socio-political environment conducive to knowledge production: medical expertise, public health know-how, crisis management ingenuity, and global economic proficiency."[16] MENA risk society is wide-ranging.

At the same time, international organizations and international democracy promoters share part of responsibility for having delivered flawed and short-sighted assistance which failed to address real needs of beneficiaries. The comprehensive framework of cooperation that international organizations have proposed did not take into account the localized realities of each country. The absence of context-specific program of assistance designed on analysis of each setting on the ground has heightened the fragility of MENA society, feeding into a cross-regional aspect of its risk society.

The response to the pandemic is a glaring example. Beside inward-looking attitudes discussed above, the World Health Organization (WHO)—the most authoritative global health organization—has failed to understand that the prevention measures and recommendation to counter and deter the spread of COVID in the industrialized world are simply unworkable for most of MENA countries, which lack infrastructure, institutional capabilities, and economic resources to comply with them.

Against this background, the spillovers of the pandemic call for an immediate shift in the EU approach to the MENA region. The time has come for EU authorities to work with their Arab counterparts for enhancing the resilience of MENA countries and confronting its risk society. This includes developing strategies of risk avoidance and risk mitigation that are tailored on contingent realities and available resources of the region. The European Union, for geostrategic and historical reasons, cultural ties, and for its identity as a civilian power in the global political scene, is the ideal actor to usher in a critical change in strategy when designing assistance and aid programs in the MENA region.

The distribution of vaccines, medical instruments, and sharing of health knowledge are key areas around which the EU can foster resilience in the MENA region, especially in light of actions from rival states such as Russia and China. Indeed, a robust EU intervention in the MENA region will help mitigate the increasing influence of authoritarian powers, including regional players such as Gulf states and Turkey, who are extending their governance to MENA countries, arguably curbing peoples' will to fight for political freedom and socioeconomic rights.

The deterrence of risks stemming from climate change is certainly another promising area of cooperation that the EU should implement in the years ahead. MENA countries are particularly vulnerable to this challenge, as many suffer from water scarcity, desertification, coastal erosion, industrial pollution, in addition to depending heavily on agriculture and tourism for their economies. Some efforts have been already made to establish wind and solar projects through European Investment Bank loans and significant ENP grants. Besides prominent environmental benefits, promoting investment in renewable energy in the MENA is crucial because it helps develop the private sector, diversify economies, and create jobs.

The EU should encourage MENA dialogue and bolster South-South cooperation. Although fostering regional integration among MENA countries is quite a complicated task, given the level of rivalry and tension across the region, the atomization of MENA country politics is clearly weakening the capacity to deal with global challenges and compounding its risk society.

Finally, civil society and activists should not be abandoned. While Europe finances MENA civil societies more than any other international donors worldwide, often assistance programs are designed in a very clinical and abstract way. The EU has to take immediate action—launching specific programs of assistance and using diplomatic resources—to support civil society activists and help hamper the authoritarian leaders across the MENA who crush peaceful protests and repress social movements.

Faced with this state of affairs, the EU should learn from the lessons of COVID-19 and orient its policies toward its neighbors, following the logic of resilience, state building, and inclusiveness. The pandemic and the responses to it have shown different capacities to counter the spread of the virus depending on the different health systems and economic capacities of individual states. At the same time, however, it has highlighted the absolute interconnectedness of EU and MENA region, as the foregoing discussion of cross-regional risk society suggests. It is simply irresponsible to believe that issues and crises lived by MENA countries such as climate change, state fragility, migration, terrorism, socioeconomic struggles, and the return of authoritarianism will not have a direct impact on EU countries and the Mediterranean region as a whole.

Conclusion

This chapter has pointed out that EU inward-looking foreign policy toward the MENA during the pandemic has deepened problems affecting the MENA region. The chapter posits that EU approach not only increases the spillover of the health crisis in the MENA region, but poses a threat to EU stability as many of the above-mentioned issues are—and will more and more—creep into the EU. Through the analysis of the EU–MENA relations since the outbreak of COVID-pandemic and cross-regional risk society, the chapter suggests that the EU has not yet come to the realization that simple injections of money in MENA struggling economies barely save these countries from immediate collapse. Moreover, cash transfers will not solve entrenched problems or foster MENA countries' capacity to manage crisis. Indeed, the EU has not designed assistance programs in a way that revamps its short-sighted policies. It has not taken action to promote sustainable economic reform and regional integration across MENA. Most importantly, the European Union is not focusing on the improvement of the Arab countries' abilities to manage risks and develop risk avoidance and risk mitigation strategies that can foster resilience to crisis.

Notes

1 Adjunct professor, Department of Human Sciences, Arts and Communication, TÉLUQ University.

2 Associate professor, Department of Civilizations and Forms of Knowledge, University of Pisa.

3 Egypt's GDP expanded by 5.6 percent in 2019 and by 3.6 percent in 2020. For more information, see World Bank Overview in Egypt, https://www.worldbank.org/en /country/egypt/overview. Also see: "How Egypt's economy can continue to thrive during a global pandemic," Ahmed Galal Ismail, June 2020. https://www.weforum.org /agenda/2020/06/egypt-economy-thrive-during-global-pandemic/.

4 See Egypt: Al-Sisi Should End Rights Abuses, Human Rights Watch, 2018. https:// www.hrw.org/news/2018/04/10/egypt-al-sisi-should-end-rights-abuses.

5 Indeed, despite Tunisia's seemingly successful transition during Arab uprisings and a number of important objectives in terms of democratic transition, on closer scrutiny, the successful narrative of the Tunisian transition falters in several domains. Above all, the shortcomings in satisfying the demands of the revolution emerge on the economic level. Nowadays citizens still continue to demonstrate for fulfilment of the promises of the revolution in order to achieve social justice, dignity, and employment (Allal and Geisser 2018). Kais Saied's takeover of power on July 25, 2021, cemented this trend of democratic backsliding.

6 In this respect indeed, in April 2020, the EU Commission launched "TEAM EUROPE" to support partner countries fighting against the pandemic. The approach is to "combine resources from the EU, member States and financial institutions, such as the European Investment Bank (EIB) and the European Bank for Reconstruction and Development (EBRD)." The goal is to propose a package of 20 billion euros to help the most vulnerable countries in Africa, Middle East, and other regions of the world, and mainly the people most at risk, including children, women, the elderly and disabled, as well as migrants, refugees and displaced persons.

7 For more information see https://www.middleeastmonitor.com/20180510-egypt-and -italys-eni-sign-agreement-for-exploration-of-oil-and-gas-in-north-sinai-worth-105 -million/.

8 France has sold to Egypt 30 sophisticated Jet-Fighter to Egypt in 2015. See https:// www.arabnews.jp/en/middle-east/article_45305/.

9 A 2016 article published by Amnesty International stated: "Almost half of European Union (EU) member states have flouted an EU-wide suspension on arms transfers to Egypt, risking complicity in a wave of unlawful killings, enforced disappearances and torture, Amnesty International said today" https://www.amnesty.org/en/latest/news /2016/05/eu-halt-arms-transfers-to-egypt-to-stop-fuelling-killings-and-torture/.

10 See Houry N. and Jeannerod B, Human Rights Watch, January 28, 2019. https://www .hrw.org/news/2019/01/28/how-french-weapons-enable-egypts-abuses, originally published on Le Monde.

11 Authors' interview with the Director of NAPI (North Africa Policy Organization). NAPI strengthens participatory governance in North Africa by building the research, writing, and advocacy capacity of youth. Among its programs, NAPI also perform charitable activities through NAPI Aid, mostly providing basic livelihood sources. In Tunisia, 2020 and 2021 saw a surge of people demanding aid from NAPI.

12 Moran (2020) The EU and the Med: Is Geography Still Destiny. The Cairo Review of Global Affairs https://www.thecairoreview.com/essays/the-eu-and-the-med-is -geography-still-destiny/.

13 On the rise of migration flows in May, see: https://www.aljazeera.com/news/2021/5/1/ more-than-800-migrants-rescued-in-mediterranean-head-to-italy.

14 For an updated analysis about the 2016 EU-Turkey migration agreement, see Kirişci (2021). As EU-Turkey migration agreement reaches the five-year mark, adda job creation element, Brooking, https://www.brookings.edu/blog/order-from-chaos/2021 /03/17/as-eu-turkey-migration-agreement-reaches-the-five-year-mark-add-a-job -creation-element/.
15 Between 2016 and 2021, Erdogan has used the "migrants card" to blackmail EU. See, for instance, https://www.dw.com/en/erdogan-warns-millions-of-refugees-heading-to -europe/a-52603580.
16 See: https://www.opendemocracy.net/en/north-africa-west-asia/arab-world-between -formidable-virus-and-repressive-state/.

References

Ait Ali, Abdelaziz, Uri Dadush, Yassine Msadfa, Yara Myachenkova and Simone Tagliapietra. (2019). "Towards EU-MENA Shared Prosperity," *Bruegel Policy Report*, March 14, https://www.bruegel.org/2019/03/towards-eu-mena-shared-prosperity-2/ (accessed March 10, 2022).

Allal, Amin and Vincent Geisser. (2018). *Tunisie. Une démocratisation au-dessus de tout soupçon?* Paris: Centre National de la Recherche Scientifique (CNRS).

Aydin, Mustafa and Sinem Acikmese. (2007). "Europeanization through EU Conditionality: Understanding the New Era in Turkish Foreign Policy," *Journal of Southern Europe and the Balkans*, 9 (3): 263–74.

Borck, Tobias (2020). "Europe and the Coronavirus Pandemic in the Middle East," *RUSI Commentary*, April 6, https://rusi.org/commentary/europe-and-coronavirus-pandemic -middle-east (accessed February 10, 2022).

Bouris, Dimitris and Tobias Schumacher, eds. (2017). *The Revised European Neighbourhood Policy: Continuity and Change in EU Foreign Policy.* Basingstoke: Palgrave Macmillan.

Bush, Sarah (2015). *The Taming of Democracy Assistance.* Cambridge: Cambridge University Press.

Cavatorta, Francesco and Paola Rivetti. (2014). "EU–MENA Relations from the Barcelona Process to the Arab Uprisings: A New Research Agenda," *Journal of European Integration*, 36 (6): 619–25.

Council of the European Union. (2015). *EU Annual Report on Human Rights.* Luxembourg: Office for Official Publications of the European Communities, https:// www.consilium.europa.eu/media/30939/hr2005en.pdf (accessed May 22, 2022).

Dandashly, Assem (2018). "EU Democracy Promotion and the Dominance of the Security–Stability Nexus," *Mediterranean Politics*, 23 (1): 62–82.

El Karoui, Hakim and Michel Duclos. (2020). "Is Covid-19 a Game-Changer for the Middle East and the Maghreb?," *Institute Montaigne, Blog*, April 23, https://www .institutmontaigne.org/en/blog/covid-19-game-changer-middle-east-and-maghreb (accessed February 10, 2022).

Fakhoury, Tamirace. (2016). "Securitising Migration: The European Union in the Context of the Post-2011 Arab Upheavals," *The International Spectator*, 51 (4): 67–79.

Ferragina, Annamaria, Stefano Iandolo and Erol Taymaz. (2021). "Migration and Comparative Advantages: New Evidence on the EU-MENA Region," *International Journal of Manpower*, https://www.emerald.com/insight/content/doi/10.1108/IJM-08 -2020-0395/full/html (accessed November 21, 2021).

Hyde-Price, Adrian. (2006). "'Normative' Power Europe: A Realist Critique," *Journal of European Public Policy*, 13 (2): 217–34.

Hoekman, Bernand, Matteo Fiorini and Aydin Yildirim. (2020). "COVID-19: Export Controls and International Cooperation," in Simon Evenett and Richard Baldwin (eds.), *COVID-19 and Trade Policy: Why Turning Inward Won't Work*, 77–88. Brussels: CEPR Press.

Kaunert, Christian and Sarah Léonard. (2011). "EU Counterterrorism and the European Neighbourhood Policy: An Appraisal of the Southern Dimension," *Terrorism and Political Violence*, 23 (2): 286–309.

Khader, Bichara. (2020). "Geopolitical Impact of the Coronavirus on the EU and the MENA Region," in Stephen Calleya (ed.), *Towards a Post Pandemic Euro-Mediterranean Strategy*, 18–36. La Valletta: University of Malta Press.

Kirişci, Kemal. (2021). "As EU-Turkey Migration Agreement Reaches the Five-Year Mark, Adda Job Creation Element," *Brooking*, March 17, https://www.brookings.edu/blog/order-from-chaos/2021/03/17/as-eu-turkey-migration-agreement-reaches-the-five-year-mark-add-a-job-creation-element/ (accessed Janaury 18, 2022).

Ispi. (2021). "The Great Game of Vaccines in the MENA Region," February 26, https://www.ispionline.it/en/pubblicazione/great-game-vaccines-mena-region-29446 (accessed October 15, 2021).

Lazaridis, Gabriella. (2016). *Security, Insecurity and Migration in Europe*. London: Routledge.

Lebl, Leslie. (2014). "The Islamist Threat to European Security," *Middle East Quarterly*, 21 (3): 1–13.

Lehne, Stephan. (2014). *Time to Reset the European Neighborhood Policy*, Vol. 4. Brussels: Carnegie Europe.

Livi Bacci, Massimo. (2018). "Does Europe Need Mass Immigration?," *Journal of Economic Geography*, 18 (4): 695–703.

Manners, Ian. (2002). "Normative Power Europe: A Contradiction in Terms?," *JCMS: Journal of Common Market Studies*, 40 (2): 235–58.

Moran, J. (2020). "The EU and the Med: Is Geography Still Destiny," *The Cairo Review of Global Affairs*, Essays, August 21, https://www.thecairoreview.com/essays/the-eu-and-the-med-is-geography-still-destiny/ (accessed November 21, 2021).

Otte, M. (2021). "The EU-MENA Partnership: Time for a Reset, Security Policy Brief," *Egmont Institute*, February 4, https://www.egmontinstitute.be/the-eu-mena-partnership-time-for-a-reset/ (accessed November 21, 2021).

Pepicelli, Renata. (2004). *2010 un nuovo ordine mediterraneo?* Messina: Mesogea.

Powel, Brieg and Larbi Sadiki. (2010). *Europe and Tunisia: Democratization via Association*. London: Routledge.

Przemysław, Osiewicz. (2020). "EU-MENA Relations in a Time of Pandemic," *Middle East Institute*, April 28, https://www.mei.edu/publications/eu-mena-relations-time-pandemic (accessed November 21, 2021).

Sadiki, Larbi and Layla Saleh. (2020). "Reflexive Politics and Arab 'Risk Society'? COVID-19 and Issues of Public Health," *Orient: German Journal for Politics, Economics and Culture of the Middle East*, 61 (2): 6–20.

Saleh, Layla and Larbi Sadiki. (2020). "The Arab World between a Formidable Virus and a Repressive State," *Open Democracy*, April 6, https://www.opendemocracy.net/en/north-africa-west-asia/arab-world-between-formidable-virus-and-repressive-state/ (accessed February 15, 2022).

Simoncini, Guendalina. (2020). "International PVE and Tunisia: A Local Critique of International Donors' Discourses," in Alice Martini, Kieran Ford and Richard Jackson (eds.), *Encountering Extremism: Theoretical Issues and Local Challenges*, 276–99. Manchester: Manchester University Press.

Süleymanoğlu-Kürüm, Rahime. (2018). *Conditionality, the EU and Turkey: From Transformation to Retrenchment*. London: Routledge.

Teti, Andrea. (2015). "Democracy Without Social Justice: Marginalization of Social and Economic Rights in EU Democracy Assistance Policy after the Arab Uprisings," *Middle East Critique*, 24 (1): 9–25.

Van Hüllen, Vera. (2015). *EU Democracy Promotion and the Arab Spring: International Cooperation and Authoritarianism*. Berlin: Springer.

Van Hüllen, Vera. (2019). "Negotiating Democracy with Authoritarian Regimes. EU Democracy Promotion in North Africa," *Democratization*, 26 (5): 869–88.

Woertz, Eckart and Roie Yellinek. (2021). *Vaccine Diplomacy in the MENA Region, Middle East Institute*, April 14, https://www.mei.edu/publications/vaccine-diplomacy-mena-region (accessed December 20 2021).

Wolff, Sarah and Stella Ladi. (2020). "European Union Responses to the Covid-19 Pandemic: Adaptability in Times of Permanent Emergency," *Journal of European Integration*, 42 (8): 1025–40.

13

The Post-Pandemic Bifurcation

Democratization versus Oligarchy Radicalization in the Arab World

Mudar Kassis[1]

Introduction

After record-breaking durations of political power retention in Arab countries for which the Algerian novelist Waciny Laredj used the coined term *repubdoms*,[2] rulers who had ruled for decades were falling because of the revolts that erupted starting in late 2010. *The Arab Dignity Revolutions* were not only an expression of misery and disenchantment with the existing order, a feeling that a threat is to be confronted, but also a belief that change is possible:

> People . . . knew that a time had ended, and that another time was set on the horizon with a lot of certainty, perhaps more merciless, but they swore to change everything, even the deceptive timings and times that were set to the pulse of the ruler by self-command, the owner of the Repubdom of Arabia. (الأعرج 2011، 11)

The revolts have undoubtedly created a temporal-spatial break with the political past in spite of being undermined by the counterrevolutions. In addition, the pandemic interrupted a second wave of political turmoil, including 2019 uprisings in Algeria and Sudan. COVID-19 added a layer of threat and misery to the masses, created an additional temporary fortification for regimes, and produced some skepticism concerning the revolts' and the *hiraks'* outcomes.

The pandemic stalled some of the techniques of regime contestation: physical collective protest in the squares was not a choice anymore. Meanwhile the state, with its security apparatus, was deemed necessary by many. However, the pandemic will not last forever, and a "new life" will supervene it. "Historically, pandemics have forced humans to break with the past and imagine their world anew. This one is no different. It is a portal, a gateway between one world and the next" (Roy 2020). What require answers are the questions about the nature of the new world—the Arab region in particular—and about the actors who shall shape it.

The Arab World is witnessing a popular demand for restructuring. It is also witnessing a new wave of proxy wars (e.g., Libya, Syria, and Yemen), and escalating regional tensions. A significant novelty in the scene is that the "silent masses" have shrunk (and keep shrinking) and are speaking out. Conversely, those who are satisfied with the status quo and display an animus to change are still resourceful. A clear division has emerged between them and those who believe that the time has come to reshape their countries upon new foundations. This polarization process will affect the dynamics of its unfolding through, for instance, new alliances and political cleavages, political undercurrents, and conflicts. Throughout this phase of polarization, everyone will position themselves in a way which will maximize their role in shaping the next order, because the struggle for the future is a struggle between the forces of the present. COVID-19 has added to these tensions.

In 2010, Muhammad Al-Bouazizi set himself on fire, instigating a revolt in Tunisia which echoed in several Arab countries, creating *The Arab Dignity Revolutions*. Ten years later, George Floyd was killed in cold blood in a manifestation of racism, instigating a global wave of protest exemplified in the movement "Black Lives Matter." In some ways, the reaction to the 2010 incident was a blueprint of that of 2020. Both are joined by the demand for dignity. One might wonder if the Global South will initiate the change toward the "next world," and whether the *dignity revolutions* have been the prelude of this change. "Evidence of commonality abounds in the global squares of protest and in the triggers of discontent. All of these protest groups seem to embrace, at least rhetorically, an emancipatory mantra of freedom and dignity" (Sadiki 2016, 327).

This mantra of dignity indicated a transformative threshold, which with the "notion of 'reflexive modernization' [that] panders to a moral agenda, which remains unfulfilled in the Arab world on count of the undeniable persistence of inequity and discrimination" (Sadiki and Saleh 2020, 6). The revolution deems to achieve this moral agenda through the shaping of the public will and reshaping the public sphere in a manner that allows the moral dimension to be transposed from the private sphere to the public sphere, and de-monopolize the political. The popular chant of "dignity" is a signifier of protesting the old "dignitaries." It carries an epochal significance indicating the need for foundational change that amounts to the reformulation of the social contract through "reflexivity," which "demands measuring up to moral standards that consider the right to safety for all and matching ethics that resist top-down and exclusionary orders of governmentality" (Sadiki and Saleh 2020, 15).

Dignity revolutions are thus a reflexive quest for a new order that overcomes the current state of inequality, vulnerability, and societal fragmentation and exclusion. They are a quest for radical democratization that does not necessarily conform to the prevailing perceptions of Western liberal democracy. This nonconformity lends global significance to these revolutions. Years after 2011, the COVID-19 pandemic has a dual effect on the quest for democratization: stagnation and radicalization. The pandemic's effect on the counterrevolutionary forces, meanwhile, is radicalizing. Thus, Arab "risk society" in the COVID era has placed more barriers before the dignity revolutions.

Outlining or sketching the "reflexive" rethinking of the social contract is an impossible task, but the "dignity" slogan signposts some of its intended ingredients and trends. These include the universalization of equality (beyond civil-political to the socioeconomic and cultural, and hence beyond precarity); freedom; and the autonomy of will which once collectivized creates (popular) sovereignty.

In this chapter, understanding the *dignity revolutions* as a phenomenon of global significance, we will sketch the active counterrevolutionary powers; look into the (possible) impact of the COVID-19 pandemic on the dynamics of sociopolitical change in the Arab World; and finally, speculate on the chances of the creation of a "new world" from a regional (MENA) perspective. The chapter commences with these tasks with the realization that neither the *dignity revolutions* nor the pandemic is behind us, and we cannot evaluate either of them before we observe their finale. This intervention is, therefore, speculative about what is still unfolding.

The Revolution

The *dignity revolutions*[3] can serve as a point of reference for this discussion. The dignity frame sets the stage for understanding counterrevolution, and thus the impact on the revolution–counterrevolution dynamic and Arab "risk society." "Starting points" in history are contestable, but the turmoil that erupted in the Arab World in late 2010 is itself a culmination and a prelude. The *dignity revolutions* had multiple interrelated characteristics: scale, concentration, significance, direction, suddenness, and peacefulness. However, the most relevant for our analysis is their revelation that is inscribed in the transnational slogan "dignity," the use of which as a political slogan in the region is novel. The slogans of the *dignity revolutions* encompassed a range of demands that in essence contested the entirety of the status quo in the Arab World. The "dignity" slogan introduced a socioeconomic dimension to political movements that had been missing for decades, and represented the bond between the social and the political. In addition, "dignity" moved beyond the nation and the state.

Revolutions result from structural failures. Their slogans reflect the nature and depth of existing defects as identified by revolutionaries. The breadth of the "dignity" chant urges the discovery of its signified. It was voiced in many countries, but in this chapter we confine this discussion to the revolutions in Tunisia and Egypt. These cases were, unlike Syria, Yemen, and Libya, void of blatant foreign intervention, and experienced a quantum leap (even if the new orbit was pushed back) toward ending (authoritarian) regime perpetuity.

The revolutions that occurred in Tunisia and Egypt embraced the most archetypical representative of the state—the army. They did not take place as a result of an emergent condition, rather, they took place in response to two regimes plunged into methodical and, arguably, successful reform programs.[4] They were as much revolutions against these reforms as they were revolutions against the status quo maintained by the two regimes.

Revolutionary Demands

The centrality of the dignity slogan signifies that the policies of the former regimes, including the reforms they were undertaking, tampered with the dignity of society.

Dignity revolutions were "not just a revolt against authoritarian regimes but also expressions of a systemic crisis, a structural crisis of the social order of neoliberal globalization" (Bogaert 2013, 214). People did not believe that the reform processes would improve their chances of becoming respectable citizens. The regime infringed on their dignity. It not only meddled with the living circumstances of citizens but with them directly. The nature of the security doctrine imposed by the globalized unipolar neoliberal world order made tampering with dignity inevitable.

Dignity, as a signifier, does not have a well-defined or concrete signified. It expresses insistence on some values concerning people with different, sometimes contradicting, connotations. While democracy was an obvious popular demand, and dignity was a widely chanted slogan during the peaks of protest and revolt, a retrospective sorting of public priorities does not give dignity or democracy a significant weight. In Table 13.1, only some 8 percent of those who provided a positive response chose democracy or dignity as the most important reason for the outbreak of *dignity revolutions*.

The majority of the answers in the above table identify what respondents *do not* want: corruption, poverty, dictatorship, and oppression. This is a typical reflection of "doxastic anxiety." As Table 13.1 demonstrates, no respondents to the question about the causes of the revolts opted for the answer "no other choice"—that is, respondents were consciously seeking purposeful change, or a drive toward a new order.

The Significance of the Slogan

The chanting of dignity designates a call to overcome exclusionary features of states and by extension the contemporary world order. This is not the first time in modern history that it surfaces. It was used for supporting the cancellation of slavery in Tunisia in the mid-nineteenth century, and by Tunisian president Habib Bourguiba, who used the phrase "once women regain their dignity . . ." (Al-Argash 2013).

Table 13.1 Most Important Reasons for the Outbreak of the Arab Spring in Polls across Arab Countries According to Poll of 2019–2020

The Reasons	Most Important Reasons
Against corruption	31
Due to poor economic conditions	16
Against dictatorship	16
For political freedoms	6
To end oppression	6
For justice and equality	4
For democracy	3
For dignity	4
Other	1
don't know, decline to respond	13
No other choice	0
Total	100

Source: Arab Center for Research and Policy Studies—Results of Arab Opinion Index 2019–2020 (Arab Center for Research and Policy Studies 2020, 11).

There is reason to assume that the dignity slogan surfaces when the aspired change is "epochal"—seeking to move to a new historical phase. The demand is not only for regime change, but rather for changing its foundations, demanding the termination and reformulation of the existing social contract (قسيس 2012).

The use of the dignity slogan for revolution or by popular movements indicates a shift of the realm in which it operates, from the private (individual, moral) to the public (political). Such a shift that takes place spontaneously reflects the will of the private (individual, family, group) entity to participate in the shaping of the public (social, political, national) entity. It assumes the existence of a drive to realize the private will outside the private sphere. It assumes the cognition of a historical moment that has a claim on making history—a transformative historical process.

While acknowledging the importance of the shift of the concept of dignity to the political sphere, one must distinguish clearly between the elite initiative to centrally position the concept in the state super-structures (e.g., legislation) and the popular demand for dignity. The central question here is: what instigates the popular demand for something that might seem to obscure "its economic and social aspects and the aspirations of its initiators" (Beinin 2016, 101)? Why does the popular common sense, which usually avoids abstraction, embrace this slogan at times? The public utilizes this concept to express and condense the entirety of popular demand—achieving a new historical era. A comparison between the *bread revolutions* in the late 1980s and the *dignity revolutions* can easily expose the differences, including the latter's insistence on ousting and destroying regime symbols.

To summarize, we can formulate three conclusions. The first is that the popular use of the dignity slogan indicates the desire to trigger change of "epochal" nature. Thus, when "dignity" is not realized, dissatisfaction and demands persist. We have seen this in the COVID era. The second conclusion is that the revolutionary form of political expression signifies an irreversible process of the objectification of collective subjective wills, that is, there is no going back from the new epoch to the old one (even if they look similar). The third conclusion is that the demands of the *dignity revolutions* go beyond the Arab political regimes: slogans pointed to the world order. *Dignity revolutions* are Arab revolutions that belong to a globalized era. They simultaneously confronted their local totalitarian regime and the oligarchical world order. Their emancipatory dimensions are dual as well, challenging the prevailing perceptions of Western liberal democracy (in its neoliberal form). Hence, the use of the dignity slogan also found global resonance. These demands have only strengthened since COVID "risk society" took hold, and states have been unable to see to their citizens' health and other socioeconomic needs.

The Significance of the Achievements and Shortcomings of the *Dignity Revolutions*

The forces of revolution are not homogenous, and their consensus over the dignity slogan does not signify one single signified. One can imagine various perspectives ranging from ones of a liberal nature (related mainly to individual civil rights) to others of a social nature, related primarily to economic and social rights because "many of the socio-economic grievances remain, or are worse in 2021 than in 2010" (Sadiki and Saleh 2021). Taking one without the other is a betrayal of some of the forces. Deepening social inequalities since COVID's onset are reflected on this second emphasis of dignity.

The *dignity revolutions* interacted with at least three traits: (1) the impact of globalization on the nature of the state; (2) the redistribution of labor and wealth among countries due to the hegemony of unadorned market values over the globalization process; and (3) the new security doctrine, which (over)empowered the coercive state, and shifted the main function of the state to the protection of external interests to the detriment of its original role of serving as a security and protection umbrella for its citizens, national identity, and sovereignty. Thus, safeguarding dignity, including since the pandemic, became an urgent and vital popular demand to divert the nature of globalization from corporate globalization to solidarity.[5]

What constitutes the success or failure of the *dignity revolutions* is not the form of the emerging regime, but its potential and capacity to enact radical democratization by adopting economic and political programs that can overcome or counterbalance neoliberal policies. The distinctive attribute of such democratization is inclusion and not market liberalization. In this sense and context, any regime that cannot safeguard dignity is, by the definition adopted here, counterrevolutionary.

"Everyone (almost without exception) agrees . . . to condemn the economic and social policies of the ousted President Hosni Mubarak's regime, as well as to talk somehow about their bias towards 'social justice' . . . And they conclude the same conclusion: the need to encourage the private sector" (2015 كساب). This also applies to "third way" regimes that took the form of political Islam, which provides (and imposes) an identity, but hides its positions concerning welfare. In a similar fashion, civil society organizations had, and will continue to have, an extremely limited impact on the revolutionary process.[6]

The *dignity revolutions* succeeded in declaring the decay of the old regimes, in challenging the monopoly over politics, in forcing change, and in declaring the advent of a new era. The revolt against the monopoly over politics was evident, not only in the insistence of ousting Mubarak, Ben Ali, Bouteflika, and Albashir, but more so in the massive protest[7] against popularly elected Egyptian president Morsi on June 30, 2013, one year after electing him.

Between the years 2011 and 2020, more than two-thirds and up to three-fourths of poll respondents expressed support for democracy, and between 6 and 18 percent declined to express a position. As Figure 13.1 shows, support for democracy is rising slowly, while skepticism is declining.

The most evident shortcoming of the *dignity revolutions* is their inability to provide a replacement regime, or a new leadership. This problem was building up in the years before COVID. The "third way" politics and the accompanying "political corporations" that prevailed in the three decades preceding the *dignity revolutions* are still in place. Political opposition groups in the Arab World were, and still are, largely part of the regime system. They have different answers to the questions posed by the establishment, but they do not pose their own questions. The fate of Egypt under Sisi, the threat to the nascent Tunisian democracy by Saied, and the military coup of October 2021 in Sudan are witness to the price of the political immaturity of revolutions.

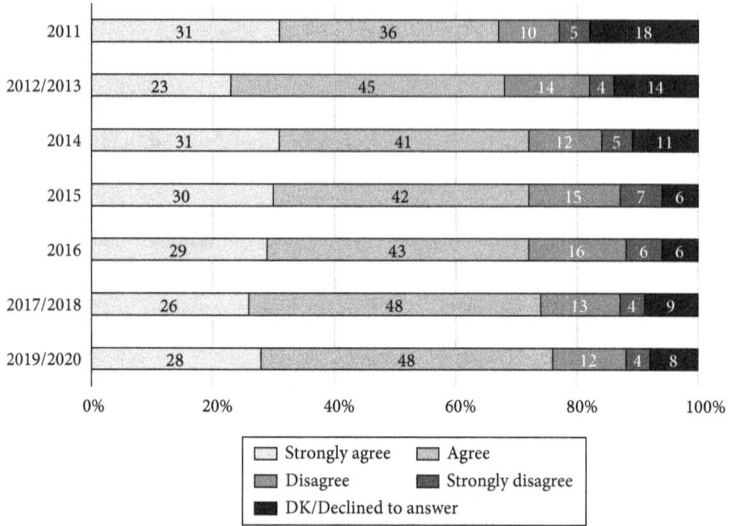

Year					
2011	31	36	10	5	18
2012/2013	23	45	14	4	14
2014	31	41	12	5	11
2015	30	42	15	7	6
2016	29	43	16	6	6
2017/2018	26	48	13	4	9
2019/2020	28	48	12	4	8

Legend: Strongly agree · Agree · Disagree · Strongly disagree · DK/Declined to answer

Figure 13.1 Support for the statement "Democracy remains better than other forms of government, despite its shortcomings" in polls across Arab countries during the years 2011–2020. *Source*: Reconstructed using data from source: Arab Center for Research and Policy Studies—Results of Arab Opinion Index 2019–2020 (Arab Center for Research and Policy Studies 2020, 2).

"Political corporations" act as ruling parties that do not operate in accordance with known party structures. They control all the branches of political authority, the job market, security, culture, and media. By monopolizing the political realm, they undermine the very notion of opposition, whose efficacy hinges on defeating the entirety of the system. Opposition, thus, has to either suffice with low profile, inefficient, verbal opposition with an ever-shrinking constituency; or resort to radical forms of protest and organization frequently utilizing violence, and adopting an ideological blanket of populist and conspiracy theory discourse. For that, it utilizes various types of identitarian mantras, which reshape politics by transforming struggle by contesting politics through splitting rather than sharing it. In such a situation, political participation becomes meaningless, and the very idea of citizenship loses ground.

In the absence of a political alternative to the regime, the revolutionary forces were deprived of political organization and leadership to the extent that they had no choice but to resort to the army for political leadership, most clearly in the example of Egypt. Militaries have similarly played a significant role in measures to fight the pandemic. The army, being the archetypical representation of the "political establishment"—a corporation itself, volunteered to lend itself to the revolution as a bridge to power. It was not perceived as a replacement, nor did it pretend to be one, but it conditioned its "bridging" role on ensuring that the other end of the bridge leads to where its allies stay operative and powerful. The army was ready for this role for at least three reasons: (a) its "low profile" role in politics; (b) it has a relatively autonomous network of external relations instrumental in importing external legitimacy for a "future regime"; and (c)

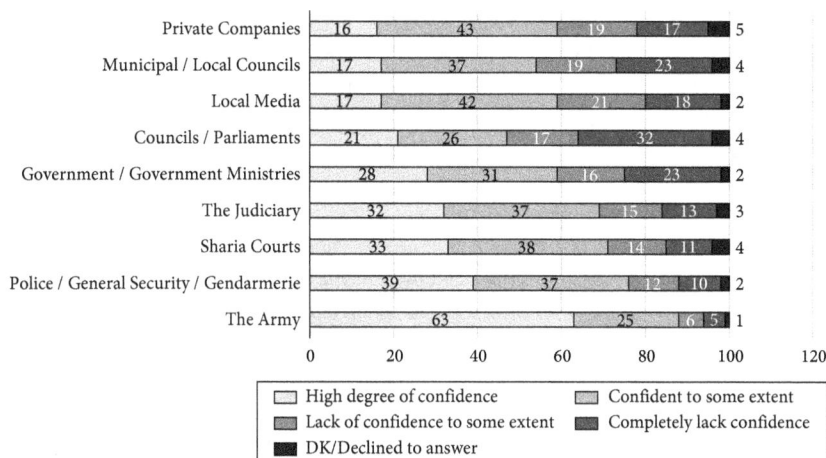

Figure 13.2 Citizens' trust in major state institutions (aggregate of 13 Arab countries). *Source*: Reconstructed using data from source: Arab Center for Research and Policy Studies—Results of Arab Opinion Index 2019–2020 (Arab Center for Research and Policy Studies 2020, 6).

it bases its legitimacy on capacity and merit and not on any form of representation. As Figure 13.2 demonstrates, trust in the army and other security institutions is significantly higher than all other institutions (including representative institutions and judiciaries).

The *dignity revolutions* failed to set the direction of change. The maximum they achieved in the four Arab countries where they succeeded in ousting a regime, without jumping into a civil/proxy war (Tunisia, Egypt, Sudan, and Algeria), was enforcing tools for political change that are not, on their own, sufficient to ensure change. In Egypt, in combination with the army, they produced a Muslim Brotherhood regime that was popularly rejected a year later. This opened the door to a ferocious return of the old regime with army blessing and protection, and external intervention to the detriment of democratization. In Tunisia, dignity revolution produced a political system built on the liberal assumptions of elite contestation with little consideration for popular will (outside of elections). The system has not been stable since its emergence and stumbled into a series of crises until it came to a point when President Saied liquidated the central structures of liberal democracy in July 2021. In Sudan, the revolution had to come to a transitional arrangement that could provide room for either fostering the revolutionary powers, or buying time for counterrevolutionary powers supported by an assortment of external forces. The military coup that took place on October 25, 2021, confirmed the latter tendency, while the massive protests against the military rule provide hope for a revolutionary revival.

It is still early to evaluate the eventual impact of the *dignity revolutions*, but the status of the countries where they bore fruit, with reference to their demands and slogans, does not reflect success. COVID's detrimental impact on economies and state budgets, when social spending on public health was already inadequate, made matters worse for the publics seeking dignity since 2010. The lack of accountability repudiated political liberalization and warranted its reversibility. Not long after liberalizations were instigated in the late 1980s, a new security doctrine throve, and political liberalization was moved to a back-burner until it was completely abandoned in favor of neoliberalization. "[T] he years between 2003 through the beginning of 2011 saw a dramatic increase in the speed, depth, and seeming dominance of neoliberal reforms" (Haddad 2017, 75). This neoliberalization process was a major factor in prompting the *dignity revolutions*, but at the same time, served as their embedded limitation. Internal and external factors and actors facilitated the post-revolutionary triumph of alliances involving the Brotherhood and allies and protégés of old regimes, resulting in reducing revolutionary demands to their textual and formal dimensions. As a result, post-revolutionary regimes faltered.

The *dignity revolutions* were full of turmoil themselves, and created uncertainty and upheaval. The prevailing neoliberal policies and their "post-political culture" came to a dead end. Like every decay, they became self-destructive. The *dignity revolutions* utilized the "master's tools to dismantle the master's house," but they could not master its reconstruction because they lacked adequate political organization, and because of the strengths of the counterrevolutionary forces which had access to resources that the *dignity revolutions* did not. Having said this, the Arab World today is not similar to that of 2010. The revolutions turned out to be contagious in the short and the long terms. Arab countries are not seen, at least by the populace, as isolated. The revolutions in Sudan and Algeria clearly demonstrated a pattern of lesson-learning from the successes and failures of their predecessors. Yet, the direction and pace of change in both countries indicates that there is more to learn.

The *dignity revolutions* set new thresholds that are yet to be achieved. They seem even more distant since the pandemic. These include, inter alia: (a) political pluralism—the rejection of monopoly over politics; (b) universality and unity of rights—the criticality of social, economic, and cultural rights; (c) political engagement—the need for political organization beyond civil society activism and social movements; (d) inclusiveness of democracy—the insufficiency of procedures for democracy, and the necessity of a moral component in politics; and (e) preeminence of community-based collective rights and action, and the irreducibility of democracy to Western liberal democracy. Multiple aspects of the second wave of the *dignity revolutions* confirm "progress" toward the set thresholds. As Alyssa Miller writes in her analysis of the role of the anticorruption campaign *Manish Msamah* (I do not forgive) which emerged in Tunisia in 2015:

> The campaign is revealed as an early participant in the "second wave" of the Arab Spring, which has refused the lure of procedural democracy in favor of deeper structural change. (Miller 2021, 205)

Dignity revolutions, acquiring global significance, made clear that the Arab World cannot be researched in isolation, nor can it be solely a "recipient" of global impacts, that "we must guard against mono-causal explanations of politics in the Arab Middle East" (Sadiki 2016, 338), and that the nation-state approach to analysis cannot alone explain the political processes in the region. (Sadiki 2016, 336). It also made clear that modernization theory is incapable of unrolling a roadmap for reshaping the Global South, the Arab region included. On the contrary, the Global South is taking part in reshaping democracy globally.

The Counterrevolution

Counterrevolution is an inevitable reaction to any revolution. *Dignity revolutions* are not an exception either collectively or in the particularity of each of the countries where they erupted. Powers whose interests are threatened by the revolution instigate counteractions to protect and maintain their pre-revolution status and benefits. They embark on counteractions to stop revolutionary potential, reverse its realized impact or redirect it, and dry out its resources. The argument here is that counterrevolution has intensified in the wake of COVID in regime responses to the pandemic.

The preliminary success of the *dignity revolutions* in Egypt, Tunisia, Sudan, and Algeria, led the counterrevolutionary powers to declare initially their support for the revolution. They turned their back to regime symbols, but acted to protect those components of the political system that constituted their source of interest, secure their privilege, and maintain tools for control. They opted to desert the regime, but salvage the establishment. According to Kais Saied (interviewed six years before he became Tunisia's president), the slogan "*Tunis hurra hurra w Bin Ali barra*" (Tunis is free, Bin Ali out) was replaced, after the establishment of the Higher Authority for Realisation of the Objectives of the Revolution, Political Reform and Democratic Transition in March 2011, with the slogan "*alsha'b ureed isqat al-hukouma*" (the people want to topple the government) because the street saw in the "Higher Authority" a manoevre to maintain the old regime, as if they are telling the people "go back to your homes and we will take care of you." Saied qualified the establishment of the "Higher Authority" as an "attempt to transform the *hirak* into something like a space shuttle that is launched by several engines [after which] the shuttle gets rid of them [the *hiraks*]" (Saied 2013). Salvaging the establishment, which is vital for the planned comeback of counterrevolutionary forces, involves the protection of its support structures, such as the markets, the media, and the security apparatus(es).

The Arab Democracy Index of 2016 shows that four years after the eruption of *dignity revolutions*, the scores for indicators concerning respect of rights and freedoms, equality and social justice, and strong and accountable institutions are down respectively by 49, 32, and 16 points (5 percent, 3 percent, and 1.5 percent accordingly), while score for the indicators concerning rule of law significantly increased by 114 points (11.5 percent) (الشقاقي، قسيس و حرب 2017، 7).

A closer look at the sub-indicators of the Index in the Tunisian case (Figure 13.3) shows that post-revolutionary change was not homogeneous. The direction of change in practice was oriented toward fostering the state apparatus, and providing impunity for governmental institutions. The change process was highly reliant on legislative and judicial reforms—the most obvious increase was in the score of indicators related to the rule of law. This, apparently, facilitated the increase of indicators reflecting the

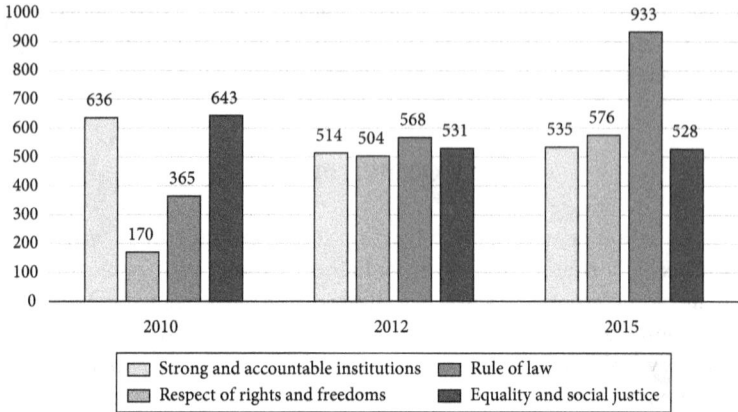

Figure 13.3 Classification of scores according to democratic practices in Tunisia: Comparison of readings between 2010, 2012, and 2015. *Source*: Arab Reform Initiative, Date set of the Arab Democracy Index—5 (2017 5 -العربي الديمقراطية مقايس ،حرب و قسيس ،الشقاقي).

respect of rights and freedoms, albeit not those rights that provide for equality and social justice. The single ever-dwindling indicator over the four-year period leading to 2015 is the one that is most representative of the demands of the revolution (equality and social justice).

The Tunisian case demonstrates that the changes that take place after a revolution, measured at a point in time, are the (temporary) resultant of the dynamics of the revolution and the counterrevolution. While local actors undertake revolution, the counterrevolution involves local as well as external actors who implement their agendas in legalized forms such as sanctions, loans, or through trade agreements, or through extra-judicial means involving the dispatching, financing, or support of militias. Counterrevolutionary actors are not only those who acted to terminate the revolution but also those who acted in contradiction with the anti-neoliberal demands of the revolution by promoting and radicalizing neoliberal policies instead of furthering justice through socioeconomic equality. What became dangerously apparent in 2020 onward was that the counterrevolution and its preservation of neoliberal policies left states much less able to confront COVID or mitigate people's suffering (in health and economic well-being).

Internal Actors

Both Egypt and Tunisia have undergone significant transformations under arrays of neoliberal reforms that preceded the *dignity revolutions*. Both were ranking high on the success scale according to various international reports. Tunisia was listed under the high human development countries with an HDI value of 0.683 in the Human Development Index of the UNDP, while Egypt was listed under the medium human development with an HDI value of 0.620 (United Nations Development

Programme 2010, 144). The ongoing (successful) neoliberal reforms led to the emergence of a nouveau-riche class that treated government and security officials as their nomenklatura. The revolution posed a serious threat for them, but its success was unescapable. Hence, they resorted to diverting the *dignity revolutions'* goals—a task eased by the absence of direction and leadership in the revolutions. This trend has magnified the counterrevolutionary "risk society" in the areas of COVID preparedness and response.

The readiness of some forces that took part in the *dignity revolutions* to shrink and transform revolutionary goals facilitated the counterrevolutionary task. Among these forces were the Muslim Brothers in Egypt and the Ennahda Movement in Tunis (both right-wing, economically liberal, socially conservative, and Islamist) in addition to some liberal forces. These forces contested the old regime's monopoly, but not its neoliberal politics. They posed as candidates for replacing the old corrupt regime. In essence, the actions of these parties diverted the meaning and significance of "dignity" from inclusion to exclusion. They downsized revolutionary demands by excluding their socioeconomic elements and solely maintaining the procedural, political dimensions (e.g., elections). A main tool for the realization of the diversion technique was the media. Both local and regional media presented the dilemma of the nascent post-2011 regime as being religious or civil. "Amongst the manoeuvres used by the regime to maintain itself was the indoctrination of public opinion that the main conflict is between Islam and unbelief . . . and the relegating of all key social, and even political issues" (Saied 2013). Yusra Ghannouchi, the international spokesperson for the Tunisian Ennahdha Party noted that "otherwise serious media" exaggerates the "ideological polarisation" by "cloaking every possible . . . issue in the reductionist Islamist-secularist dichotomy while ignoring other more insightful dimensions" (Ghannouchi 2014). This dichotomization is one of the common denominators for those who wanted to avoid the actual anti-neoliberal quests of the *dignity revolutions*. Those manipulating this supposed polarity included protégés of the old regime, liberals, Islamists, the security apparatus, and the army (especially in the case of Egypt).[8]

The Islamic movements characterized the old regimes as secular rather than nationalist, capitalist, neoliberal, proxy, or any other quality of relevance to their failure. The global wave of Islamophobia that the "clash of civilizations" doctrine nourished, created an environment, in which sticking to Islamic identity seemed a dignified choice. The term "civil" in the context of post-revolutionary debates implicitly discounted secularity as an acceptable option. The (neo)liberal and leftist forces characterized elected parties as "Islamist," rather than socially reactionary, or economically and politically mainstreamers (capitalist). The secular/religious divide helped camouflage the agendas of liberal political parties that also fell short of representing revolutionary demands. The result was a contestation between apolitically defined parties fostering the neoliberal post-political stance. Major media outlets like Aljazeera supported the indoctrination of the Islamist post-political identity. Director of Amnesty International Tunisia Lutfi Azzouz said:

> the revolution uncovered many things and revealed many wrong stereotypes. Examples are such beliefs that the Tunisian society is an open society that accepts

equality, while the reality is the existence of racist discrimination based on colour, and agitation against Jews and Christians; and that Tunisian Islam is Zaitounian [in reference to the Zaitouna School], while the reality is the emergence of Takfiri [ex-communicational] trends. (Azzouz 2013)

Most likely these phenomena existed before the revolution (the involvement of some Tunisians in the ranks of the *Mujahedeen* in Afghanistan may have something to do with this). The dominant post-revolutionary discourse may have simply boosted these phenomena.

The new political landscape allowed for what was referred to in Egypt as a "safe exit"—a smooth "transition" to a "controlled democracy" (Kandil 2016, 375) through the ballot box. The same applied to Tunisia. Both Islamist parties achieved unquestionable success in the elections before people became quickly disenchanted with them. "Morsi had given the SCAF [Supreme Council of the Armed Forces], the secularists, the *fulool* [remnants of the old regime], and, most importantly, the revolutionaries, a reason to return to Tahrir, which led to his removal from power by the military on July 3, 2013" (Fahmy 2016, 91). Neither of the two parties was responsive to the *dignity revolutions'* socioeconomic demands. Their platforms did not involve equality, social welfare, inclusion, provisions for state-sponsored health and education, or poverty eradication. The new political leaders were not less neoliberal than the old regime. They even sacrificed the narrow platform of procedural democracy. In Egypt, President Morsi waged an attack on labor unions offering "to share control of ETUF [Egyptian Trade Union Federation] with former Mubarak supporters" (Beinin 2016, 117), and "by December 2012, the Brotherhood was already flexing its muscles: snubbing military mediation and employing armed supporters to repress opposition . . . Brothers not only endorsed the repression of attempts to reignite the revolt, but they actually blamed the victims" (Kandil 2016, 331–2). The agony between the various forces that played different roles in the post-revolutionary process turned into antagonism after the Rabaa massacre of August 14, 2013. The bloody act was a play of radicalization within the anti-revolutionary camp. The army executed a coup against Brotherhood after the alliance between the two forces became unnecessary (Sika 2022). Similar dynamics involved attempts to supress the unions (Beinin 2016, 121–8), and popular protests against Ennahda took place in Tunisia.

The similarities between the ways the revolutions and counterrevolutions played out in Tunisia and Egypt do not mean there were no differences. Revolutions took multiple paths in different countries. Counterrevolutionary tactics also have similarities as well as differences. A common tactic is reframing the revolutionary quest and transforming it by highlighting some new (invented or unearthed) frontier to replace revolution's designation. In Egypt and Tunisia, the new regimes "invented" a legislative front that served reframing revolutionary demands, and achieving what Habermas calls "juridification," which signifies control through a growing body of regulatory tools (constitution, laws, and decrees). Along with an ever-growing security apparatus, this process generated new forms of governmentality: "being the 'conduct of conduct' means it conditions the very ways of people's thinking, acting and being" (Sadiki and Saleh 2020, 14).

The contestation among the new players intensified, and involved some redistribution of powers, and political realignments. According to Shawki Tabib, part of the old Tunisian oligarchy operates under the auspices of Ennahda Movement, counting on the latter's failure to come back to power (Tabib 2013). "Elites have no intention to reach a reconciliation. The dragging out of the debate over legislative texts was to cover the actual struggle" (Tabib 2013). "It is a struggle for existence under the disguise of the constitution . . . they all dream on the same pillow and share a single dream: the Carthage Palace" (Saied 2013). Political elites made laboratory rats out of the masses, experimenting on them to get to power—"bit'alamou lihjama brous el-yatama [they learn cupping with the heads of orphans]" (M'Rad 2013).

In addition to utilizing the media for indoctrination and distraction, there are other techniques that Taïeb Baccouche (general secretary of Nida' Tunis Party at the time of the interview) listed as "the main tools for the reproduction of hegemonic structures: chaos, violence, absence of security, and the fear of terrorism" (Baccouche 2013). Typically, panic and lack of security are created through market mechanisms that threaten livelihoods—like a shortage in energy sources (petrol and electricity). (The COVID pandemic has also instigated widespread panic, capitalized on by state and military elites.) Speculations in the media exacerbate the situation. *Asharq Al-Awsat* newspaper published a report in its business section three days before the coup de grâce street protests of June 30, 2013, that is exemplary in this regard:

> Egypt continues to face a deteriorating fuel crisis with the capital, Cairo, particularly hard hit, resulting in long lines of cars queuing up in front of gas stations blocking traffic.
>
> . . . Egyptian president Mohamed Mursi apologized for fuel shortages . . . Mursi blamed the fuel crisis on unfounded media speculation and the illegal hoarding of fuel by some gas stations. (Yamani 2013)

Analysts are convinced, beyond any conspiracy theory, that the army designed the fuel crisis (Sika 2022). Consolidating techniques and tools and ensuring their service to the counterrevolutionary strategy requires the reproduction and maintenance of a central power depository, as well as regaining initiative through coercion, clientelism, and the constant fear of threats. "Counter-revolutionary forces act through the deep state, and seek to maintain chaos" (Saied 2013).

The deep state hinges on two pillars: civil bureaucracy and the army. The counterrevolutionary inversion requires the concentration of these two pillars through their unification, balancing, and subordination to a regulator/guardian of the old/new regime: typically, a bloated security apparatus. After the revolution, the Tunisian state succeeded in establishing the broad set of democratic institutional structures, but the counterrevolutionary forces managed to keep these changes hostage to their interests under the threat of coercion and chaos:

> Almost all vital sectors in the country have undergone some change, but the impact is barely felt by Tunisians. The one area that has escaped change is security.

...

The Tunisian Police and National Guard have seen their numbers increase by more than 25,000 men between 2011 and 2015. (Boussen 2021, 4–5)

Furthermore, security forces are pushed into a confrontational relation with the masses through various means like the identification of security with the regime, and security provision with impunity:

Political complacency with police violence, coupled with inflammatory rhetoric from the police unions, is a perfect recipe for abuse. (Guellali 2021)

The direct impact of the internal counterrevolution is destabilization, creating a favorable situation for oligarchy. The existence of armed and quasi-military structures outside the state also creates a strong feeling of instability while providing extra-judicial protection to certain segments of the population. This recreates inequality, fosters the notion of being a minority, and eventually results in destabilization. The Arab Security Index of 2016 highlighted the "correlation between these [sectarian] affiliations and the attitudes and impressions of the public towards the security sector" (الشقاقي، حرب و لدادوة 2016). These and other techniques are supported and further exacerbated by the acts of external anti-revolutionary actors.

External Actors

Counterrevolutionary "risk society" has arguably been more problematic due to external intervention. Such problems as the deficit of fuel (whether real or not, and whether new or recurring) are frequently politically orchestrated/instrumentalized both on the internal and external fronts. For example, toward the end of 2014, Dr. Ahmed Mokhtar, deputy editor in chief of Al Ahram Al Massai wrote in *Khaleej Times* magazine:

The 25th January revolution in 2011 and its security implications that reflected on [the] investment climate made several international corporations suspend any new projects they planned to carry out in Egypt . . .
. . . As the Egyptian government planned to attract huge investments during the coming period, it has become a challenge to provide the necessary fuel that would supply new factories. . . (Mokhtar 2014)

In the same article, another line points to the importance of certain regional coalitions of the Egyptian regime, which benefited from "large quantities of oil products as an economic aid" (Mokhtar 2014).

On the security level, the most effective and widespread technique of external counterrevolutionary intervention is the involvement of foreign or local militias that act upon foreign command and agendas. Frequently these militias, while challenging the regime, provide it with legitimacy by creating "demand" on combating what represents an "external enemy" of the state. This is the case in almost all countries were *dignity revolutions* erupted. When counterrevolutionary powers do not get a full grip on the state, the delineation of state and non-state actors becomes hazy. Together, they form a sort of a network of actors. The centrality of the state as a provider of security is revealed as a fiction. Because the essence of statehood is security provision, when the state shares it with non-state actors, it is weakened, thus creating a situation where social revolutionary acts are not feasible or rational. Moreover, such weakened states (e.g., Libya and Syria) have less capacity to deal with crises such as the pandemic onslaught.

At the level of governance, external (especially military) intervention is the antithesis of democratization. Out of four countries where the dignity revolutions took down regime symbols, two (Yemen and Libya) are in wars involving external military interventions. According to some analysts, the external intervention in Syria is what prevented a democratic outcome of the revolts, and turned the democratic *Hirak* into a civil (and internationalized) war (2020 مَنَاع). In another example, the Bahraini government invited forces from some seven countries to suppress protests in 2011 (Zarcom Media 2011), thus evading change.

In addition, there exists a "passive counterrevolution"—the insistence of external actors to maintain the course of their intervention with disregard to popular demands. The pandemic has allowed us to "discover anew the ubiquity of international power players that shape and dictate policy" (Saleh and Sadiki 2020). Even earlier, European Union foreign aid policy in the aftermath of the *dignity revolutions* showed no responsiveness, other than lip service to the demands chanted in revolutionary squares. EU support can be characterized as "marginalizing the question of social and economic rights as well as—to a slightly lesser extent—. . . marginalizing the potential role of labour organizations" (Teti 2015, 22). It has continued in the neoliberal vein of pre-2011 regime reforms. Directly or indirectly, external actors thus strengthen counterrevolutionary "risk society" before and during COVID.

The red line of external intervention is built on conjoining the interests and efforts of internal and external counterrevolutionary forces. Some seek to maintain or regain power through destabilization, and others seek to create beneficial geopolitical positions at the cost of the livelihoods of other nations. This confluence leads to a multifaceted anti-revolutionary hegemony that furthers imperialist interests. Moreover, it pushes "dignity" further down the road for publics struggling to (literally) survive shocks such as COVID.

The Pandemic as a Bummer and a Catalyst

Arab "risk society" complicates the quest for dignity. However, the pandemic's challenges cannot be understood as causing or resulting from democratic change in the wake of the dignity revolutions. "[V]ulnerability to crises (in this case, a global pandemic) in the Arab states is structural" (Sadiki and Saleh 2020, 6). In the Arab world and globally, problems and solutions existed before the pandemic. Countries worldwide were poorly prepared as the pandemic broke out in early 2020 (Schiller and Hellmann 2021). The pandemic simply exacerbated the situation. The economy was hit and poverty hiked, but this was not new: "the [Arab] region is more unequal than even Africa or Latin America" (Partridge 2021 [2011]).

Education suffered. The poorer suffered more, and became more deprived. Remote schooling is not the same as going to school in-person, but even that is not accessible to more than half of the children in the Arab World:

> [E]except for Gulf countries, the percentage of internet users varies between 2% to 78% in the Arab region, less than half of the population has an access to the internet in 9 countries. (UNFPA ASRO 2021, 27)

This means that the future generation of democracy builders are less educated, less healthy, and more unemployed since COVID. Nevertheless, they may have better clarity concerning the problem because the pandemic has deepened and exposed neoliberal politics entangled with (returns to) authoritarianism. A comment by an Egyptian expert addressed to researchers from Freedom House is characteristic:

> The military regime has used COVID-19 as an opportunity to further repress political activists, rights defenders, lawyers, journalists, and doctors, arresting dozens, denying them basic assistance in places of detention, and placing several on terrorist lists. (Repucci and Slipowitz 2020, 3)

Security and intelligence were at the frontline of procurement of COVID-related items globally. Egypt's Trade and Industry Ministry coordinated with the Military Production Ministry to expand the production of medical masks and to open a production line for cloth masks (Ahram online 2020). In Palestine, the Minister of Health declared that her ministry received COVID testing-related material from the chief of intelligence (عكس التيار 2020). This phenomenon of security and army involvement in civil domains (the health system being a vivid example) is not observable only to an unexpected pandemic. On the backdrop of a "failure" in the Tunisian health system leading to a surge in COVID-19 cases and deaths, on July 2021, one and a half years after the emergence and spread of the COVID-19, the Tunisian president ordered the army to manage the pandemic (بحر 2021). That was shortly before he suspended the parliament, and took over the government less than a week later (Parker 2021). The army and other internal, and possibly external, forces supported Saied's acts. The pandemic was an initial excuse for the president's monopolization of power. Multiple excuses, not related to the pandemic, followed.

> COVID-19's perils have augmented the risks of human existence, especially for the have-nots: individuals, communities and states. Arabs are scrambling for new mediums—material, immaterial, moral and political—to weather the pandemic and its manifold socio-economic-political repercussions. Reflexivity as dialogue and debate can be one step in blunting the blows wrought by COVID-19. Risk might engender an opening for civic, political, and economic players to ponder policies and activisms that can begin to reign in inequality, vulnerability, and exclusion in the Arab region. (Sadiki and Saleh 2021)

As was the case in Egypt and in Sudan, counterrevolution (emboldened by the COVID crisis) can stagnate democratization and even temporarily move it out of the horizon. Nevertheless, the next quest for democratization will likely be more radical. The lesson to be learned is that sidelining questions of justice and inclusion becomes a recipe for revolutionary failure.

The pandemic created a situation where the state of exception became normal rather than requiring normalization. "In some contexts, leaders and politicians have used the situation to advance nationalist political agendas, spread extremist ideologies, or find advantage in an ongoing contest for hegemony in the global political order" (Bonotti and Zech 2021, xiii). With limited healthcare capacities during the peak of the pandemic, the loss of jobs, and the need for vaccination—all managed by public healthcare systems of mostly clientelist regimes—the government became the conferrer of "let live" largesse. The pandemic seems to have provided ruling "oligarchs" with a raison d'être for their hegemony, legitimized the build-up of their coercion, provided an augmented reality repetition in real time for a life where expression of opinion is likely to prove an excessive and futile exercise, made incarceration/lockdown a matter of command, and made doctors depend, in their professional practice, on security officials.

On the other hand, the pandemic translucently exposed the (under)performance of Arab regimes, their political systems, government structures, and capacities. It underlined all that the *dignity revolutions* contested. The exhibited inability and lack of capacity during the pandemic reduced the trustworthiness of these regimes to a zilch. The story of a young Iraqi civil servant is characteristic:

> The vaccine has come here so fast, . . . but that's so strange. In Iraq, with things like this, you usually can't get access without some corruption, or you have to pay somebody. But it [the vaccine] is for free and it's available for everybody. It's a bit suspicious. (Schaer 2021)

The emerging picture is ironic. The regime acts to control the lives of the citizens. It requires loyalty, which the neoliberal traditions transpose into one-way compliance (involuntary loyalty). A dilemma arises: on one hand, the government promotes policies where each is responsible for their own fate. On the other hand, lockdowns and the unavailability of, or lack of access to, vaccination and hospitalization threaten people's fates. Pandemic-era "risk society" makes dignity even more difficult to realize.

Conclusion: The Post-Pandemic Bifurcation

This chapter has taken stock of the Arab "dignity revolutions" and their prospects in light of COVID. The pandemic further polarized the Arab political landscape across countries. Political conflicts that were concealed by compromises and temporary solutions are up for an essential resolution. Managing or camouflaging conflicts under the disguise of development, peacebuilding, state building, and reconciliation is exposed as ineffective. The twinning of liberalism and democracy has exhausted itself. Liberalism has grown into neoliberalism, which is prone to oligarchy—not democracy; liberalism does not assume equality, while democracy does; the peak of liberal democracy in the West was conditioned on the divide of the three worlds that were reorganized; and the increasing spread of populism will not leave much room for plurality, or rights. Any direction that does not prioritize equality and inclusion is in effect counterrevolutionary.

The ways in which these global dynamics might express themselves in the Global South, including the Arab World are multiple. The end game will depend on the battle between democratic and "oligarchic" camps. The current era in the Arab World is one of change. The pandemic put a clutch on its speed, but increased it torque. "Longstanding uprisings that have brought down leaders from Lebanon to Iraq have largely left the streets as COVID-19 stifles public life. But that hasn't stopped protesters from pursuing political change" (Allinson and Sanders 2020). The forced delay of street action led to a "hibernation" of the *hiraks*, but the devastation and poverty that dominated the scene, together with the weakening of the middle class, are likely to facilitate a stronger next burst of the *dignity revolutions*. Albeit this will not guarantee the success of the *hiraks*, nor their success in achieving democratization, equality, protection of dignity, and emancipation. The war over the future is not teleological. It can take unforeseen turns as the revolts, *hiraks*, the pandemic, and the counterrevolution unfold.

The goals of a next round of the *dignity revolutions* will, likely, be more fundamental after the readily available liberal democracy blue print has stopped being a satisfactory model of sociopolitical organization. Now Arab rebels are tasked with the invention of a new model—even a new world order. The current order is more stable in the Global North, and the Global South is the weak link in the chain. The simple reproduction of the neoliberal order in the conditions of crony capitalism, rentier economy, surging unemployment, low quality education, debt, high consumption, and external hegemony is unlikely to succeed. Thus, there are chances that an aggravated global turmoil will start in the Global South. Since the eruption of the *dignity revolutions*, the Arab World became a strong and trained candidate for igniting the quest for change. What the globalization achieved is that no part of the world can be isolated any more, but the global chain is as strong as its weakest link.

The Arab oligarchy and its allies regionally and globally, recognizing this scenario, are likely to radicalize. The rules of the game might become more brutal, delaying the change process, resulting in bloodier battles, and requiring a more comprehensive range of resources for fighting the oligarchy. The emotional urge for revolt as a reaction to indignation, even strengthened by COVID's destruction, will not be sufficient:

> The very logic of the emergency state, then, is to prevent us from doing what really should be done. Today more than ever, we need a thinking which is not a simple reflexive response to the state of emergency. (Zizek 2009)

In the final account, the democratic emancipatory mission of the Arab street is a sophisticated and complex one. The pandemic has only crystallized the need for a change at a number of levels. Success hinges on securing an array of conditions:

the invention and shaping of a next epoch; the invention of new modes of political organization; the fostering of broader and stronger coalitions of emancipatory powers on grounds of solidarity; the twinning of local struggle against the local oligarchies with the struggle against neocolonial arrangements that nourish the global oligarchic hegemony; and the theoretical development of a revolutionary strategy.

Notes

1 I would like express my gratitude for the helpful comments from the reviewers and the editors.
2 *Jumlukiyyat* (جُمْلُكِيَات) is a term that combines (in plural) syllables from the two terms republic *"Jumhourieh"* (جمهورية), and kingdom *"mamlakah"* (مملكة).
3 For a more elaborate analysis of the Arab Dignity Revolutions by the author, see "Arab Dignity Revolutions: A Post-Neoliberal View" [in Arabic]. (قسيس، ثورات الكرامة العربية ومفهوم الكرامة 2012).
4 It is worth noting here that Tunisia had the highest national per capita income among the non-oil-producing Arab countries, except for Lebanon. Egypt witnessed high-growth rates in the years preceding the revolution (around 7 percent on average annually since 1980).
5 Google N-grams show a 44 percent growth in the frequency of the presence of "solidarity" in Google's text corpora in English between 1991 and 2016. (https://books.google.com/ngrams/graph?content=solidarity&year_start=1991&year_end=2016&corpus=26&smoothing=0).
6 For a discussion of CSOs future choices, see (قسيس 2020).
7 It is important not to mix up the massive protest of June 30, 2013, with the military takeover of power of July 3, 2013. It is obvious that protests of June 30 were a culmination of a process, contaminated with various internal and external counterrevolutionary elements. However, exploiting the disillusionment of the masses does not negate the fact of disillusionment. Joel Benin cites strikes of nearly 40,000 workers in December 2012, and "1,972 collective actions during the first six months of 2013, the last months of Morsi's rule" (Beinin 2016, 117). The eventual capture of power by Sisi on July 3 is a separate process that served as the culmination of the counterrevolutionary conspiracy that accompanied the protests.
8 For an account on the positions of various political actors combining historical presentation with a discussion of the most prominent writings on the issue see (Smet 2016).

References

Ahram Online. (2020). "Egypt Eyes Production of 30 million Cloth Masks per Month Through Textile Factories," *Ahram Online*, June 7, https://english.ahram.org.eg/News/371632.aspx (accessed July 10, 2021).

Al-Argash, Abdel-Hamid, interview by Mudar Kassis. (2013). *Professor of History at Manouba University*, December 29.

Allinson, Tom and Lewis Sanders. (2020). "Coronavirus: Arab Uprisings Struggle Amid Lockdowns," *DW*, April 6, https://www.dw.com/en/arab-uprisings-struggle-amid-coronavirus/a-53027193 (accessed July 10, 2021).

Arab Center for Research and Policy Studies. (2020). "ACRPS Announces the Results of the Arab Opinion Index," *Arab Center for Research and Policy Studies*, October 6, https://arabindex.dohainstitute.org/AR/Documents/AOI-In-Depth-News-Story-2019 -2020-en.pdf (accessed July 1, 2021).

Azzouz, Lutfi, interview by Mudar Kassis. (2013). *Director of Amnesty International Tunisia*, December 24.

Baccouche, Taïeb, interview by Mudar Kassis. (2013). *Tunisian Minister of Education (2011); Secretary General of Nida' Tunis Party (2013); Minister of Foreign Affairs (2015); Secretary-General of the Arab Maghreb Union (2016)*, December 27.

Beinin, Joel. (2016). *Workers and Thieves: Labor Movements and Popular Uprisings in Tunisia and Egypt*. Stanford: Stanford University Press.

Bogaert, Koenraad. (2013). "Contextualizing the Arab Revolts: The Politics behind Three Decades of Neoliberalism in the Arab World," *Middle East Critique*, 22 (3): 213–34, https://doi.org/10.1080/19436149.2013.814945.

Bonotti, Matteo and Steven T. Zech. (2021). *Recovering Civility during COVID-19*. Singapore: Palgrave Macmillan.

Boussen, Zied. (2021). *The Unfinished Revolution: Police Brutality at the Heart of the 10th Anniversary of the Tunisian Revolution*. Bawader: Arab Reform Initiative, https://www .arab-reform.net/wp-content/uploads/pdf/Arab_Reform_Initiative_en_the-unfinished -revolution-police-brutality-at-the-heart-of-the-10th-anniversary-of-the-tunisian -revolution_19205.pdf?ver=e68314dc44e18ffeb793b1d3d46104ab (accessed March 10, 2022).

Fahmy, Dalia. (2016). "The Muslim Brotherhood: Between Opposition and Power," in Bessma Momani and Eid Mohamed (eds.), *Egypt beyond Tahrir Square*, 76–94. Bloomington: Indiana University Press.

Ghannouchi, Yusra. (2014). "The Media and its Role in Spreading a Dichotomous Narrative in Tunisia," *Middle East Monitor*, January 27, https://www.middleeastmonitor .com/20140127-the-media-and-its-role-in-spreading-a-dichotomous-narrative-in -tunisia/ (accessed February 4, 2022).

Guellali, Amna. (2021). "A Return to the Police State in Tunisia ?" *Nowaa*, February 9, https://nawaat.org/2021/02/09/a-return-to-the-police-state-in-tunisia/ (accessed July 10, 2021).

Haddad, Bassam. (2017). "Toward an Agenda for Critical Knowledge Production in Political Economy," in Arab Council for the Social Sciences (ed.), *Questioning Social Inequality and Difference in the Arab Region*, 69–89. Beirut: Arab Council for the Social Sciences.

Kandil, Hazem. (2016). *The Power Triangle: Military, Security, and Politics in Regime Change*. New York: Oxford University Press.

Miller, Alyssa. (2021). "'I Do Not Forgive!': Hope and Refusal in Tunisia's Democratic Transition," *Comparative Studies of South Asia, Africa and the Middle East*, 41 (2): 205–21, https://doi.org/10.1215/1089201X-9127089 (accessed August 14, 2021).

Mokhtar, Ahmed. (2014). "It's Time for Egypt to Diversify its Energy Resources," *Khaleej Times*, December 14, https://www.khaleejtimes.com/editorials-columns/the-fuel-crisis (accessed July 10, 2021).

M'Rad, Chiraz Ben, interview by Mudar Kassis. (2013). *Founder and Manager of the site www.jomhouria.com and the Company Médias Plus*, December 24.

Parker, Claire. (2021). "Tunisia's President Fires Prime Minister, Dismisses Government, Freezes Parliament," *The Washington Post*, July 25, https://www.washingtonpost.com/ world/middle-east/?itid=nb_world_middle-east (accessed July 26, 2021).

Partridge, Matthew. (2021 [2011]). "How the Economic Policies of a Corrupt Elite Caused the Arab Spring [Living standards in the region must rise if the political momentum is to be kept up]," *NewStatesman*, February 9–June 7, https://www.newstatesman .com/2021/02/ns-archive-how-economic-policies-corrupt-elite-caused-arab-spring (accessed July 10, 2021).

Repucci, Sarah and Amy Slipowitz. (2020). *Democracy under Lockdown: The Impact of COVID-19 on the Global Struggle for Freedom*. Washington, DC: Freedom House.

Roy, Arundhati. (2020). "The Pandemic is a Portal," *Financial Times*, April 3, www.ft.com/ content/10d8f5e8-74eb-11ea-95fe-fcd274e920ca (accessed March 10, 2022).

Sadiki, Larbi. (2016). "The Arab Spring: The 'People' in International Relations," in Louise L'Estrange Fawcett (ed.), *International Relations of the Middle East*, 324–55. New York: Oxford University Press.

Sadiki, Larbi and Layla Saleh. (2020). "Reflexive Politics and Arab 'Risk Society'? COVID-19 and Issues of Public Health," *Orient: German Journal for Politics, Economics and Culture of the Middle East*, 61 (2): 6–20.

Sadiki, Larbi and Layla Saleh. (2021). "The COVID-19 Pandemic and Possibilities for Arab 'risk society,'" *The Mebourne Asia Review,* May 10, https://doi.org/10.37839/ MAR2652-550X6.11 (accessed October 10, 2021).

Saied, Kais, interview by Mudar Kassis. (2013). *Professor of Constitutional Law at the University of Tunis (tunisian president 2019 -)*, December 28.

Saleh, Layla and Larbi Sadiki. (2020). "The Arab World between a Formidable Virus and a Repressive State," *openDemocracy*, April 6, https://www.opendemocracy.net/en/ north-africa-west-asia/arab-world-between-formidable-virus-and-repressive-state/ (accessed July 10, 2021).

Schaer, Cathrin. (2021). "Coronavirus: Arab Countries Struggle with High Vaccine Hesitancy," *DW*, April 16, https://www.dw.com/en/middle-east-covid-vaccine-rollout -hesitancy/a-57227395 (accessed July 10, 2021).

Schiller, Christof and Thorsten Hellmann. (2021). *Corona Pandemic Shows That Many States are Poorly Prepared*. Policy Brief, Berlin: Bertelsmann Stiftung, https://www .bertelsmann-stiftung.de/en/publications/publication/did/major-differences-in-the -conditions-for-successful-covid-19-crisis-management-all.

Sika, Nadine, interview by Mudar Kassis. (2022). *Associate Professor of Comparative Politics at The American University in Cairo*, February 5.

Smet, Brecht de. (2016). *Gramsci on Tahrir: Revolution and Counter-Revolution in Egypt*. London: Pluto Press.

Tabib, Shawki, interview by Mudar Kassis. (2013). *Head of the Bar Association 2010–2013*, December 26.

Teti, Andrea. (2015). "Democracy Without Social Justice: Marginalization of Social and Economic Rights in EU Democracy Assistance Policy after the Arab Uprisings," *Middle East Critique*, 24 (1): 9–25, https://doi.org/10.1080/19436149.2014.1000076.

UNFPA ASRO. (2021). "The Population Development Composite Index 2020 Report," *UNFPA - Algeria*, July, https://algeria.unfpa.org/sites/default/files/pub-pdf/pdci_2020 _report_-_web_version_0.pdf (accessed February 12, 2022).

United Nations Development Programme. (2010). *Human Development Report 2010*. New York: Palgrave Macmillan.

Yamani, Sharif. (2013). "Egypt Endures Fuel Crisis," *Asharq Al-Awsat*, June 27, https://eng -archive.aawsat.com/sharif-yamani/business/fuel-crisis-paralyzes-egypt (accessed July 10, 2021).

Zarcom Media. (2011). "Thousands of Jordanian Forces Enter Bahrain to Help Manama
	Suppress Protests," *Zarcom Media*, July 31, http://www.zarcommedia.com/2011/07/31
	/thousands-of-jordanian-forces-enter-bahrain-to-help-manama-suppress-protests/
	(accessed July 10, 2021).
Zizek, Slavoj. (2009). "'. . . I cek On Udi Aloni's Forgiveness," *International Journal of
	Applied Psychoanalytic Studies*, 6 (1): 80–3.

أيمن بحر. (2021). "قيس سعيد يصدر أوامره للجيش بإدارة أزمة تفشي فيروس كورونا," الأهرام الدولي. 21
	تموز/يوليو. تاريخ الوصول 22 تموز/يوليو, 2021 ,https://alahramaldawly.com/2021/07/21/147812/.
بيسان كساب. (2015). "'الهوية '.. عجل مقدس يعبده المصريون," السفير العربي. 19 أبريل. تاريخ
	الوصول 15 فبراير, 2022 ,https://bit.ly/kassab-holy_calf.
خليل الشقاقي، جهاد حرب، وليد لدادوة. (2016). مقياس قطاع الأمن وتوجهات المواطنين، 2016. رام الله: المركز
	الفلسطيني للبحوث السياسية والمسحية.
خليل الشقاقي، مضر قسيس، وجهاد حرب. (2017). مقايس الديمقراطية العربي- 5. باريس: مبادرة الإصلاح
	العربي.
عكس التيار. (2020). "المخابرات الفلسطينية العامة وصفقة كورونا .. ما القصة؟" عكس التيار. 1
	نيسان/أبريل. تاريخ الوصول 10 تموز/يوليو, 2021 .http://bitly.ws/fHXI.
مضر قسيس. (2012). "ثورات الكرامة العربية ومفهوم الكرامة." ثورات الكرامة العربية (رؤى لما بعد
	النيوليبرالية). القاهرة: روافد، 13–25.
مضر قسيس. (2020). "مراهقة وفرص بلوغ المؤسسات غير الحكومية: الإنتاج المعرفي في حقبة النظام العالمي
	الجديد." تأليف رصد وتوثيق تجارب التعليم وإنتاج المعرفة حول المجتمع المدني في الجامعات العربية
	ومراكز أبحاثها، تحرير دينا خواجا، 31-21. بيروت: معهد الأصفري للمجتمع المدني والمواطنة ـ الجامعة
	الأمريكية في بيروت.
هيثم منّاع. (2020). الحركة المدنية الديمقراطية في سورية: من أين وإلى أين؟ حوارية في الفضاء الرقمي: معهد
	مواطن للديمقراطية وحقوق الإنسان ـ جامعة بيرزيت، 4 آب/أغطس,
		https://www.youtube.com/watch?v=eaX--Dt9gg4.
واسيني الأعرج. (2011). جُمْلُكِيَّة آرابيا. بيروت-بغداد: منشورات الجمل.

Conclusion

14

A Matter of Pandemics, Politics, and Academics

The Conundrums of Researching COVID-19 in MENA

Larbi Sadiki and Layla Saleh

In this brief chapter, we comment on the book's findings, its contributions, and pathways for future and further research on MENA risk society. We highlight the importance of our 'risk society' angle, a novel and appropriate frame through which to examine the "pandemic condition" in the region (Sadiki and Saleh 2020). Situating our findings within recent research on COVID-19, we also dialog comparatively with other regional accounts. The goal is to succinctly flag similar and dissimilar trajectories explored by other scholars from around the world. That investigations of MENA risk society should stop with these final pages of the book is an idea anathema to us, however. We close the chapter by considering the future of risk society research. "Situated interventions" can be a next step in policy-relevant work that can (we hope) improve lives while conferring gains in practical-theoretical knowledge.

Revisiting Risk Society

It is not far-fetched to state that COVID-19 represents a watershed in the lives of MENA states and societies. Two ideas are compelling. One is that postcolonial rule may be represented as an experiment in and of modernization. It proceeded as a kind of "lab" for weaning tradition, as it were, and inducing West-centric brands of modernity. The other idea is that the COVID pandemic has been a second "lab," as if to confirm failure of MENA states and societies in the first "lab." That is, the tests undertaken to seek modernization and ease the region into modernity. The first lab was by contrivance and choice, after independence. The second, fortuitous as it might have been, carried over the atrophy of modernization plans and expectations into times of the pandemic, aggravating existing perils for states, collectivities, and individuals. Here criticism of MENA's own failed postcolonial experiments in modernization and modernity intersects with Beck's critique of modernity in its entirety. His "new modernity," is doubled reality, as it were. It is fraught with both scientific advancement but also nuclear endangerment, high-tech advancement and socioeconomic underdevelopment and environmental degradation, opportunities and perils. These paradoxes inhere in his "risk society." Such a risk society excludes no one, being as expansive as the systemic processes (industrialization, liberalization, globalization) that have diffused it to all corners of the globe. In this instance, the local is not immured from the global.

The risk society of colonial times has ceded to that of postcolonial/independence reality, the high expectations of which initially transfigured minds and souls. Instead of emancipation, new shackles of inequality, authoritarianism, Western tutelage (Saleh 2020), and Western technical know-how yielded fates imperiled by risk to culture, family, autonomy, freedom, national resources, and even national unity and solidarity. Richer, more democratic, globalized, industrialized, and high-tech societies have always fared better. What risk society has done is to relativize risk—risk everywhere among rich and poor nations, ex-colonizers and ex-colonized. The difference, as the COVID-19 pandemic has shown, in MENA at least, is that the advanced societies retain a competitive edge of wealth, health, know-how, high-tech, knowledge, security, and autonomy. Scientific and technological advancement are at the root of the problem of globalizing risk, Beck avers. However, those states and societies endowed with them possess the means of risk management and risk solving—the antidote, as it were. MENA states and societies share in the insecurities, flaws, and mishaps that come with new modernity's risk society, but not in the problem-solving skills, scientific and research capacities, or institutionalized instruments of debating, limiting risk, adjusting to it, much less keeping it at bay. MENA regional coordination remains feeble even during COVID, for instance (Fawcett 2021). Risk management skills have lacked historical moorings and structures, according to Beck, that cushion society and individuals against vulnerabilities in new modernity. For example, in MENA, charity networks have been over-securitized under global risks of battling terrorism (Benthall and Lacey 2014), ceasing to exist as sanctified structures (May 2021) that enable solidaristic potentialities. In the United States (ACLU 2009) and elsewhere, this has amounted to almost knocking down a pillar of faith that is *Zakat* (mandatory alms-giving) complemented by voluntary *sadaqah* (charity). Centuries-old habitual practices of the religious *mujtama' ahli* (traditional civil society-type associations) are increasingly monitored, constrained, and even discouraged by states. Charitable groups' relative absence during the COVID-19 pandemic has eliminated local and bottom-up skills of risk debate, assessment and management, pre- and post-COVID. This is especially the case in areas of socioeconomic inequalities, perhaps one of the most manifest types of risk in Arab and Middle Eastern societies. State obsession with monopolistic control and penetration of society, including in the realm of value allocation and distribution, has deprived regimes of civic and social margins of existence for burden-sharing.

Absent Social Protection

The COVID-19 pandemic has exposed MENA states and societies in two ways: first, by throwing into sharp relief material and immaterial problems having to do with all things "distributive". The distribution of wealth and health within societies and states and between them, distribution of power, and of knowledge are all relevant here. MENA states and societies, accordingly, feature as quasi-risk societies, meaning settings where risks outweigh opportunity along three interconnected dimensions: social justice, democracy, economy and development. The postcolonial order failed to deliver either contractual goods having to do with governance, or distributive/social justice, to the detriment of equality between regions and individuals. For both, COVID-19 made existing discrepancies worse. Lack of access to equal opportunities, welfare, hospital beds and good healthcare, water, a share of the development cake, and employment including for youth, worsened under the pandemic. If these deficiencies tend to unleash public indignation, it is because they were preceded by decades of poor trust in brands of rule whose reproduction of power did not equate with reproduction of welfare values and practices, much less power-sharing. Many of the historical welfare measures of income have since the 1980s increasingly come under attack. That period marked the rise of structural adjustment and liberalization templates of economic management in most MENA states (Sadiki 2000). Dismantling earlier welfarist structures, and failure to bridge them on the back of the 2011 uprisings that swept the region, meant absence of ready-made foundations for lessening the pandemic's deleterious effects on vulnerable social groups. This has also widened the gap of income and wealth between social groups, individuals and regions within states, but also among them.

Even before the devastating impact of the pandemic, unemployment was on the rise, causing "multiple marginalization" (Sadiki 2019) to increase too. Across the board, formal jobs dwindled, and in the absence of welfare and social protection structures, governmental and nongovernmental, relief of such pressures, was noted mostly by absence rather than presence. Heavily policed lockdown responses, adding to the number of jobless days in countries such as Jordan, Morocco, Tunisia, Egypt, disproportionately added risk to the most vulnerable individuals and groups whose savings were zilch. Low-income households who once upon a time extracted benefits from charity money pots, including Islamic, found themselves most in need of traditional structures of support—family, tribe, and religious organizations. The global fed into the local; thus, regions whose natural resources depended on external investment were not spared from pandemic hardship. Examples are legion: Tunisia's Kamour protests, for example, escalated during COVID Sadiki (2021). Pandemic shocks over the course of two years exposed the absence of resilient development devoid of distributive and inclusive mechanisms, formal and informal.

Dialoguing with Emerging Research

Energizing our investigations of MENA risk society is the pressing nature of a still unfolding pandemic and its many repercussions, predictable and unpredictable. A number of studies exploring COVID-19's sociopolitical fallout cropped up in the months during which we conceived of and drafted this book. Given what we see as the policy relevance of this volume, for actual people's actual lives and well-being, we attempt here to briefly "dialogue" with such scholarship. Contradictory findings by scholars investigating the link between regime type and effective responses to the pandemic indicate that the question is far from settled. Across a vast thousand-year history, Stasavage (2020) has expounded on the comparative advantages of democracy and autocracy in crisis governance. Speedier, centralized decision-making under authoritarianism vies with more transparent processes slowed down by democratic institutions, he argues. On the other hand, Frey et al. (2020) dispute the view that democracies have been less competent enactors of COVID containment policies. This is a salient problematic for MENA countries. We have (indirectly) grappled with it in the book.

Like Koehler and Schulhofer-Wohl's (2021) study, the book's chapters demonstrate collectively and alongside one another how MENA countries have differed in their COVID-19 responses. Koheler and Schulhofer-Wohl (2021) argue that governments in the region varied in their containment measures (such as lockdowns and mosque closures) because of differing incentives to proffer containment as either a "private" (benefiting the few) or "public" good (benefiting the many). The structure and make-up of governing institutions is not uniform throughout MENA, and neither are pandemic policies, they suggest. However, "public good" is an ambiguous concept. Arab states' practices of provision provide reliable evidence to this effect. A "public good" can become "privatized"—it is not just a matter of universal availability and collective consumption but also a matter of equitable distribution. In the Arab world, distribution remains an unsolved, twofold problem: from the West to the rest (MENA), and from the state to the public. Many variables can interfere. Moreover, is "publicness" an attribute of democratic, accountable, and representative institutions? In MENA, Gulf countries were the first to procure and vaccinate, some inoculating citizens *before* resident migrants. Small non-democratic GCC states then moved to disseminate the vaccine regionally and globally, as Milton-Edwards illustrates in Chapter 2. Demand for the vaccine is not governed locally. The intensity of demand is driven by external bodies and knowledge and research regimes, as well as production orders unrelated to domestic demand or institutional settings. The amount of the public good produced and distributed (e.g., the vaccine) depends more on Pfizer and other pharmaceutical companies than parliamentary arrangements in GCC states, Tunisia or Egypt. The global dependencies, a manifestation of risk society, that Moussa and Yokota highlight in Egypt (Chapter 7) and Dandashly touches upon in discussing Lebanon's sovereignty-eroding economic crisis (Chapter 9), help explain state stumbling in providing COVID treatments and healthcare.

As a set of investigations, this book's various chapters have shown that the Arab states within MENA are divided into two blocs. The relatively wealthy and strictly authoritarian (with the qualitative exception of Kuwait) GCC states (Chapters 2–4) contrast with the rest (Maghreb and Mashreq both, Chapters 5–9) in their capacity to *fund* public health containment measures. Risk society's afflictions, however, do not stop at physical infection and spread, as we have attempted to argue. The social/political "cost" in the Gulf can be thought of in terms of compromising on (or neglecting) human rights and democratic space (Chapter 4). The remaining countries explored in Chapters 5–9 experience risk society as a double bind of democratic deficit and socioeconomic hardship. One irony is of course that Tunisia's democratic experiment, most advanced in the region, has been "frozen" (Chapter 5), its unraveling not unrelated to COVID-spurred popular unrest. Kassis (Chapter 13) attributes this regression as counterrevolution triumphant, its neoliberal, corrupt appendages strengthened by the pandemic. Conflict-produced insecurities cross national boundaries, from Syria to Lebanon (Chapter 9) and Turkey (Chapter 10).

Cross-Regional Linkages

MENA risk society forms the topic of this book, but the travails of the pandemic condition are not unique to the region. The risk society framework averts the trap of "exceptionalizing" the Middle East. Beck examines the problems of modernity as they assail Western, industrialized countries. He implicitly seems to rule out that regions such as MENA face different difficulties in grappling with modernization processes and its negative externalities. By a similar token, the empirical record so far shows that regions outside MENA face parallel challenges to the ones outlined by our collective foray into pandemic-era risk society. Certainly, regional interconnections are unavoidable in practice. What we consider pandemic "risk" crosses the Mediterranean to the EU and back. COVID touches new and old predicaments of migration, receding economies, political turbulence, and conflict (resolution) in Libya, Egypt, Algeria, and Tunisia (Mezren et al. 2020). Marzo and Pepicelli's conclusion (Chapter 12) that the EU's prioritization of its member states' needs over cooperation with and support of the Southern neighborhood is a nod to the power disparities permeating these entanglements.

Latin American countries face a heady brew of social inequality, fiscal imbalances, popular unrest, and even populism (Goldfajn and Yeyati 2021) that similarly plague MENA's risk society and its "pandemic condition." Like the non-Gulf Arab members of the MENA region (Chapters 5–9), Latin America's journey into a "middle-class society" that climbs out of rampant inequalities, becoming more inclusive and resilient at micro and macro scales, has steepened during COVID-19 (Bolch et al. 2022). This book's various contributions (especially Chapters 3–10) have demonstrated how differing degrees of state-imposed lockdowns (further) shuttered MENA economies, rendering the marginalized even more vulnerable. African states saw an analogous pattern where lockdowns aggravated existing poverty (UNECA 2020).

In another form of risk, the pandemic poses magnified problems of food security in Asia and the Pacific (Susantono, Sawada, and Park 2020). Similar insecurities loom not only for the Gulf's water resources (Chapter 4). As the war in Ukraine heats up, Arab importers of wheat (especially Egypt, Tunisia, and Lebanon) already buckling under COVID-19's economic havoc (Chapters 5, 7, and 9) face a pressing food security dilemma (Sabaghi 2022). Intra-regional variation is not unique to MENA. Like some Asian countries such as Malaysia (2022), the switch to online teaching and learning in the Gulf (Chapter 4) has been relatively successful. Syrian (women) refugees in Turkey (Chapter 10), or some dwellers of urban areas of Egypt, Morocco, and Tunisia, have not fared so well. However, risk society does not imply total submission to biological calamities, socioeconomic misfortunes, or political deficiencies. Popular adaptations and communally improvised coping mechanisms cannot be ruled out, as for instance in Iran (Chapter 11). Brazilians, too, forged solidarity through emergency actions and complementary online-offline activism during COVID (Abers and von Bülow 2021). And like the Chileans who defied quarantine measures to protest in a continuation of their 2019 uprising (Somma and Sánchez 2021), Chapters 5, 8, and 9 confirm that MENA protests did not disappear during COVID (Sadiki and Saleh 2021), from Palestine to Algeria.

Finally, COVID-19 affects men and women in congruous but also different ways. International organizations such as the World Bank and the UNDP have identified the many facets of what we might call "gendered risk society." Across various regional groupings, existing inequalities, power disparities, and social mores jeopardize the human development of women and girls more acutely and more specifically than that of men (Rivera et al. 2020). Atop higher exposure to the virus in care sectors (e.g., healthcare), the World Bank and others caution that women are more likely to suffer unemployment especially in informal sectors. They face greater setbacks in education, endangering livelihoods and futures. In the pandemic, women are more likely to experience gender-based violence from homes to raging conflict sites (World Bank 2020b, 10–14). Far from being a particularly MENA problem, the "continuum of violence" spanning the bedroom to the battlefield stretches out, imperiling women's "everyday security" in countries including the United States (Forester and O'Brien 2020). These vulnerabilities are to an extent borne out by findings in the book. Chapter 3 notes Pakistani women who form a significant pool (especially in the UAE) for Gulf labor may face particular precarity in those settings. Increased nationalization (and less migrant labor) in the pandemic thus impacts these female workers. Refugee women are especially insecure, as Chapter 10 concludes, from violence to unemployment to education. More systematic research is needed to unearth how women have lived pandemic risk in MENA, what policies have been more or less effective, and what realms of social and political life call for further attention by policymakers and civil society. Moreover, the global situated-ness of gendered risk society in the region, particularly as Arab publics in revolution engage Western policy (Saleh 2016), is a ripe field for continued investigation.

Reflexive Meditations on Writing This Book

Surviving COVID-19 and enduring its sociopolitical whirlwinds has been a wild ride for those of us privileged enough to live and tell the tale. This volume has literally taken shape amid a flurry of morphing policies and a furor of social science investigations into the pandemic's impact and responses to it at various levels of state, society, region, and the world. The book thus represents an (unfinished) attempt at real-time research. Certainly, the quasi-ethnographies of the pandemic that we have penned, as a group of scholars sprinkled across (and outside) the region, did not necessarily materialize in the ways we had anticipated. This is a "risk" of which every researcher embarking on a new project is cognizant, of course. However, a bit of self-reflexivity about the research and writing process of this volume is in order. Some of the very challenges we have written about as symptoms of MENA risk society intervened in our research plans. Foremost among them, of course, has been scheduled travel for fieldwork. Our (Sadiki and Saleh's) trips to Tunisia in spring and summer of 2021, for instance, were stalled more than once, forcing us to revise our plans. Over the course of summer 2021, on and off-again lockdown measures—curfews, blocked travel between governorates, closures of many public amenities—interrupted our mobility as researchers even when we were physically present in the 'research site'. Working online (for all contributors to this volume) has required improvisations and substitutions, including relying on uneven social media data and conducting virtual interviews. We have in our various circles and locales sought to cobble together "digital ethnography" methods outlined in the Introductory chapter.

Moreover, social science research in MENA (especially its Arab members) is constantly beset by a fundamental problem, even in the best of non-COVID times. Region-wide unavailability and inaccessibility of reliable data, so deleterious for economic growth (World Bank 2020a), regularly confound scholars of (and in) MENA. Coupled with our immobility, the lack of good data—deeper than the simple COVID stats showcased in Chapter 1—has haunted us in every step of the project. Mostly devised in secrecy without the benefit of public debate (excepting perhaps Tunisia before July 25, 2021, and Turkey) policies from pay-cuts to new travel rules to vaccination protocols would spring up suddenly. They restructured our daily lives as people (especially those living in MENA, as most of us do), further complicating our data collection, generation, and analysis. Some chapters did manage to acquire a quasi-ethnographic feel (Chapters 6, 7, 9, 10, and 11). Others have taken a stab closer to action research, offering policy recommendations and critique (Chapters 2, 3, 4, and 12) regarding MENA economies and foreign relations. Yet, published research always lag behind the turbulent pace of real-world change. Hence, our policy recommendations remain at best tentative. More than once, we had to rework our introduction, and some contributors likewise had to update their chapters.

Looking Ahead: "Situated Interventions" for MENA Risk Society

A kind of "situated intervention" can help steer the push to tackle the challenges, recounted in the chapters of this book, of MENA risk society. Moving forward, such a slant is vital for ethnographies of the pandemic that move beyond diagnosis to problem-solving. Unemployment, poor healthcare infrastructure, narrowing "migration corridors," insecure female refugees, stalling peace talks, asymmetrical trade deals with the EU, restricted civic space, and authoritarian practices are manifestations of risk society explored in this book. Problems are bigger than a single field of study. Obstacles to democracy and development are many. One discipline cannot on its own address the extent to which COVID has touched so many aspects of the social world. Situated (MENA and COVID-focused) interventions thus entail multidisciplinarity. Moreover, to bridge the gulf between theory and practice, further innovative research is needed whereby shared space is carved out with practitioners (human development, health, governance, civil society, and scholars). To this end, we suggest renormativizing the relevance of the social sciences by making them engaged through what Teun Zuiderent-Jerak calls "situated intervention" (2015). That is, without compromising the practices and norms, ethics, and approaches to knowledge-making of academic disciplines and policy practitioners. Both are needed, enriching one another for the greater sake of nuanced outcomes that inform qualitative research engagement of benefit to polity, society, and the academy. Twinning policymaking and knowledge-making is imperative. COVID-relevant knowledge-making calls for multidisciplinary research in combination with practitioner inputs.

Teun Zuiderent-Jerak takes a leaf out of the natural sciences not by leaning toward positivism, but by exploring the possibilities of social scientists' deliberate (experimental) interventions in the (social) world they study. He suggests a way out of scholars' "dual fears" when approaching the practical world. His interventions sidestep both the "fear of either being too detached from normative concerns," cold and clinical, or "being 'merely useful,'" overly pragmatic (Zuiderent-Jerak 2015, 20). In his version of engaged scholarship, normativity is central. With such an aim, he suggests that "scholarly intervention" makes room for an "experimental production of normativity," whereby "surprise[s]" of a normative kind await interventionist scholars (Teun Zuiderent-Jerak 2015, 5). His domain is healthcare quality, but the notion of situated interventions can be equally relevant for MENA risk society, the socioeconomic and political challenges of its "pandemic condition." Scholarly experimentation in design and implementation of policies and practices in such a way that loops back into research can carry over into practical, real-world efforts to confront the specific ills caused or intensified by COVID-19. Reflecting on the normative discoveries of interventions carried out as practitioner and simultaneously studied as scholar, he suggests letting go of a rigid (sometimes unrecognized) "sentimentality" regarding the "intellectual predispositions" of scholars (Teun Zuiderent-Jerak 2015, 182). Experimentation in (policy) interventions should diffuse into a flexibility of concepts and theoretical frameworks as well. In our case, this could be a stringent neoliberalist posture on the one hand, which upholds austerity or structural adjustment to eliminate subsidies or balance budgets—with disastrous consequences for the unemployed or the poor, for instance. Alternatively, an unyielding "critical" approach could be so extreme that it refuses to deal with IFIs (international financial institutions) such as the World Bank or the IMF altogether, hindering all attempts to minimize global (economic) dependencies. Absolutism in either of these intellectual-normative positions can translate into missed opportunities for theoretically, empirically, and ethically informed policymaking to make people's lives better, to shrink the vulnerabilities induced by COVID. Even the most critical scholar, policymaker, or activist cannot simply wish away the IMF or World Bank, or repeal their mandates. Critique combined with a practical sensibility toward the maneuverings of global capitalism's deputies may be a more effective combination to help protect and empower the marginalized.

Furthermore, some flexibility is in order as academics venture into the policy world and as policymakers open their ears to scholars. Here, the "ethics of specificity" that underlies situated intervention is important (Zuiderent-Jerak 2015, 189–92). This orientation "privileges authentic normativity that is adoptive to the setting it encounters," rather than attempting additive insertions of fixed normative positions (191). Arriving at the right thing to do in policy and in research practice, then, is localized and contextualized. In this way, Zuiderent-Jerak indirectly speaks to the trade-offs and ethical quandaries inextricable from policy decisions and politics itself. Who gets what, when, and how, to invoke Lasswell, comes down to decisions regarding distribution of goods. Is promoting women's employment (Khurma 2021), hiring unemployed youth, or supporting retired public sector workers, prioritized as policy, This ethics of specificity should be grounded, we would add, within broad normative principles that approach with sanctity human freedom and dignity, as the Arab Spring protesters put it. If the pandemic seems to have ransacked state coffers and stolen livelihoods, a strong (but flexible) normative rudder is needed more than ever to guide policymaker and scholar alike.

Situated interventions must, therefore, be firmly ensconced in the MENA-context. However, we do not preclude cross-regional learning, as in our brief exercise in regional comparisons, above. Interventions are not launched from a "clean slate." Other regions struggle, to varying degrees, with issues like distributing aid, identifying and supporting vulnerable populations, devising anti-COVID measures that respect human rights, conducting public awareness campaigns to facilitate vaccine rollouts, designing social welfare programs for the disadvantaged, resuscitating the small business sector, and more. Concocted by synergism between practitioners and scholars, interventions must speak to the normative, distributive, civic, and participatory. Breaking down barriers that reinforce strict binaries (theory/practice, policy/academy) is key. This is especially the case in light of decision-makers' aversion to sharing data.

Required now are collaborations along the lines of situated interventions described and adapted here, to coproduce a different kind of knowledge than is familiar to many social scientists. It is an "all hands on deck" enterprise involving the academy, society, policy, and even charity, sorely needed for distribution as states fall short. British social scientists, for instance, have moved quickly to investigate pandemic-related issues. UK Research and Innovation (UKRI) and the Economic and Social Research Council (ESCRC) have awarded grants to projects exploring businesses, economic woes, employment difficulties, geographies, supply chains, healthcare, education, voluntary associations, psychological and societal "resilience," crime, the environment, policy processes, and more (UKRI 2021). Similar breadth and depth in research can serve the MENA region. The Qatar National Research Fund's "rapid response" call for COVID-related research in 2020, or reports published by civil society groups such as Lebanon's Arab Forum for Alternatives or the Forum for Tunisian Social and Economic Rights (FTDES), are promising. Here, pandemic ethnographies can nudge an epistemic refashioning of post-COVID knowledge practices. For they are intended as a creative remobilization of a multidisciplinary division of labor for the purpose of engaging real-life global problems. Academic research cannot afford to take a back seat due to preoccupations of purist pursuits of "truth." More must be brainstormed and planned, researched and written, investigated and applied. This volume has waded into the waters of "MENA risk society" diagnoses. We cannot stop there, however. Beck's reflexive modernization awaits. Proceeding there entails innovative and cooperative debate and "communicative action" to manage and mitigate the region's risk society. The pandemic has already claimed enough lives and livelihoods. MENA researchers should heed the wake-up call. It is time to inject our research practice with a "shot" of normative and practical urgency, with evidence-based social science inquisitiveness, that risk society demands and situated interventions can offer.

References

Abers, Rebecca Naera and Marisa von Bülow. (2021). "Solidarity During the Pandemic in Brazil: Creative Recombinations in Social Movement Frames and Repertoires," in Michelle Fernandez and Carlos Machado (eds.), *COVID-19's Political Challenges in Latin America*, 87–101. Cham: Springer.

ACLU. (2009). "Blocking Faith, Freezing Charity: Chilling Muslim Charitable Giving in the 'War on Terrorism Financing,'" https://www.aclu.org/other/charitable-giving-and -war-terrorism-financing (accessed March 14, 2022).

Benthall, Jonathan and Robert Lacey, eds. (2014). *Gulf Charities and Islamic Philanthropy in the 'Age of Terror' and Beyond*. Berlin: Gerlach Press.

Bolch, Kimberly, Almudena Fernandez and Luis Felipe López-Calva. (2022). *When Juncture Meets Structure: Vignettes on Development and the COVID-19 Crisis in Latin America and the Caribbean*. New York: UNDP.

Fawcett, Louise. (2021). "The Middle East and COVID-19: Time for Collective Action," *Globalization and Health*, 17: 133, https://doi.org/10.1186/s12992-021-00786-1.

Forester, Summer and Cheryl O'Brien. (2020). "Antidemocratic and Exclusionary Practices: COVID-19 and the Continuum of Violence," *Politics and Gender*, 16 (4): 1150–7.

Frey, Carl Benedikt, Chinchih Chen and Giorgio Presidente. (2020). "Democracy, Culture, and Contagion: Political Regimes and Countries Responsiveness to Covid-19," *Covid Economics: Vetted and Real-Time Papers 18*, 222–38. London: CEPR Press.

Goldfajn, Ilan and Eduardo Levy Yeyati, eds. (2021). *Latin America: The Post-Pandemic Decade: Conversations with 16 Latin American Economists*. London: CEPR Press.

Khurma, Merissa. (2021). "Women, Work and COVID-19 in MENA: Towards an Action Agenda," *Enheduanna: Wilson Center Blog*, October 22, https://www.wilsoncenter.org/ blog-post/women-work-and-covid-19-mena-towards-action-agenda (accessed March 13, 2022).

Koheler, Kevin and Jonah Schulhofer-Wohl. (2021). "Governing the COVID-19 Pandemic in the Middle East and North Africa: Containment Measures as a Public Good," *Middle East Law and Governance*, https://doi.org/10.1163/18763375-13040003.

May, Samantha. (2021). *Islamic Charity: How Charitable Became Seen as a Threat to National Security*. London: Zed Books.

Mezran, Karim, Emily Burchfield, Paolo Alli, Emadeddin Badi, Haykel Ben Mahfoudh and Alessia Melcangi. (2020). *The Impact of COVID-19 on Either Shore of the Mediterranean*. Rafik Hariri Center for the Middle East, Atlantic Council, https://bit.ly /3t7sxZ7 (accessed March 14, 2022).

Rivera, Carolina, Yu-Chieh Hsu, Fernanda Paves Esbry and Esuna Dugarova. (2020). *Gender Inequality and the COVID-19 Crisis: A Human Development Perspective*. United Nations Development Program, https://www.worldbank.org/en/topic/gender/brief/ gender-and-covid-19-coronavirus (accessed March 14, 2022).

Sabaghi, Dario. (2022). "Middle East Faces Severe Wheat Crisis over War in Ukraine," *DW*, March 9, https://www.dw.com/en/middle-east-faces-severe-wheat-crisis-over-war-in-ukraine/a-61056418 (accessed March 13, 2022).

Sadiki, Larbi. (2000). "Popular Uprisings and Arab Democratization," *International Journal of Middle East Studies*, 32 (1): 71–95.

Sadiki, Larbi. (2019). "Regional Development in Tunisia: The Consequences of Multiple Marginalization," *Policy Briefing, Brookings Doha Center*, https://www.brookings.edu/wp-content/uploads/2019/01/Regional-development-in-Tunisia-the-consequences-of-multiple-marginalization_English-Web.pdf (accessed March 13, 2022).

Sadiki, Larbi. (2021). "Tunisia's Peripheral Cities: Marginalization and Protest Politics in a Democratizing Country," *Middle East Journal*, 75 (1): 77–98.

Sadiki, Larbi and Layla Saleh. (2020). "Reflexive Politics and Arab 'Risk Society'? COVID-19 and Issues of Public Health," *Orient: German Journal for Politics, Economics and Culture of the Middle East*, 61 (3): 6–20.

Sadiki, Larbi and Layla Saleh. (2021). "Editors' Introduction," *Protest*, 1 (1): 1–5.

Saleh, Layla. (2016). "(Muslim) Woman in Need of Empowerment: US Foreign Policy Discourses in the Arab Spring," *International Feminist Journal of Politics*, 18 (1): 80–98.

Saleh, Layla. (2020). "GCC-US Alliance-Making Reconsidered: The Travails of Dependency," *The International Spectator*, 55 (2): 49–64.

Shin, Hyun Ban, Murray Mckenzie and Do Young Oh, eds. (2022). *COVID-19 in Southeast Asia: Insights for a Post-Pandemic World*. London: LSE Press, https://doi.org/10.31389/lsepress.cov.

Somma, Nicolás M. and Felipe Sánchez. (2021). "Transformative Events and Collective Action in Chile During the Covid-19 Pandemic," in *COVID-19's Political Challenges in Latin America*, 103–18. Cham: Springer.

Stasavage, David. (2020). "Democracy, Autocracy, and Emergency Threats: Lessons for COVID-19 from the Last Thousand Years," *International Organization*, 74 (S1): E1–E17, https://doi.org/10.1017/S0020818320000338.

Susantono, Bambang, Yasuyuki Sawada and Cyn-Young Park. (2020). *Navigating COVID-19 in Asia and the Pacific*. Asian Development Bank, http://dx.doi.org/10.22617/TCS200247-2.

UK Research and Innovation. (2021). "ESRC-Funded Projects Addressing Social Science and COVID-19," https://www.ukri.org/publications/esrc-funded-projects-addressing-social-science-and-covid-19/ (accessed March 14, 2022).

United Nations Economic Commission for Africa. (2020). *COVID-19: Lockdown Exit Strategies for Africa*. United Nations, https://doi.org/10.18356/b3e7523f-en.

World Bank Group. (2020a). *How Transparency Can Help the Middle East and North Africa*. New York, https://www.worldbank.org/en/region/mena/publication/mena-economic-update-april-2020-how-transparency-can-help-the-middle-east-and-north-african (accessed March 13, 2022).

World Bank Group. (2020b). *Policy Note: Gender Dimensions of the COVID-19 Pandemic*, https://openknowledge.worldbank.org/handle/10986/33622 (accessed March 13, 2022).

Zuiderent-Jerak, Teun. (2015). *Situated Intervention: Sociological Experiments in Healthcare*. Cambridge, MA: MIT Press.

Index

Note: Page numbers followed by "n" refer notes.